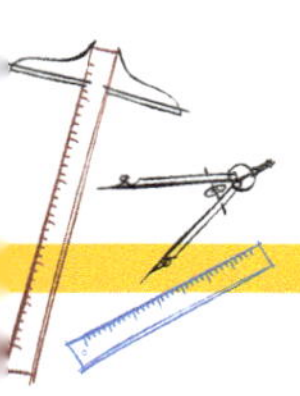

Skyline **Engineering**

CIVIL ENGINEERING DESIGN INFORMATION SYSTEMS. 2 & 3 - DIMENSIONAL AUTOCAD MODELING IN REAL COORDINATE GEOMETRY

VLADIMIR L. NEMCHENOK, P.E.

TABLE OF CONTENTS

ACKNOWLEDGEMENT

This work would not have been possible without the understanding and support of Mr. Massimo Marino, the CEO of LMH Heavy Civil Construction Company.

I am also grateful to the Surveyors - Mr. Michael Keegan, PLS, Mr. Jeffrey Romani, PE, and Mr. Graig Saunders, whom I have had the pleasure to work with at the Central Artery/Tunnel and Cabot Yard Projects. They "tested" the described method in field conditions and proved its accuracy and usefulness.

ABOUT THE AUTHOR

Vladimir Nemchenok, PE, graduated from Moscow State Mining University and worked in the former USSR as a Controlled Demolition Designer. After emigration to the USA in 1991, he worked in Boston on Central Artery/Tunnel Project.

In 2013, Vladimir founded Skyline Engineering, LLC. He is a registered Professional Engineer in the States of Connecticut, Massachusetts, New Hampshire, and Rhode Island.

He possesses around 40+ years of experience in civil engineering design of highways, tunnels, railroads, buildings, retaining walls, foundations, utility systems, septic systems, controlled demolition, and gas stations along with related construction field experience. Vladimir also has a knowledge of AutoLISP, AutoCAD, HydroCAD, Architectural and Structural Revit, Title 5, Massachusetts Stormwater and Wetland Regulations.

INTRODUCTION

The purpose of this document is to navigate through the developed set of programs to be used as a tool to help civil engineers, surveyors, and management professionals to visualize the design concept and progress of construction projects. This modeling tool proved valuable, especially with large and complex Central Artery and MBTA transportation and infrastructure projects in Boston Area, Massachusetts.

Some of the following projects this Method was developed and used for:

- Cabot Yard and Maintenance Facility Improvements
- MBTA Contract #R44CN02
- Boston, MA – $213 M

- I-93 Kneeland Street to Charles River
- Tunnels Construction, Viaduct Demolition and Surface Restoration
- (CA/T Contract C17A6)
- Boston, MA - $414 M

- I-93 High to State Street I-93 Tunnel Section (CA/T Contract C17A9) and
- MBTA Aquarium Station Modernization MBTA Contract (S0CN02)
- Boston, MA - $362 M

- I-93 High to State Street I-93 Tunnel Section (CA/T Contract C17A1) and
- MBTA Aquarium Station Modernization MBTA Contract (S0CN02)
- Boston, MA - $244 M

- Old Colony Railroad Middleborough Line Right-of-Way and Bridges
- (MBTA Contract #C4CN10)
- Braintree to Lakeville, MA - $52 M

THE METHOD:

The Method describes 2D/3D Modeling of objects with various shapes in Real Coordinate Geometry. It is based on the Project Baselines Tabulation, which allows, besides accurate Layout/3D Placement, to receive actual quantities and takeoffs along the modeling process, and reveal potential conflicts with existing Site Infrastructure.

MODULES:

I. SURVEYING
II. GEOTECHNICAL
III. STRUCTURAL
IV. UTILITIES
V. MANAGEMENT

GENERAL APPROACH.

Each module is working with the preliminary developed Database Tables from the Project Design Information.
A detailed description will be given with each module analysis.
The Database Tables include:

Module I – Surveying:
1) Baselines Alignment Tables from Tabulation Charts – Tangents, Curves, Spirals, Increment Stations, Increment Elevations.
2) Base Lines Layout, Offset & Correlation Programs; Transformation (Adjustment and Movement) of Project-Provided Templates into Cross-Sections and Profiles in Real Space.
3) 2 & 3 – Dimensional Curved Shapes – Chord Approximation Approach.
4) Vertical Curves.

Module II – Geotechnical:
1) Boring Tables – Designation, Location & Stratigraphy of Boring Holes, with Depth Indication of each strata layer.
2) Projection & Distribution Programs to draw "Real World" Soil Profile

Module III – Structural:
1) Deep Foundations & Slurry Walls
2) Excavation Support
3) Concrete & Steel Structures
4) Electronic Library of Structural Members Parameters & Geometry to be used in the Project.

Module IV – Utilities:
1) Charts showing Utility Type, Elevation, Size, and Wall Thickness.
2) Directional Approach for 3D Modeling.
3) Conflict Analysis

Module V – Management – Charts for Schedule Representation within AutoCAD:
1) Project Related Charts – Activity, Description, Duration, Start and Finish Dates.
2) Auxiliary Charts – Calendar Data.
3) Correlation of Graphical Objects with Corresponding Schedule Activities.

Graphical Illustration Sets Attached at the end of Modules II, III, IV, and V.
Corresponding References Provided throughout the Text.

MODULES DESCRIPTION

1. SURVEYING

The goal is to show accurate layout, elevation views, cross-sections and provide correlated takeoffs and calculation information throughout the project to be used by personnel in the field.

1) Survey Information Organization & Tabulation.

The meaning of tabulation is to provide the horizontal and vertical input information for Each Baseline throughout the project. Electronically, Each Baseline is organized as a separate directory in File Manager:

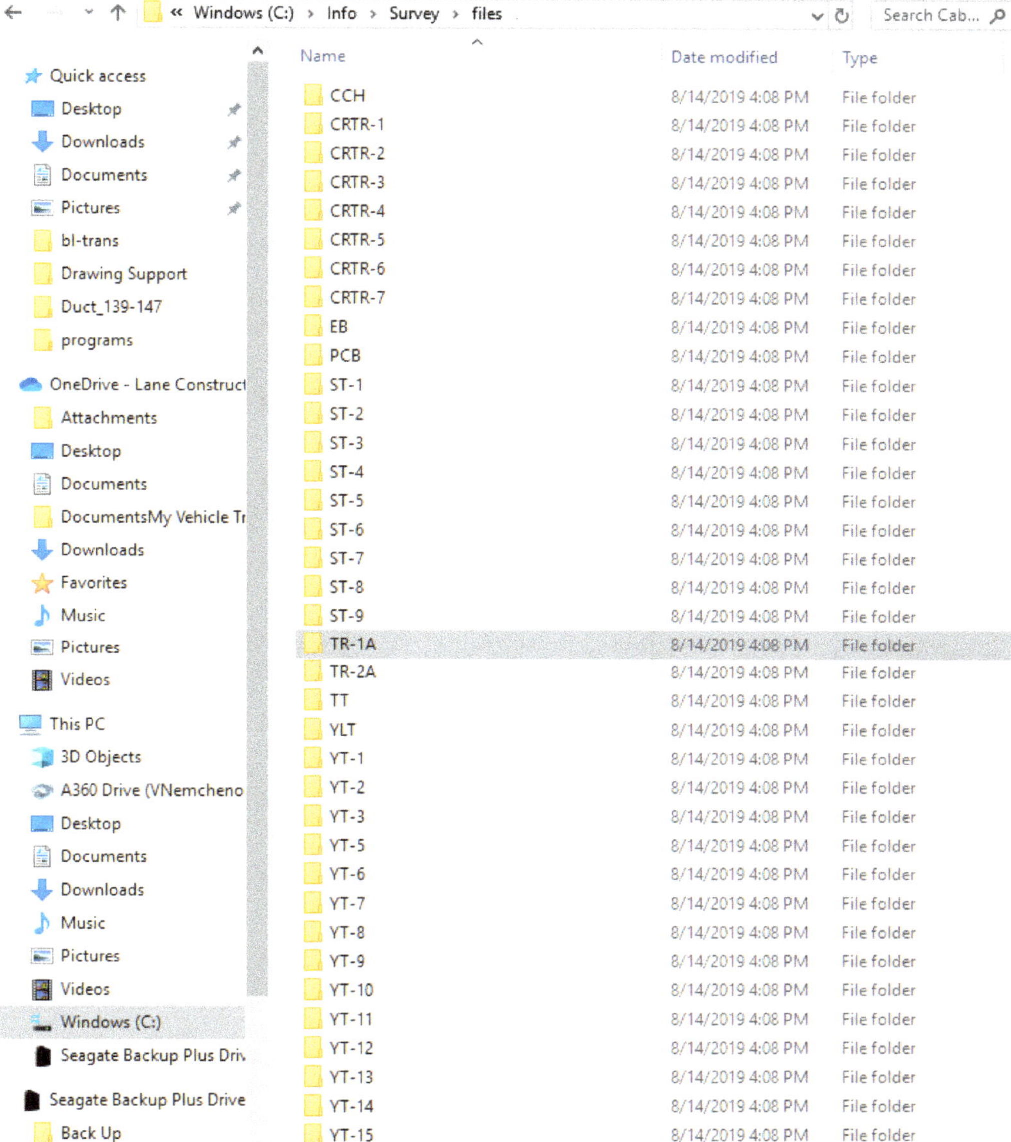

Further, Each Baseline (Directory) is organized in a uniform way:

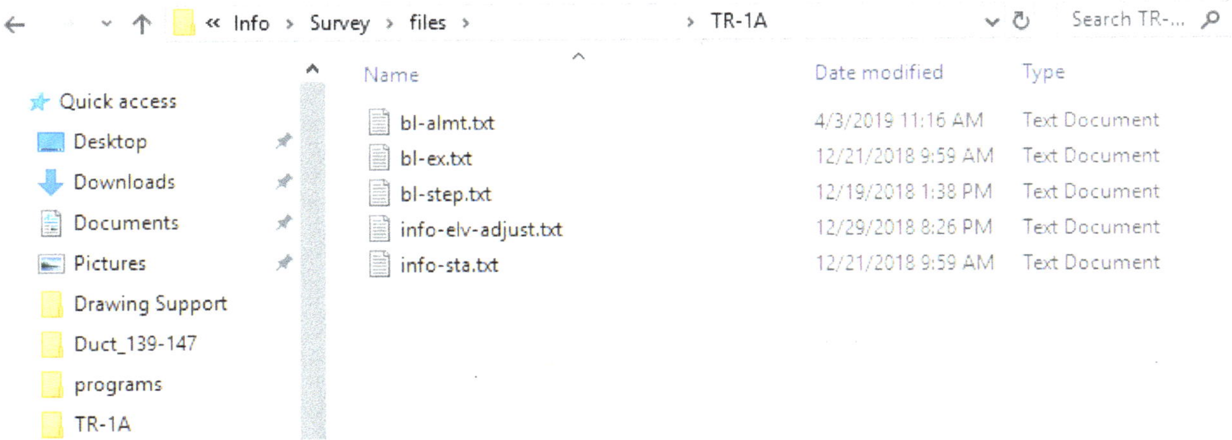

The Files in Each Directory have a typical setup for the whole Project and include:

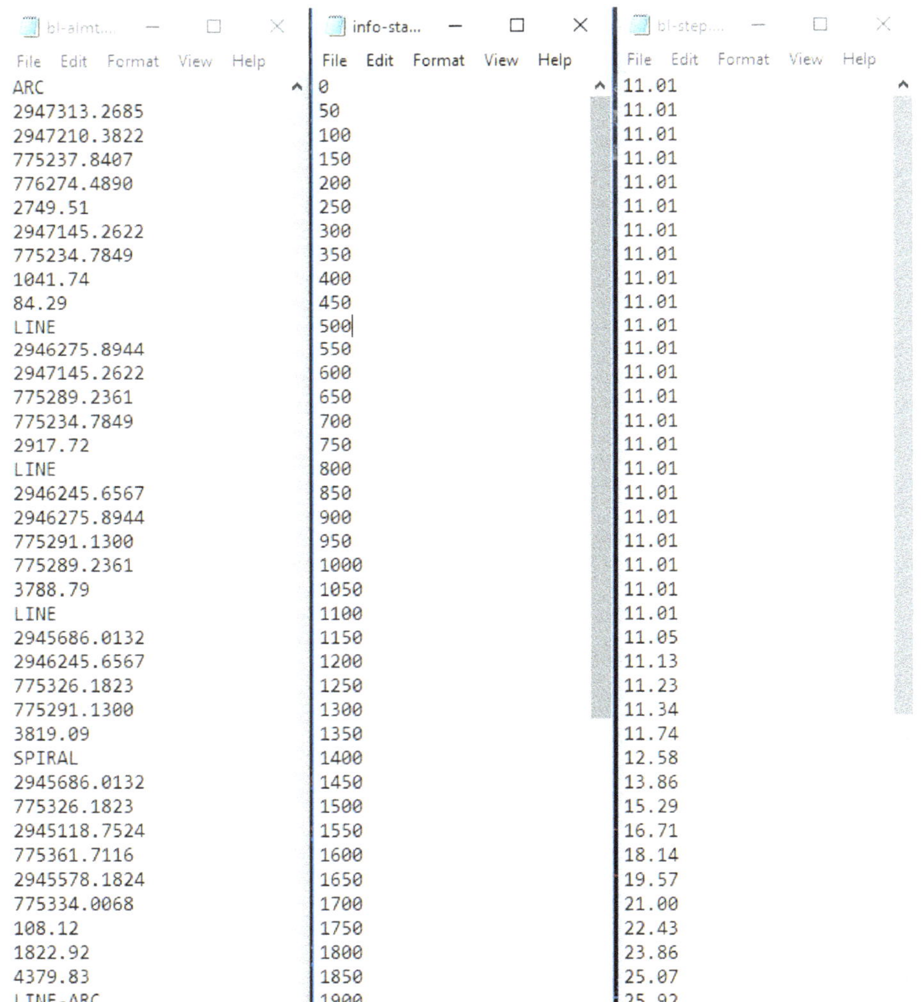

bl-almt...	info-sta...	bl-step...
ARC	0	11.01
2947313.2685	50	11.01
2947210.3822	100	11.01
775237.8407	150	11.01
776274.4890	200	11.01
2749.51	250	11.01
2947145.2622	300	11.01
775234.7849	350	11.01
1041.74	400	11.01
84.29	450	11.01
LINE	500	11.01
2946275.8944	550	11.01
2947145.2622	600	11.01
775289.2361	650	11.01
775234.7849	700	11.01
2917.72	750	11.01
LINE	800	11.01
2946245.6567	850	11.01
2946275.8944	900	11.01
775291.1300	950	11.01
775289.2361	1000	11.01
3788.79	1050	11.01
LINE	1100	11.01
2945686.0132	1150	11.05
2946245.6567	1200	11.13
775326.1823	1250	11.23
775291.1300	1300	11.34
3819.09	1350	11.74
SPIRAL	1400	12.58
2945686.0132	1450	13.86
775326.1823	1500	15.29
2945118.7524	1550	16.71
775361.7116	1600	18.14
2945578.1824	1650	19.57
775334.0068	1700	21.00
108.12	1750	22.43
1822.92	1800	23.86
4379.83	1850	25.07
LINE-ARC	1900	25.92

Alignment File – Horizontal Tabulation Components [BL-ALMT];

50' Increment Stations File [INFO-STA];
Correlating Proposed [BL-STEP] and Existing [BL-EX] Elevation Files

The Following Block-Scheme illustrates the Project Survey Database Structure - Transfer Data from Project Survey Library Structure to Survey Working Files:

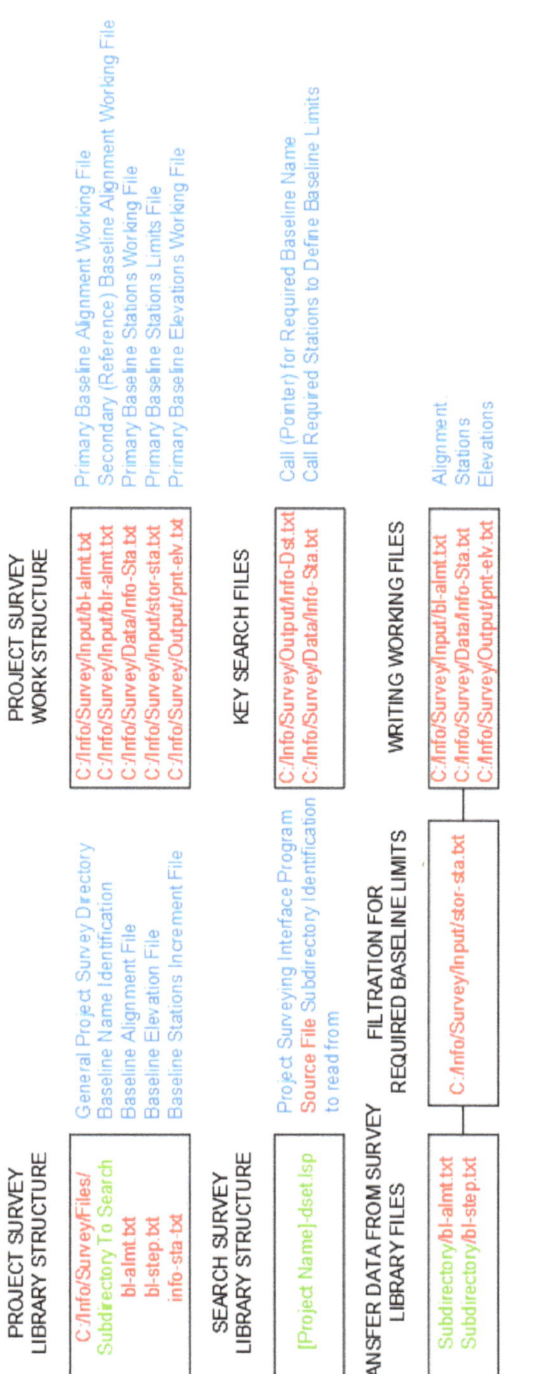

The Tabulation horizontal components include tangents (lines), curves (arcs), and, for railroad projects, spirals (combination of approach tangents and an arc between them).

2) In the current modeling system, the horizontal components are defined as follows (as the implementation program reads the chart):

Tangents:

The Component Type - **LINE**;
Backsight (Reference Point) North Coordinate - **bsN**;
Occupation Point (Instrument Location) North Coordinate - **occN**;
Backsight (Reference Point) East Coordinate - **bsE**;
Occupation Point (Instrument Location) East Coordinate - **occE**;
Occupation Point (Instrument Location) Station - **CSTA**;

An example of a Tangent definition from Tabulation Chart:

LINE
2950150.5919
2950212.6861
775166.7510
775177.9747
303.04

Curves:

The Component Type - **ARC**;
Point of Curvature (Beginning of the Arc) North Coordinate - **pcN**;
Radii Point (Center of the Arc) North Coordinate - **radN**;
Point of Curvature (Beginning of the Arc) East Coordinate - **pcE**;
Radii Point (Center of the Arc) East Coordinate - **radE**;
Point of Curvature (Beginning of the Arc) Station - **PCSTA**;
Point of Tangency (End of the Arc) North Coordinate - **ptN**;
Point of Tangency (End of the Arc) East Coordinate - **ptE**;
Arc Radius - **R**;
Arc Tangent (Distance from Point of Tangents Extended Intersection to End and Start Points of Ach) – **T**;

An example of a Curve definition from Tabulation Chart:

ARC
2950423.8071
2950070.3908
775247.5154
775965.2180
80.04
2950212.6861

775177.9747
800.00
112.23

Spirals:

The Component Type - **SPIRAL**;
Tangent to Spiral Pont (Beginning of Spiral) North Coordinate - **tsstN**;
Tangent to Spiral Pont (Beginning of Spiral) East Coordinate - **tsstE**;
Point of Intersection (Point of Approach Tangents Intersection) North Coordinate - **psiN**;
Point of Intersection (Point of Approach Tangents Intersection) East Coordinate - **psiE**;
Spiral to Curve Pont (End of Spiral) North Coordinate - **csscN**;
Spiral to Curve Pont (End of Spiral) East Coordinate - **csscE**;
Length of Spiral - **LS**;
Circular Curve (Arc) Radius - **RD**;
Spiral Start Station - **CSTA**;
Spiral Flag (Line-Arc – before the Circular Curve, Arc-Line – after the Circular Curve) - **FLAG**;

An example of a Spiral definition from the Tabulation Chart:

SPIRAL
2945686.0132
775326.1823
2945118.7524
775361.7116
2945578.1824
775334.0068
108.12
1822.92
4379.83
LINE-ARC

CHAPTER I: SURVEYING

I.1. SURVEYING BASIC CORRELATIONS FOR PROGRAMMING

I.1.1 BACKSIGHT POINT (BS), BACK DISTANCE (DK), & AZIMUTH (AZ).

The position of instrument occupation point (**OCC**) and backsight point (**BS**) is defined by Northern (**occN, bsN**), and Eastern (**occE, bsE**) coordinates. Initially, these coordinates are read by the program from input tabulation charts.

The major calculation components between these points are BACK DISTANCE (**DK**) and AZIMUTH (**AZ**). The BACK DISTANCE (**DK**) is determined by Pythagorean theorem as the hypotenuse of the right triangle, where two other sides are defined as the difference of Northern (**DN**) and Eastern (**DE**) Coordinates (Figure 1):

DN = bsN – occN;
DE = bsE-occE;

$$DN^2 + DE^2 = DK^2$$

For the AZIMUTH (**AZ**) definition, it is practical to imagine the instrument occupation point (**OCC**) at the intersection of the **E** and **N** axis and analyze the position of the backsight point (**BS**):

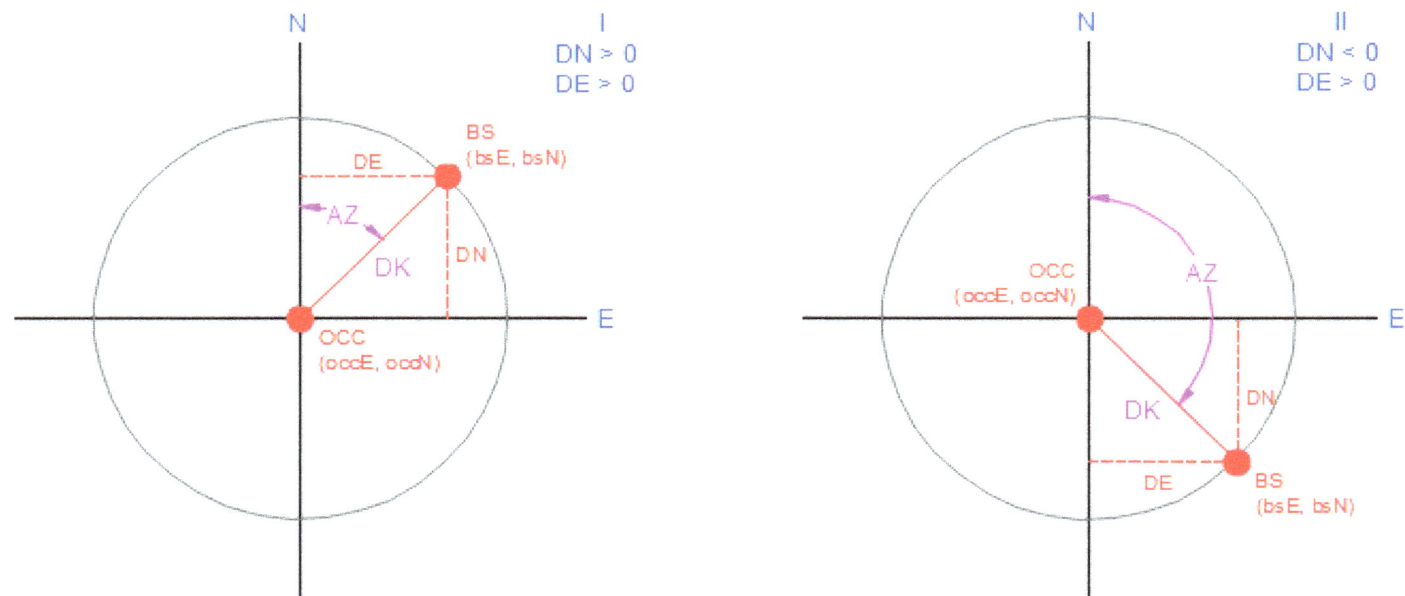

Figure I.1.1A (above). Quadrant I & II Combinations of Occupation and Backsight Points Positions.
Figure I.1.1B (below) Quadrant III & IV Combinations of Occupation and Backsight Points Positions.

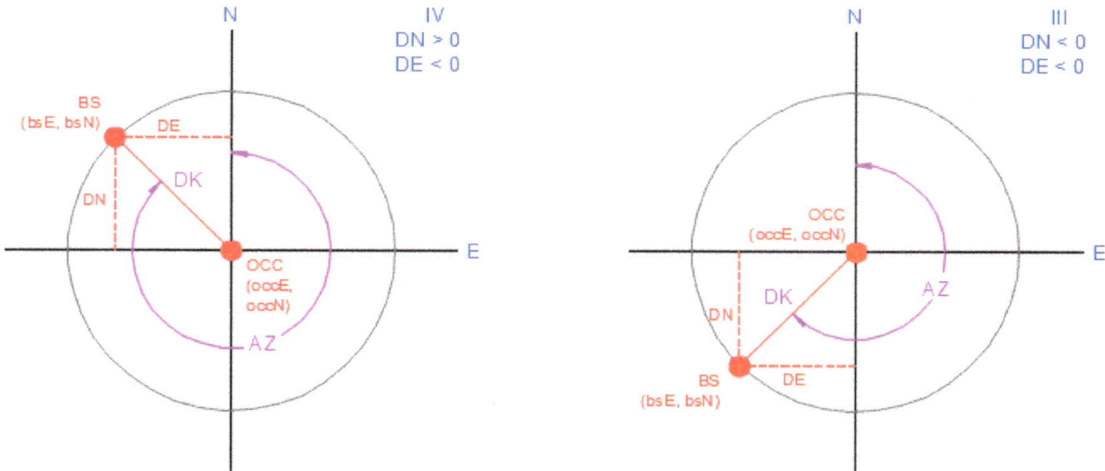

Figures I.1.1C (below) show all possible combinations of backsight point (**BS**) location relative to instrument occupation point (**OCC**), AZIMUTH (**AZ**), and BEARING (**BRG**) in the calculation program.

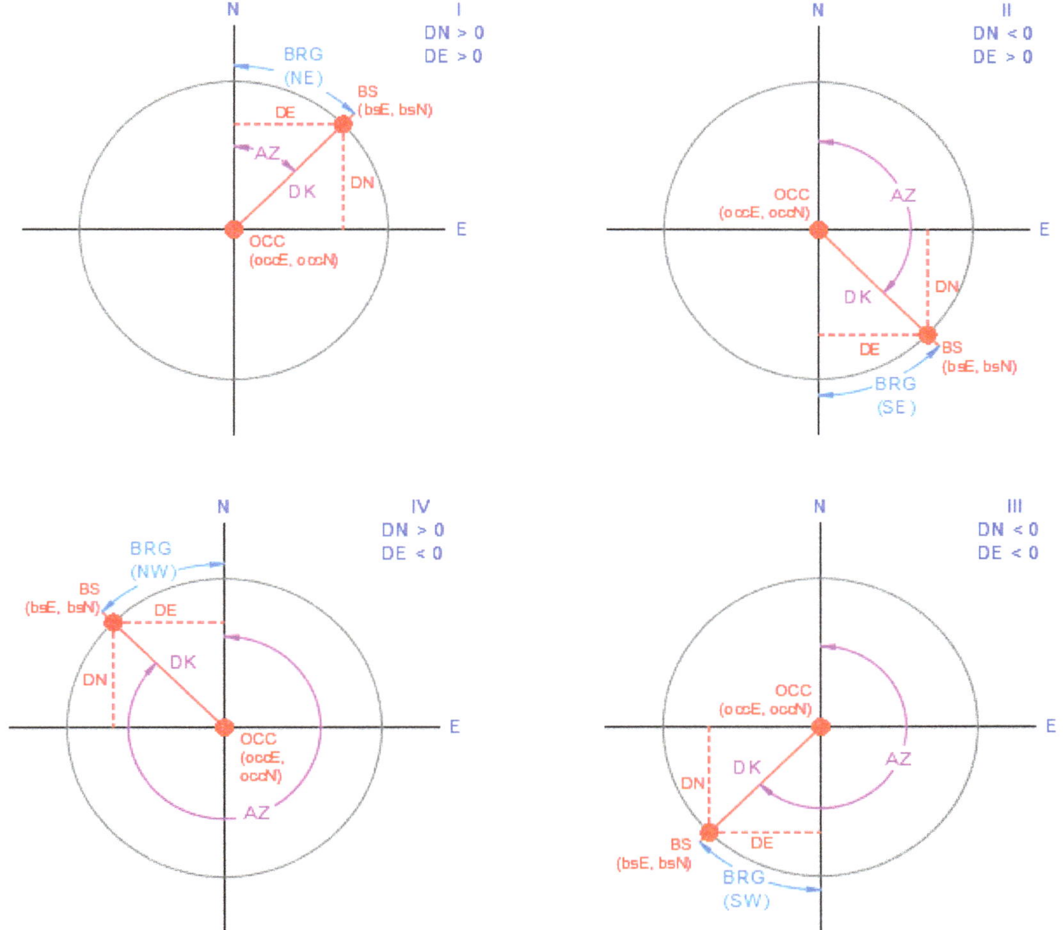

Figure I.1.1D. The AZIMUTH program block scheme is shown below.

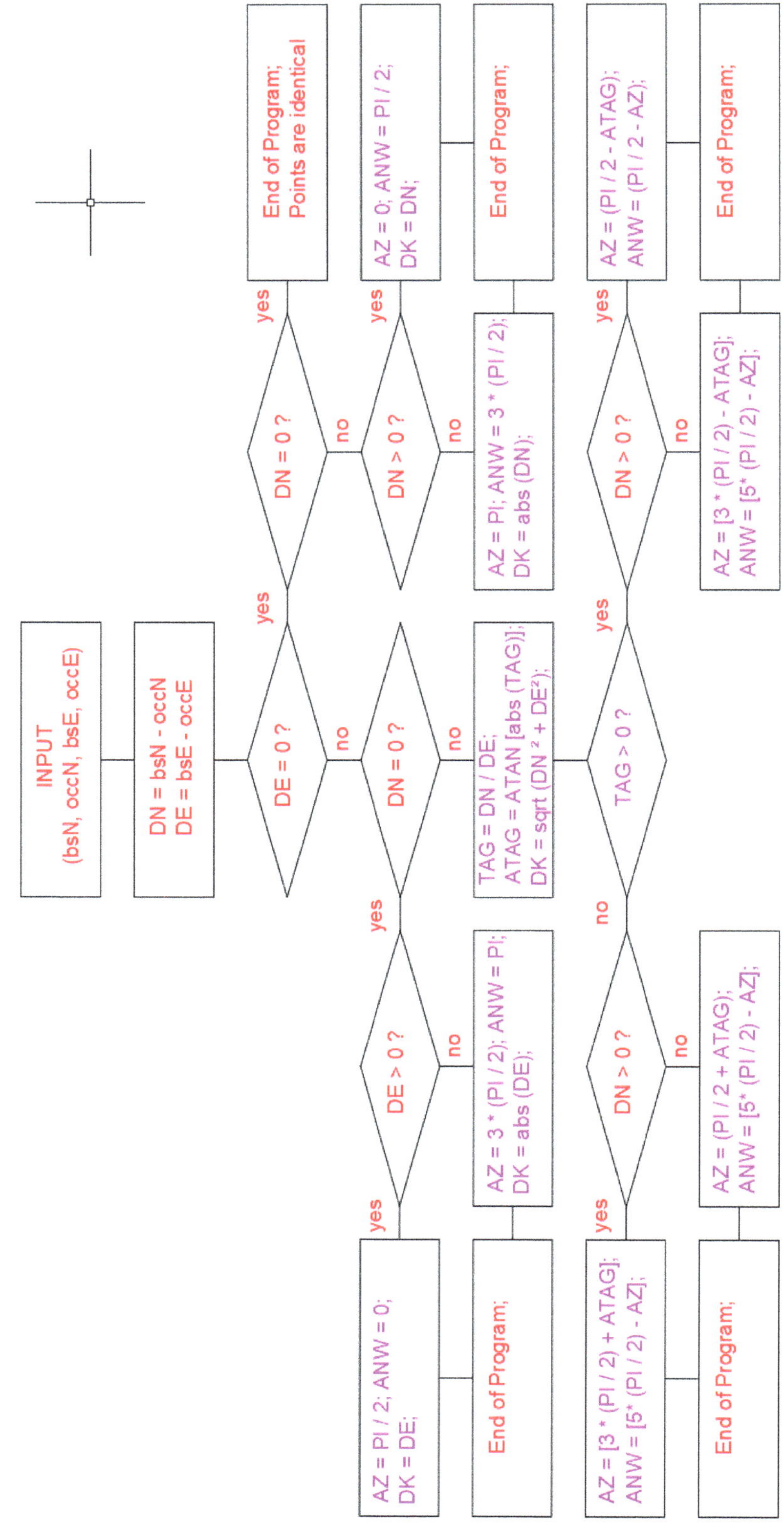
INPUT
(bsN, occN, bsE, occE)
DN = bsN - occN
DE = bsE - occE
DE = 0 ?
yes
no
DN = 0 ?
yes
no
End of Program;
Points are identical
DN > 0 ?
AZ = 0; ANW = PI / 2;
DK = DN;
End of Program;
AZ = PI; ANW = 3 * (PI / 2);
DK = abs (DN);
DN = 0 ?
TAG = DN / DE;
ATAG = ATAN [abs (TAG)];
DK = sqrt (DN ² + DE²);
TAG > 0 ?
DN > 0 ?
AZ = (PI / 2 - ATAG);
ANW = (PI / 2 - AZ);
End of Program;
AZ = [3 * (PI / 2) - ATAG];
ANW = [5* (PI / 2) - AZ];
DE > 0 ?
AZ = PI / 2; ANW = 0;
DK = DE;
End of Program;
AZ = 3 * (PI / 2); ANW = PI;
DK = abs (DE);
DN > 0 ?
AZ = [3 * (PI / 2) + ATAG];
ANW = [5* (PI / 2) - AZ];
End of Program;
AZ = (PI / 2 + ATAG);
ANW = [5* (PI / 2) - AZ];

I.1.2. FORESIGHT POINT (FS) COORDINATES (fsE, fsN), DISTANCE (DIST), & ANGLE-ON-LINE (ONL)

Known: OCC, BS, AZ, ONL, DIST;
Determine: FS (fsE, fsN)

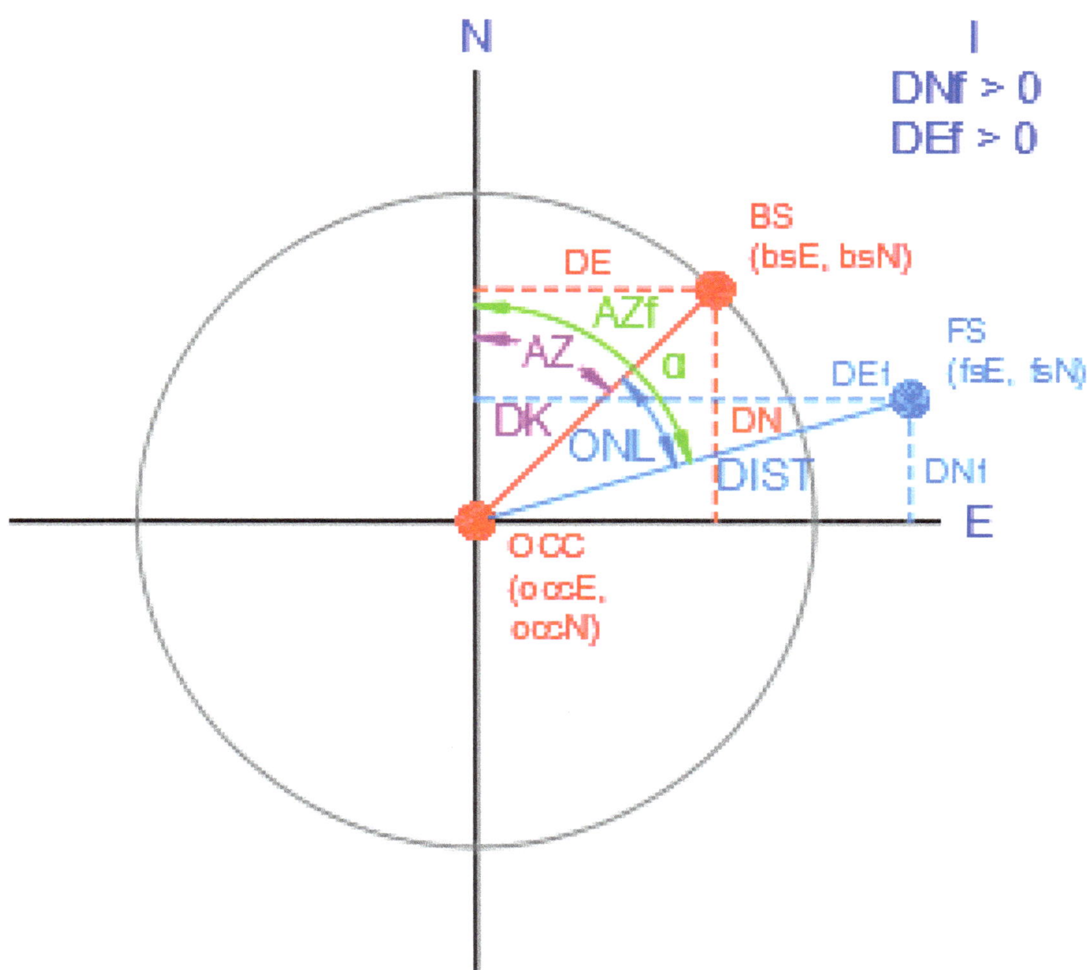

Figure I.1.2A. Foresight Point (FS) Definition. I Quadrant. **a<π/2**

a= AZ + ONL;

DEf = DIST * sin(**a**) > 0;
DNf = DIST * cos(**a**) > 0;

fsE = occE + DEf;
fsN = occN + DNf;

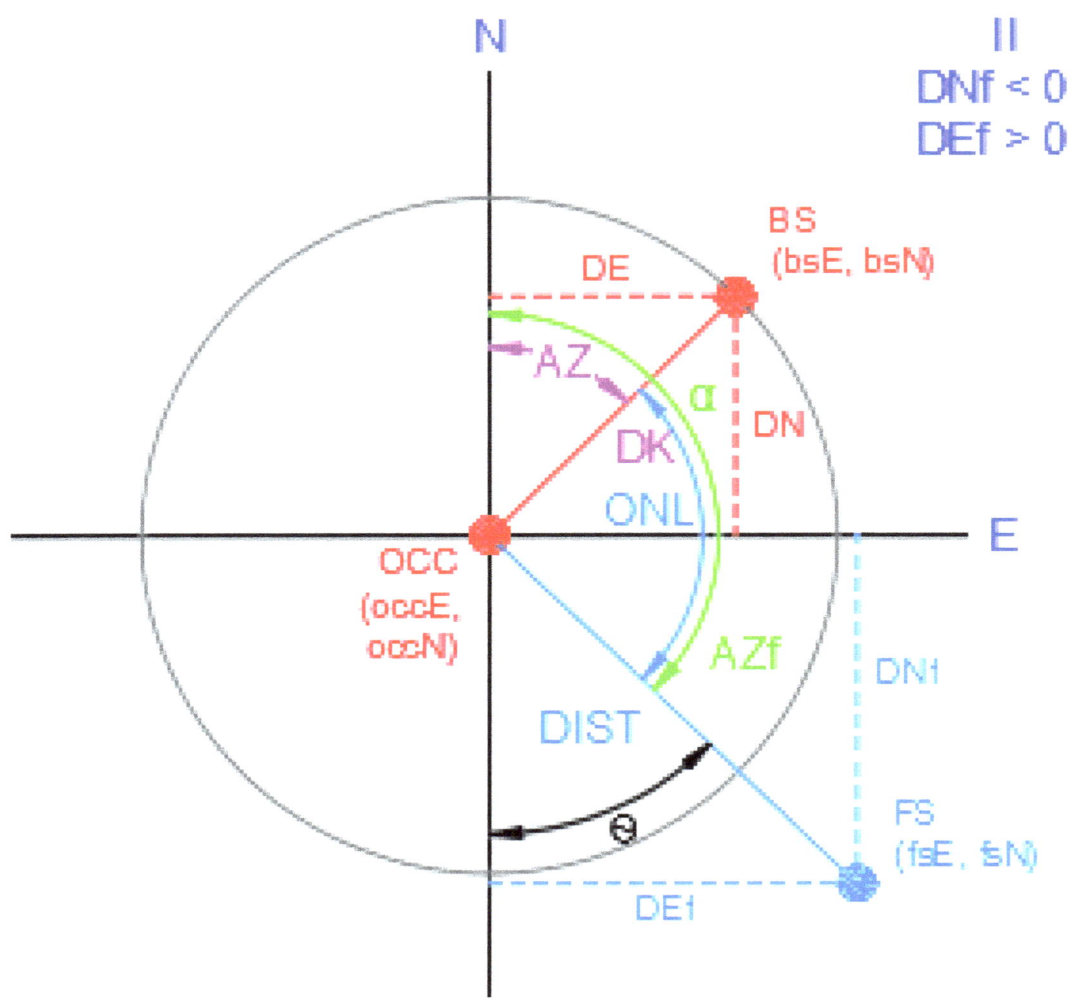

Figure I.1.2B. Foresight Point (FS) Definition. II Quadrant. **π/2** < **a**<**π;**

a=π -**Q**;

cos(**a**)=cos (**π** -**Q**) = cos (**π**) * cos (**Q**)+sin (**π**) * sin (**Q**)=- cos (**Q**);
sin(**a**)=sin (**π** -**Q**) = sin (**π**) * cos (**Q**)-cos (**π**) * sin (**Q**)= sin (**Q**);

DEf = DIST * sin(**a**) > 0;
DNf = DIST * cos(**a**) < 0;

fsE = occE + DEf;
fsN = occN + DNf;

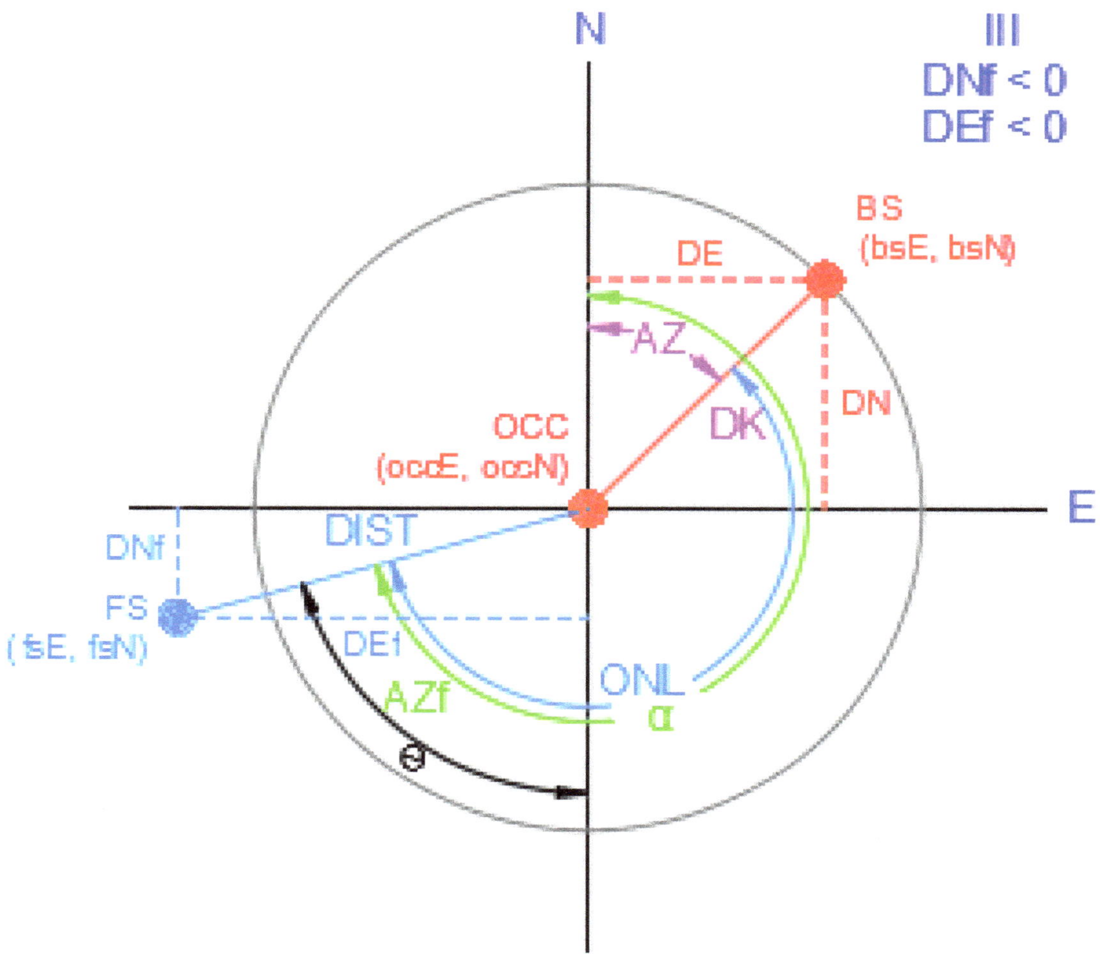

Figure I.1.2C. Foresight Point (**FS**) Definition. III Quadrant. **π < a<3*π/2**

a=π +**Q**;
cos(**a**)=cos (π+**Q**) = cos (π) * cos(**Q**)-sin (π) * sin (**Q**)=- cos (**Q**);
sin(**a**)=sin (π+**Q**) = sin (π) * cos(**Q**)+cos (π) * sin (**Q**)=- sin (**Q**);

DEf = DIST * sin(**a**) < 0;
DNf = DIST * cos(**a**) < 0;

fsE = occE + DEf;
fsN = occN + DNf;

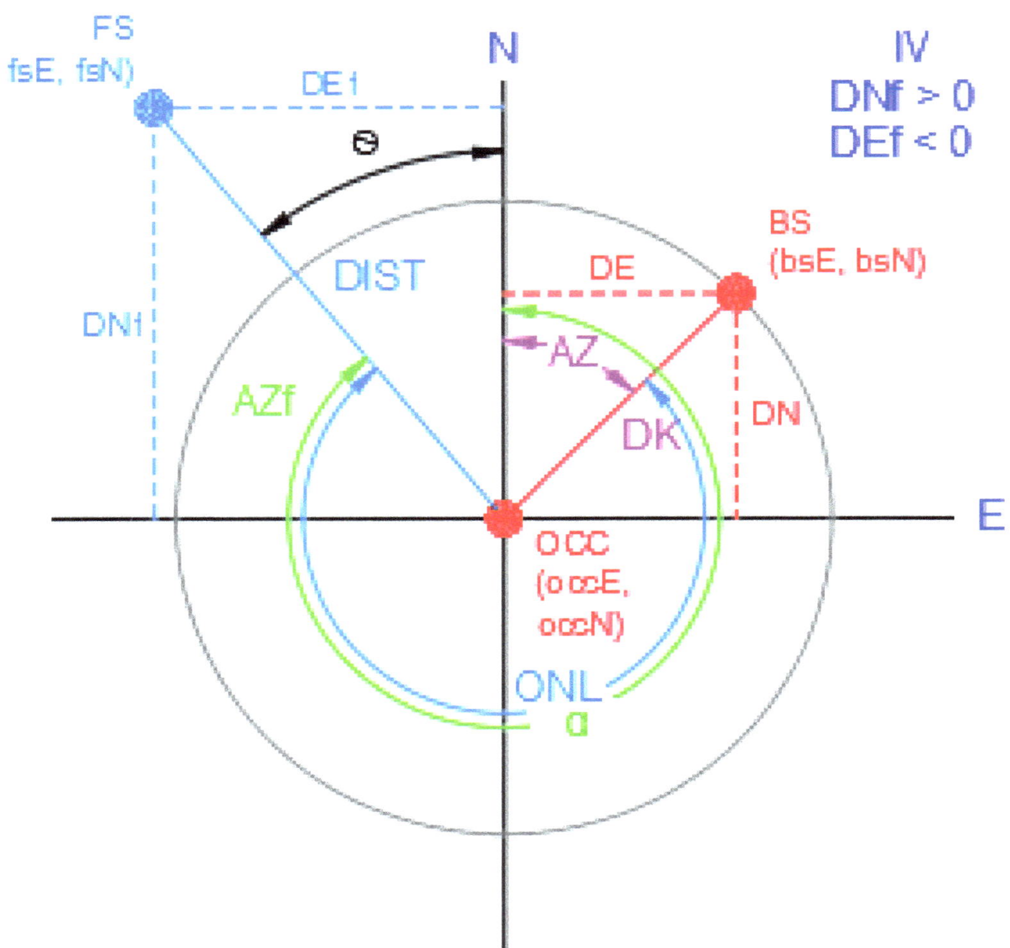

Figure I.1.2D. Foresight Point (**FS**) Definition. IV Quadrant. **3*π/2** < **a**< **2*π**

a=2*π -**Q**;

cos(**a**)=cos (2*π -**Q**) = cos **(2*π)** * cos (**Q**)+sin (2*π) * sin (**Q**)=cos (**Q**);
sin(**a**)=sin (2*π -**Q**) = sin (2*π) * cos (**Q**)-cos (2*π) * sin (**Q**)= - sin (**Q**);

DEf = DIST * sin(**a**) < 0;
DNf = DIST * cos(**a**) > 0;

fsE = occE + DEf;
fsN = occN + DNf;

Figure I.1.2E. The Foresight Point Coordinates program block scheme is shown below.

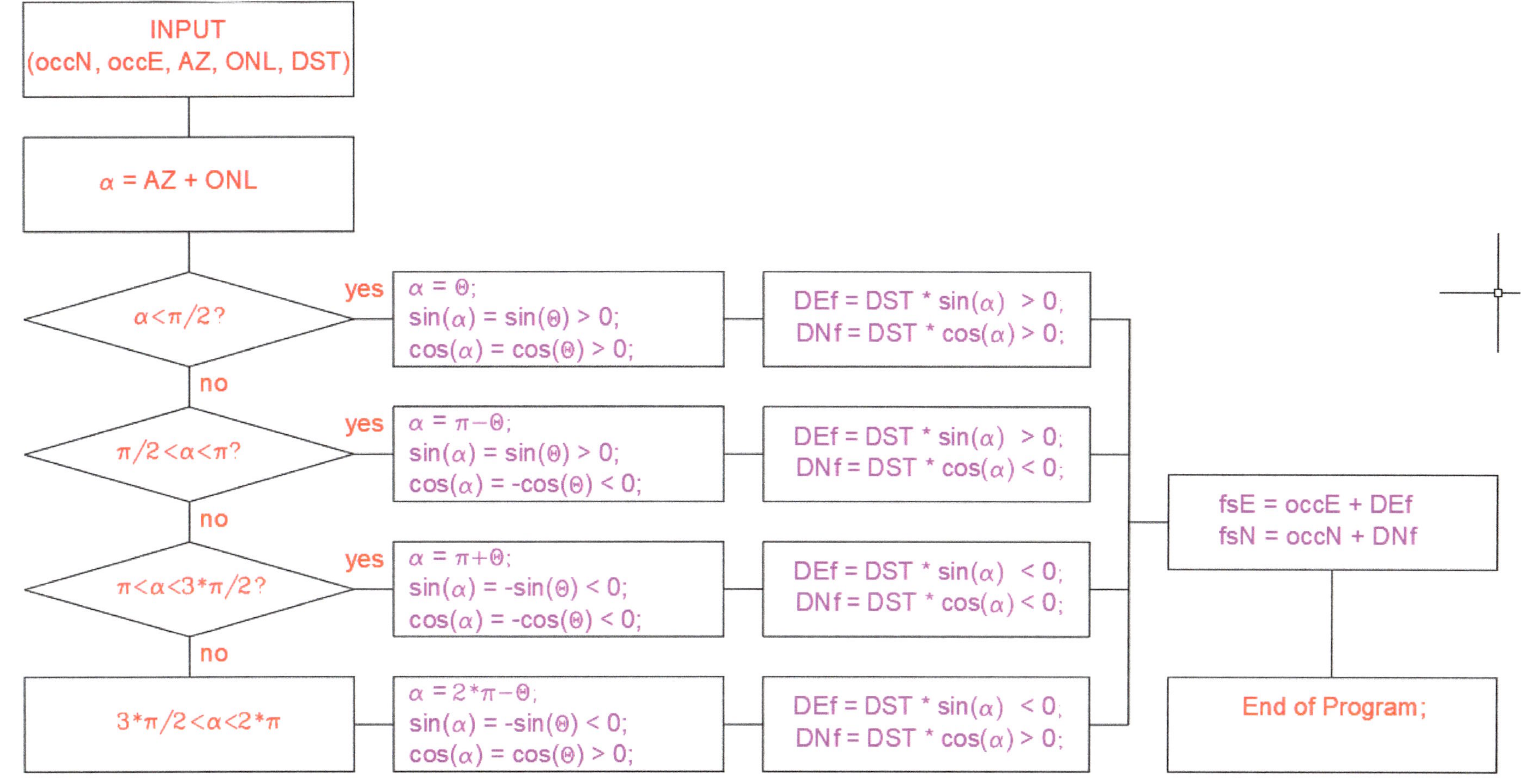

INPUT
(occN, occE, AZ, ONL, DST)
α = AZ + ONL
α<π/2?
yes
α = Θ;
sin(α) = sin(Θ) > 0;
cos(α) = cos(Θ) > 0;
DEf = DST * sin(α) > 0;
DNf = DST * cos(α) > 0;
no
π/2<α<π?
yes
α = π−Θ;
sin(α) = sin(Θ) > 0;
cos(α) = -cos(Θ) < 0;
DEf = DST * sin(α) > 0;
DNf = DST * cos(α) < 0;
no
π<α<3*π/2?
yes
α = π+Θ;
sin(α) = -sin(Θ) < 0;
cos(α) = -cos(Θ) < 0;
DEf = DST * sin(α) < 0;
DNf = DST * cos(α) < 0;
no
3*π/2<α<2*π
α = 2*π−Θ;
sin(α) = -sin(Θ) < 0;
cos(α) = cos(Θ) > 0;
DEf = DST * sin(α) < 0;
DNf = DST * cos(α) > 0;
fsE = occE + DEf
fsN = occN + DNf
End of Program;

Known: OCC, BS, FS, AZ;
Determine: ONL, DIST

1) Determine Foresight Point AZIMUTH (**AZf**) and Foresight Point Distance (**DIST**) - Using AZIMUTH Algorithm with Foresight Point Coordinates (**fsE, fsN**) and an Instrument Occupation Point Coordinates (**occE, occN**)
2) Graphically **AZf** = (a), as shown on Figures 2A, 2B, 2C, 2D
3) An ANGLE-ON-LINE (**ONL**) is defined as a difference between the Backsight and Foresight Points AZIMUTHS (**AZ, AZf**), and illustrated by the ANGLE-ON-LINE program block scheme:

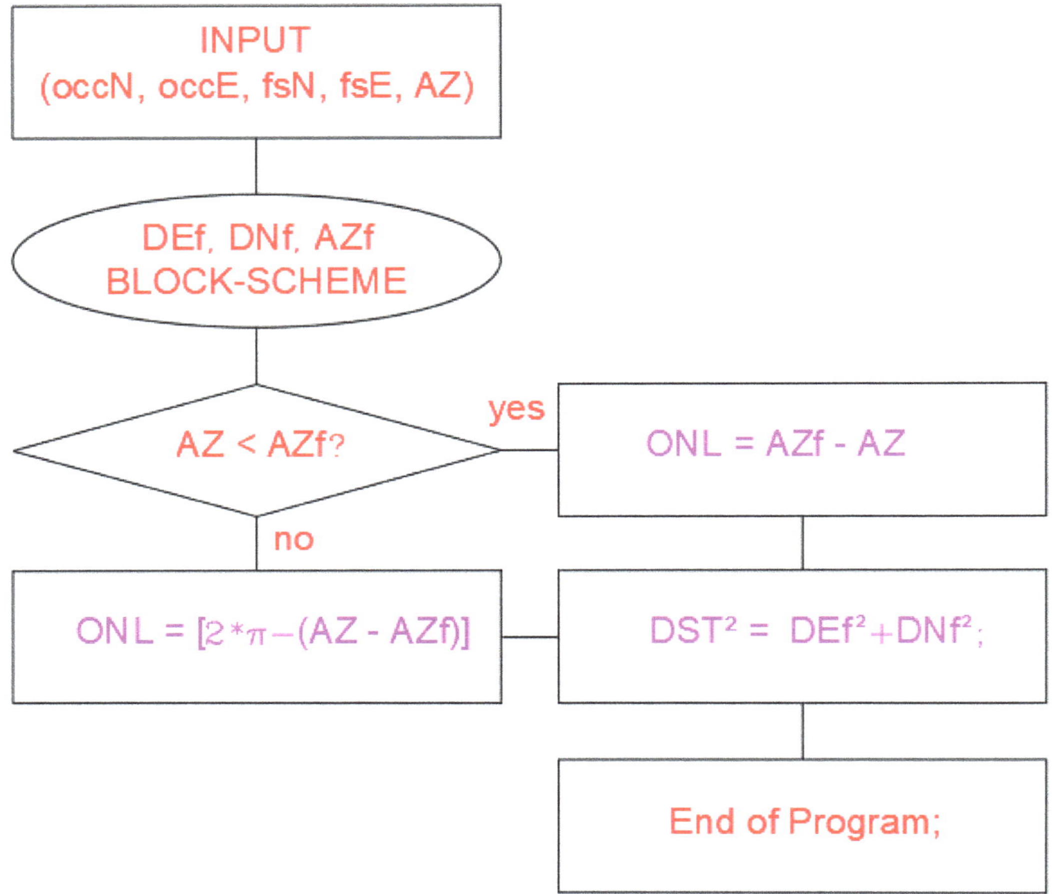

Figure I.1.2F. ANGLE-ON-LINE & FS POINT DIST. Definition Block Scheme

I.2. WORK WITH ALIGNMENTS

Now, as correlations between an Instrument (Occupation), Backsight, and Foresight Points have been established, it is feasible to use them to work with the project's survey baseline alignments.

I.2.1. TANGENTS

An example of input tangent parameters is shown on Page 11 – Backsight BS (**bsN, bsE**) & Occupation Point OCC (**occN, occE**) coordinates, Segment Starting Station (**CSTA**)

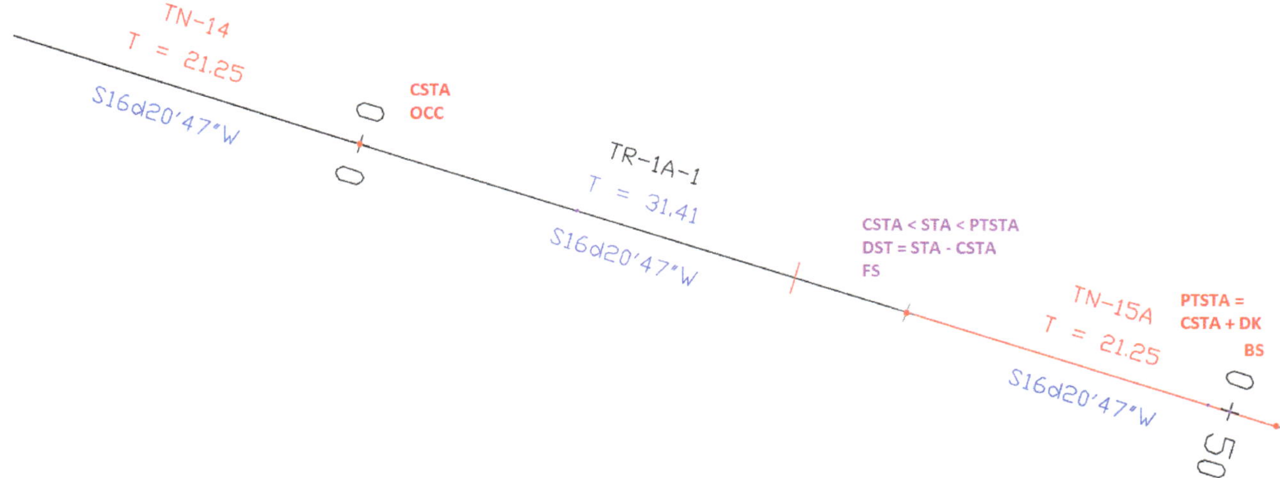

Figure I.2.1A Tangent Segment Baseline Definition – Limits, Designation, Bearing, Block-Scheme.

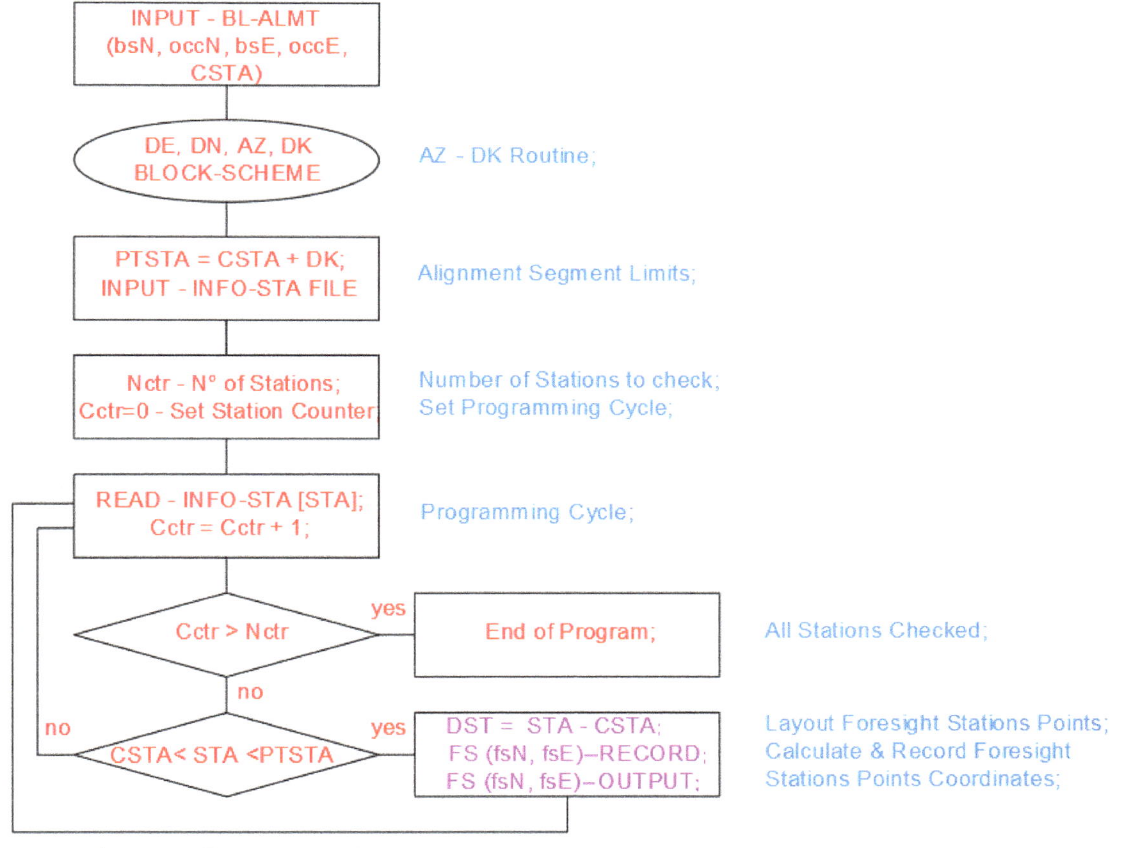

Example #1

Given:
Baseline TR-1A.
Stations 0+12.50, 0+32.15, 0+48.75.

Required:
Based on Block-Scheme (Figure I.2.1.A), determine:

1) Baseline Alignment Segment containing shown above Stations;
2) Coordinates and Bearings of shown above Stations;

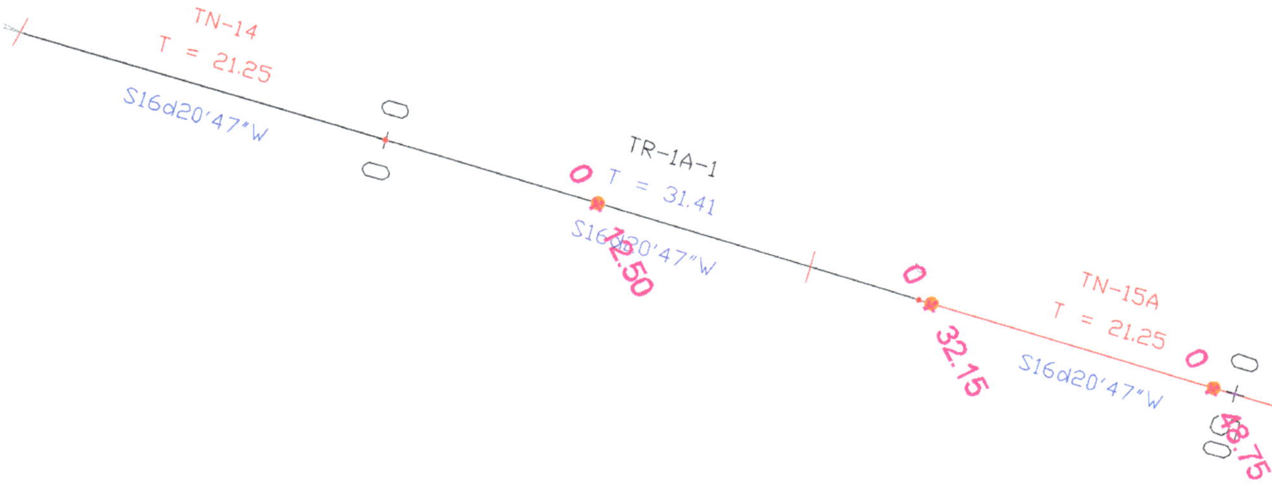

Figure I.2.1.B (below) illustrates the solution – CAD File with printed Stations, Working Text Files with Input Stations [INFO-STA], Corresponding Alignment Segment [BL-ALMT], and printed Stations Coordinates and Bearings [LINE-OCC]. Note that with Tangent Alignment, the previously defined Bearing coincides by definition with calculated station bearings.

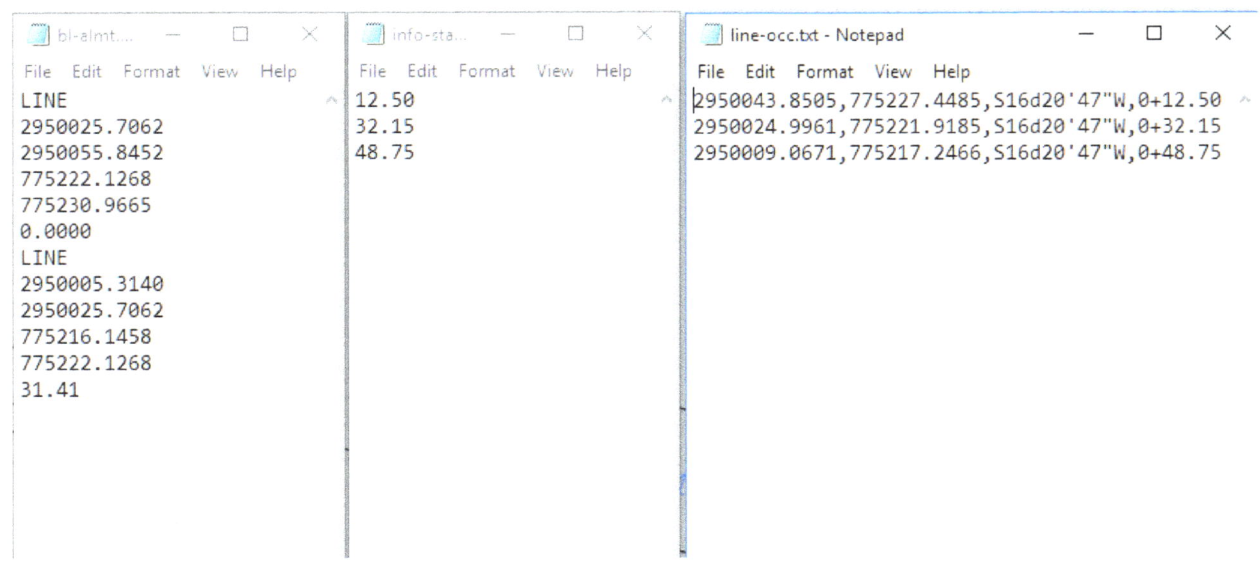
bl-almt....

File Edit Format View Help

```
LINE
2950025.7062
2950055.8452
775222.1268
775230.9665
0.0000
LINE
2950005.3140
2950025.7062
775216.1458
775222.1268
31.41
```

info-sta...

File Edit Format View Help

```
12.50
32.15
48.75
```

line-occ.txt - Notepad

File Edit Format View Help

```
2950043.8505,775227.4485,S16d20'47"W,0+12.50
2950024.9961,775221.9185,S16d20'47"W,0+32.15
2950009.0671,775217.2466,S16d20'47"W,0+48.75
```

I.2.2. CURVES

An example of input curve parameters is shown on pages 11 & 12 – Subsequently PC (**pcN, pcE**) - Point of Curvature and PT (**ptN, ptE**) – Point of Tangency - as Backsight Points, RAD (**radN, radE**) – Radius Point as an Occupation Point, PC Starting Station (**PCSTA**), Radius (**R**), Tangent (**T**).

Figure I.2.2.A shows a CURVE definition drawing and a calculation Block-Scheme for Central Angle (CANG), Length of Curve (TL), and Point of Tangency (PTSTA) Station with the above-mentioned input parameters.

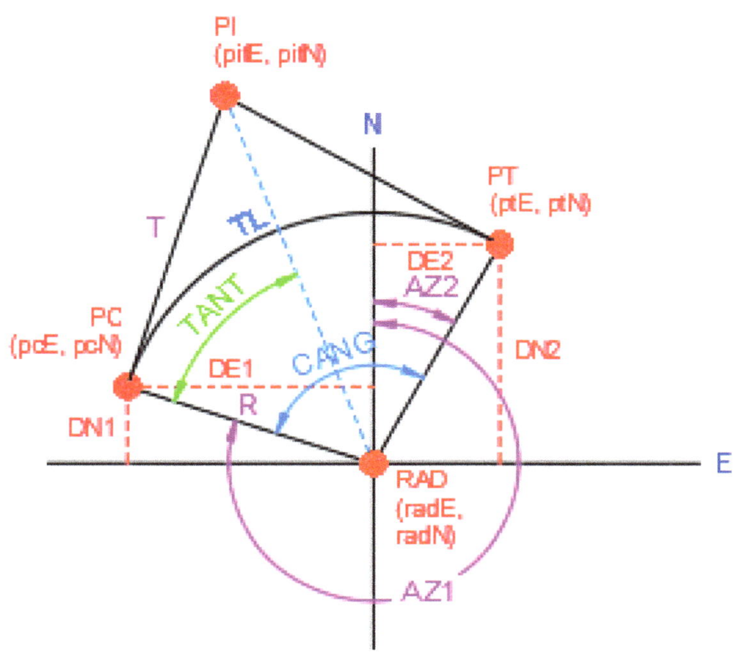

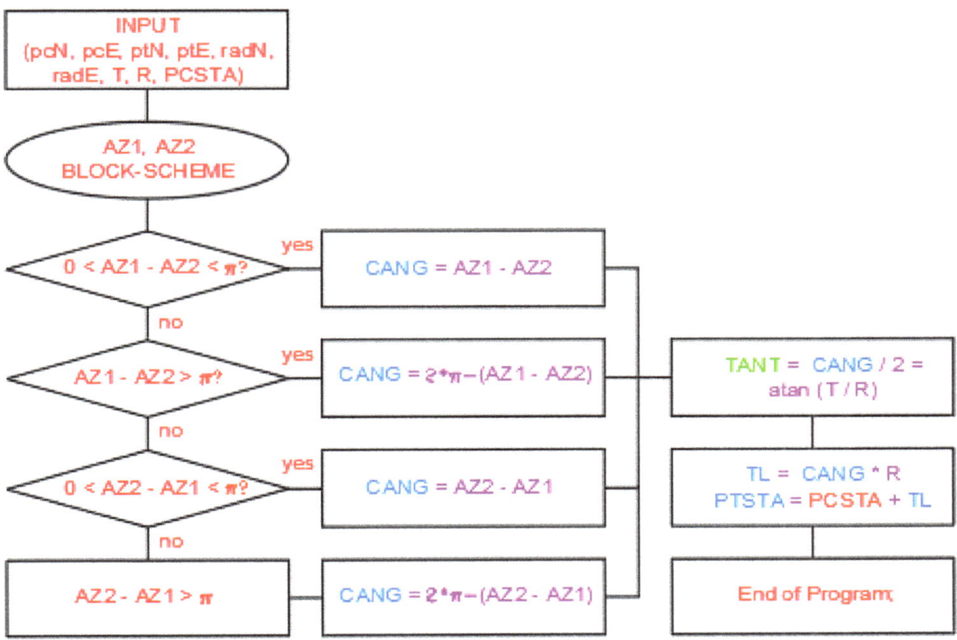

As a tabulation option, the project might use a curve Point of Intersection PI (**pitN, pitE**) coordinates instead of those for a Radius Point. In this case, the input parameters are as follows:

Subsequently, Point of Intersection PI (**pitN, pitE**) and Point of Tangency PT (**ptN, ptE**) – as Backsight Points, Point of Curvature PC (**pcN, pcE**) - as an Occupation Point, PC Starting Station (**PCSTA**), Radius (**R**), Tangent (**T**).

Figure I.2.2.B shows a CURVE definition drawings (cases A, B, C, D) and a calculation Block-Scheme for Radius Point RAD (**radN, radE**) coordinates, Central Angle (CANG), Length of Curve (TL), and Point of Tangency (PTSTA) Station with the above-mentioned input parameters.

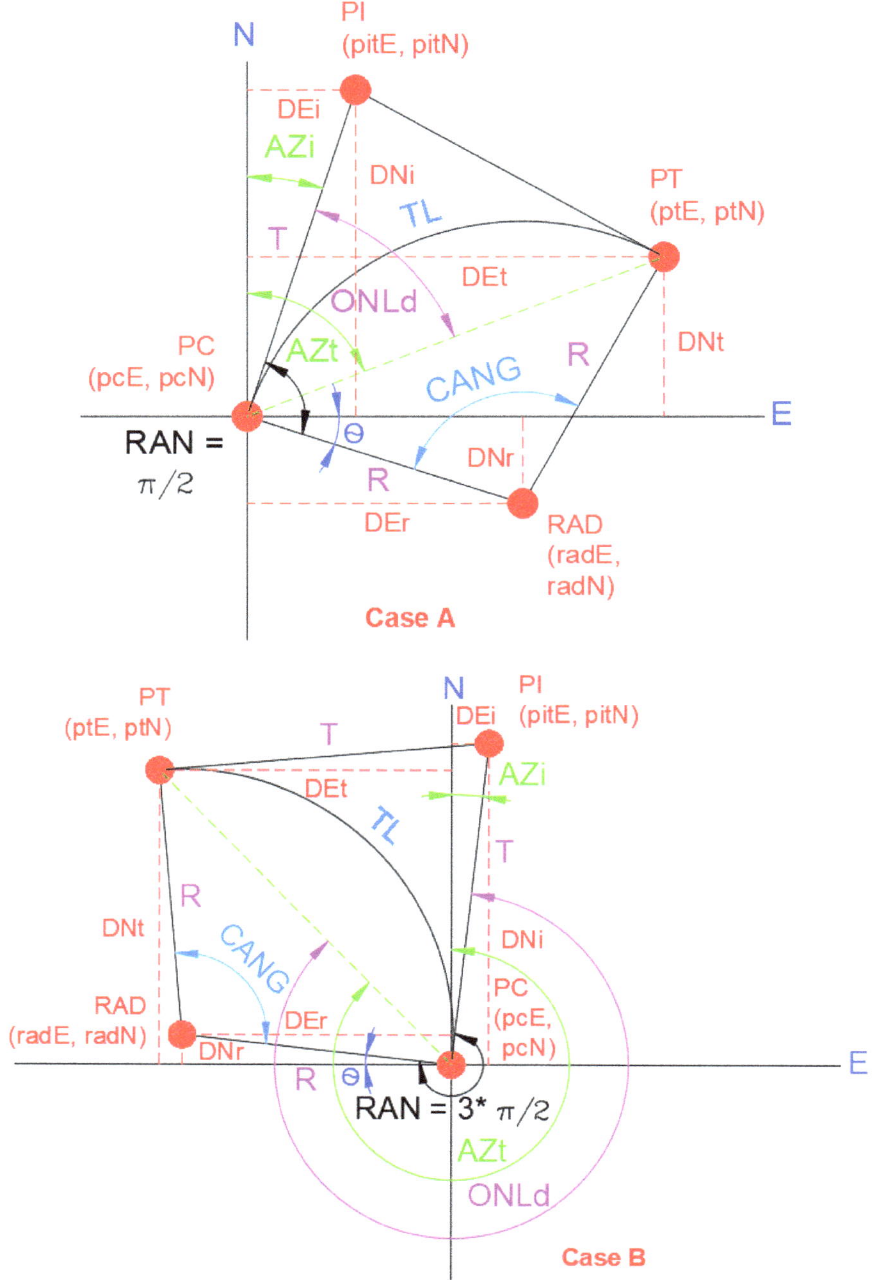

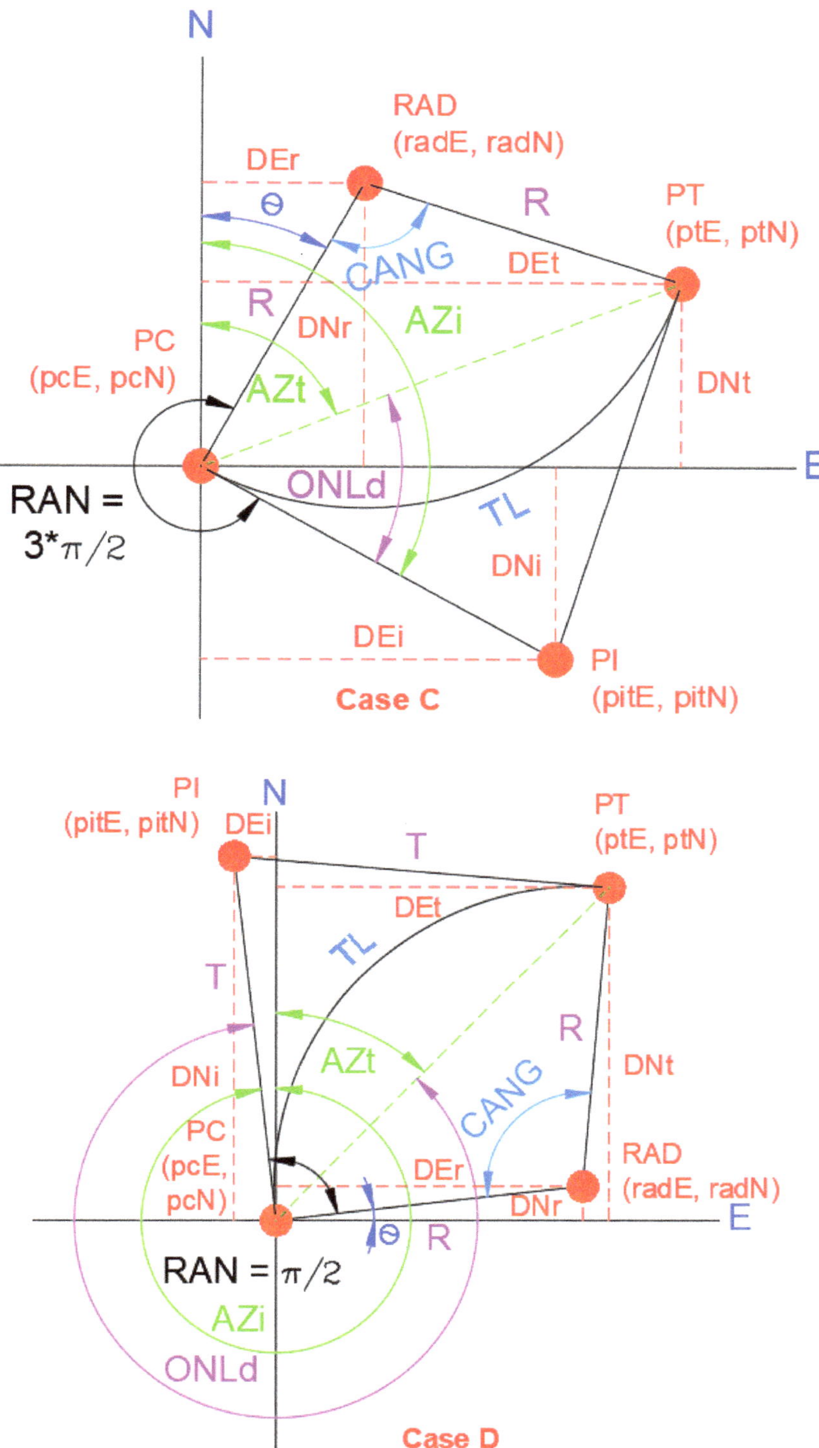

Figure I.2.2.B Curve definition options PC - PI - PT

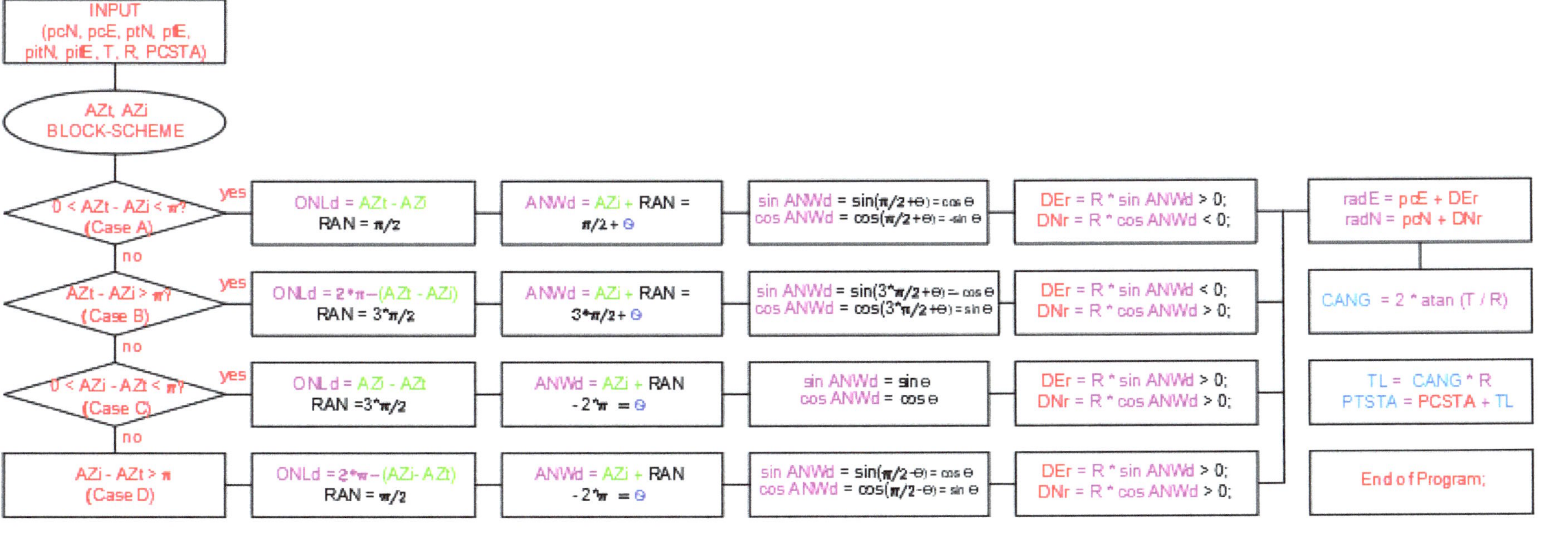

Curve Definition Options - Block-Scheme

Figure I.2.2.C Curve Segment Baseline Definition – Limits, Designation, Length, Radius, Running Block-Scheme.

3+00
PCSTA
TR-1A-8
ω = 74.38
Rл= 375.03
PTSTA
4+00

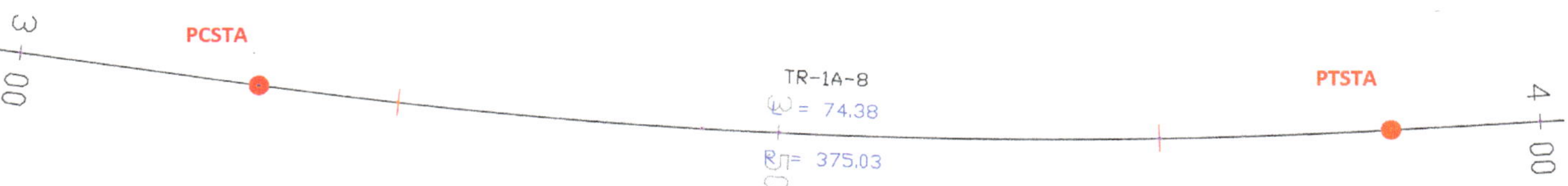

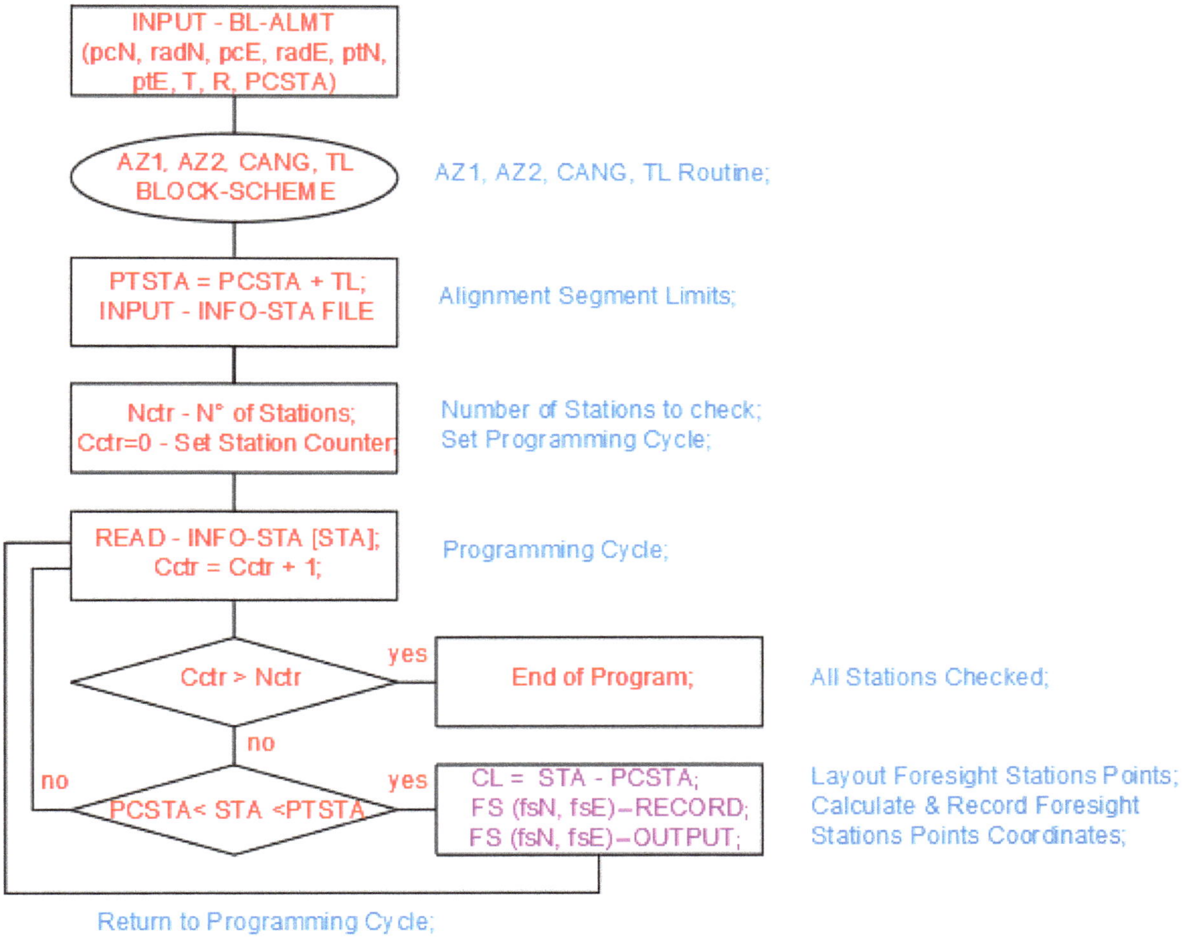

INPUT - BL-ALMT (pcN, radN, pcE, radE, ptN, ptE, T, R, PCSTA)
AZ1, AZ2, CANG, TL BLOCK-SCHEME
AZ1, AZ2, CANG, TL Routine;
PTSTA = PCSTA + TL; INPUT - INFO-STA FILE
Alignment Segment Limits;
Nctr - N° of Stations; Cctr=0 - Set Station Counter;
Number of Stations to check; Set Programming Cycle;
READ - INFO-STA [STA]; Cctr = Cctr + 1;
Programming Cycle;
Cctr > Nctr
yes
End of Program;
All Stations Checked;
no
PCSTA< STA <PTSTA
yes
no
CL = STA - PCSTA; FS (fsN, fsE)–RECORD; FS (fsN, fsE)–OUTPUT;
Layout Foresight Stations Points; Calculate & Record Foresight Stations Points Coordinates;
Return to Programming Cycle;

Example #2

Given:
Baseline TR-1A.
Stations 3+00.00, 3+15.80, 3+45.00, 3+75.00, 3+90.18, 4+00.00

Required: Based on Block-Scheme (Figure I.2.2.C), determine:
3) Baseline Alignment Segments containing shown above Stations;
4) Coordinates and Bearings of shown above Stations;

Figure I.2.2.D (below) illustrates the solution – CAD File with printed Stations, Working Text Files with Input Stations [INFO-STA], Corresponding Alignment Segment [BL-ALMT], and printed Stations Coordinates and Bearings [LINE-BS]. Note that the Stations within Curve Alignment have defined Bearings perpendicular (by definition) to station bearings at adjacent Tangent Segments.

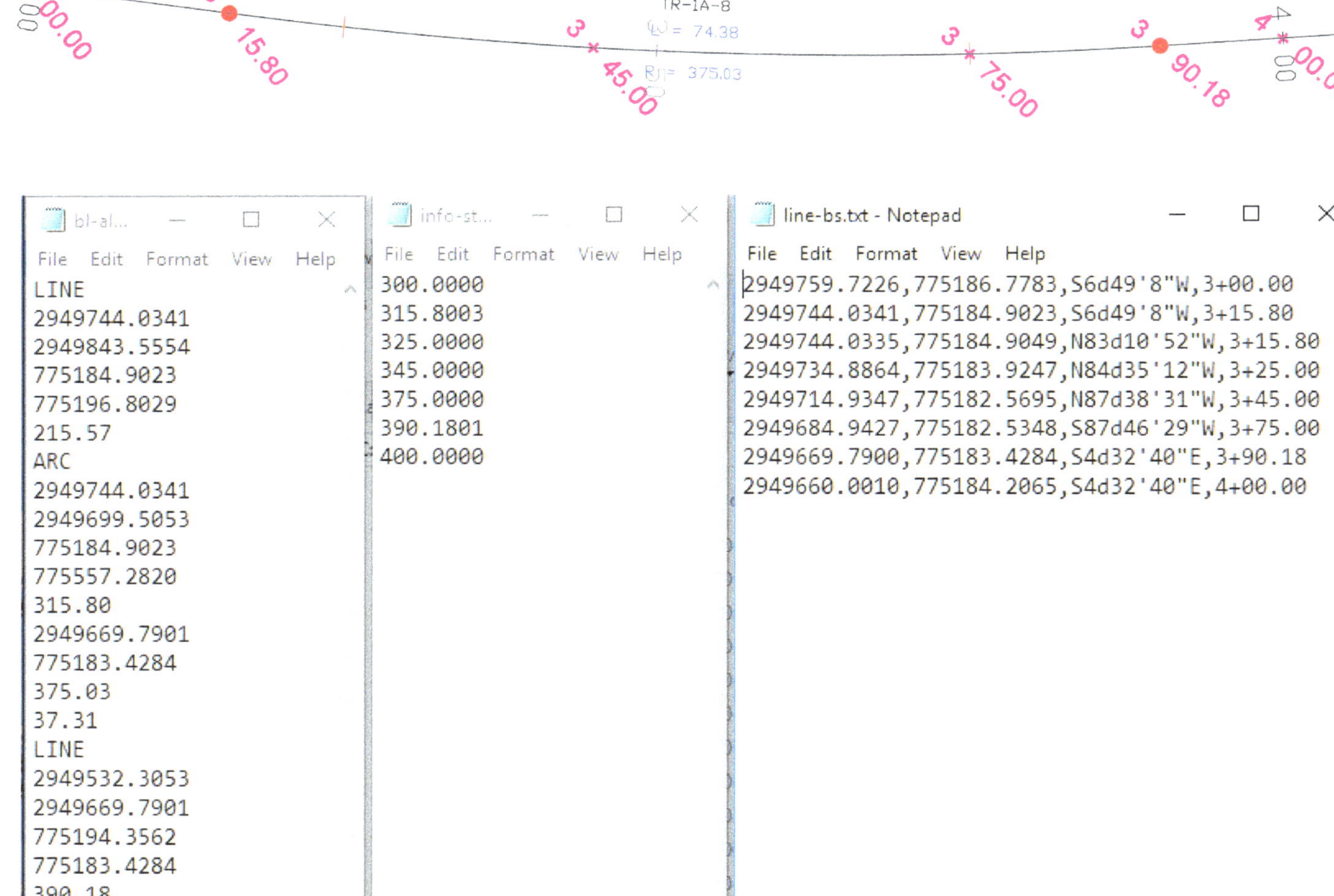

I.2.3. SPIRALES

An example of input spiral parameters is shown on Page 12 – Subsequently - Tangent to Spiral Point (Beginning of Spiral) TS (**tsstN, tsstE**), Point of Intersection (Point of Approach Tangents Intersection) PI (**psiN, psiE**), Spiral to Curve Pont (End of Spiral) SC (**csscN, csscE**), Length of Spiral – **LS,** Circular Curve (Arc) Radius – **RD,** Spiral Start Station – **CSTA,** Spiral Flag (Line-Arc – before the Circular Curve, Arc-Line – after the Circular Curve) - **FLAG**;

Figures I.2.3.A-C show Spiral Definition and Detail drawings and a calculation Block-Scheme for Point-on-Spiral PNTC coordinates (ptnN, ptnE) with the above-mentioned input parameters.

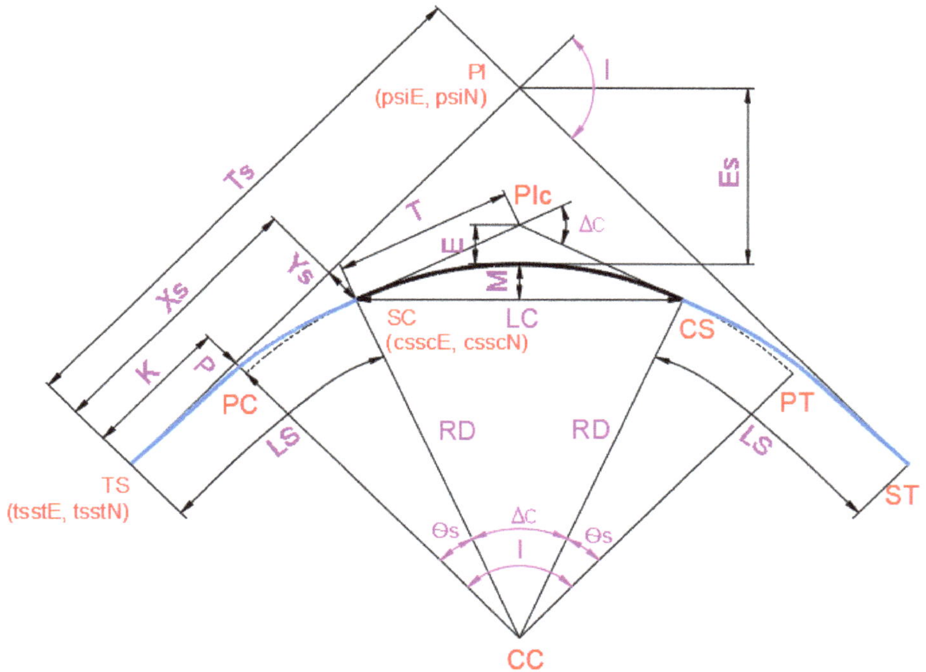

DEFINITIONS

PTNC	ARBITRARY POINT ON SPIRAL
CC	CENTER OF CIRULAR CURVE
CS	POINT OF CHANGE FROM CIRULAR CURVE TO SPIRAL
Da	DEGREE OF CIRULAR CURVE (ARC DEFINITION)
E	EXTERNAL DISTANCE FROM PIc
Es	EXTERNAL DISTANCE FROM PI
I	TOTAL CENTRAL ANGLE
K	DISTANCE FROM TS/ST TO PC/PT OF CIRULAR CURVE MEASURED ALONG MAIN TANGENT
L	LENGTH OF SPIRAL AR FROM TS TO ANY POINT (POINT "A") ON SPIRAL
Ls	TOTAL LENGTH OF SPIRAL MEASURED ALONG CURVE
LC	LONG CHORD OF CIRULAR CURVE
La	LENGTH OF CIRULAR CURVE
LTs	LENGTH OF LONG TANGENT OF SPIRAL
M	MID ORDINATE DISTANCE OF CIRULAR CURVE
P	OFFSET OF PC/PT OF CIRULAR CURVE MEASURED FROM MAIN TANGENT OR RADIAL SHIFT OF COMPOUND CONNECTING SPIRAL (COMPOUND CURVE)
PC	POINT OF CIRULAR CURVE
PI	POINT OF INTERSECTION OF MAIN TANGENTS
PIc	POINT OF INTERSECTION OF CIRULAR CURVE TANGENTS
PT	POINT OF TANGENT OF CIRULAR CURVE
R	RADIUS OF CIRULAR CURVE
SC	POINT OF CHANGE FROM SPIRAL TO CIRULAR CURVE
SI	POINT OF INTERSECTION OF SPIRAL TANGENTS
ST	POINT OF CHANGE FROM SPIRAL TO TANGENT
STs	LENGTH OF SHORT TANGENT OF SPIRAL
T	TANGENT LENGTH OF CIRULAR CURVE
TS	POINT OF CHANGE FROM TANGENT TO SPIRAL
Ts	TANGENT LENGTH FROM TS/ST TO PI
X	DISTANCE FROM TS/ST OF ANY POINT (POINT "A") ON SPIRAL PROJECTED TO MAIN TANGENT
Xs	DISTANCE FROM TS/ST TO SC/CS PROJECTED TO MAIN TANGENT
Y	OFFSET OF ANY POINT (POINT "A") ON SPIRAL MEASURED FROM MAIN TANGENT
Ys	OFFSET OF SC/CS MEASURED FROM MAIN TANGENT
θ	CENTRAL ANGLE OF SPIRAL ARC L
θs	CENTRAL ANGLE OF SPIRAL ARC Ls
ϕ	DEFLECTION ANGLE OF A CHORD BETWEEN TS/ST AND ANY POINT (POINT "A") ON SPIRAL
Δc	CENTRAL ANGLE OF CIRULAR CURVE

Figure I.2.3.A. Spiral Segment Definitions.

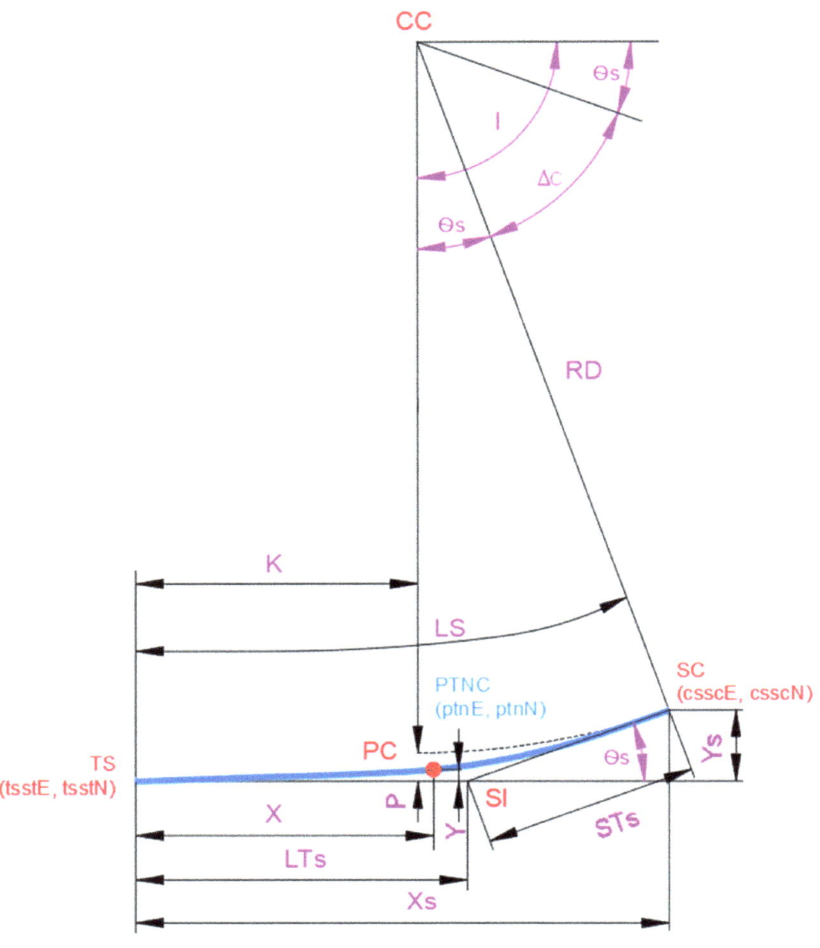

SPIRAL TRANSITION CURVE EQUATIONS

$X = \frac{L}{100}[100 - 0.3046174198\,\theta^{2}(10)^{-2} + 0.429591539\,\theta^{4}(10)^{-7} - 0.301987076\,\theta^{6}(10)^{-12}]$ = Xs AT THE SC/CS

$Y = \frac{L}{100}[0.5817764173\,\theta - 0.126585165\,\theta^{3}(10)^{-4} + 0.122691057\,\theta^{3}(10)^{-9}]$ = Ys AT THE SC/CS

$\Delta c = I - 2\theta s$

$Es = (R+P)\,EXSEC\frac{I}{2} + P$

$M = R(1 - COS\frac{\Delta c}{2})$

$\theta s = \frac{Ls}{200}(\frac{36{,}000}{2\,\pi R})$

$K = Xs - R\,SIN\theta s$

$P = Ys - R(1 - COS\theta s)$

$\theta = (\frac{L}{Ls})^{2}\theta s$

$LC = 2\,R\,SIN\frac{\Delta c}{2}$

$STs = \frac{Ys}{SIN\,\theta s}$

$\phi = ARTAN\frac{Y}{X}$

$Lc = 100\frac{\Delta c}{Dc}$

$T = RTAN\frac{\Delta c}{2}$

$Da = \frac{5729.58}{R}$

$LTs = Xs - \frac{Ys}{TAN\,\theta s}$

$Ts = (R+P)TAN\frac{I}{2} + K$

$E = R(\frac{1}{COS(\Delta c/2)} - 1)$

Figure I.2.3.B. Spiral Segment Equations.

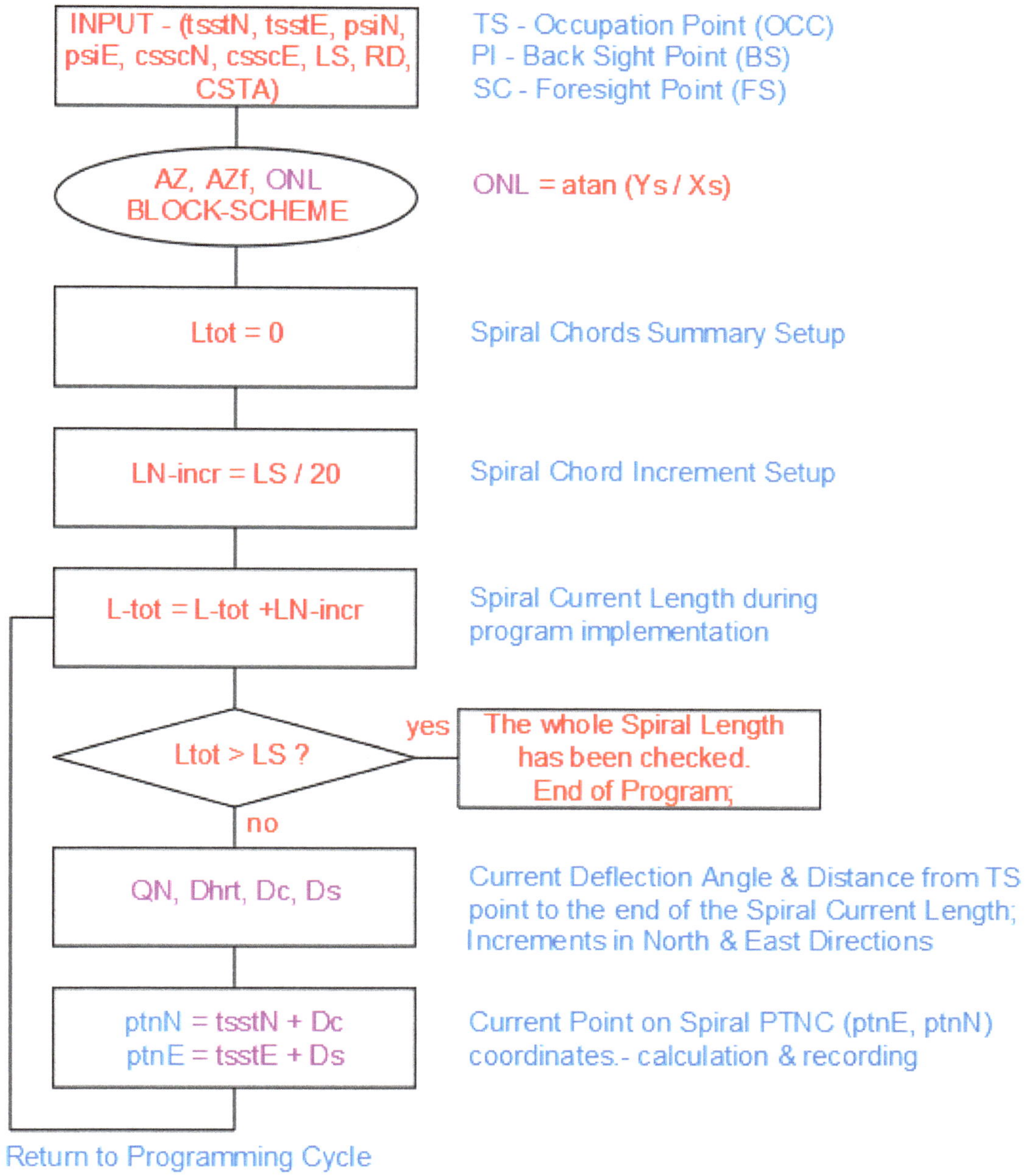

INPUT - (tsstN, tsstE, psiN, psiE, csscN, csscE, LS, RD, CSTA)
TS - Occupation Point (OCC)
PI - Back Sight Point (BS)
SC - Foresight Point (FS)
AZ, AZf, ONL BLOCK-SCHEME
ONL = atan (Ys / Xs)
Ltot = 0
Spiral Chords Summary Setup
LN-incr = LS / 20
Spiral Chord Increment Setup
L-tot = L-tot +LN-incr
Spiral Current Length during program implementation
Ltot > LS ?
yes
The whole Spiral Length has been checked. End of Program;
no
QN, Dhrt, Dc, Ds
Current Deflection Angle & Distance from TS point to the end of the Spiral Current Length; Increments in North & East Directions
ptnN = tsstN + Dc
ptnE = tsstE + Ds
Current Point on Spiral PTNC (ptnE, ptnN) coordinates.- calculation & recording
Return to Programming Cycle

Figure I.2.3.C. Spiral Segment Calculation Block-Scheme

Figure I.2.3.D. Spiral Segment Baseline Layout – Limits, Designation, Length, Running Block-Scheme

44+00
TR-1A-32
SPIRAL
LS = 108.12
44+50
45+00

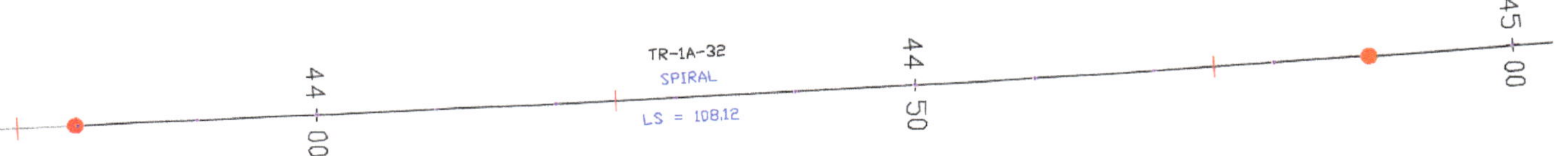

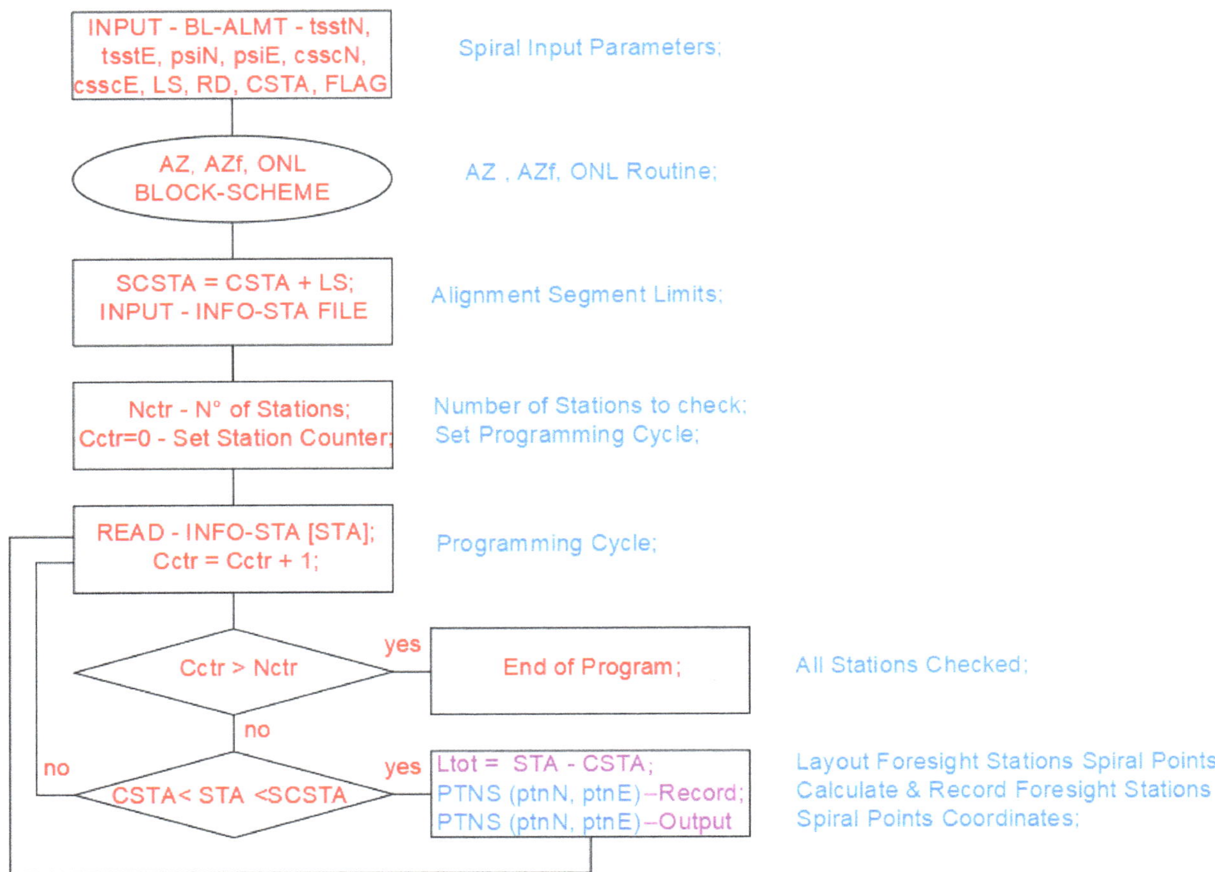

<u>Example #3</u>

Given:
Baseline TR-1A.
Stations 43+75.00, 43+80.00 thru 44+90.00 with 10' increments

Required: Based on Calculation Block-Scheme (Figure I.2.3.C), determine:

5) Baseline Alignment Segments containing shown above Stations;
6) Coordinates and Bearings of shown above Stations;

Figure I.2.3.E (below) illustrates the solution – CAD File with printed Stations, Working Text Files with Input Stations [INFO-STA], Corresponding Alignment Segment [BL-ALMT], and printed Stations Coordinates and Bearings [LINE-STR].

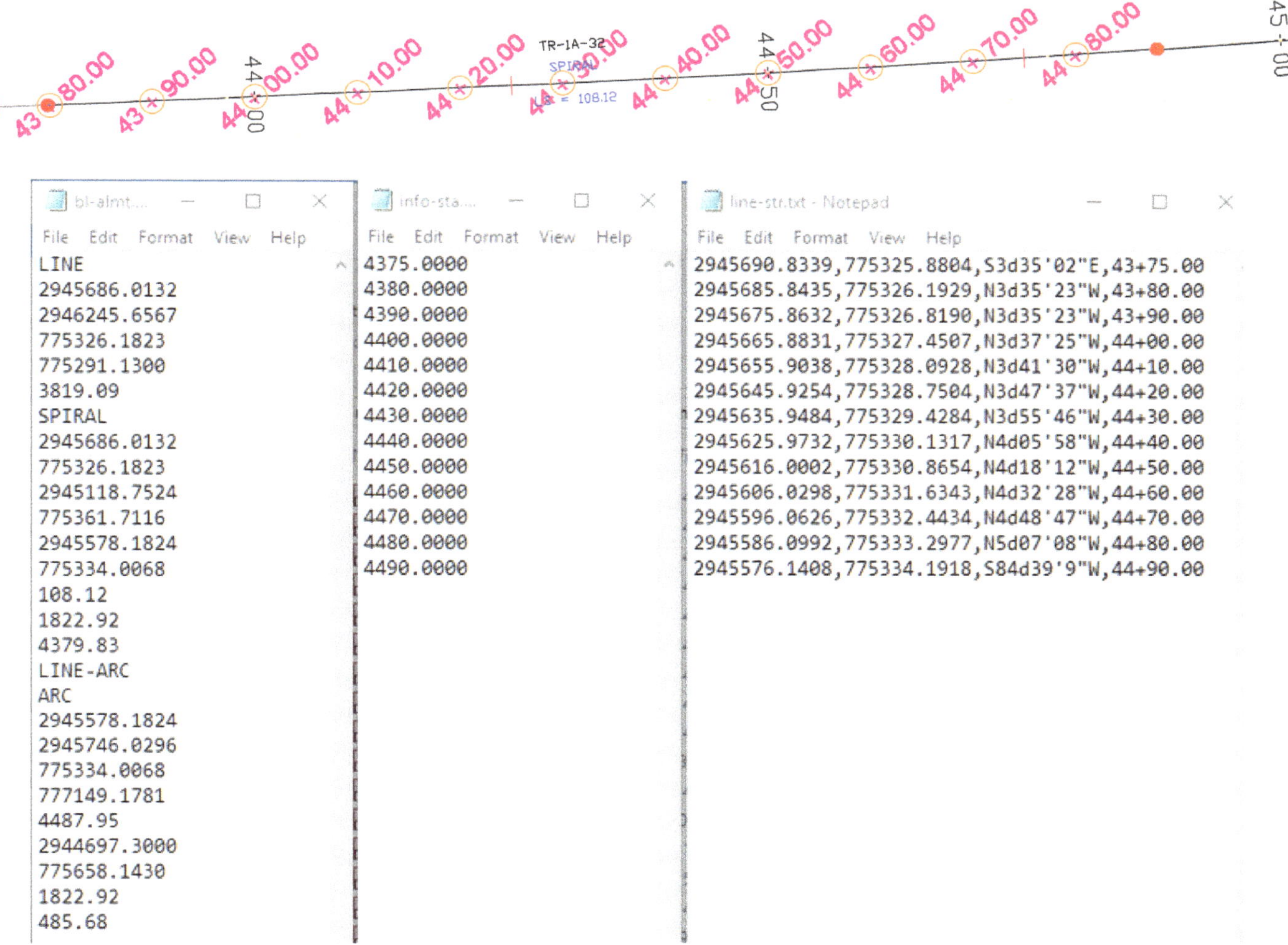


```
LINE
2945686.0132
2946245.6567
775326.1823
775291.1300
3819.09
SPIRAL
2945686.0132
775326.1823
2945118.7524
775361.7116
2945578.1824
775334.0068
108.12
1822.92
4379.83
LINE-ARC
ARC
2945578.1824
2945746.0296
775334.0068
777149.1781
4487.95
2944697.3000
775658.1430
1822.92
485.68
```

```
4375.0000
4380.0000
4390.0000
4400.0000
4410.0000
4420.0000
4430.0000
4440.0000
4450.0000
4460.0000
4470.0000
4480.0000
4490.0000
```

```
2945690.8339,775325.8804,S3d35'02"E,43+75.00
2945685.8435,775326.1929,N3d35'23"W,43+80.00
2945675.8632,775326.8190,N3d35'23"W,43+90.00
2945665.8831,775327.4507,N3d37'25"W,44+00.00
2945655.9038,775328.0928,N3d41'30"W,44+10.00
2945645.9254,775328.7504,N3d47'37"W,44+20.00
2945635.9484,775329.4284,N3d55'46"W,44+30.00
2945625.9732,775330.1317,N4d05'58"W,44+40.00
2945616.0002,775330.8654,N4d18'12"W,44+50.00
2945606.0298,775331.6343,N4d32'28"W,44+60.00
2945596.0626,775332.4434,N4d48'47"W,44+70.00
2945586.0992,775333.2977,N5d07'08"W,44+80.00
2945576.1408,775334.1918,S84d39'9"W,44+90.00
```

I.3. BASELINE OFFSETS.

The common way to represent an object location in civil engineering design - is by station and offset. For this modeling instrument, the input information also includes the Offset & Direction File [INFO-NUM], besides already known Alignment [BL-ALMT] and Station [INFO-STA] files.

The Figure I.3.A - I.1.3.B below demonstrates the Layout Plan for the area along with Input – Alignment, Stations, Offsets [BL-ALMT, INFO-STA, INFO-NUM] and Output - Coordinates [LINE-STR] text files.

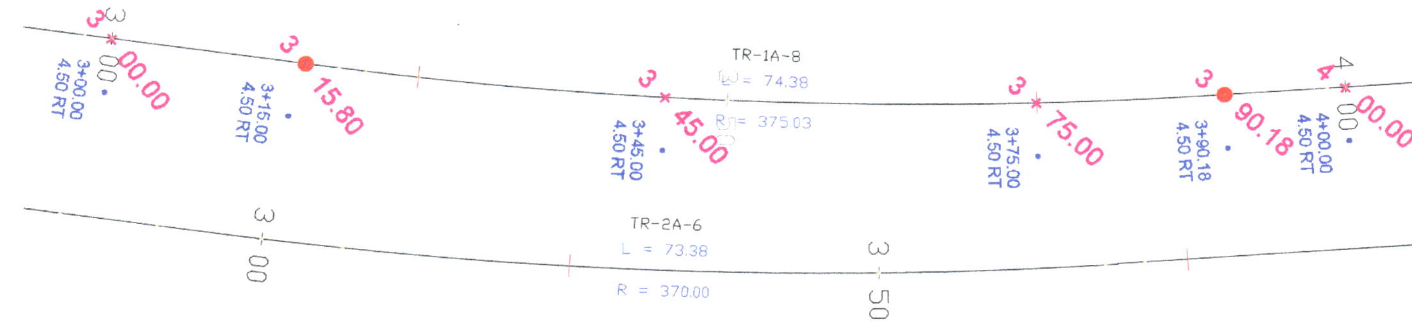

Figure I.3.A – Offset Layout Plan.

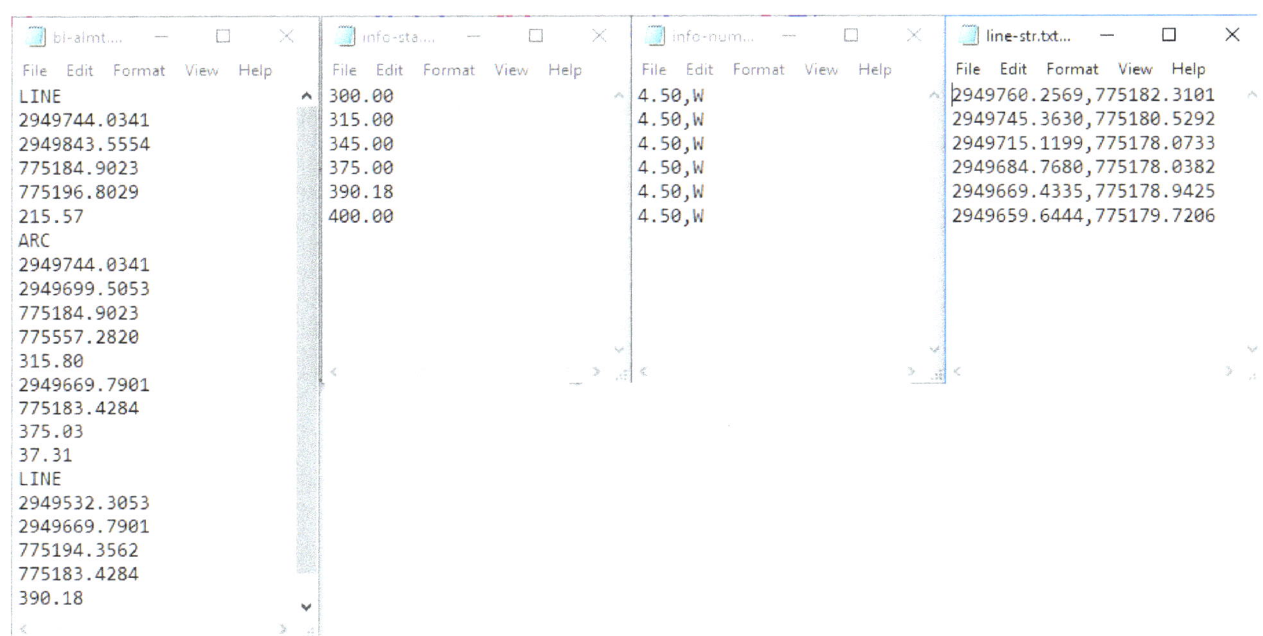

bi-almt....
File Edit Format View Help

```
LINE
2949744.0341
2949843.5554
775184.9023
775196.8029
215.57
ARC
2949744.0341
2949699.5053
775184.9023
775557.2820
315.80
2949669.7901
775183.4284
375.03
37.31
LINE
2949532.3053
2949669.7901
775194.3562
775183.4284
390.18
```

info-sta....
File Edit Format View Help

```
300.00
315.00
345.00
375.00
390.18
400.00
```

info-num...
File Edit Format View Help

```
4.50,W
4.50,W
4.50,W
4.50,W
4.50,W
4.50,W
```

line-str.txt...
File Edit Format View Help

```
2949760.2569,775182.3101
2949745.3630,775180.5292
2949715.1199,775178.0733
2949684.7680,775178.0382
2949669.4335,775178.9425
2949659.6444,775179.7206
```

Figure I.3.B – Offset Layout Input & Output Data

I.4. BASELINE CORRELATIONS

Another common task is to determine a point coordinates and/or station on an auxiliary or adjacent baseline from the known station on the main or working baseline.

The Figures I.4.A – I.4.C below shows a combination of Baselines Correlations – Tangents, Curves, and Spirals, along with corresponding Alignment, Stations, Distances and Points Coordinates information.

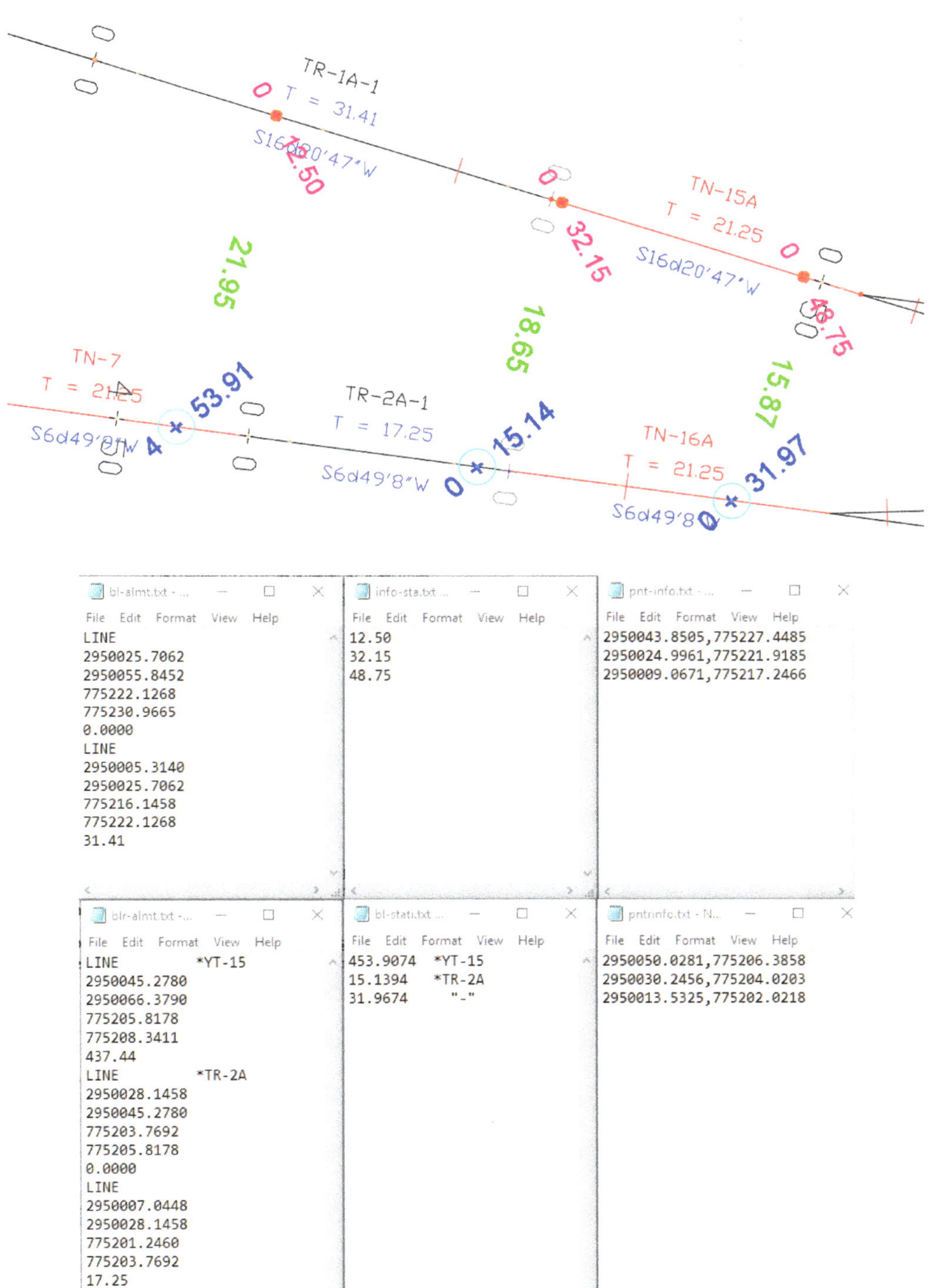

Figure I.4.A – Tangent Correlation Baselines Plan & Data

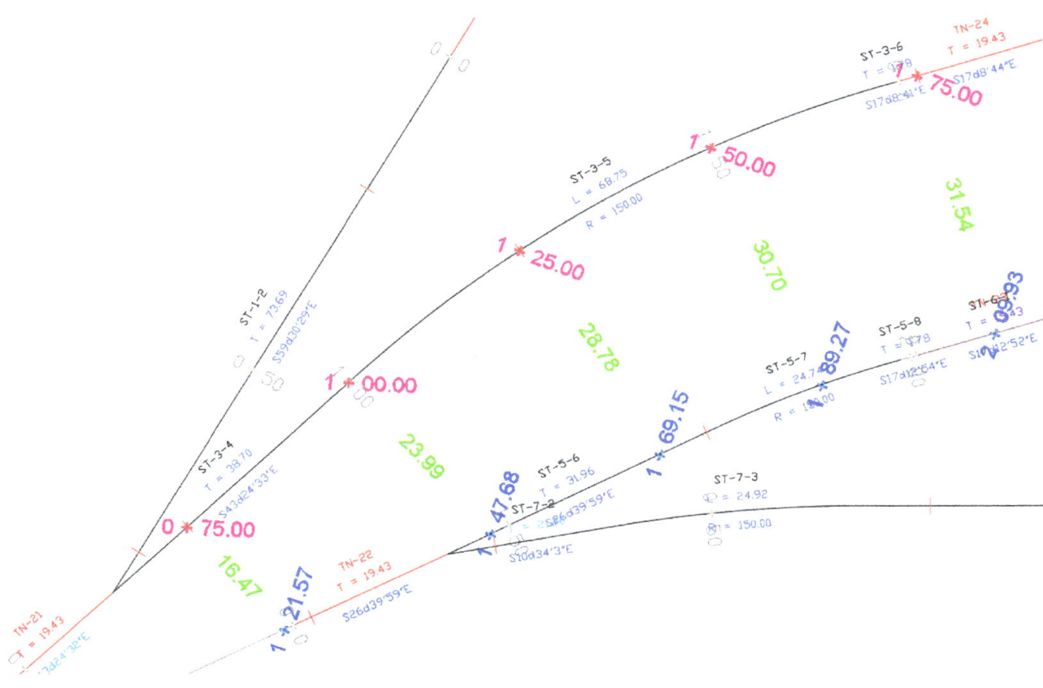

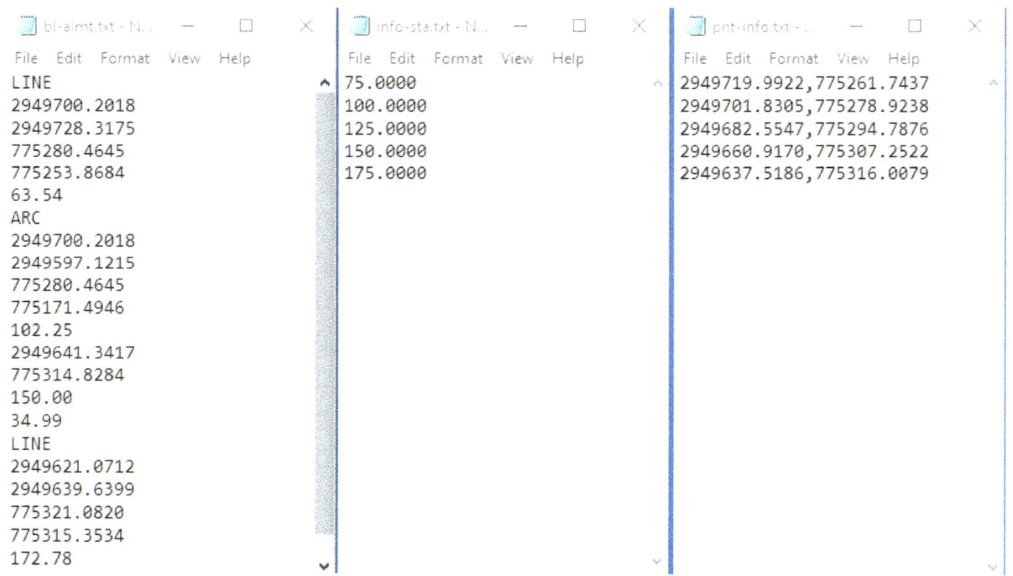

bl-aimt.txt

```
LINE
2949700.2018
2949728.3175
775280.4645
775253.8684
63.54
ARC
2949700.2018
2949597.1215
775280.4645
775171.4946
102.25
2949641.3417
775314.8284
150.00
34.99
LINE
2949621.0712
2949639.6399
775321.0820
775315.3534
172.78
```

info-sta.txt

```
75.0000
100.0000
125.0000
150.0000
175.0000
```

pnt-info.txt

```
2949719.9922,775261.7437
2949701.8305,775278.9238
2949682.5547,775294.7876
2949660.9170,775307.2522
2949637.5186,775316.0079
```

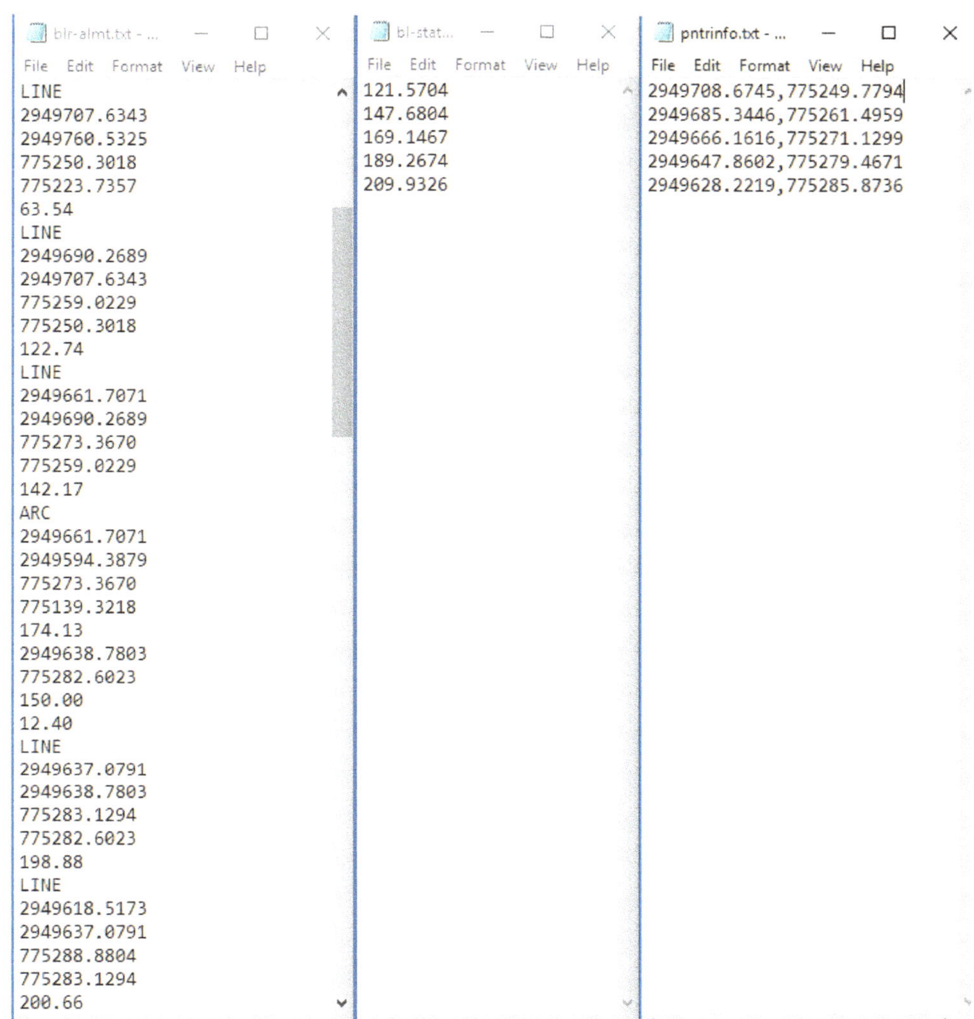

blr-almt.txt

```
LINE
2949707.6343
2949760.5325
775250.3018
775223.7357
63.54
LINE
2949690.2689
2949707.6343
775259.0229
775250.3018
122.74
LINE
2949661.7071
2949690.2689
775273.3670
775259.0229
142.17
ARC
2949661.7071
2949594.3879
775273.3670
775139.3218
174.13
2949638.7803
775282.6023
150.00
12.40
LINE
2949637.0791
2949638.7803
775283.1294
775282.6023
198.88
LINE
2949618.5173
2949637.0791
775288.8804
775283.1294
200.66
```

bl-stat...

```
121.5704
147.6804
169.1467
189.2674
209.9326
```

pntrinfo.txt

```
2949708.6745,775249.7794
2949685.3446,775261.4959
2949666.1616,775271.1299
2949647.8602,775279.4671
2949628.2219,775285.8736
```

Figure I.4.B – Curve /Tangent Correlation Baselines Plan & Data

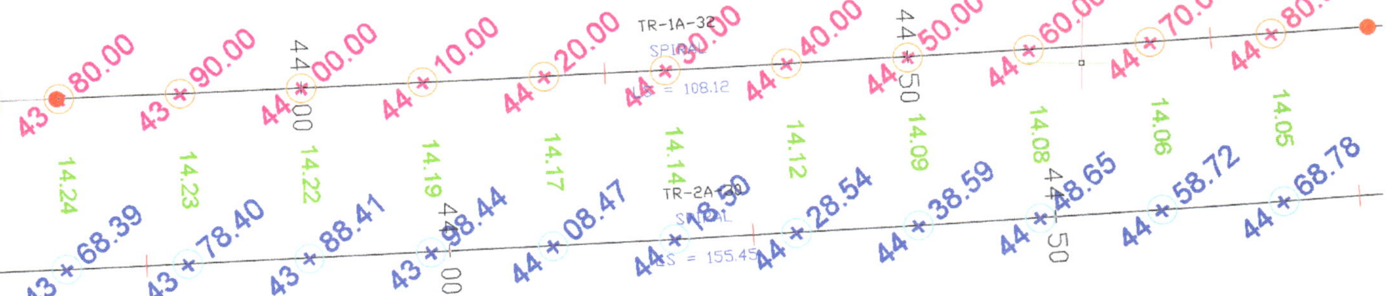

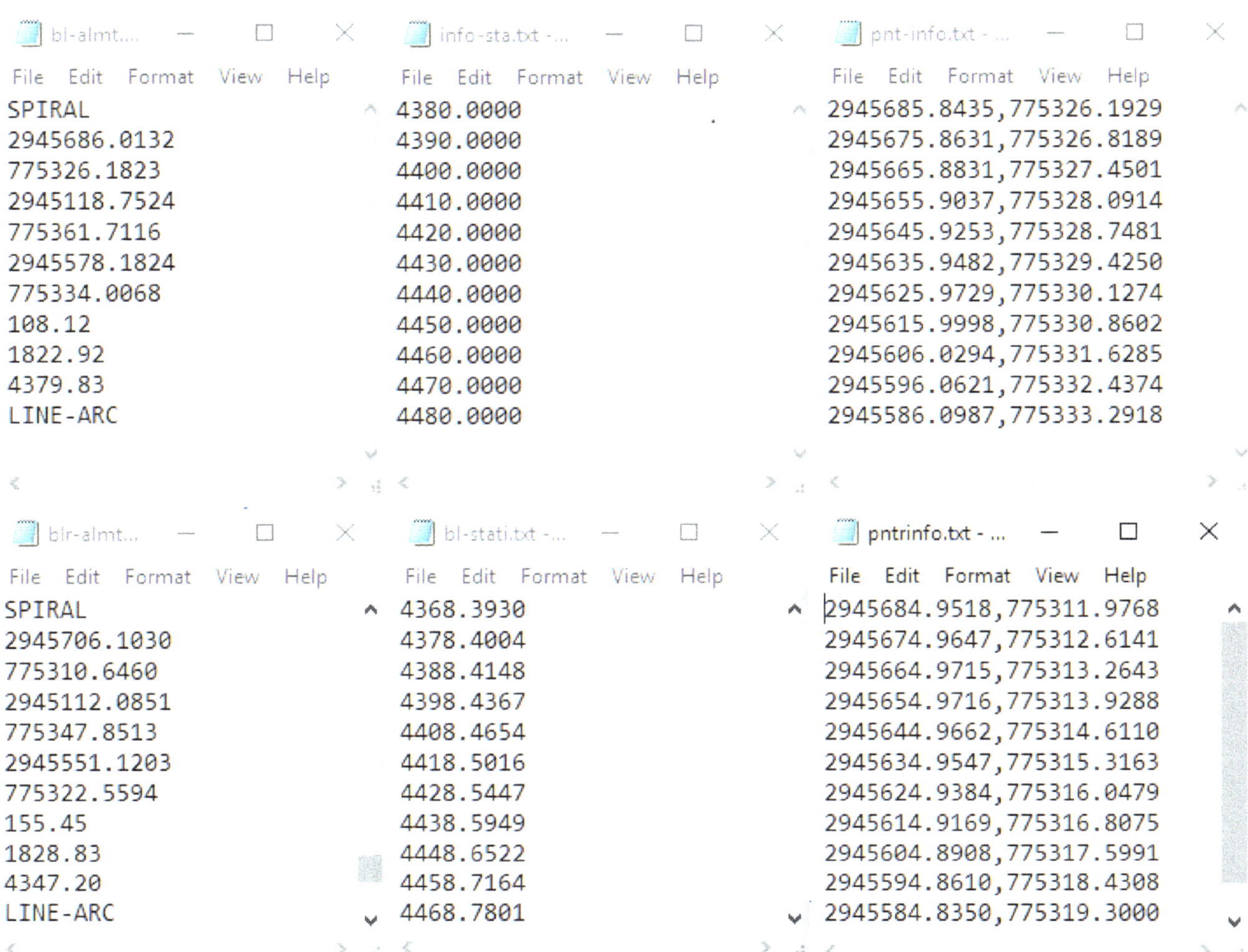

Figure I.4.C – Spiral Correlation Baselines Plan & Data

Figure I.4.D below shows the Block – Scheme for combination of Baselines Correlations

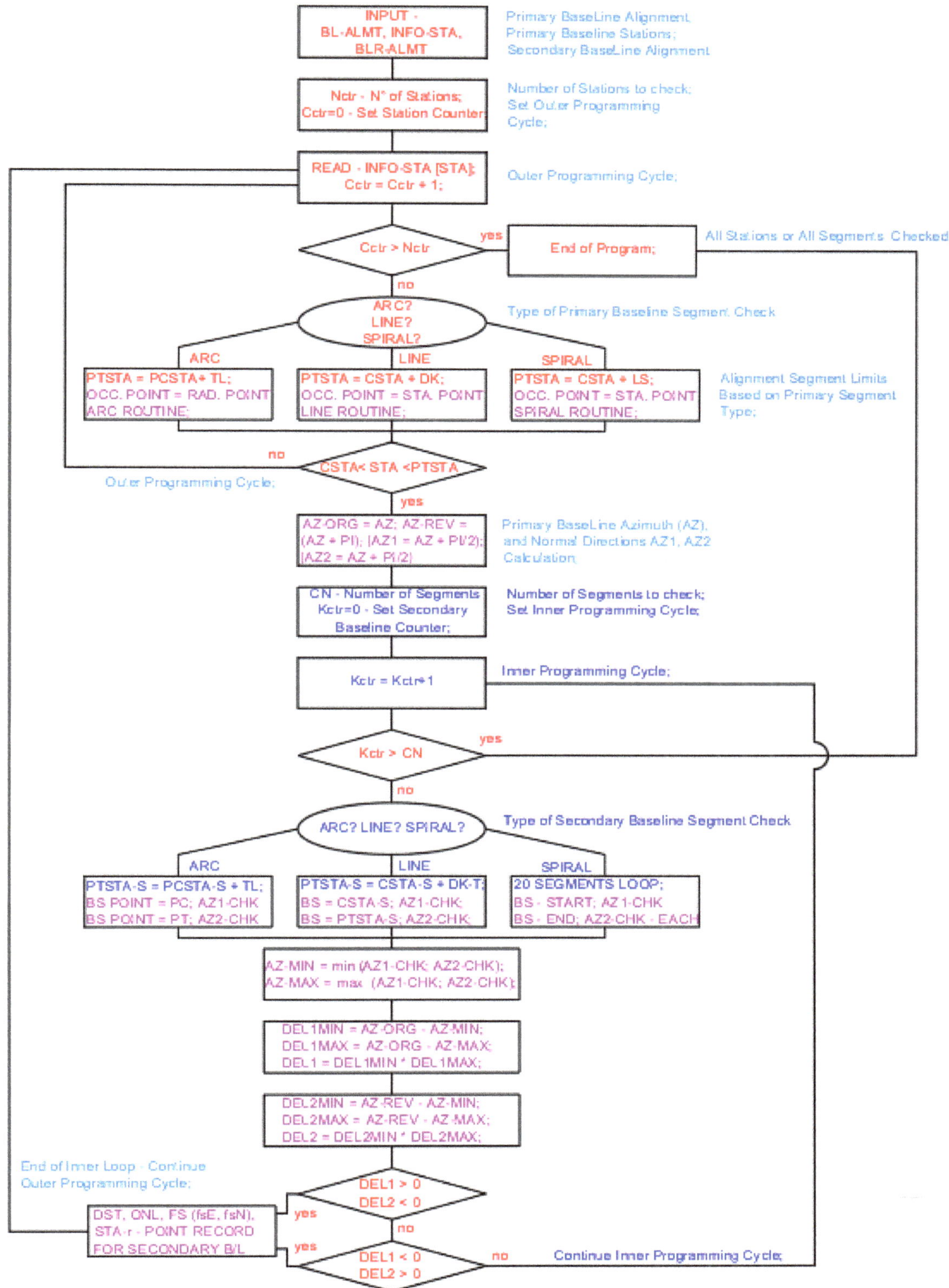

I.5. CROSS-SECTION VIEWS

Base Lines Correlations procedure is essential for creating cross-sections in project real space. It is a common situation when the Cross-Section is to reflect information from 2 or more project baselines. The current Modeling instrument considers two methods of creating cross-section:

1) Using the Project-provided templates (blocks), adjust (and scale) the block per the result of the baseline correlation program and move it into real space by known baselines' coordinates.
2) Create the new cross-section using coordinates derived from Baselines Correlation and Offset Programs.

In this Module, we consider only the first method. The second method will be described in detail in Module III – Structural.

The Figure I.5.A shows the Detailed Plan & the Cross-Section, cut through stations 1+25.00 (Track ST-3) and 1+69.15 (Track ST-5) – based on Figure I.4.B. The coordinates and the distance between the baselines are the same on both plan and section views; the cut line crosses exactly through the stations.

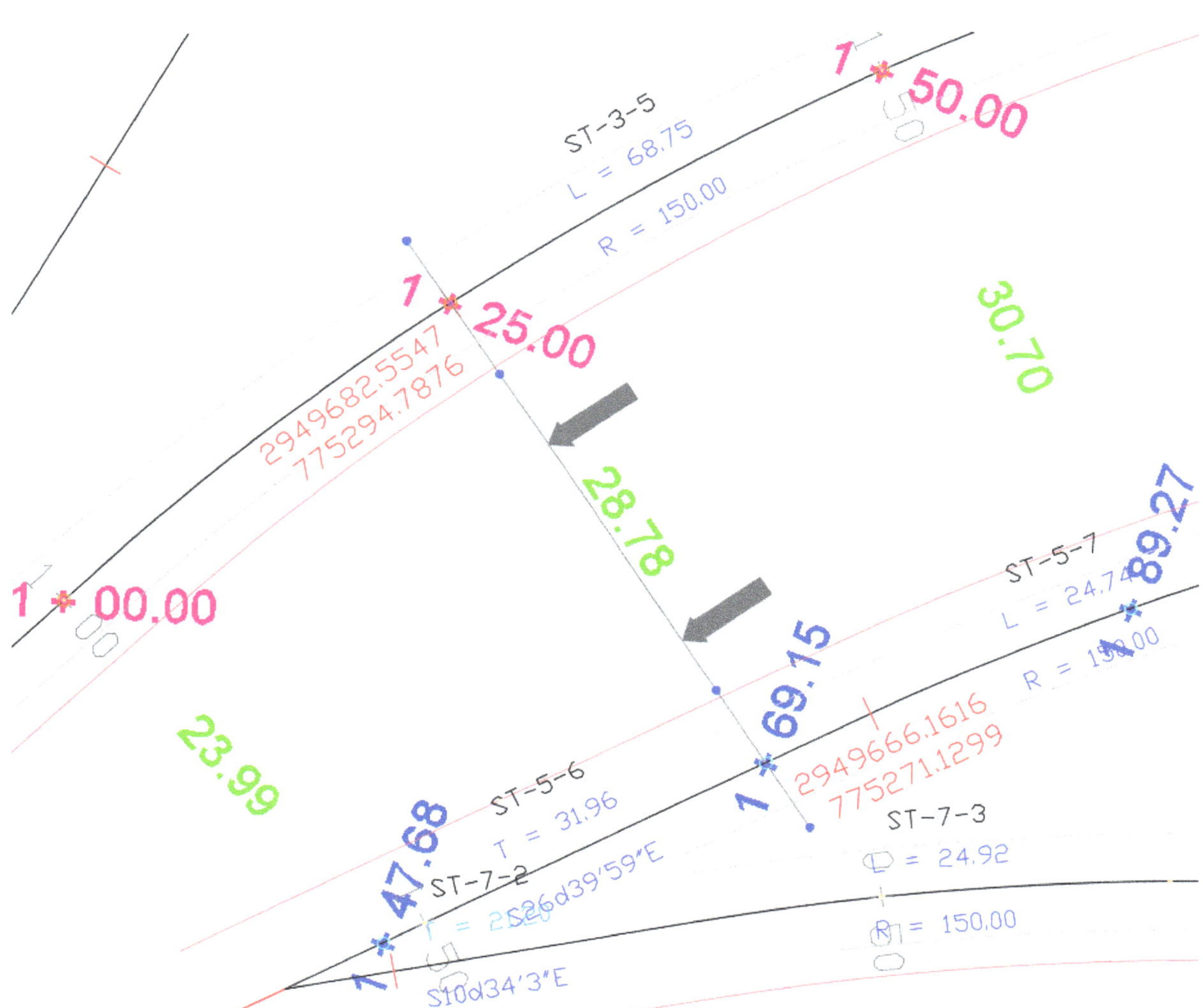

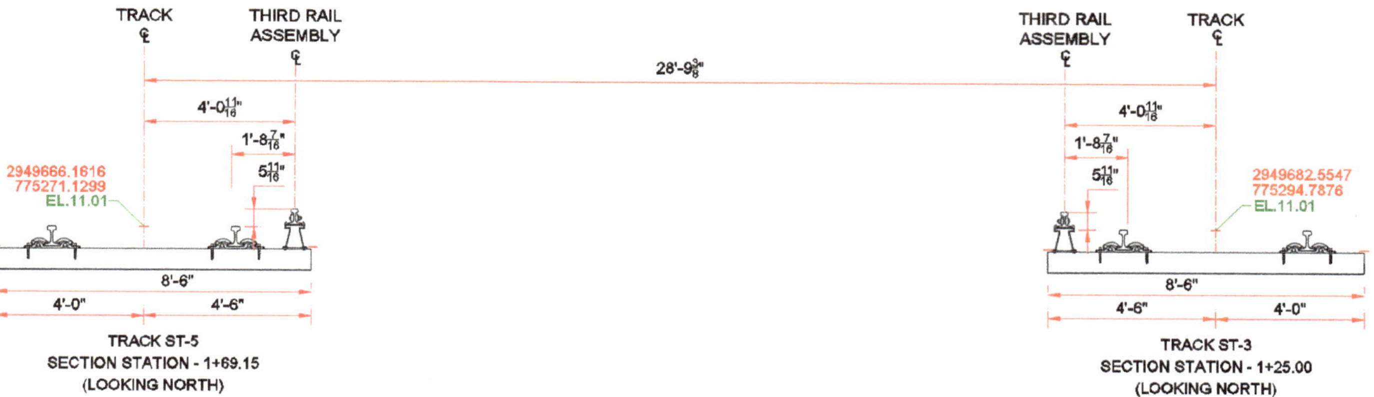

The Figures I.5.B & I.5.C. below illustrate the Block-Schemes for:

1) Project Provided Template/Block Movement into Real Space
2) Base Line Stations calculation for Cross-Section View.

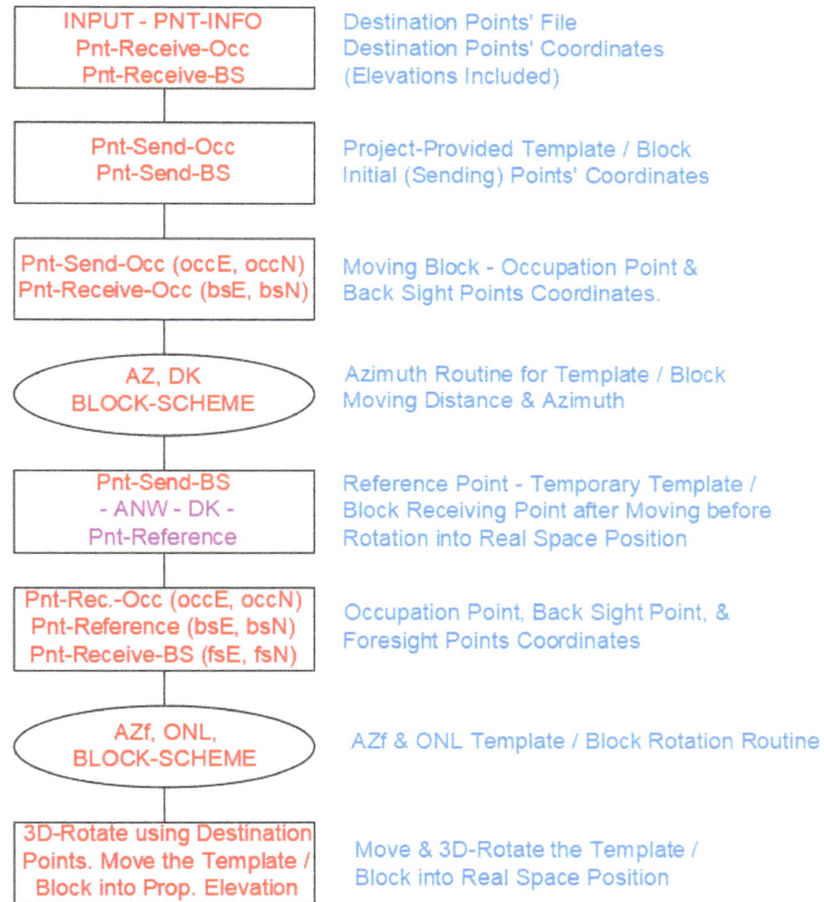

Figure I.5.B. Template/Block Movement Block-Scheme.

Figure I.5.C. (below) Base Line Stations calculation for Cross-Section View Block-Scheme.

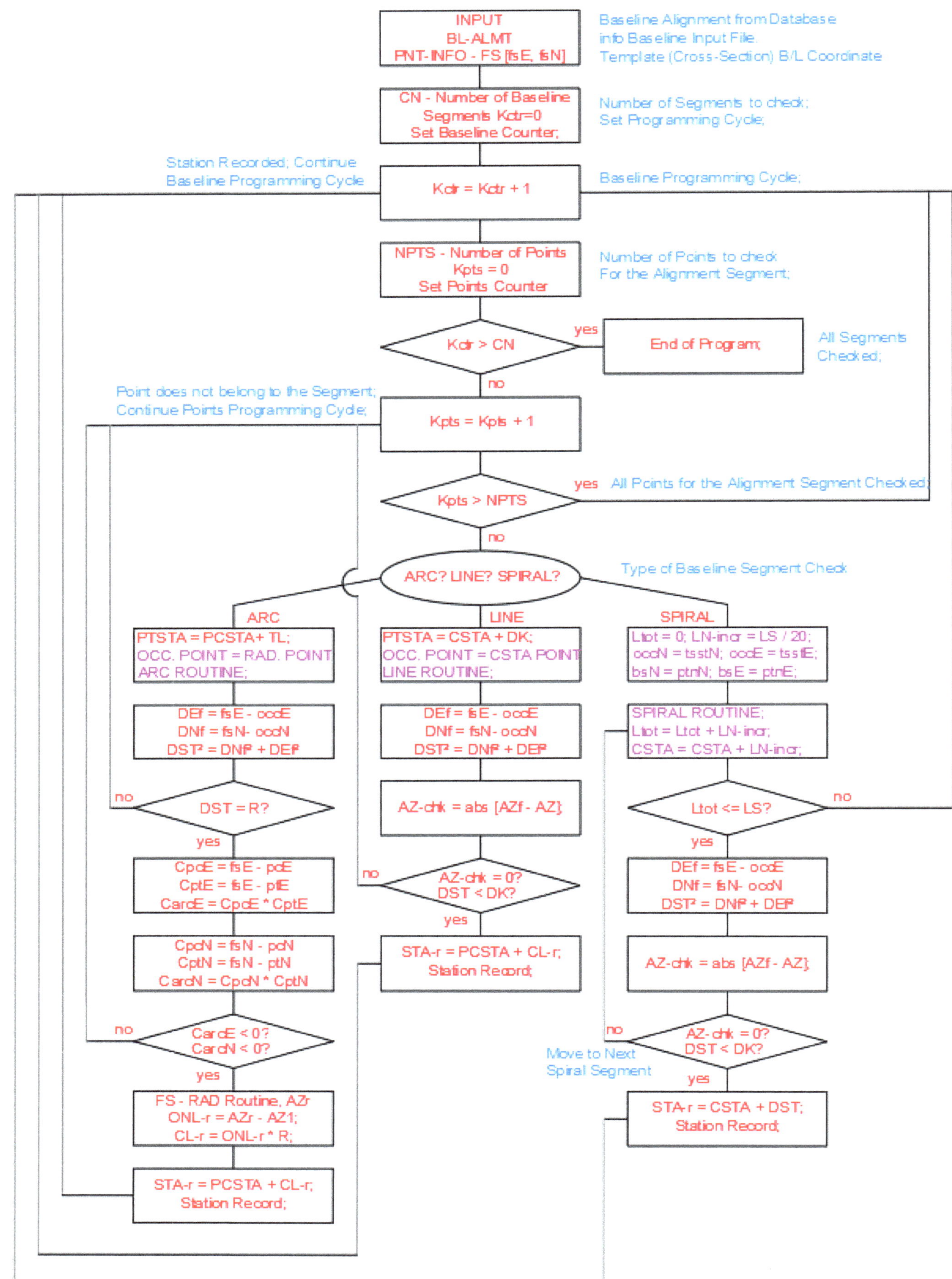
INPUT
BL-ALMT
PNT-INFO - FS [fsE, fsN]
Baseline Alignment from Database
info Baseline Input File.
Template (Cross-Section) B/L Coordinate
CN - Number of Baseline
Segments Kctr=0
Set Baseline Counter;
Number of Segments to check;
Set Programming Cycle;
Station Recorded; Continue
Baseline Programming Cycle
Kctr = Kctr + 1
Baseline Programming Cycle;
NPTS - Number of Points
Kpts = 0
Set Points Counter
Number of Points to check
For the Alignment Segment;
Kctr > CN
yes
End of Program;
All Segments
Checked;
no
Point does not belong to the Segment;
Continue Points Programming Cycle;
Kpts = Kpts + 1
yes
All Points for the Alignment Segment Checked;
Kpts > NPTS
no
ARC? LINE? SPIRAL?
Type of Baseline Segment Check
ARC
LINE
SPIRAL
PTSTA = PCSTA+ TL;
OCC. POINT = RAD. POINT
ARC ROUTINE;
PTSTA = CSTA + DK;
OCC. POINT = CSTA POINT
LINE ROUTINE;
Ltot = 0; LN-incr = LS / 20;
occN = tsstN; occE = tsstE;
bsN = ptnN; bsE = ptnE;
DEf = fsE - occE
DNf = fsN - occN
DST² = DNf² + DEf²
DEf = fsE - occE
DNf = fsN - occN
DST² = DNf² + DEf²
SPIRAL ROUTINE;
Ltot = Ltot + LN-incr;
CSTA = CSTA + LN-incr;
no
DST = R?
AZ-chk = abs [AZf - AZ]
Ltot <= LS?
no
yes
yes
CpcE = fsE - pcE
CptE = fsE - ptE
CardE = CpcE * CptE
no
AZ-chk = 0?
DST < DK?
DEf = fsE - occE
DNf = fsN - occN
DST² = DNf² + DEf²
yes
CpcN = fsN - pcN
CptN = fsN - ptN
CardN = CpcN * CptN
STA-r = PCSTA + CL-r;
Station Record;
AZ-chk = abs [AZf - AZ]
no
CardE < 0?
CardN < 0?
no
AZ-chk = 0?
DST < DK?
Move to Next
Spiral Segment
yes
yes
FS - RAD Routine, AZr
ONL-r = AZr - AZ1;
CL-r = ONL-r * R;
STA-r = CSTA + DST;
Station Record;
STA-r = PCSTA + CL-r;
Station Record;

I.6. VERTICAL CURVES

The Modeling Instrument Tool Vertical Curve Application is shown on Block-Scheme below – Figure I.6.A:

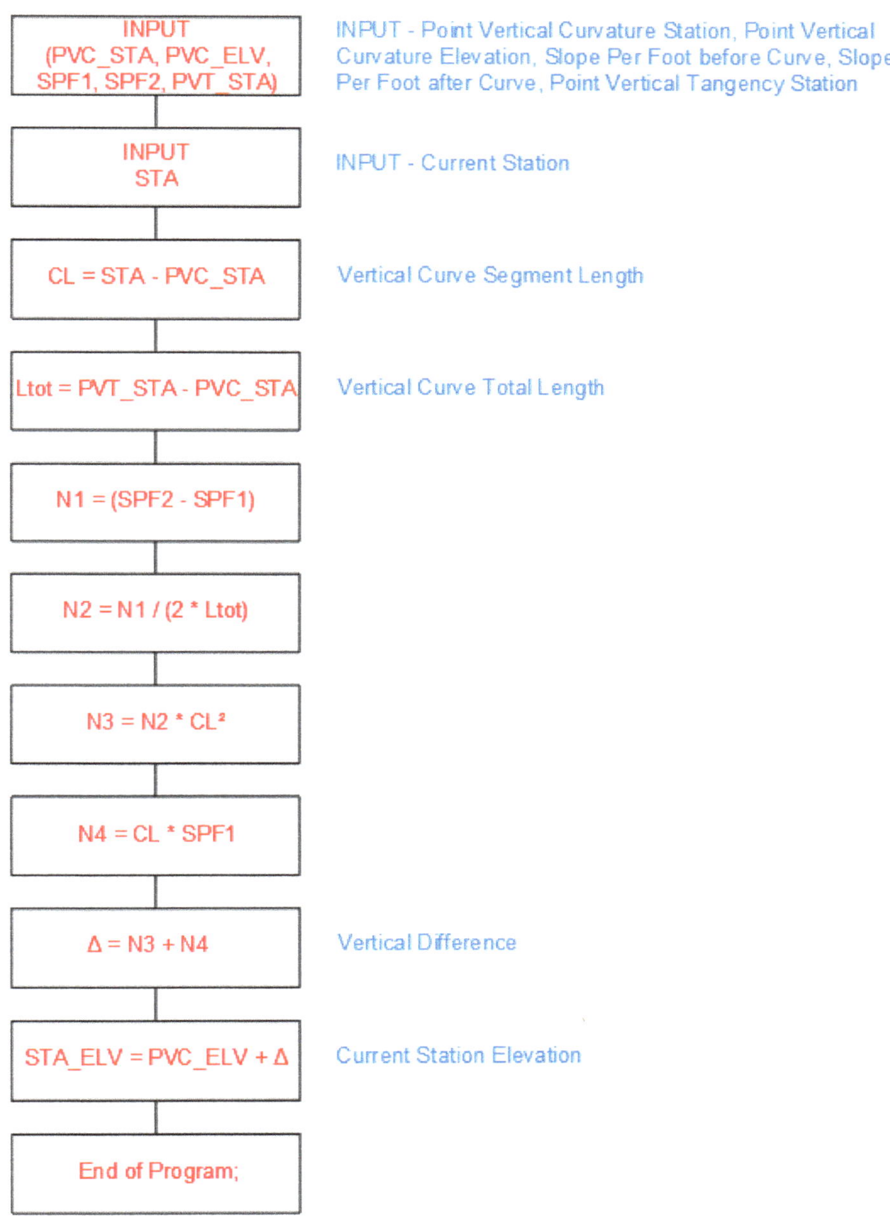

The Project Example shows the Vertical Curve Calculation for the Segment of Track TR-1A within Stations 12+91.30 – 14+41.30 with 10' Station increments – Figure I.6.B:

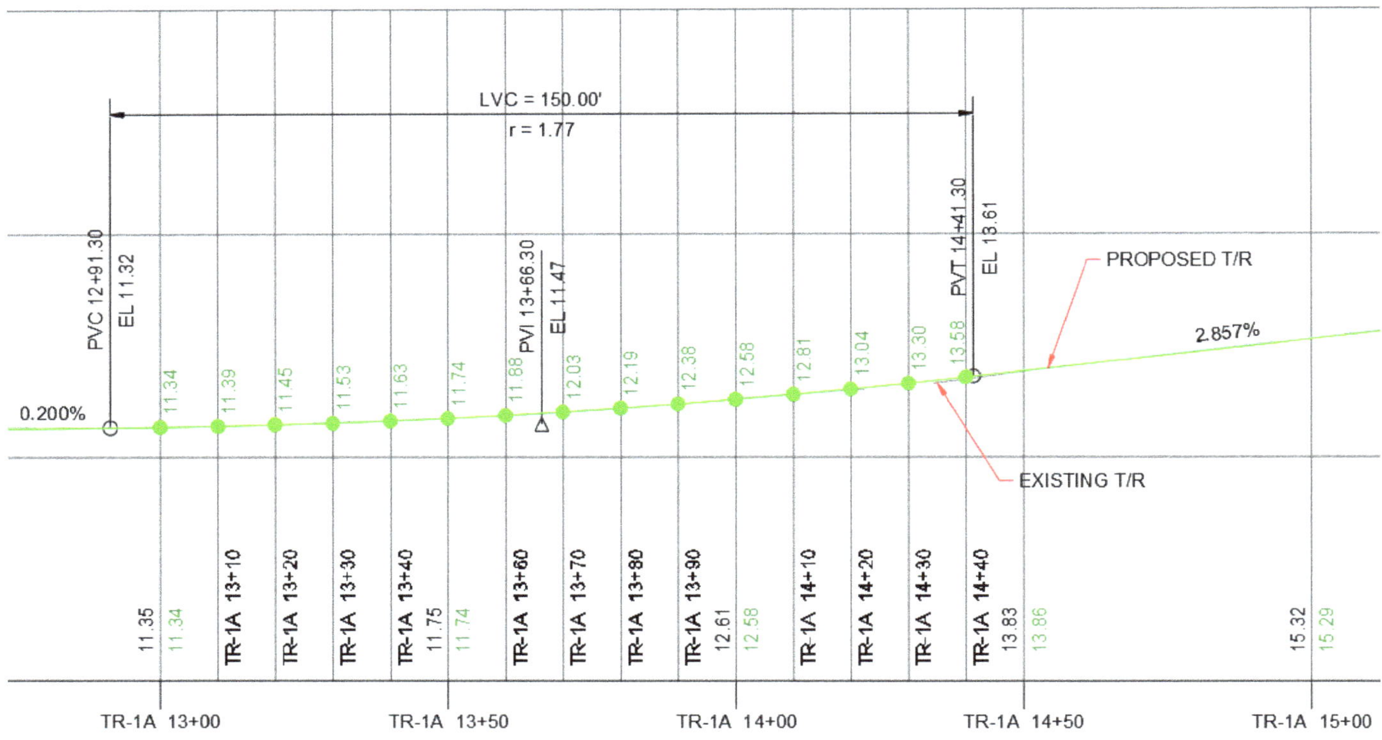

Refer to paragraph I.2, set up an Alignment - for the Track Segment shown above – Figure I.6.C:

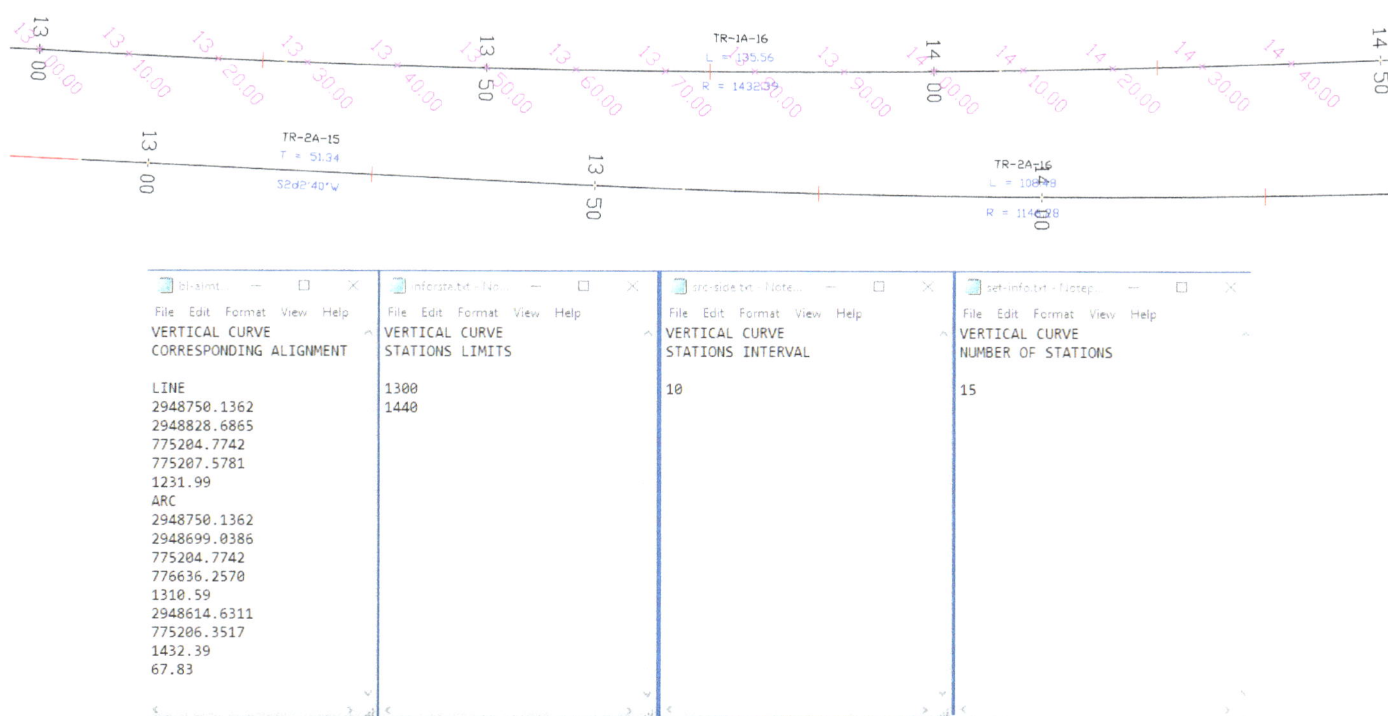

The Vertical Curve Increment Stations, Coordinates, and Calculated Elevations Files:

info-sta.txt - Notepad

```
VERTICAL CURVE
STATIONS WITHIN LIMITS

1300.0000
1310.0000
1320.0000
1330.0000
1340.0000
1350.0000
1360.0000
1370.0000
1380.0000
1390.0000
1400.0000
1410.0000
1420.0000
1430.0000
1440.0000
```

line-str.txt - Notepad

```
VERTICAL CURVE
STATIONS - COORDINATES

2948760.7198,775205.1520,S2d2'40"W,13+00.00
2948750.7262,775204.7953,S2d2'40"W,13+10.00
2948740.7310,775204.4739,N88d19'55"W,13+20.00
2948730.7343,775204.2177,N88d43'55"W,13+30.00
2948720.7361,775204.0313,N89d7'55"W,13+40.00
2948710.7368,775203.9148,N89d31'55"W,13+50.00
2948700.7369,775203.8680,N89d55'55"W,13+60.00
2948690.7369,775203.8911,S89d40'5"W,13+70.00
2948680.7374,775203.9839,S89d16'5"W,13+80.00
2948670.7387,775204.1466,S88d52'5"W,13+90.00
2948660.7414,775204.3791,S88d28'5"W,14+00.00
2948650.7460,775204.6813,S88d4'5"W,14+10.00
2948640.7530,775205.0533,S87d40'5"W,14+20.00
2948630.7628,775205.4951,S87d16'5"W,14+30.00
2948620.7759,775206.0067,S86d52'5"W,14+40.00
```

pnt-elv.txt - Notepad

```
VERTICAL CURVE
STATIONS - ELEVATIONS

11.34
11.39
11.45
11.53
11.63
11.74
11.88
12.03
12.19
12.38
12.58
12.81
13.04
13.30
13.58
```

Using the Format PNEZD [P - Point Number, N, E -North & East Coordinates, Z – Elevations, D – Description], create the Text File for Surveyors to use in the Field for Layout:

pnt-crd.txt - Notepad

```
1011,2948760.7198,775205.1520,11.34,13+00.00
1012,2948750.7262,775204.7953,11.39,13+10.00
1013,2948740.7310,775204.4739,11.45,13+20.00
1014,2948730.7343,775204.2177,11.53,13+30.00
1015,2948720.7361,775204.0313,11.63,13+40.00
1016,2948710.7368,775203.9148,11.74,13+50.00
1017,2948700.7369,775203.8680,11.88,13+60.00
1018,2948690.7369,775203.8911,12.03,13+70.00
1019,2948680.7374,775203.9839,12.19,13+80.00
1020,2948670.7387,775204.1466,12.38,13+90.00
1021,2948660.7414,775204.3791,12.58,14+00.00
1022,2948650.7460,775204.6813,12.81,14+10.00
1023,2948640.7530,775205.0533,13.04,14+20.00
1024,2948630.7628,775205.4951,13.30,14+30.00
1025,2948620.7759,775206.0067,13.58,14+40.00
```

CHAPTER II: GEOTECHNICAL

The goal is to show accurate Stratigraphy Information as a Base for Separate Soil Layers Excavation Quantity Takeoffs for the project. The meaning of geotechnical tabulation is to reflect the boring data in Real Space throughout the project. The information is obtained from Contract Drawings and organized in a Civil Directory of the File Manager as follows:

- BORING TITLE – Boring Holes Designation.
- BORING POINTS – Boring Holes Coordinates and Surface Elevation.
- BORING DATA – Boring Holes Soil Layers (Stratigraphy)
- BORING DEPTH – Boring Holes – Depth of Each Soil Layer from Surface Elevation

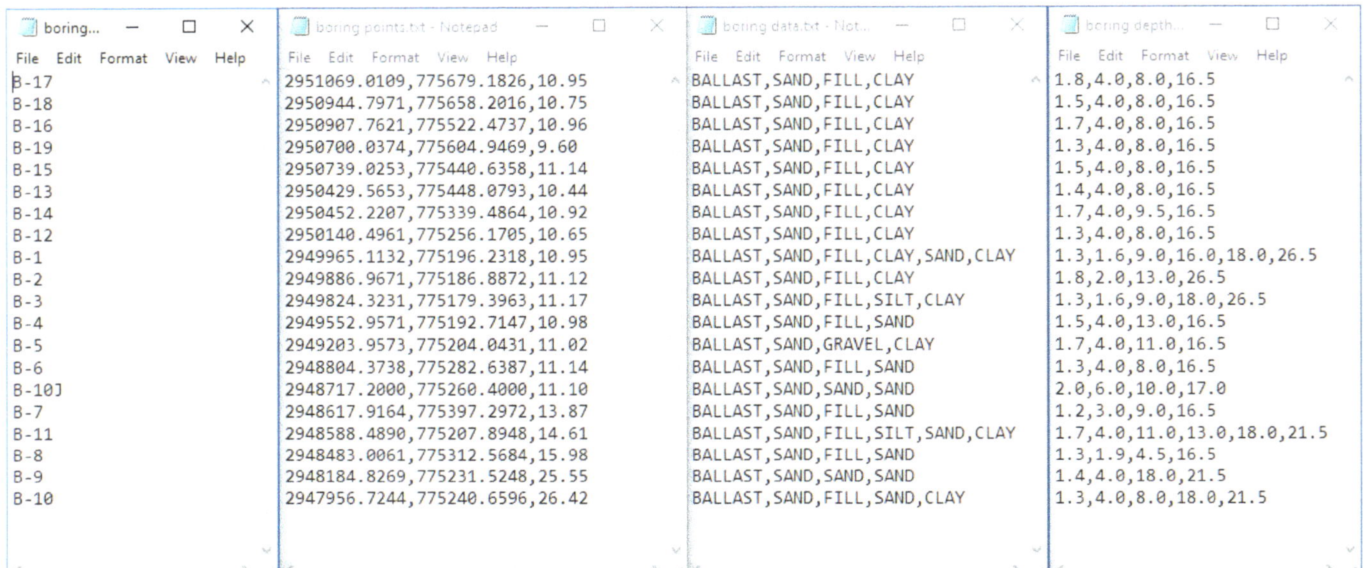

boring...	boring points.txt - Notepad	boring data.txt - Not...	boring depth...
B-17	2951069.0109,775679.1826,10.95	BALLAST,SAND,FILL,CLAY	1.8,4.0,8.0,16.5
B-18	2950944.7971,775658.2016,10.75	BALLAST,SAND,FILL,CLAY	1.5,4.0,8.0,16.5
B-16	2950907.7621,775522.4737,10.96	BALLAST,SAND,FILL,CLAY	1.7,4.0,8.0,16.5
B-19	2950700.0374,775604.9469,9.60	BALLAST,SAND,FILL,CLAY	1.3,4.0,8.0,16.5
B-15	2950739.0253,775440.6358,11.14	BALLAST,SAND,FILL,CLAY	1.5,4.0,8.0,16.5
B-13	2950429.5653,775448.0793,10.44	BALLAST,SAND,FILL,CLAY	1.4,4.0,8.0,16.5
B-14	2950452.2207,775339.4864,10.92	BALLAST,SAND,FILL,CLAY	1.7,4.0,9.5,16.5
B-12	2950140.4961,775256.1705,10.65	BALLAST,SAND,FILL,CLAY	1.3,4.0,8.0,16.5
B-1	2949965.1132,775196.2318,10.95	BALLAST,SAND,FILL,CLAY,SAND,CLAY	1.3,1.6,9.0,16.0,18.0,26.5
B-2	2949886.9671,775186.8872,11.12	BALLAST,SAND,FILL,CLAY	1.8,2.0,13.0,26.5
B-3	2949824.3231,775179.3963,11.17	BALLAST,SAND,FILL,SILT,CLAY	1.3,1.6,9.0,18.0,26.5
B-4	2949552.9571,775192.7147,10.98	BALLAST,SAND,FILL,SAND	1.5,4.0,13.0,16.5
B-5	2949203.9573,775204.0431,11.02	BALLAST,SAND,GRAVEL,CLAY	1.7,4.0,11.0,16.5
B-6	2948804.3738,775282.6387,11.14	BALLAST,SAND,FILL,SAND	1.3,4.0,8.0,16.5
B-10J	2948717.2000,775260.4000,11.10	BALLAST,SAND,SAND,SAND	2.0,6.0,10.0,17.0
B-7	2948617.9164,775397.2972,13.87	BALLAST,SAND,FILL,SAND	1.2,3.0,9.0,16.5
B-11	2948588.4890,775207.8948,14.61	BALLAST,SAND,FILL,SILT,SAND,CLAY	1.7,4.0,11.0,13.0,18.0,21.5
B-8	2948483.0061,775312.5684,15.98	BALLAST,SAND,FILL,SAND	1.3,1.9,4.5,16.5
B-9	2948184.8269,775231.5248,25.55	BALLAST,SAND,SAND,SAND	1.4,4.0,18.0,21.5
B-10	2947956.7244,775240.6596,26.42	BALLAST,SAND,FILL,SAND,CLAY	1.3,4.0,8.0,18.0,21.5

II.1 Boring Map

The Figure II.1.A below illustrates the Block-Scheme for Boring Map Program – Create Boring Holes Reference Map with Attached Project Baselines within Established Work Limits.

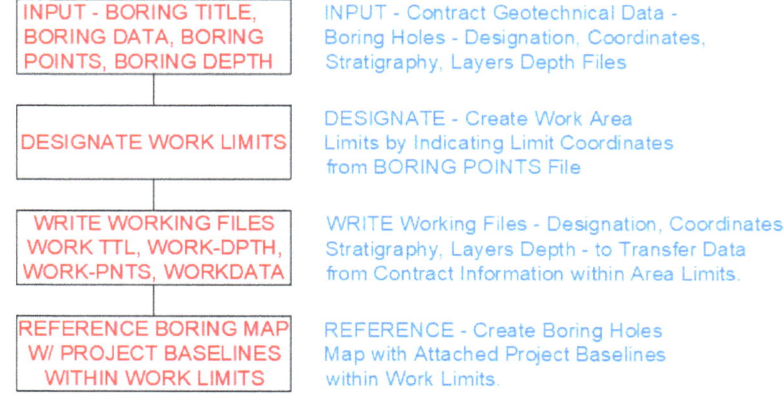

The Attached Figure II.1.B (Drawings 1-6) shows the Boring Map & Detail Groups - North to South.

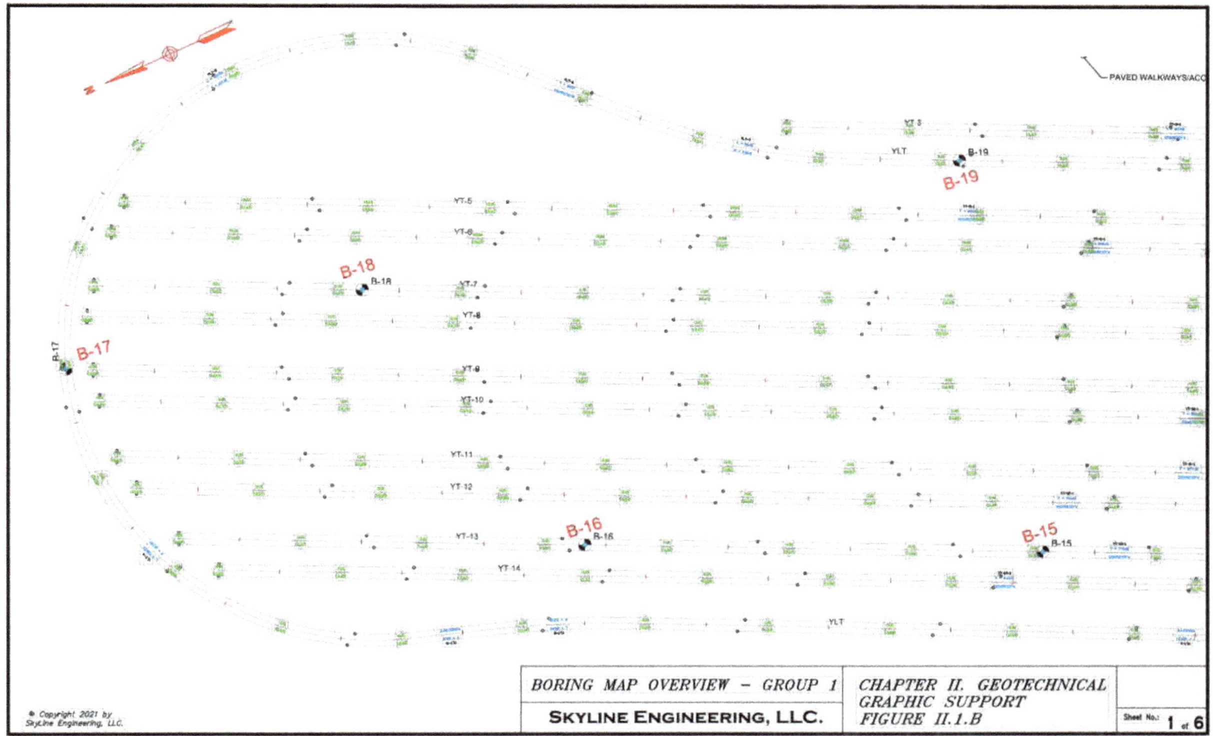

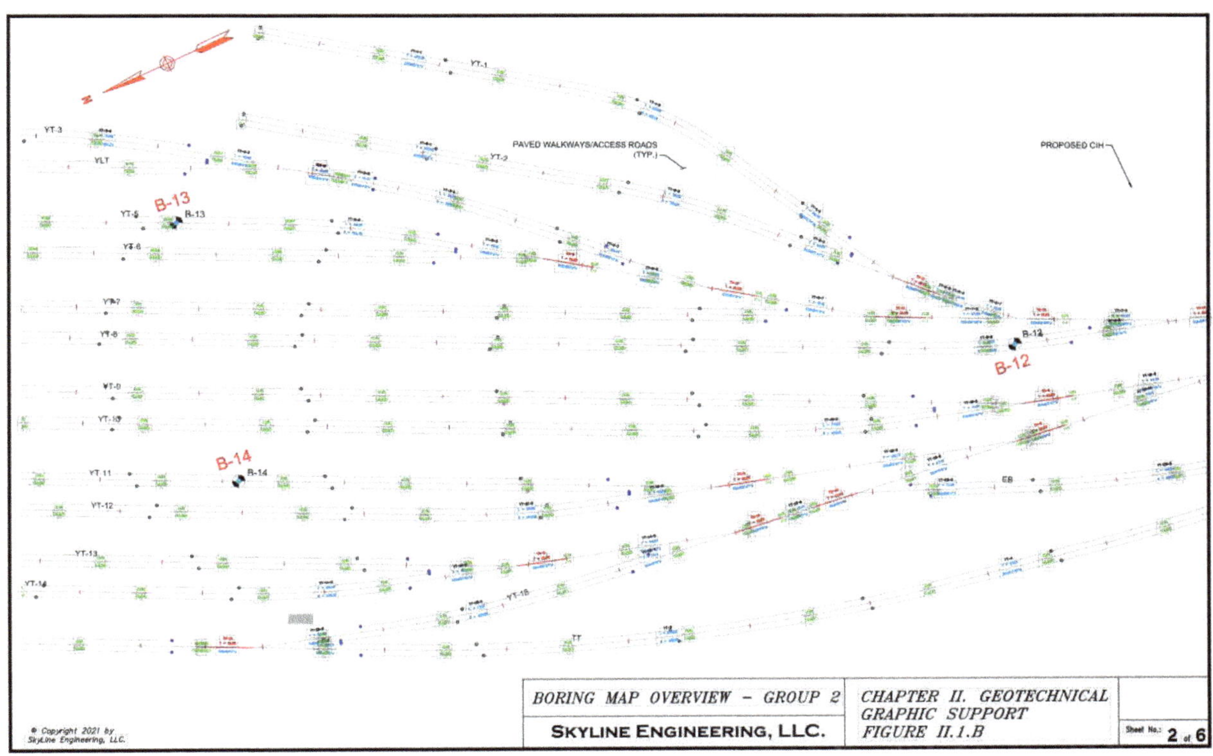

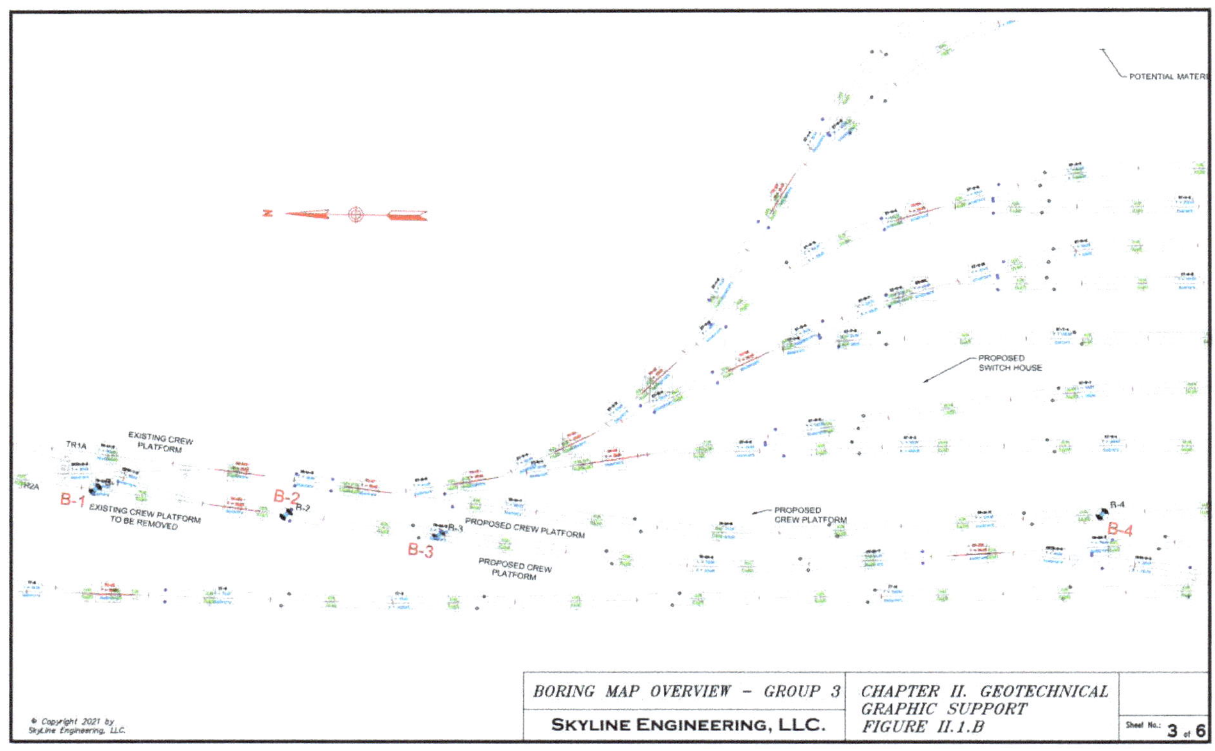
POTENTIAL MATERI
PROPOSED
SWITCH HOUSE
TR1A
EXISTING CREW
PLATFORM
B-1
EXISTING CREW PLATFORM
TO BE REMOVED
B-2
B-3
PROPOSED CREW PLATFORM
PROPOSED CREW
PLATFORM
PROPOSED
CREW PLATFORM
B-4
BORING MAP OVERVIEW – GROUP 3
SKYLINE ENGINEERING, LLC.
CHAPTER II. GEOTECHNICAL
GRAPHIC SUPPORT
FIGURE II.1.B
Sheet No.: 3 of 6
© Copyright 2021 by
SkyLine Engineering, LLC.

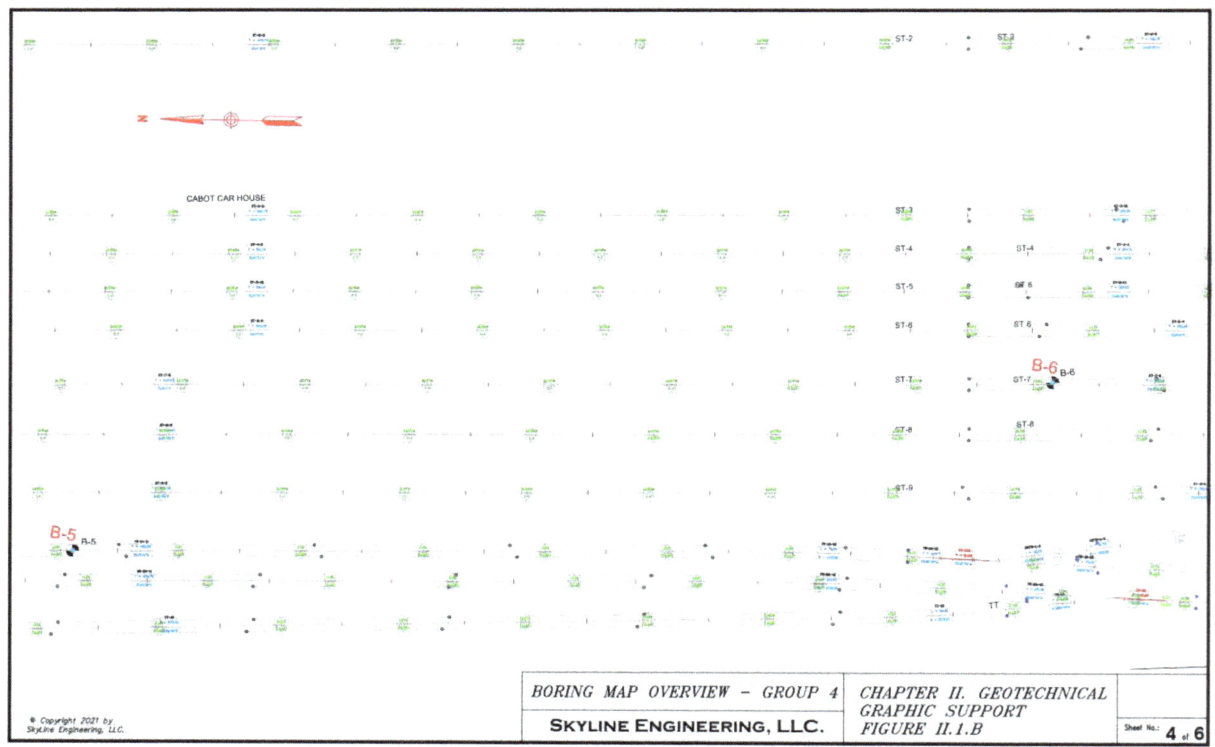
CABOT CAR HOUSE
ST-2
ST-3
ST-4
ST-5
ST-6
ST-7
ST-8
ST-9
B-6
B-5
TT
BORING MAP OVERVIEW – GROUP 4
SKYLINE ENGINEERING, LLC.
CHAPTER II. GEOTECHNICAL
GRAPHIC SUPPORT
FIGURE II.1.B
Sheet No.: 4 of 6
© Copyright 2021 by
SkyLine Engineering, LLC.

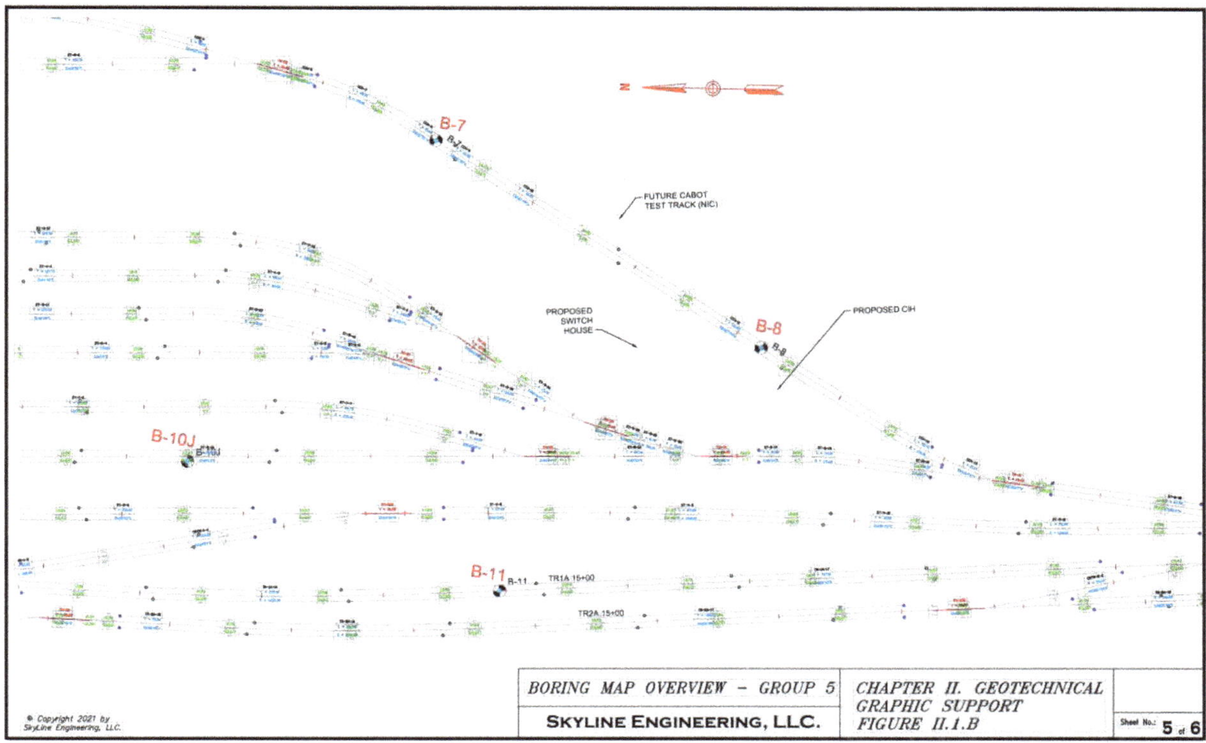
B-7
FUTURE CABOT TEST TRACK (NIC)
PROPOSED SWITCH HOUSE
PROPOSED CIH
B-8
B-10J
B-11
TR1A 15+00
TR2A 15+00
BORING MAP OVERVIEW – GROUP 5
SKYLINE ENGINEERING, LLC.
CHAPTER II. GEOTECHNICAL GRAPHIC SUPPORT FIGURE II.1.B
Sheet No.: 5 of 6
© Copyright 2021 by SkyLine Engineering, LLC.

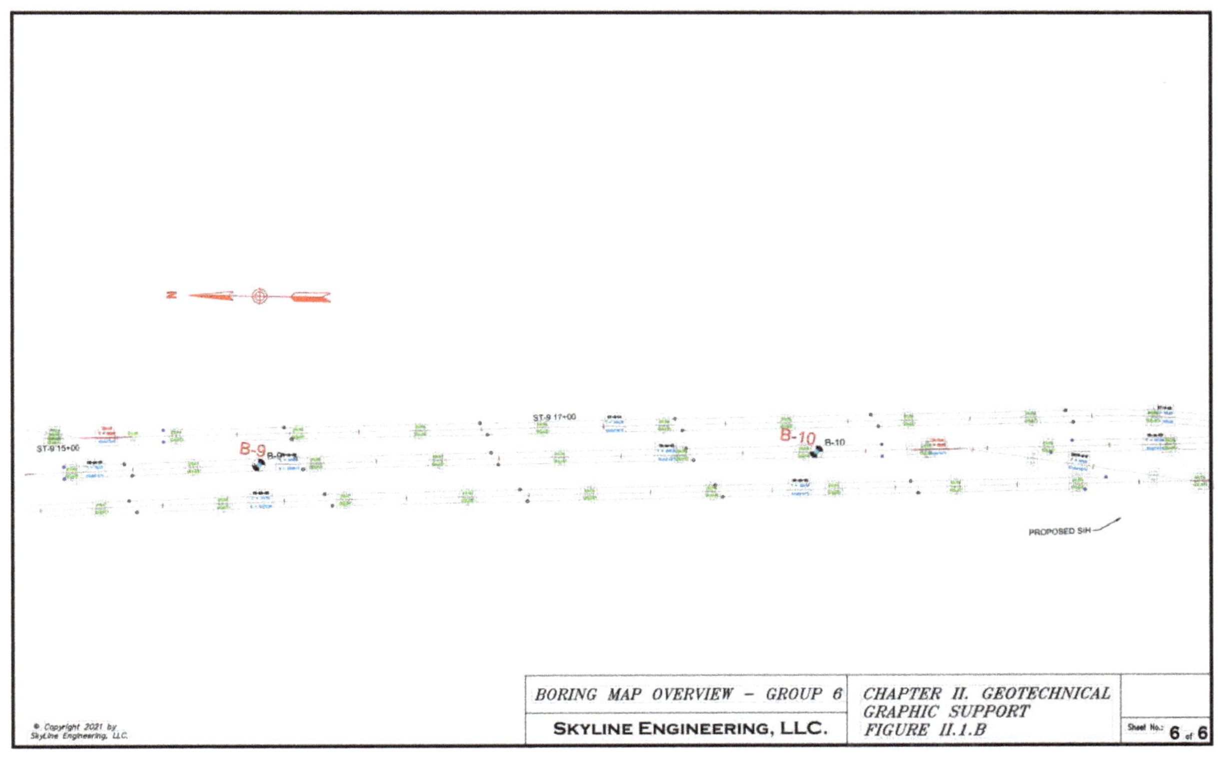
ST-9 15+00
ST-9 17+00
B-9
B-10
PROPOSED SIH
BORING MAP OVERVIEW – GROUP 6
SKYLINE ENGINEERING, LLC.
CHAPTER II. GEOTECHNICAL GRAPHIC SUPPORT FIGURE II.1.B
Sheet No.: 6 of 6
© Copyright 2021 by SkyLine Engineering, LLC.

II.2. Boring Projection.

The next logical step is to choose the Project Baseline to extrapolate the boring holes soil parameters.

PICK WORKING BASELINE TO CREATE PROJECTION POINTS FOR SOIL PROFILE

PICK - Working Baseline for Layout Boring Holes Projection Points to Create Reference Soil Profile.

The Combined Base Line for Tracks YT-8 & TR-1A, satisfying the working area limits, has been established from the Database:

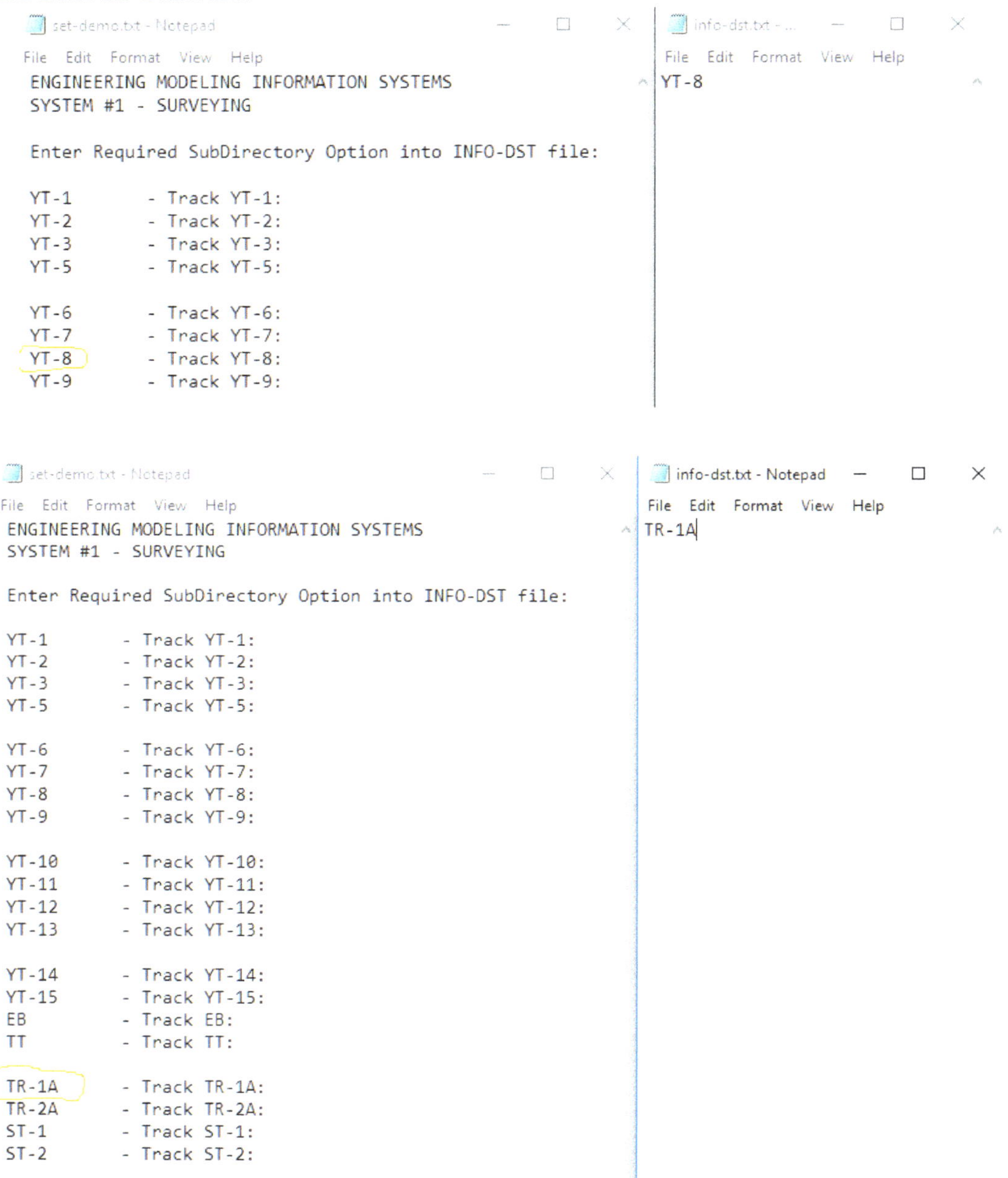

set-demo.txt - Notepad

File Edit Format View Help

```
ENGINEERING MODELING INFORMATION SYSTEMS
SYSTEM #1 - SURVEYING

Enter Required SubDirectory Option into INFO-DST file:

YT-1        - Track YT-1:
YT-2        - Track YT-2:
YT-3        - Track YT-3:
YT-5        - Track YT-5:

YT-6        - Track YT-6:
YT-7        - Track YT-7:
YT-8        - Track YT-8:
YT-9        - Track YT-9:
```

info-dst.txt - ...

File Edit Format View Help

```
YT-8
```

set-demo.txt - Notepad

File Edit Format View Help

```
ENGINEERING MODELING INFORMATION SYSTEMS
SYSTEM #1 - SURVEYING

Enter Required SubDirectory Option into INFO-DST file:

YT-1        - Track YT-1:
YT-2        - Track YT-2:
YT-3        - Track YT-3:
YT-5        - Track YT-5:

YT-6        - Track YT-6:
YT-7        - Track YT-7:
YT-8        - Track YT-8:
YT-9        - Track YT-9:

YT-10       - Track YT-10:
YT-11       - Track YT-11:
YT-12       - Track YT-12:
YT-13       - Track YT-13:

YT-14       - Track YT-14:
YT-15       - Track YT-15:
EB          - Track EB:
TT          - Track TT:

TR-1A       - Track TR-1A:
TR-2A       - Track TR-2A:
ST-1        - Track ST-1:
ST-2        - Track ST-2:
```

info-dst.txt - Notepad

File Edit Format View Help

```
TR-1A
```

The Combined Baseline for Reference Soil Profile & Projection Limits Dialog Box:

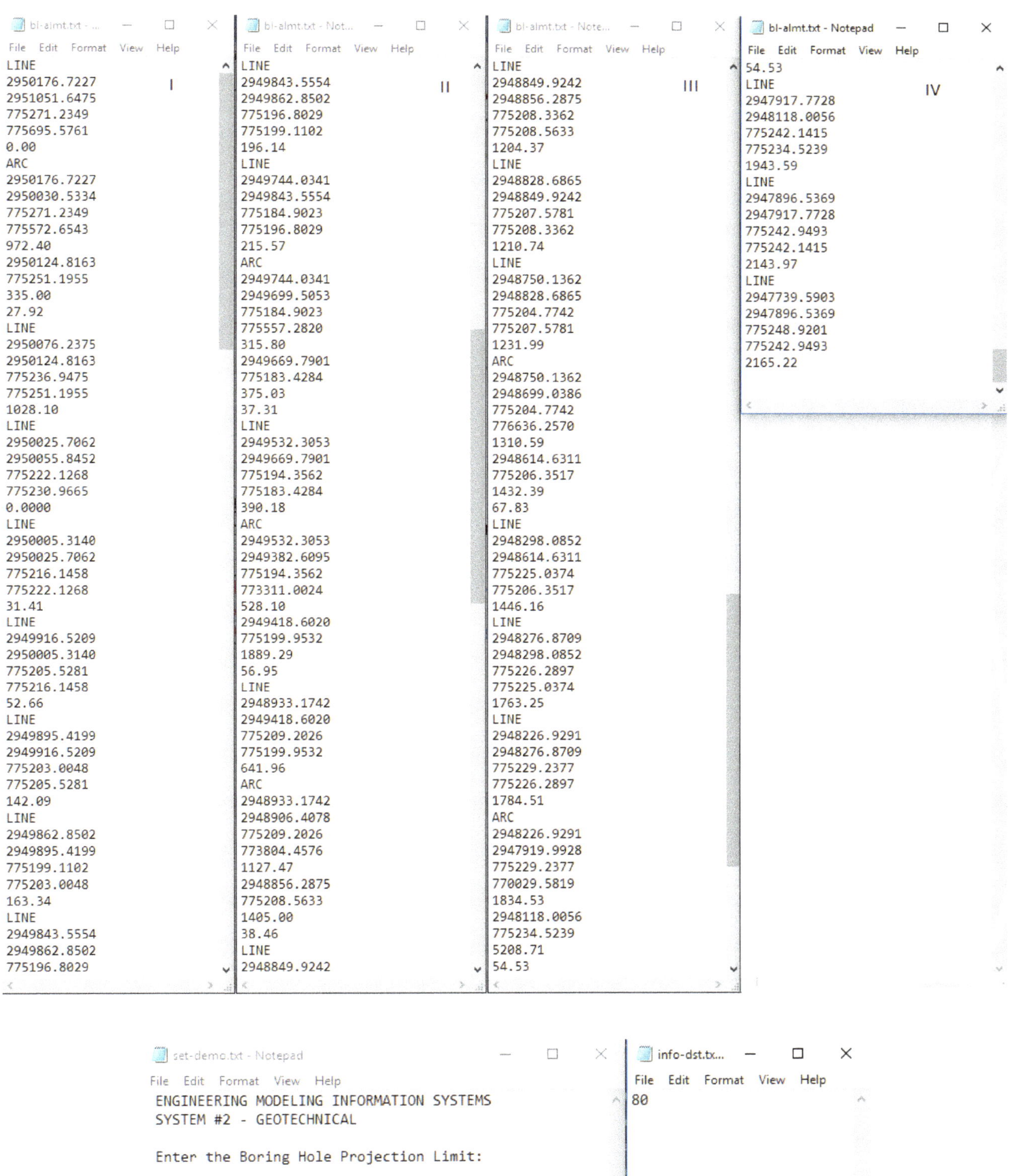

The Figure II.2.A below shows Baseline Projection Points Program Block – Scheme.

PICK WORKING BASELINE TO CREATE PROJECTION POINTS FOR SOIL PROFILE
PICK - Working Baseline for Layout Boring Holes Projection Points to Create Reference Soil Profile.
INPUT Rdst PROJECTION LIMIT
Input - Required Projection Limit - an Established Distance From Boring Holes - Normal To Combined Base Line
INPUT - BL-ALMT Nctr - N° of Segments; Cctr = 0
INPUT - Combined Baseline Alignment Set Outer Programming Cycle
Cctr = Cctr + 1 Read Alignment Segment Head
Run Outer Programming Cycle
continue outer programming cycle - move to the next baseline segment
Cctr > Nctr
yes
End of Program;
All Baseline Segments Checked;
no
ARC? LINE?
Type of Primary Baseline Segment Check
ARC
LINE
PTSTA = PCSTA+ TL; OCC. POINT = RAD. POINT ARC ROUTINE - AZ1 & AZ2
PTSTA = CSTA + DK-ORG; OCC. POINT = CSTA POINT LINE ROUTINE - AZ-ORG;
Ictr = 0; SET INNER PROGRAMMING CYCLE
continue inner programming cycle
OPEN WORKING FILES WORK TTL, WORK-DPTH, WORK-PNTS, WORKDATA
continue inner programming cycle
Nctr = Number of WORKING POINTS TO CHECK
READ WORKING FILES Ictr = Ictr + 1 - RUN INNER PROGRAMMING CYCLE
BS POINT = PNT; DEL1 = AZ - AZ1; DEL2 = AZ - AZ2;
BS POINT = PNT; LINE ROUTINE; DEL = AZ-ORG - AZ;
DEL=DEL1* DEL2 DEL < 0?
DEL<= π/2 or DEL>= 3*(π/2)?
R <= Rdst?
DK <= DK-ORG?
Ictr <= Nctr?
Ictr <= Nctr?
yes
no
FS POINT COORDINATES & CORRESPONDING TITLE, DEPTH, DATA RECORD

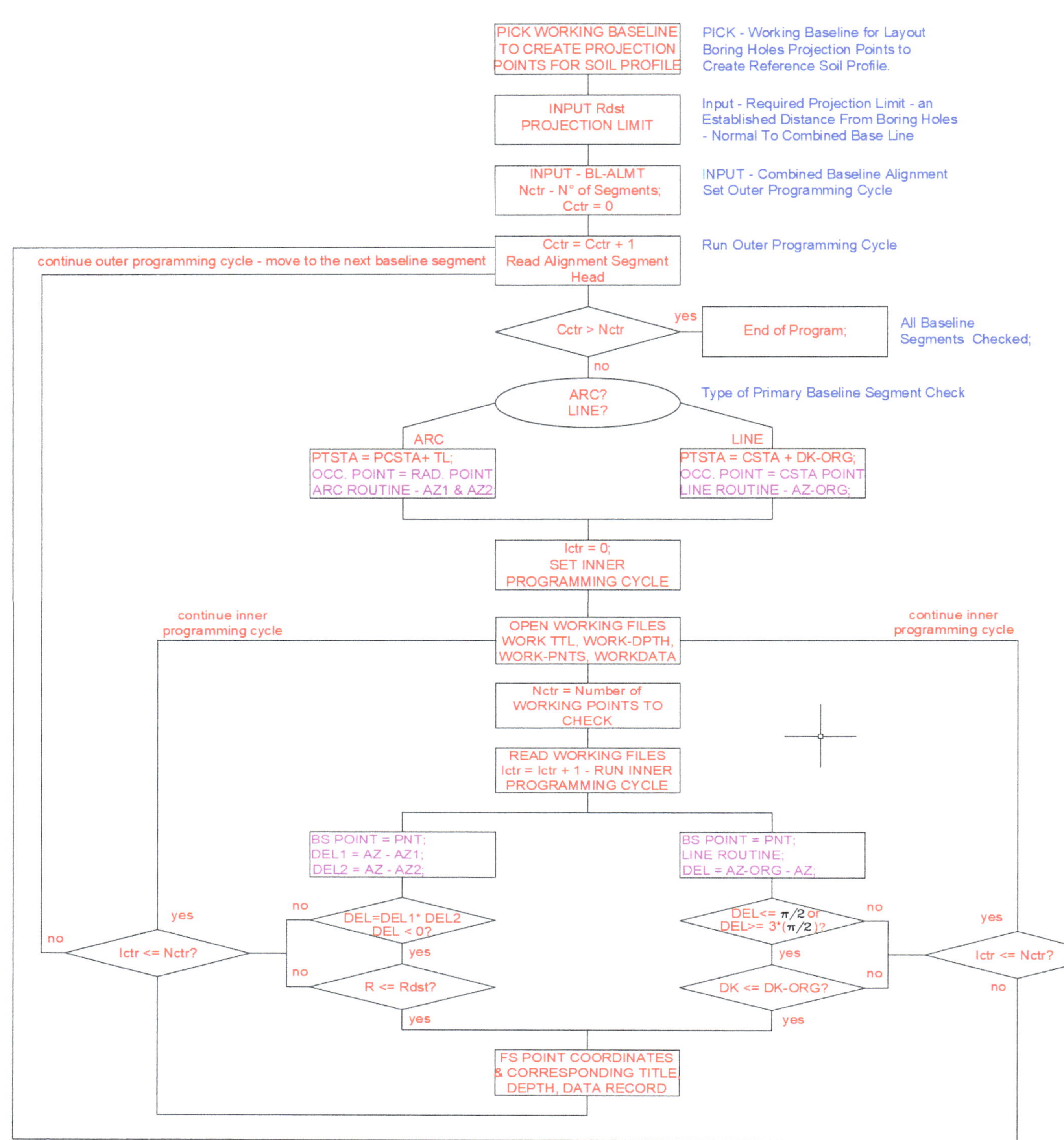

Figure II.2.A.

The Attached Figure II.2.B (Drawings 1-6) illustrates Baseline Projection Points on Combined Baseline YT-8 / TR-1A, located within 80’ of actual Boring Holes.

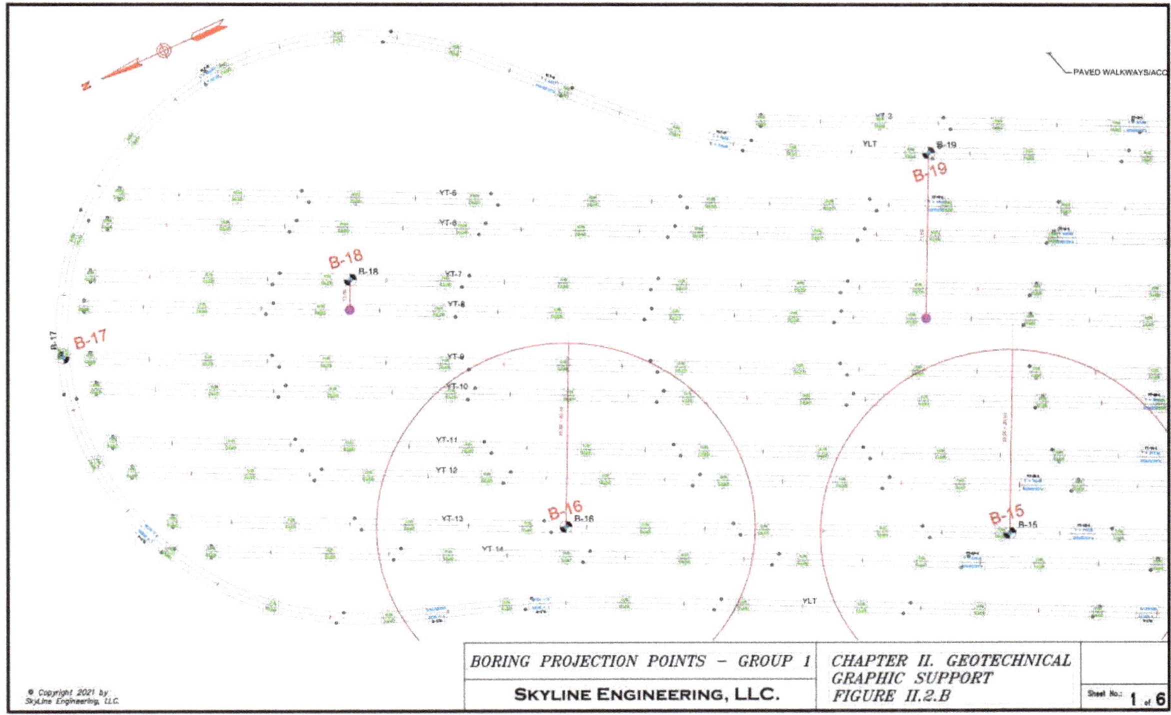

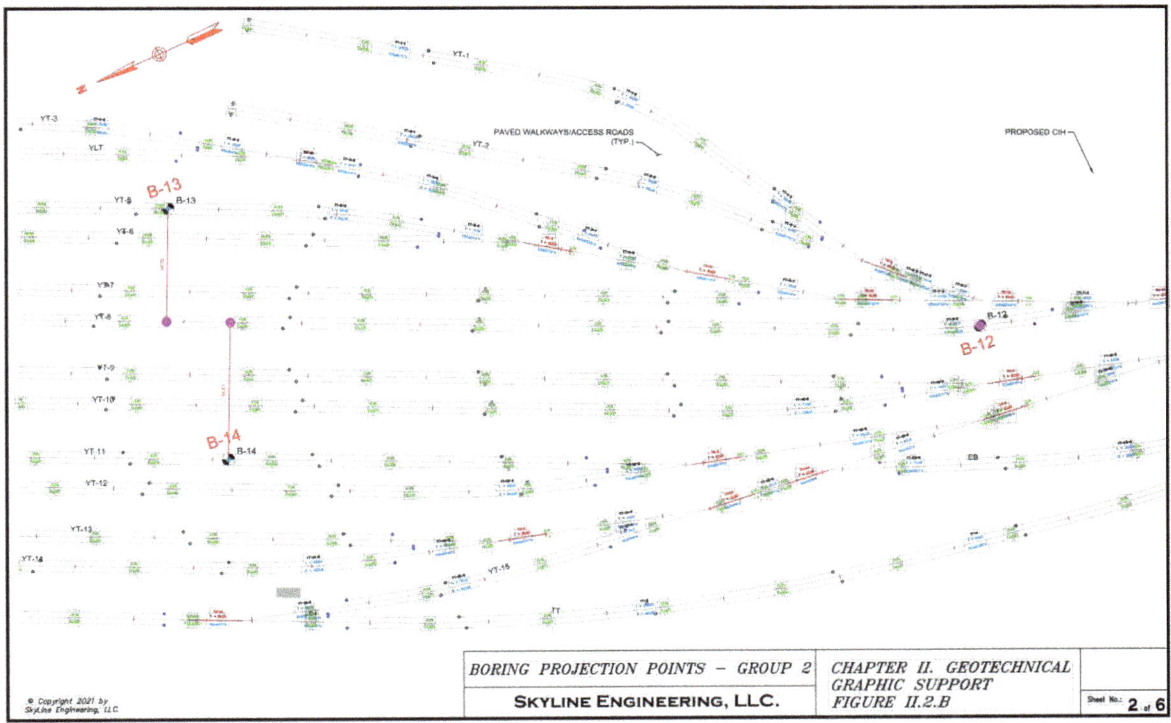

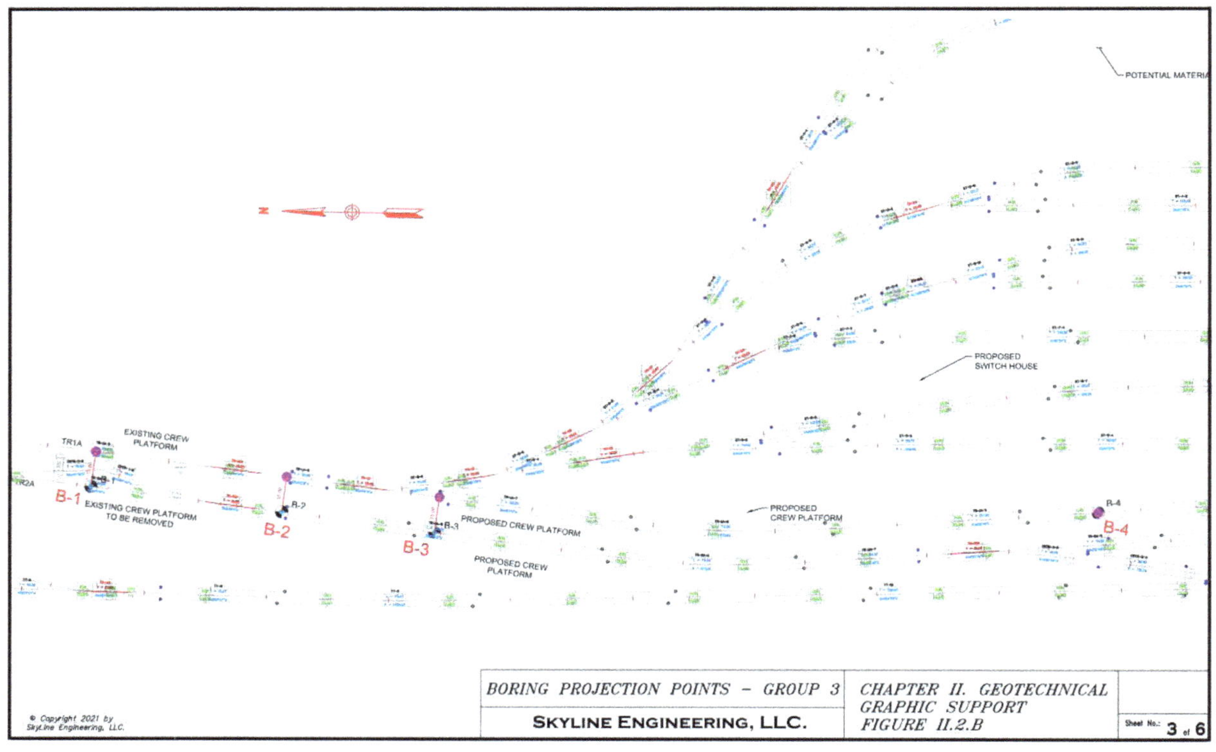
POTENTIAL MATERIA
PROPOSED SWITCH HOUSE
TR1A
EXISTING CREW PLATFORM
B-1
EXISTING CREW PLATFORM TO BE REMOVED
B-2
B-3
PROPOSED CREW PLATFORM
PROPOSED CREW PLATFORM
PROPOSED CREW PLATFORM
B-4
BORING PROJECTION POINTS – GROUP 3
SKYLINE ENGINEERING, LLC.
CHAPTER II. GEOTECHNICAL GRAPHIC SUPPORT FIGURE II.2.B
Sheet No.: 3 of 6
© Copyright 2021 by SkyLine Engineering, LLC.

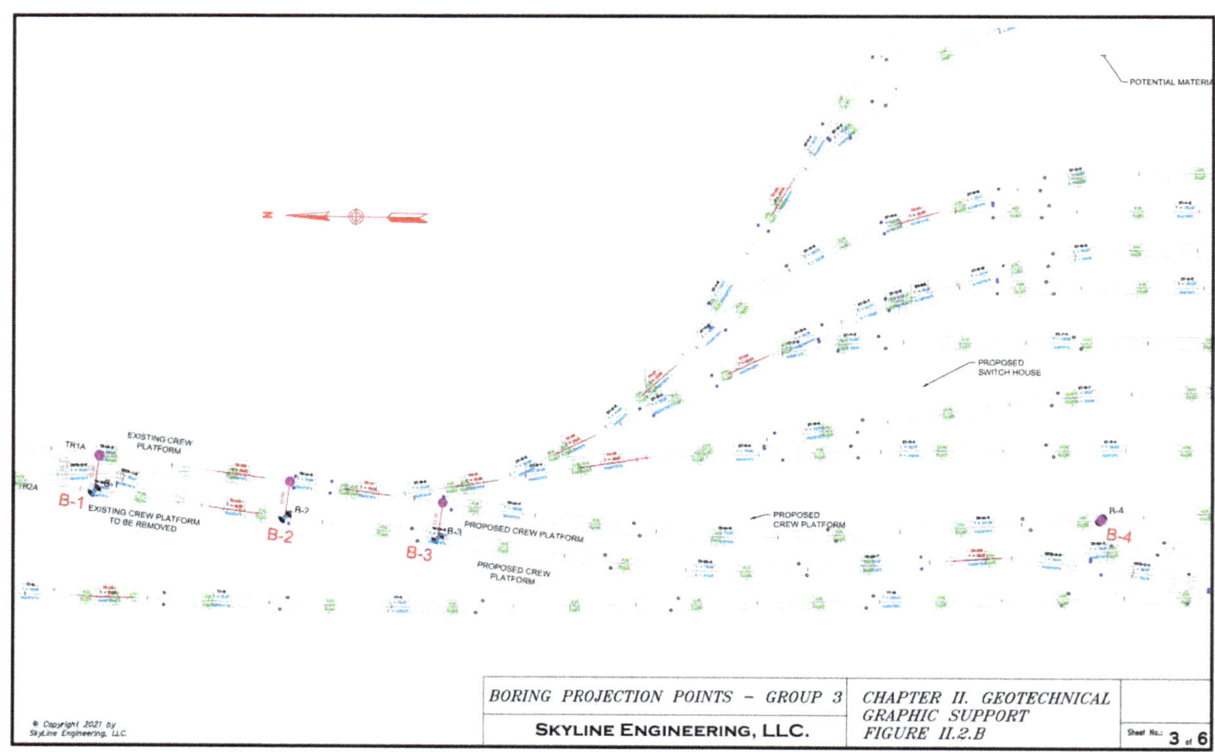
POTENTIAL MATERIA
PROPOSED SWITCH HOUSE
TR1A
EXISTING CREW PLATFORM
B-1
EXISTING CREW PLATFORM TO BE REMOVED
B-2
B-3
PROPOSED CREW PLATFORM
PROPOSED CREW PLATFORM
PROPOSED CREW PLATFORM
B-4
BORING PROJECTION POINTS – GROUP 3
SKYLINE ENGINEERING, LLC.
CHAPTER II. GEOTECHNICAL GRAPHIC SUPPORT FIGURE II.2.B
Sheet No.: 3 of 6
© Copyright 2021 by SkyLine Engineering, LLC.

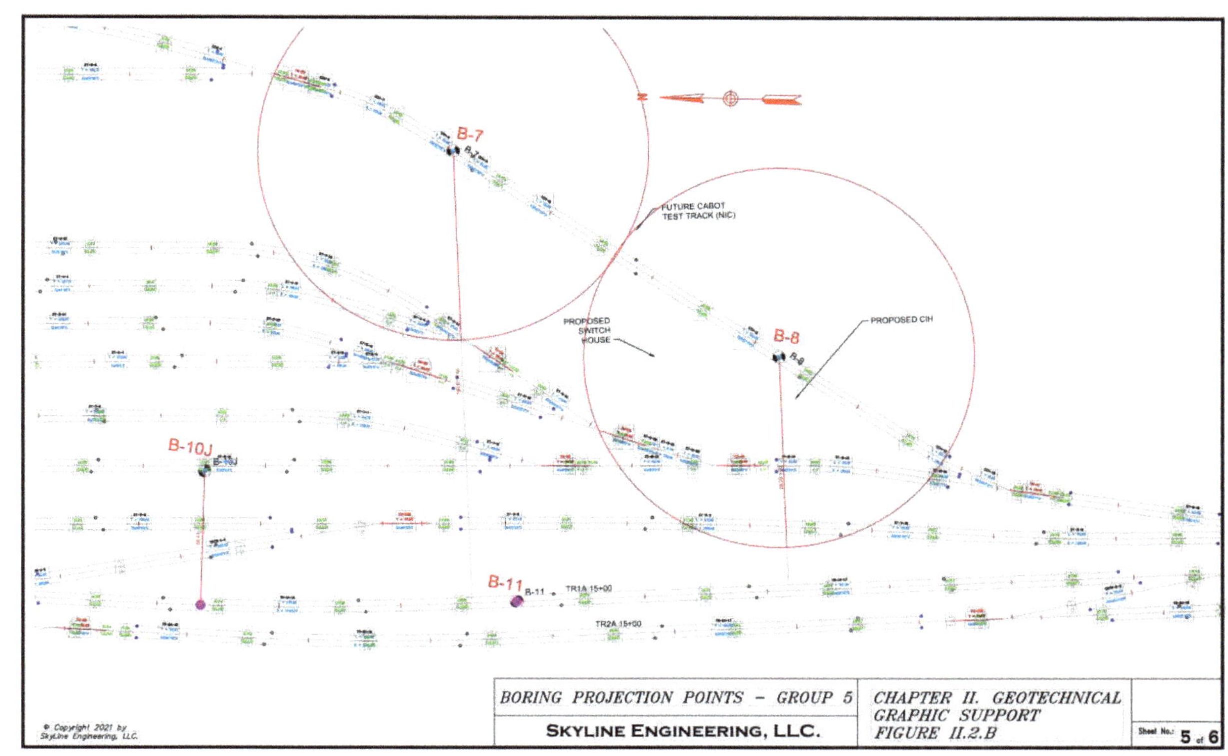
B-7
FUTURE CABOT TEST TRACK (NIC)
PROPOSED SWITCH HOUSE
B-8
PROPOSED CIH
B-10J
B-11
TR1A 15+00
TR2A 15+00
BORING PROJECTION POINTS – GROUP 5
SKYLINE ENGINEERING, LLC.
CHAPTER II. GEOTECHNICAL GRAPHIC SUPPORT FIGURE II.2.B
Sheet No.: 5 of 6
© Copyright 2021 by SkyLine Engineering, LLC.

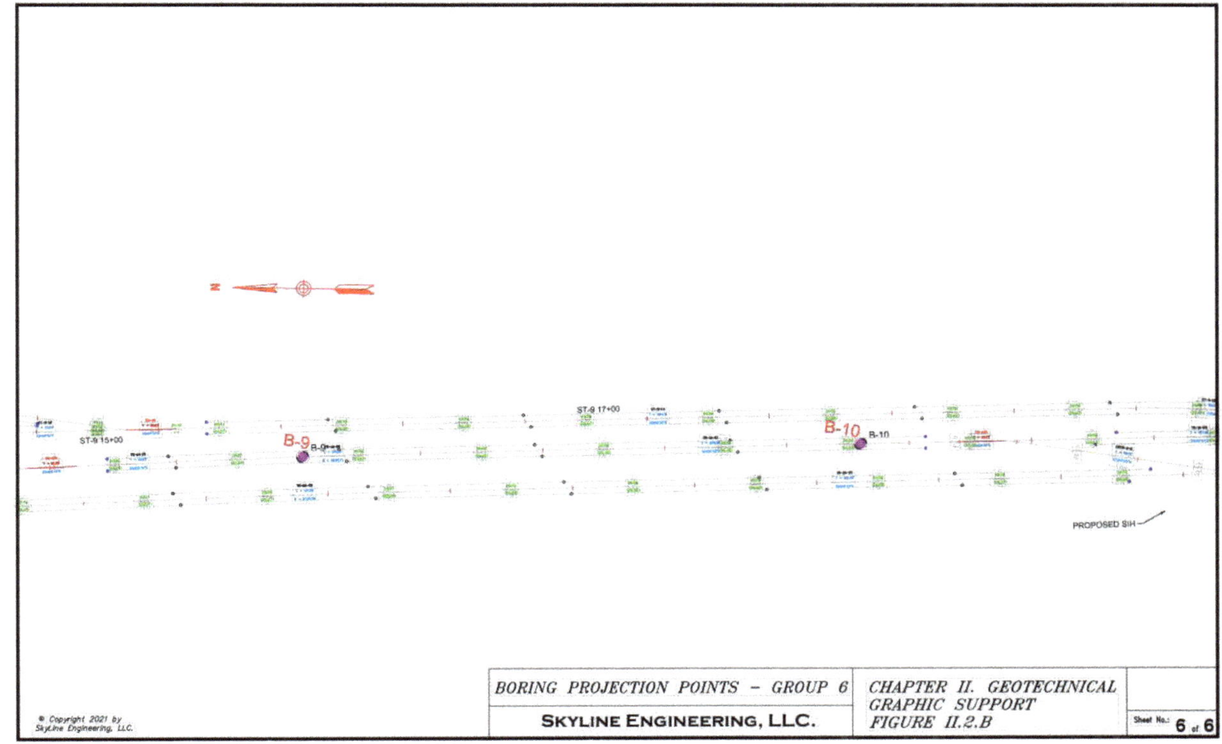
ST-9 17+00
ST-9 15+00
B-9
B-10
PROPOSED SIH
BORING PROJECTION POINTS – GROUP 6
SKYLINE ENGINEERING, LLC.
CHAPTER II. GEOTECHNICAL GRAPHIC SUPPORT FIGURE II.2.B
Sheet No.: 6 of 6
© Copyright 2021 by SkyLine Engineering, LLC.

Distribution Option for File Recording:

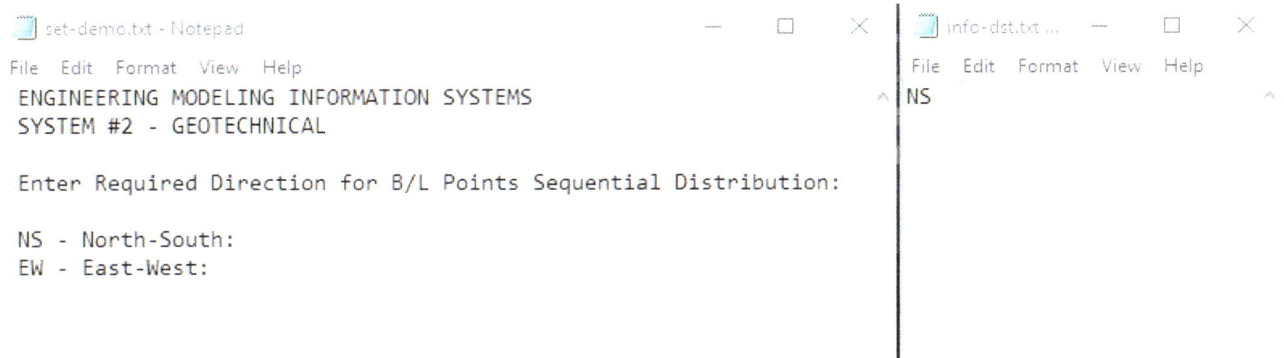

set-demo.txt - Notepad

```
ENGINEERING MODELING INFORMATION SYSTEMS
SYSTEM #2 - GEOTECHNICAL

Enter Required Direction for B/L Points Sequential Distribution:

NS - North-South:
EW - East-West:
```

info-dst.txt

```
NS
```

Baseline Projection Distribution (South to North) Input Files:

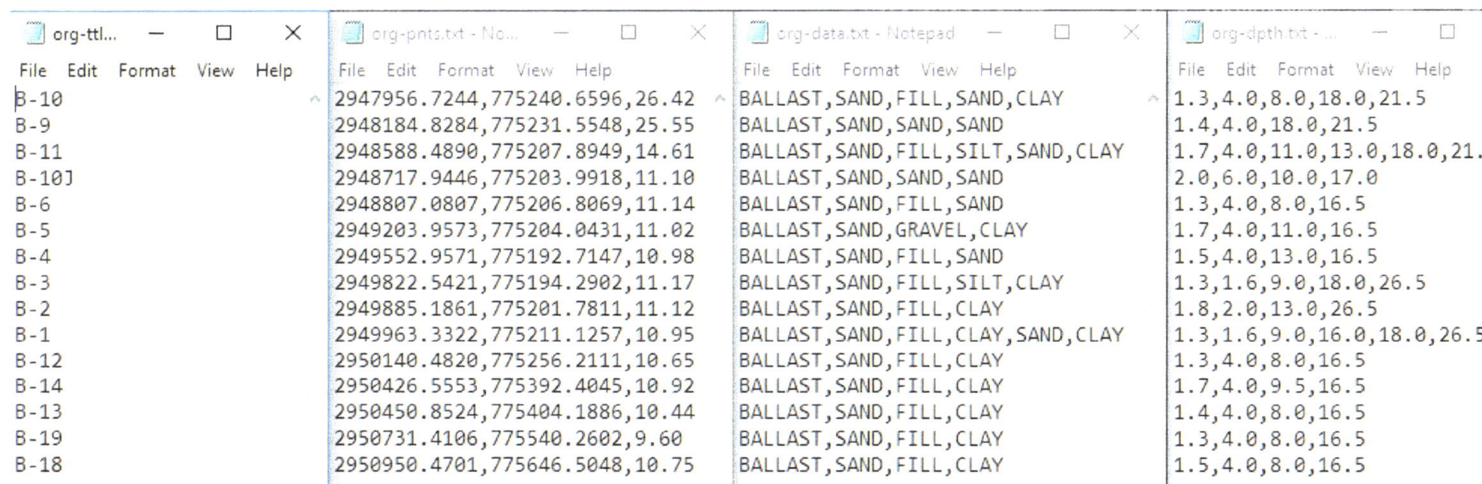

org-ttl...	org-pnts.txt - No...	org-data.txt - Notepad	org-dpth.txt - ...
B-10	2947956.7244,775240.6596,26.42	BALLAST,SAND,FILL,SAND,CLAY	1.3,4.0,8.0,18.0,21.5
B-9	2948184.8284,775231.5548,25.55	BALLAST,SAND,SAND,SAND	1.4,4.0,18.0,21.5
B-11	2948588.4890,775207.8949,14.61	BALLAST,SAND,FILL,SILT,SAND,CLAY	1.7,4.0,11.0,13.0,18.0,21.
B-10J	2948717.9446,775203.9918,11.10	BALLAST,SAND,SAND,SAND	2.0,6.0,10.0,17.0
B-6	2948807.0807,775206.8069,11.14	BALLAST,SAND,FILL,SAND	1.3,4.0,8.0,16.5
B-5	2949203.9573,775204.0431,11.02	BALLAST,SAND,GRAVEL,CLAY	1.7,4.0,11.0,16.5
B-4	2949552.9571,775192.7147,10.98	BALLAST,SAND,FILL,SAND	1.5,4.0,13.0,16.5
B-3	2949822.5421,775194.2902,11.17	BALLAST,SAND,FILL,SILT,CLAY	1.3,1.6,9.0,18.0,26.5
B-2	2949885.1861,775201.7811,11.12	BALLAST,SAND,FILL,CLAY	1.8,2.0,13.0,26.5
B-1	2949963.3322,775211.1257,10.95	BALLAST,SAND,FILL,CLAY,SAND,CLAY	1.3,1.6,9.0,16.0,18.0,26.5
B-12	2950140.4820,775256.2111,10.65	BALLAST,SAND,FILL,CLAY	1.3,4.0,8.0,16.5
B-14	2950426.5553,775392.4045,10.92	BALLAST,SAND,FILL,CLAY	1.7,4.0,9.5,16.5
B-13	2950450.8524,775404.1886,10.44	BALLAST,SAND,FILL,CLAY	1.4,4.0,8.0,16.5
B-19	2950731.4106,775540.2602,9.60	BALLAST,SAND,FILL,CLAY	1.3,4.0,8.0,16.5
B-18	2950950.4701,775646.5048,10.75	BALLAST,SAND,FILL,CLAY	1.5,4.0,8.0,16.5

Now all required conditions are satisfied to build the Baseline projected Soil Profile.

II.3. Boring Profile.

Figure II.3.A below demonstrates the Baseline Projected Soil Profile Program Block-Scheme.

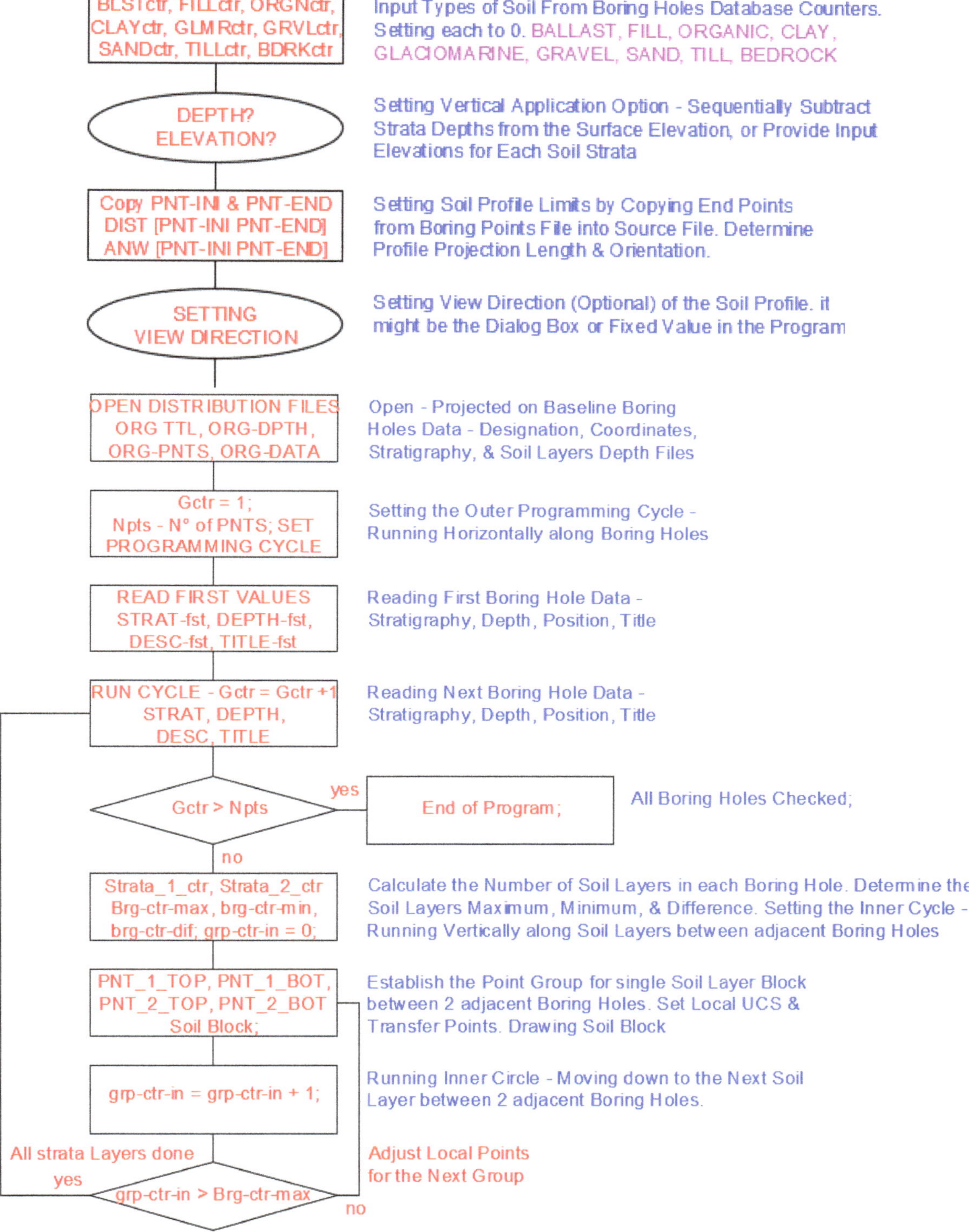

As an output of the Soil Profile Program, the Attached Figure II.3.B (Drawings 1-10) shows Boring Holes and continuous Soil Profile Segments through Combined Baseline YT-8/TR-1A.

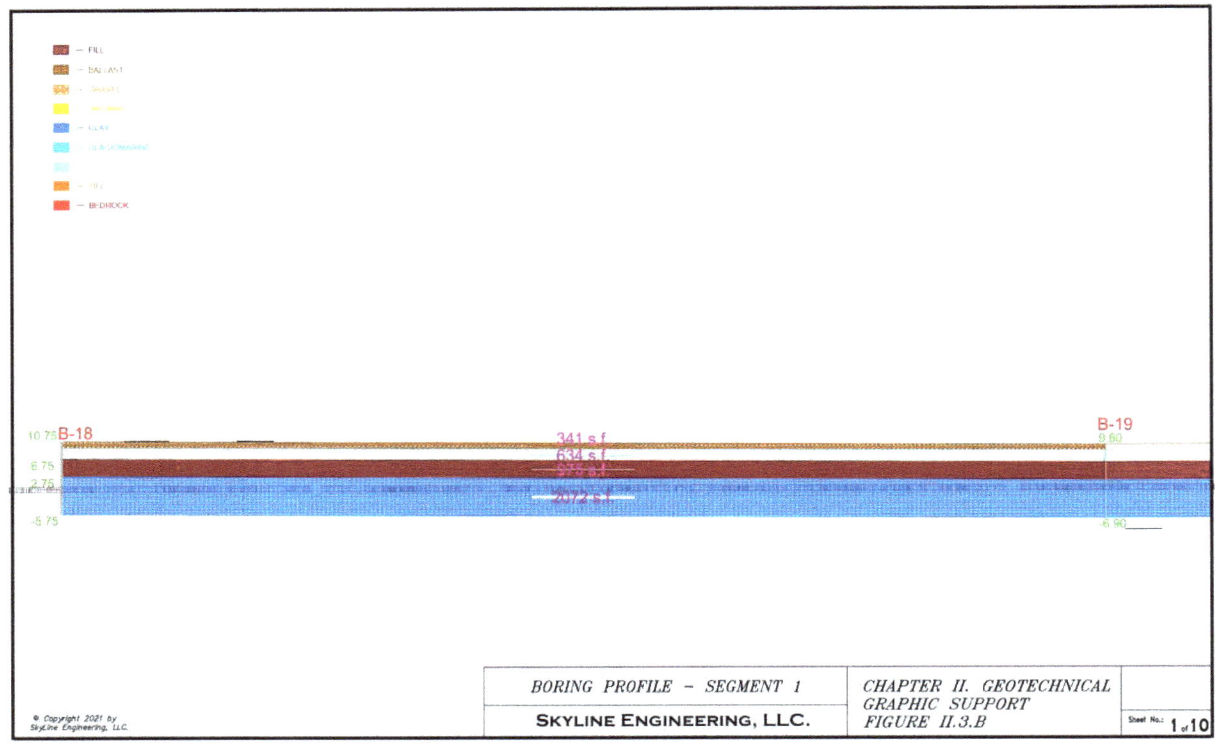

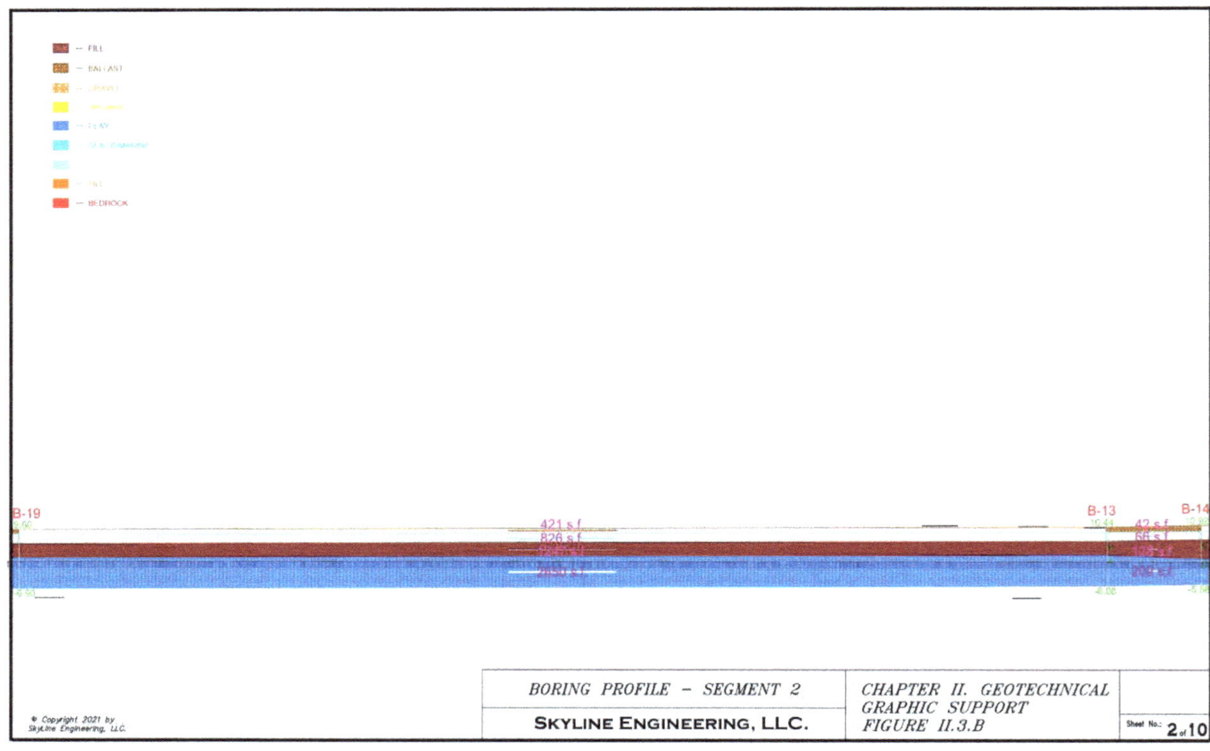

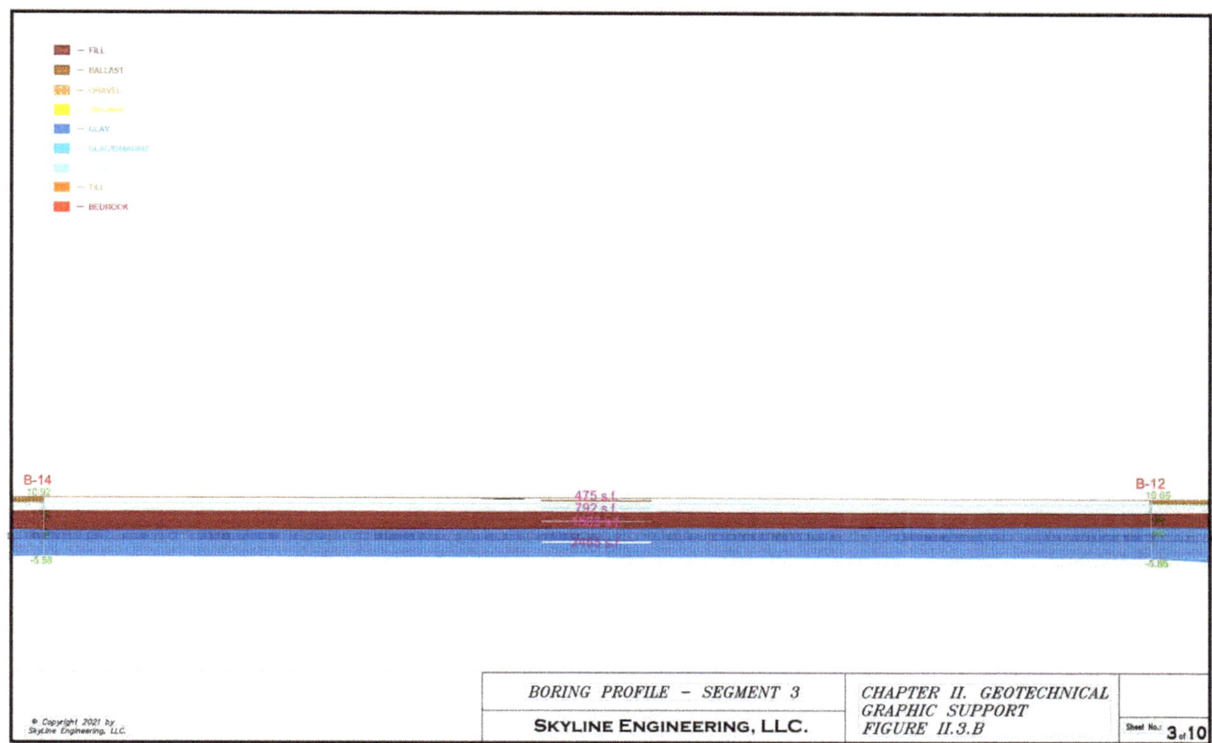
— FILL
— BALLAST
— CLAY
— BEDROCK
B-14
10.92
-5.58
475 s.f.
792 s.f.
B-12
10.85
-5.85
BORING PROFILE – SEGMENT 3
SKYLINE ENGINEERING, LLC.
CHAPTER II. GEOTECHNICAL
GRAPHIC SUPPORT
FIGURE II.3.B
Sheet No.: 3 of 10
© Copyright 2021 by
SkyLine Engineering, LLC.

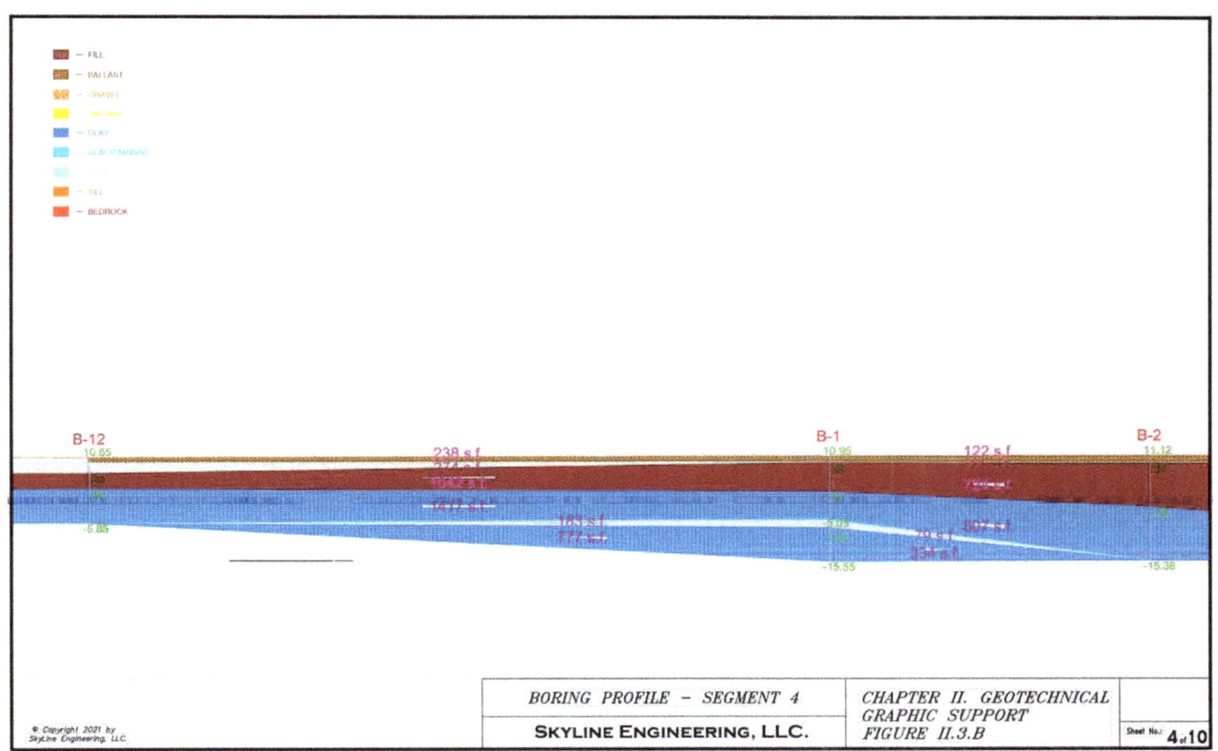
— FILL
— BALLAST
— BEDROCK
B-12
10.85
-5.85
238 s.f.
1042 s.f.
1417 s.f.
183 s.f.
777 s.f.
B-1
10.95
-5.05
-15.55
122 s.f.
807 s.f.
79 s.f.
334 s.f.
B-2
11.12
-15.38
BORING PROFILE – SEGMENT 4
SKYLINE ENGINEERING, LLC.
CHAPTER II. GEOTECHNICAL
GRAPHIC SUPPORT
FIGURE II.3.B
Sheet No.: 4 of 10
© Copyright 2021 by
SkyLine Engineering, LLC.

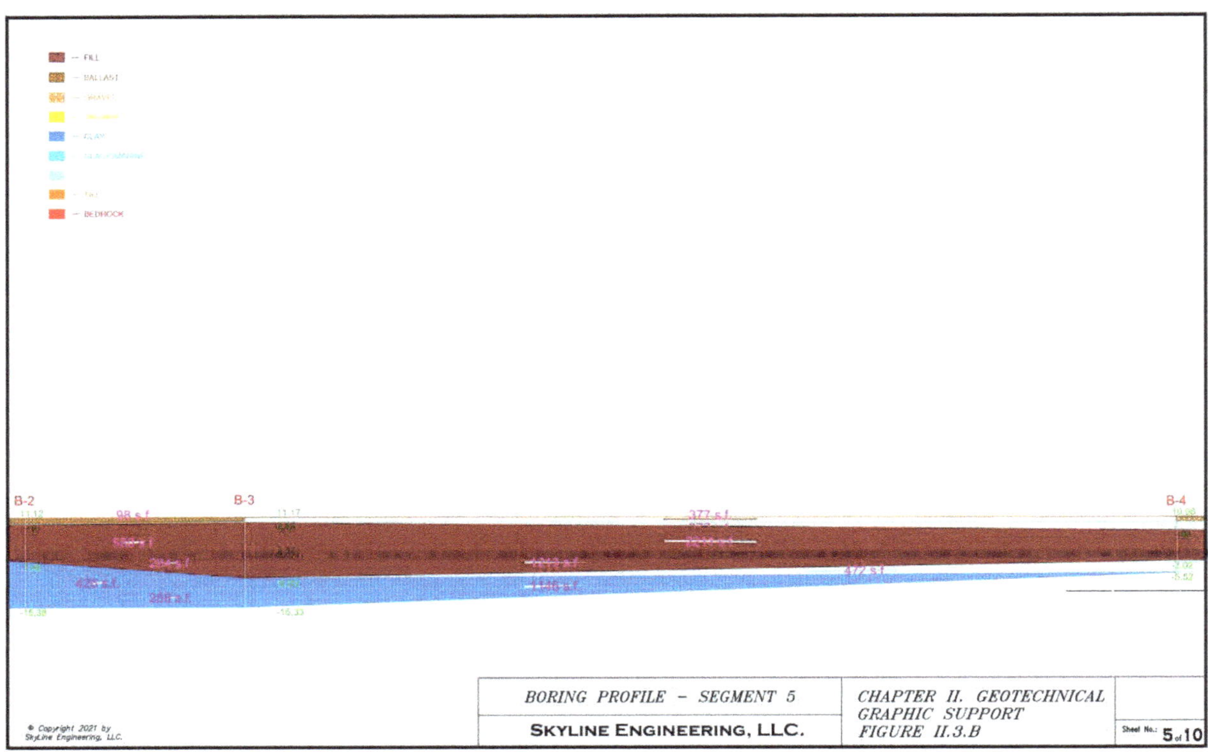
FILL
BALLAST
BEDROCK
B-2
B-3
B-4
98 s.f.
377 s.f.
472 s.f.
© Copyright 2021 by SkyLine Engineering, LLC.
BORING PROFILE – SEGMENT 5
SKYLINE ENGINEERING, LLC.
CHAPTER II. GEOTECHNICAL GRAPHIC SUPPORT FIGURE II.3.B
Sheet No.: 5 of 10

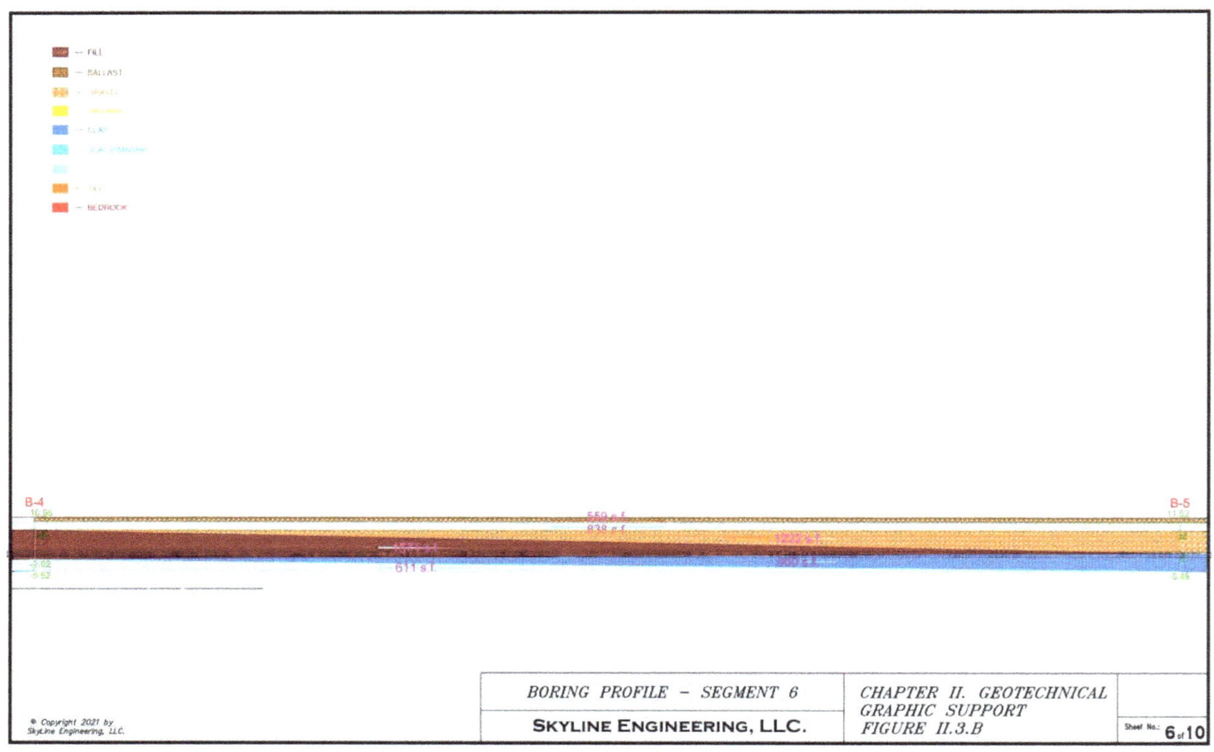
FILL
BALLAST
BEDROCK
B-4
B-5
611 s.f.
© Copyright 2021 by SkyLine Engineering, LLC.
BORING PROFILE – SEGMENT 6
SKYLINE ENGINEERING, LLC.
CHAPTER II. GEOTECHNICAL GRAPHIC SUPPORT FIGURE II.3.B
Sheet No.: 6 of 10

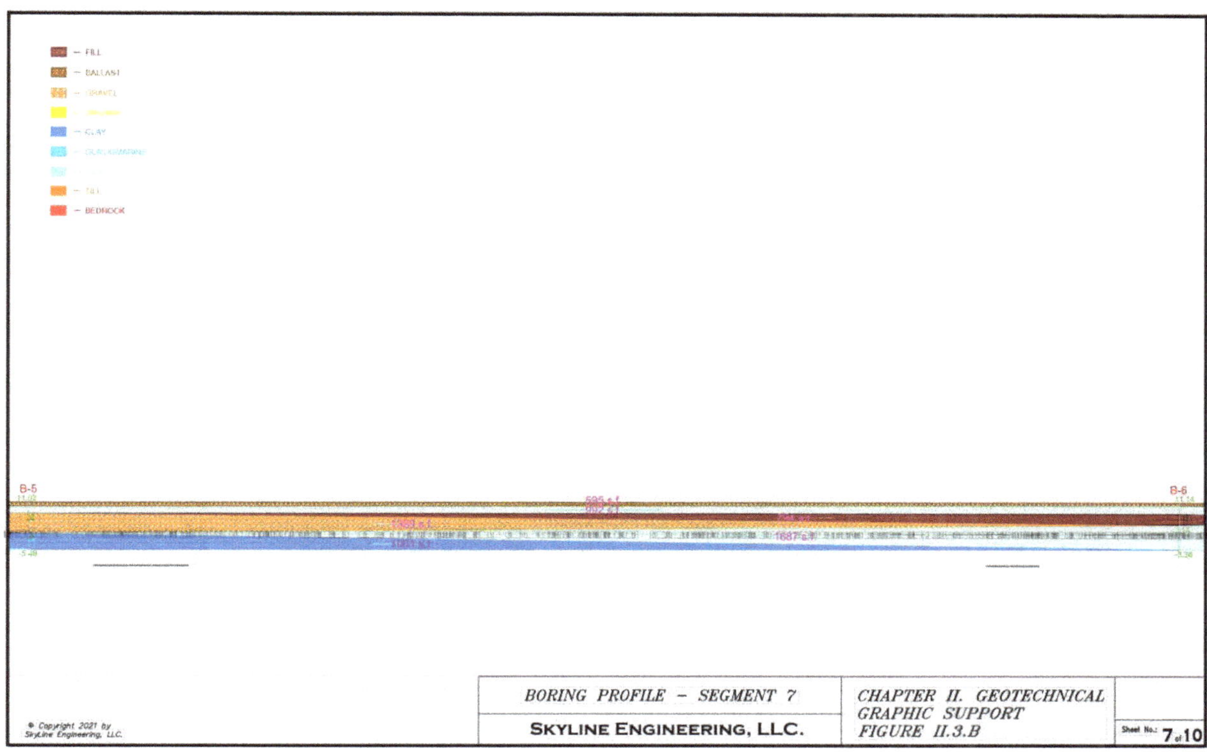
FILL
BALLAST
CLAY
BEDROCK
B-5
B-6
BORING PROFILE – SEGMENT 7
SKYLINE ENGINEERING, LLC.
CHAPTER II. GEOTECHNICAL
GRAPHIC SUPPORT
FIGURE II.3.B
Sheet No.: 7 of 10
© Copyright 2021 by
SkyLine Engineering, LLC

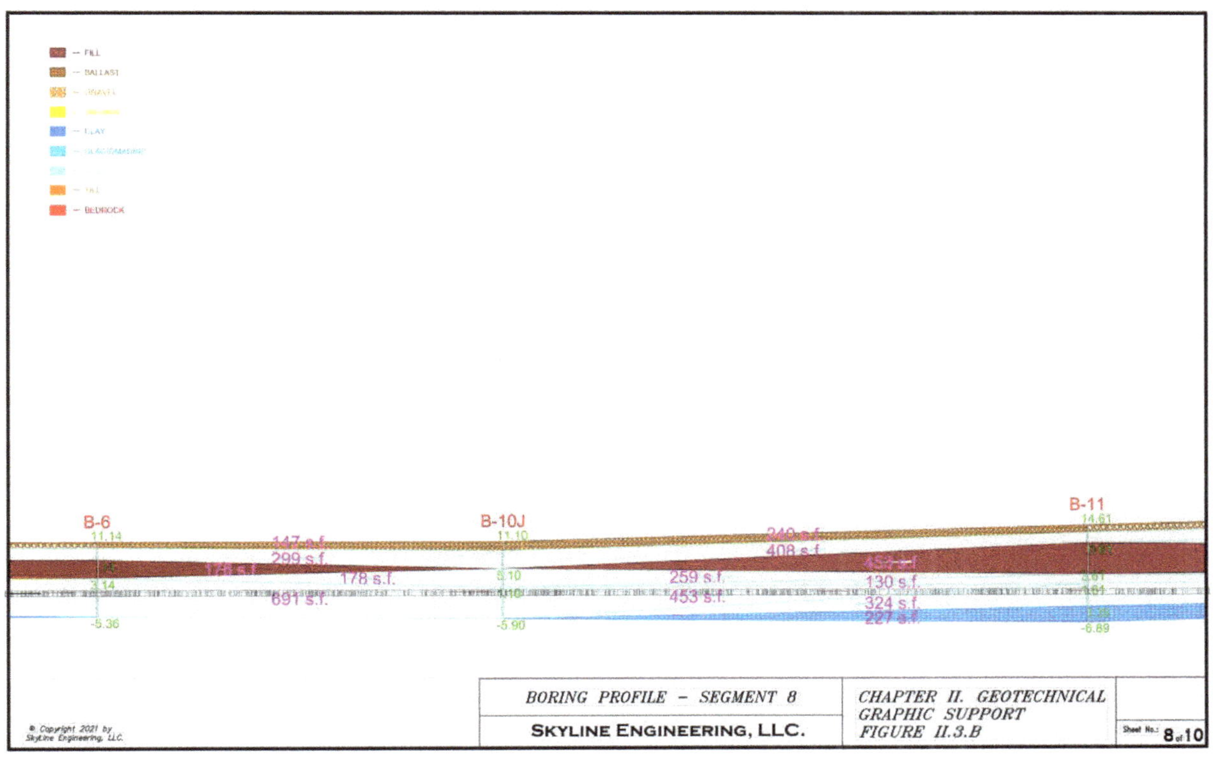
FILL
BALLAST
CLAY
BEDROCK
B-6
11.14
B-10J
11.10
B-11
14.61
147 s.f.
299 s.f.
178 s.f.
691 s.f.
240 s.f.
408 s.f.
259 s.f.
453 s.f.
452 s.f.
130 s.f.
324 s.f.
227 s.f.
3.14
-5.36
-5.90
-6.89
BORING PROFILE – SEGMENT 8
SKYLINE ENGINEERING, LLC.
CHAPTER II. GEOTECHNICAL
GRAPHIC SUPPORT
FIGURE II.3.B
Sheet No.: 8 of 10
© Copyright 2021 by
SkyLine Engineering, LLC

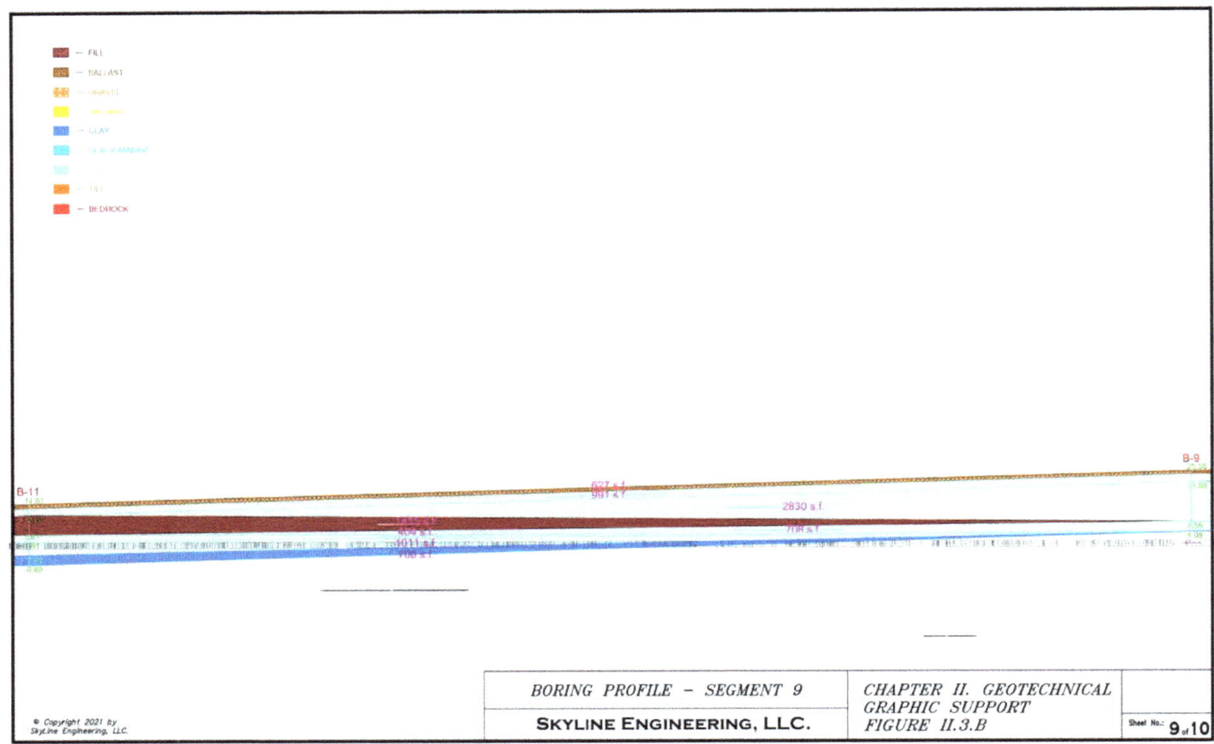
FILL
BALLAST
B-11
B-9
2830 s.f.
BORING PROFILE – SEGMENT 9
SKYLINE ENGINEERING, LLC.
CHAPTER II. GEOTECHNICAL GRAPHIC SUPPORT FIGURE II.3.B
Sheet No.: 9 of 10
© Copyright 2021 by SkyLine Engineering, LLC.

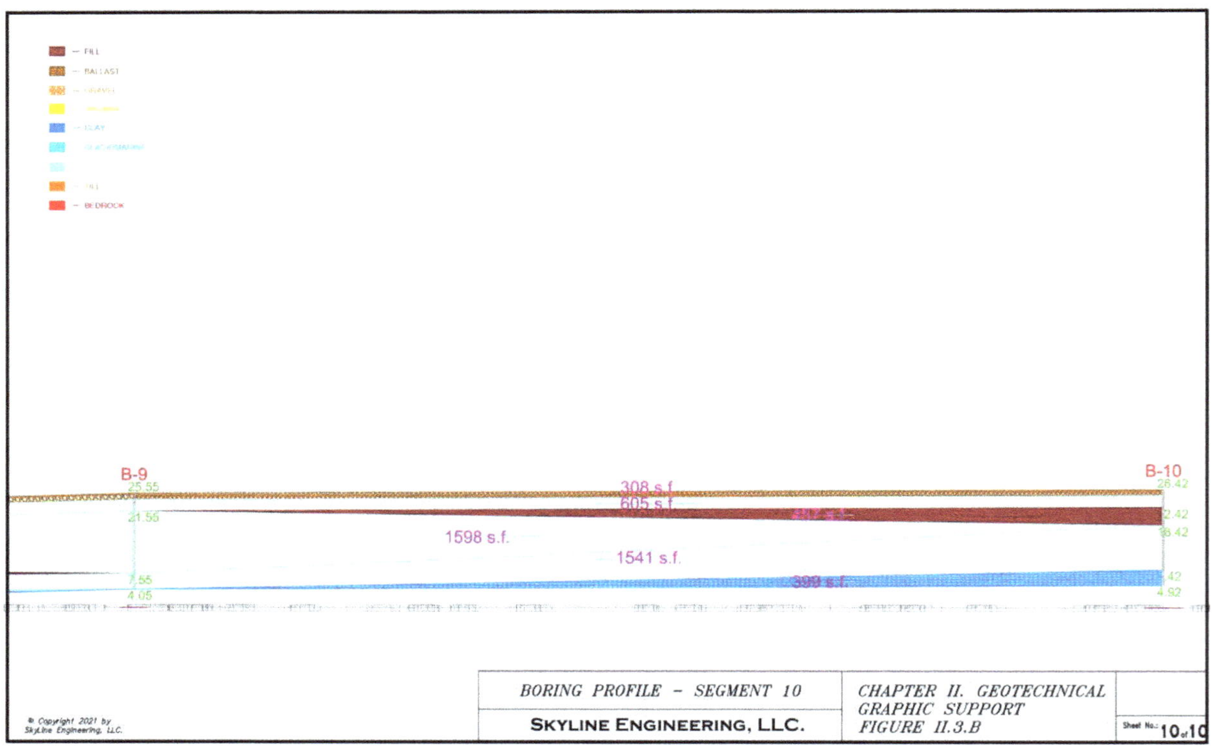
FILL
BALLAST
B-9
B-10
25.55
21.55
7.55
4.05
26.42
308 s.f.
605 s.f.
1598 s.f.
1541 s.f.
399 s.f.
BORING PROFILE – SEGMENT 10
SKYLINE ENGINEERING, LLC.
CHAPTER II. GEOTECHNICAL GRAPHIC SUPPORT FIGURE II.3.B
Sheet No.: 10 of 10
© Copyright 2021 by SkyLine Engineering, LLC.

The Profile Calculation reflects the summary of areas of each soil layer along the Baseline:

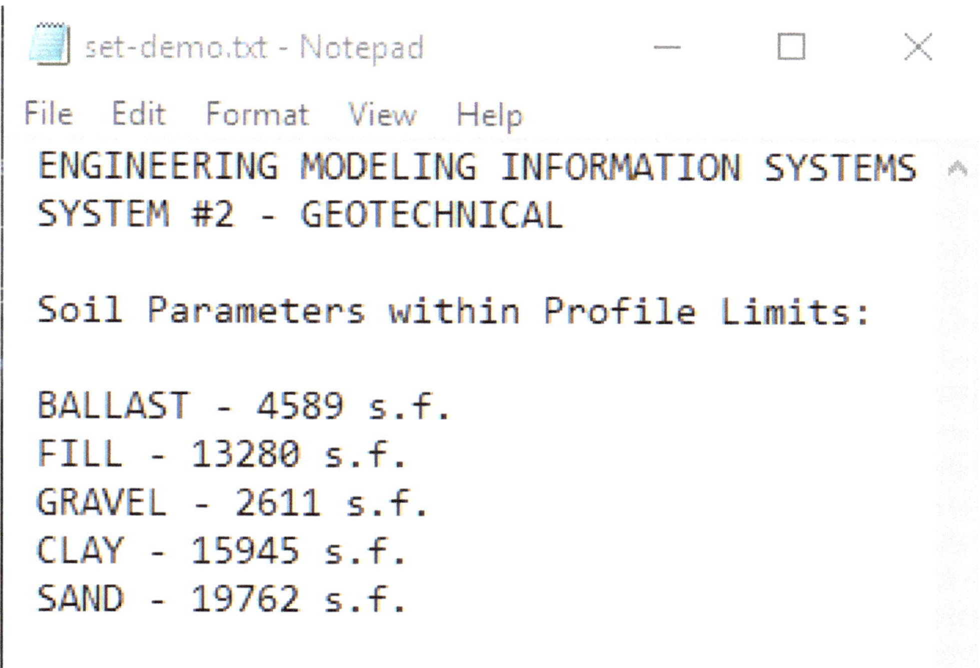
set-demo.txt - Notepad

File Edit Format View Help

ENGINEERING MODELING INFORMATION SYSTEMS
SYSTEM #2 - GEOTECHNICAL

Soil Parameters within Profile Limits:

BALLAST - 4589 s.f.
FILL - 13280 s.f.
GRAVEL - 2611 s.f.
CLAY - 15945 s.f.
SAND - 19762 s.f.

II.4 Central Artery/Tunnel Project

Figure II.4. below illustrates the Atlantic Avenue Boring Map for the Central Artery/Tunnel Project, followed by Enlarged Boring Map Segment on Middle & East Slurry Wall Baselines:

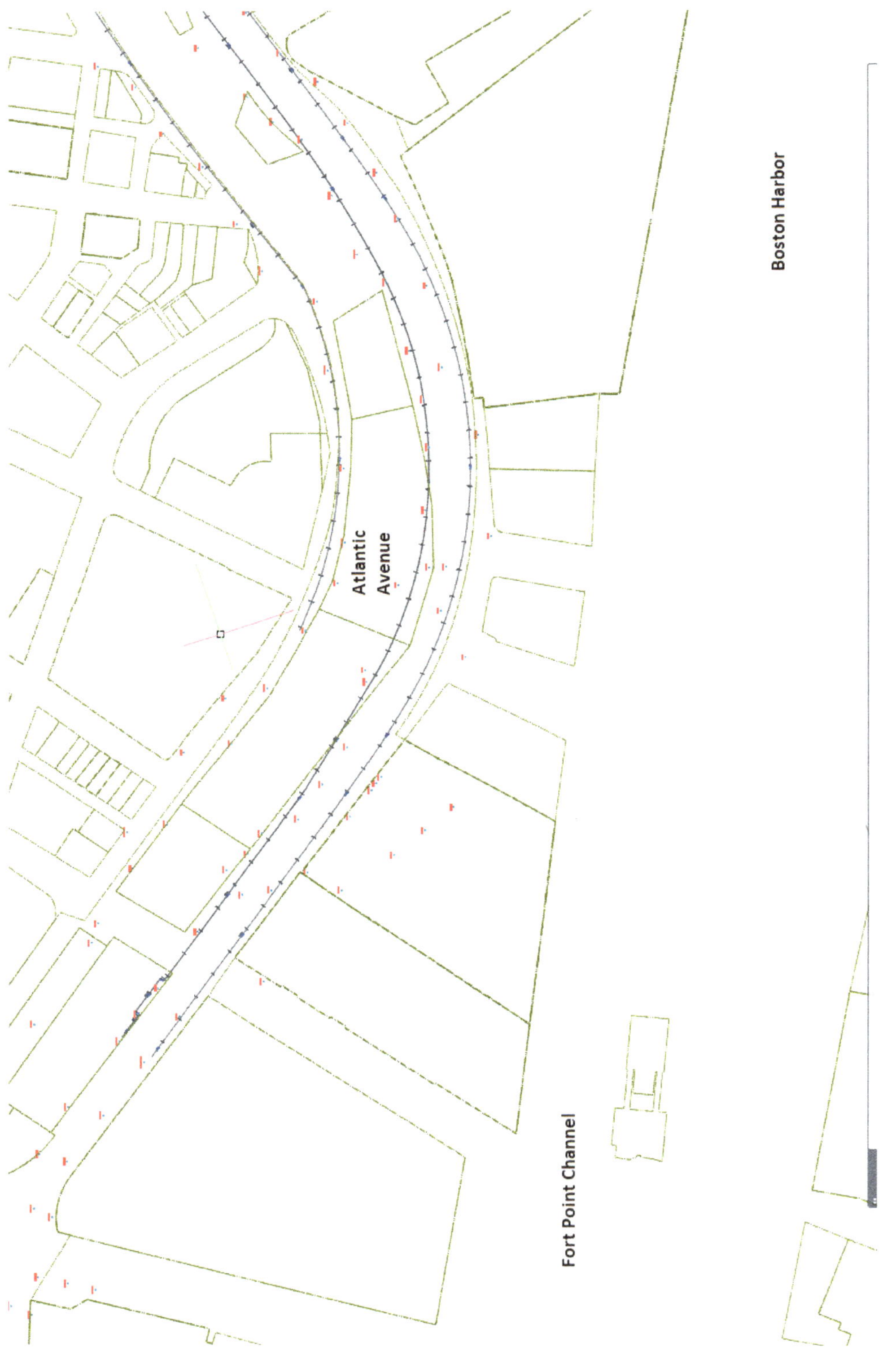

Figure II.4. – Enlarged Boring Map Segment – Middle & East Slurry Walls Baselines.

East Slurry Wall Baseline Projection Files:

bl-ttl.t...

```
AC10-4
AC10-5
AC11-1
AC11-4
AC11-5
AC10-6
AC10-7
AC11-8
AC13-5
AC13-6
AC13-9
AC10-8
AC10-11
AC11-14
AC3-2
AC5-4
AC5-6
AC10-15
AC11-18
AC5-9
AC11-20
AC3-11
AC10-19
AC11-23
AC3-12
AC10-21
AC11-26
AC10-23
AC10-27
AC10-34
AC11-33
AC5-17
AC5-18
AC5-19
AC5-35
AC10-37
AC5-34
AC11-38
AC11-40
AC11-41
AC3-15
AC10-40
```

bl-pnts.txt - Notepad

```
2954336.4693,777040.1990,111.20
2954374.9620,777094.9364,112.80
2954141.4101,776762.8213,110.60
2954300.5539,776989.1266,110.70
2954279.5346,776959.2369,111.80
2954460.2612,777212.5072,112.90
2954467.2524,777221.7812,113.80
2954418.8806,777156.5116,113.30
2954407.6520,777140.9808,111.90
2954451.6954,777201.0724,112.80
2954442.8132,777189.1301,112.70
2954743.6795,777484.3201,114.60
2954963.2195,777578.4587,112.50
2955091.6202,777602.9783,113.60
2954676.4859,777439.0985,115.40
2954801.5037,777516.3938,113.40
2955242.6186,777606.5933,113.50
2955372.0559,777588.2582,115.40
2955458.3701,777567.4070,113.20
2955555.7741,777539.9130,112.60
2955640.8463,777513.9407,111.60
2955716.8063,777490.3757,110.60
2955890.4299,777439.6272,110.60
2955984.5871,777416.2275,110.50
2955807.7669,777462.6239,110.70
2956064.1728,777398.5741,109.80
2956166.1138,777376.4678,109.70
2956289.1575,777349.4941,110.30
2956445.3047,777299.7733,108.50
2956800.5337,777073.1295,110.60
2956712.9637,777147.5393,110.80
2956344.0146,777334.8474,109.80
2956544.4943,777254.4146,110.10
2956690.6707,777164.1814,109.90
2956892.2747,776975.9528,109.20
2956930.7100,776928.4926,110.40
2956985.4962,776854.2543,109.90
2956972.0344,776811.2602,110.60
2957094.3497,776635.8610,115.90
2957079.2640,776657.7187,110.90
2957021.2093,776741.8346,111.60
2957141.6142,776567.4424,112.80
```

bl-dptn.txt - Notepad

```
96.20,89.70,64.40,37.20,-40.00
91.30,81.30,33.80,-40.00
94.60,92.60,90.60,27.60,10.40,-40.00***
97.20,92.20,64.90,40.20,-40.00
81.80,76.10,36.80,-40.00
98.40,94.90,88.90,25.90,-40.00
98.80,39.80,34.80,24.80,-40.00
91.30,39.30,-40.00
93.40,85.90,38.90,-40.00
95.80,92.80,33.80,-40.00
94.70,32.70,-40.00
104.60,27.60,14.60,-40.00
88.50,-2.50,-40.00
102.60,-6.40,-40.00
102.40,0.40,-40.00
101.40,93.40,7.90,-40.00
100.50,3.00,-40.00
98.80,-4.30,-40.00
90.20,-1.80,-40.00
93.60,89.60,84.60,-5.40,-40.00
91.60,80.60,0.10,-40.00
91.60,74.60,-2.30,-40.00
88.60,81.60,47.60,10.10,-40.00
83.50,77.50,39.70,7.50,-40.00
87.70,62.20,0.50,-40.00
87.80,76.30,29.80,11.30,-40.00
89.70,74.70,39.20,35.70,25.70,15.70,-40.00
95.30,74.30,41.80,35.30,25.80,18.50,-40.00
94.50,80.50,31.50,22.50,-40.00
98.60,89.60,73.60,61.60,57.60,51.60,47.60,37.60,31.60,25.60,-40.00
91.80,85.80,77.80,40.80,30.80,25.80,-40.00
84.80,73.30,49.80,43.30,28.30,21.80,-40.00
86.10,70.10,62.10,51.10,47.10,36.10,25.00,-40.00
91.90,86.90,69.90,50.40,40.90,34.90,27.90,-40.00
91.20,58.70,40.20,35.20,29.20,-40.00***
98.90,90.90,64.20,61.40,50.40,46.40,37.40,33.60,31.40,-40.00
93.40,90.40,35.90,30.40,-40.00
92.60,30.60,24.30,-40.00
92.40,65.90,57.90,42.40,33.90,30.90,22.40,-40.00
93.90,36.90,25.90,20.90,-40.00
93.10,31.60,26.60,-40.00
94.80,71.30,39.80,36.30,18.30,-40.00
```

bl-data.txt - Notepad

```
FILL,ORGANIC,CLAY,TILL,BEDROCK
FILL,CLAY,TILL,BEDROCK
FILL,ORGANIC,CLAY,TILL,SAND,BEDROCK***
FILL,ORGANIC,CLAY,TILL,BEDROCK
FILL,CLAY,TILL,BEDROCK
FILL,ORGANIC,CLAY,TILL,BEDROCK
FILL,TILL,CLAY,TILL,BEDROCK
FILL,TILL,BEDROCK
FILL,CLAY,TILL,BEDROCK
FILL,CLAY,TILL,BEDROCK
FILL,TILL,BEDROCK
FILL,TILL,CLAY,BEDROCK
FILL,TILL,BEDROCK
FILL,TILL,BEDROCK
FILL,TILL,BEDROCK
FILL,CLAY,TILL,BEDROCK
FILL,TILL,BEDROCK
FILL,TILL,BEDROCK
FILL,TILL,BEDROCK
FILL,CLAY,SAND,TILL,BEDROCK
FILL,CLAY,TILL,BEDROCK
FILL,CLAY,TILL,BEDROCK
FILL,ORGANIC,CLAY,TILL,BEDROCK
FILL,ORGANIC,CLAY,TILL,BEDROCK
FILL,CLAY,TILL,BEDROCK
FILL,ORGANIC,CLAY,TILL,BEDROCK
FILL,ORGANIC,CLAY,SAND,CLAY,TILL,BEDROCK
FILL,ORGANIC,CLAY,SAND,CLAY,TILL,BEDROCK
FILL,ORGANIC,CLAY,TILL,BEDROCK
FILL,ORGANIC,CLAY,GLACIOMARINE;SAND,GLACIOMARINE;SAND,GLACIOMARINE;CLAY,TILL,BEDROCK
FILL,ORGANIC,CLAY,GLACIOMARINE;CLAY,TILL,BEDROCK
FILL,ORGANIC,CLAY,SAND,CLAY,TILL,BEDROCK
FILL,CLAY,GLACIOMARINE;CLAY,SAND,CLAY,TILL,BEDROCK
FILL,ORGANIC,CLAY,SAND,GLACIOMARINE;CLAY,TILL,BEDROCK
FILL,CLAY,GLACIOMARINE;CLAY,TILL,BEDROCK
FILL,ORGANIC,CLAY,SAND,GLACIOMARINE;SAND,GLACIOMARINE;CLAY,TILL,BEDROCK
FILL,ORGANIC,CLAY,TILL,BEDROCK
FILL,CLAY,TILL,BEDROCK
FILL,CLAY,GLACIOMARINE,CLAY,GLACIOMARINE;CLAY,TILL,BEDROCK
FILL,CLAY,GLACIOMARINE;CLAY,BEDROCK
FILL,CLAY,TILL,BEDROCK
FILL,CLAY,GLACIOMARINE;CLAY,TILL,BEDROCK
```

East Slurry Wall Baseline Boring Holes Distribution (South to North) Files:

org-ttl...	org-pnts.txt - Notep...	org-dpth.txt - Notepad	org-data.txt - Notepad
AC11-1	2954141.4101,776762.8213,110.60	94.60,92.60,90.60,27.60,10.40,-40.00***	FILL,ORGANIC,CLAY,TILL,SAND,BEDROCK***
AC11-5	2954279.5346,776959.2369,111.80	81.80,76.10,36.80,-40.00	FILL,CLAY,TILL,BEDROCK
AC11-4	2954300.5539,776989.1266,110.70	97.20,92.20,64.90,40.20,-40.00	FILL,ORGANIC,CLAY,TILL,BEDROCK
AC10-4	2954336.4693,777040.1990,111.20	96.20,89.70,64.40,37.20,-40.00	FILL,ORGANIC,CLAY,TILL,BEDROCK
AC10-5	2954374.9620,777094.9364,112.80	91.30,81.30,33.80,-40.00	FILL,CLAY,TILL,BEDROCK
AC13-5	2954407.6520,777140.9808,111.90	93.40,85.90,38.90,-40.00	FILL,CLAY,TILL,BEDROCK
AC11-8	2954418.8806,777156.5116,113.30	91.30,39.30,-40.00	FILL,TILL,BEDROCK
AC13-9	2954442.8132,777189.1301,112.70	94.70,32.70,-40.00	FILL,TILL,BEDROCK
AC13-6	2954451.6954,777201.0724,112.80	95.80,92.80,33.80,-40.00	FILL,CLAY,TILL,BEDROCK
AC10-6	2954460.2612,777212.5072,112.90	98.40,94.90,88.90,25.90,-40.00	FILL,ORGANIC,CLAY,TILL,BEDROCK
AC10-7	2954467.2524,777221.7812,113.80	98.80,39.80,34.80,24.80,-40.00	FILL,TILL,CLAY,TILL,BEDROCK
AC3-2	2954676.4859,777439.0985,115.40	102.40,0.40,-40.00	FILL,TILL,BEDROCK
AC10-8	2954743.6795,777484.3201,114.60	104.60,27.60,14.60,-40.00	FILL,TILL,CLAY,BEDROCK
AC5-4	2954801.5037,777516.3938,113.40	101.40,93.40,7.90,-40.00	FILL,CLAY,TILL,BEDROCK
AC10-11	2954963.2195,777578.4587,112.50	88.50,-2.50,-40.00	FILL,TILL,BEDROCK
AC11-14	2955091.6202,777602.9783,113.60	102.60,-6.40,-40.00	FILL,TILL,BEDROCK
AC5-6	2955242.6186,777606.5933,113.50	100.50,3.00,-40.00	FILL,TILL,BEDROCK
AC10-15	2955372.0559,777588.2582,115.40	98.80,-4.30,-40.00	FILL,TILL,BEDROCK
AC11-18	2955458.3701,777567.4070,113.20	90.20,-1.80,-40.00	FILL,TILL,BEDROCK
AC5-9	2955555.7741,777539.9130,112.60	93.60,89.60,84.60,-5.40,-40.00	FILL,CLAY,SAND,TILL,BEDROCK
AC11-20	2955640.8463,777513.9407,111.60	91.60,80.60,0.10,-40.00	FILL,CLAY,TILL,BEDROCK
AC3-11	2955716.8063,777490.3757,110.60	91.60,74.60,-2.30,-40.00	FILL,CLAY,TILL,BEDROCK
AC3-12	2955807.7669,777462.6239,110.70	87.70,62.20,0.50,-40.00	FILL,CLAY,TILL,BEDROCK
AC10-19	2955890.4299,777439.6272,110.60	88.60,81.60,47.60,10.10,-40.00	FILL,ORGANIC,CLAY,TILL,BEDROCK
AC11-23	2955984.5871,777416.2275,110.50	83.50,77.50,39.70,7.50,-40.00	FILL,ORGANIC,CLAY,TILL,BEDROCK
AC10-21	2956064.1728,777398.5741,109.80	87.80,76.30,29.80,11.30,-40.00	FILL,ORGANIC,CLAY,TILL,BEDROCK
AC11-26	2956166.1138,777376.4678,109.70	89.70,74.70,39.20,35.70,25.70,15.70,-40.00	FILL,ORGANIC,CLAY,SAND,CLAY,TILL,BEDROCK
AC10-23	2956289.1575,777349.4941,110.30	95.30,74.30,41.80,35.30,25.80,18.50,-40.00	FILL,ORGANIC,CLAY,SAND,CLAY,TILL,BEDROCK
AC5-17	2956344.0146,777334.8474,109.80	84.80,73.30,49.80,43.30,28.30,21.80,-40.00	FILL,ORGANIC,CLAY,SAND,CLAY,TILL,BEDROCK
AC10-27	2956445.3047,777299.7733,108.50	94.50,80.50,31.50,22.50,-40.00	FILL,ORGANIC,CLAY,TILL,BEDROCK
AC5-18	2956544.4943,777254.4146,110.10	86.10,70.10,62.10,51.10,47.10,36.10,25.00,-40.00	FILL,CLAY,GLACIOMARINE;CLAY,SAND,CLAY,TILL,BEDROCK
AC5-19	2956690.6707,777164.1814,109.90	91.90,86.90,69.90,50.40,40.90,34.90,27.90,-40.00	FILL,ORGANIC,CLAY,SAND,GLACIOMARINE;CLAY,TILL,BEDROCK
AC11-33	2956712.9637,777147.5393,110.80	91.80,85.80,77.80,40.80,30.80,25.80,-40.00	FILL,ORGANIC,CLAY,GLACIOMARINE;CLAY,TILL,BEDROCK
AC10-34	2956800.5337,777073.1295,110.60	98.60,89.60,73.60,61.60,57.60,51.60,47.60,37.60,31.60,25.60,-40.00	FILL,ORGANIC,CLAY,GLACIOMARINE;SAND,GLACIOMARINE;SAND,GLACIOMARINE;CLAY,TILL,BEDROCK
AC5-35	2956892.2747,776975.9528,109.20	91.20,58.70,40.20,35.20,29.20,-40.00***	FILL,CLAY,GLACIOMARINE;CLAY,TILL,BEDROCK
AC10-37	2956930.7100,776928.4926,110.40	98.90,90.90,64.20,61.40,50.40,46.40,37.40,33.60,31.40,-40.00	FILL,ORGANIC,CLAY,SAND,GLACIOMARINE;SAND,GLACIOMARINE;CLAY,TILL,BEDROCK
AC11-38	2956972.0344,776811.2602,110.60	92.60,30.60,24.30,-40.00	FILL,CLAY,TILL,BEDROCK
AC5-34	2956985.4962,776854.2543,109.90	93.40,90.40,35.90,30.40,-40.00	FILL,ORGANIC,CLAY,TILL,BEDROCK
AC3-15	2957021.2093,776741.8346,111.60	93.10,31.60,26.60,-40.00	FILL,CLAY,TILL,BEDROCK
AC11-41	2957079.2640,776657.7187,110.90	93.90,36.90,25.90,20.90,-40.00	FILL,CLAY,GLACIOMARINE;CLAY,BEDROCK
AC11-40	2957094.3497,776635.8610,115.90	92.40,65.90,57.90,42.40,33.90,30.90,22.40,-40.00	FILL,CLAY,GLACIOMARINE,CLAY,GLACIOMARINE;CLAY,TILL,BEDROCK
AC10-40	2957141.6142,776567.4424,112.80	94.80,71.30,39.80,36.30,18.30,-40.00	FILL,CLAY,GLACIOMARINE;CLAY,TILL,BEDROCK

The Attached Figure II.4.A (Drawings 1-7) illustrates Baseline Projection Points on East Slurry Wall Baseline, located within 50' of actual Boring Holes.

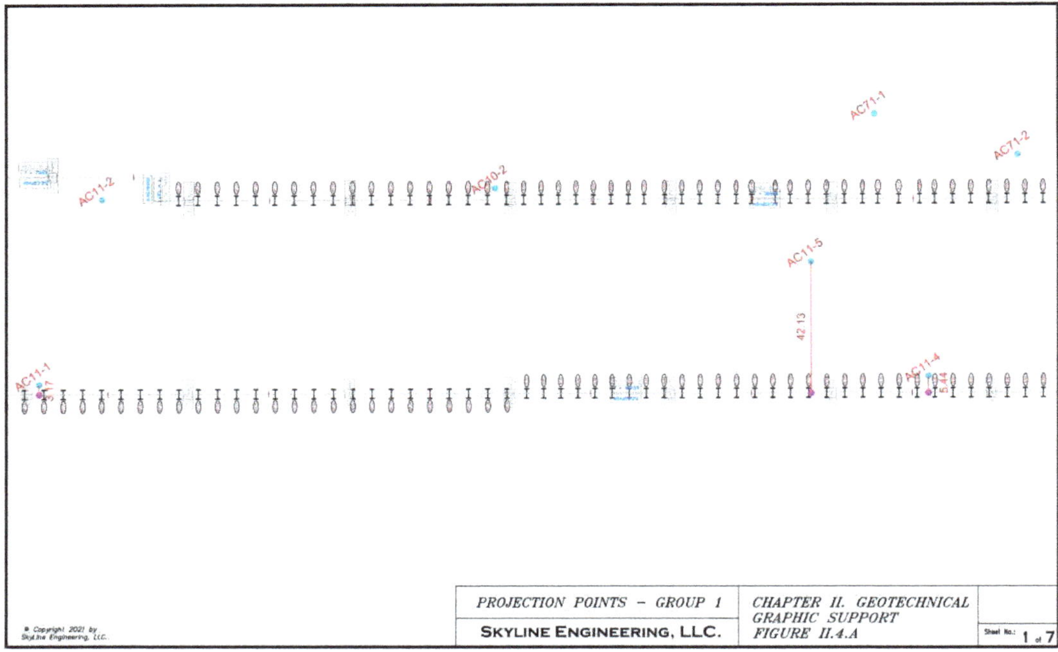

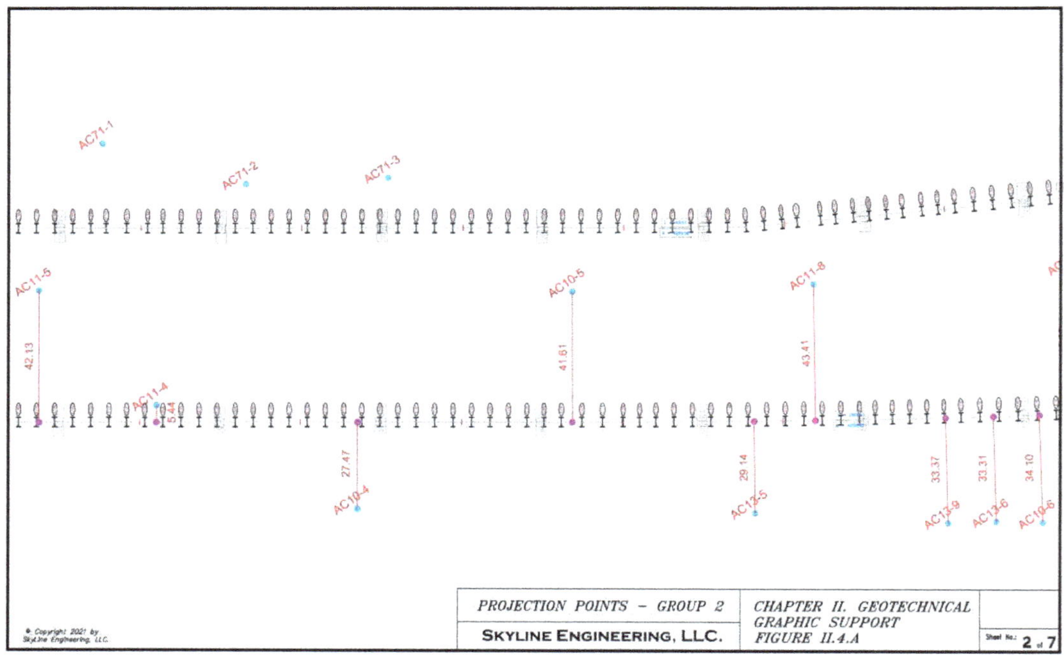

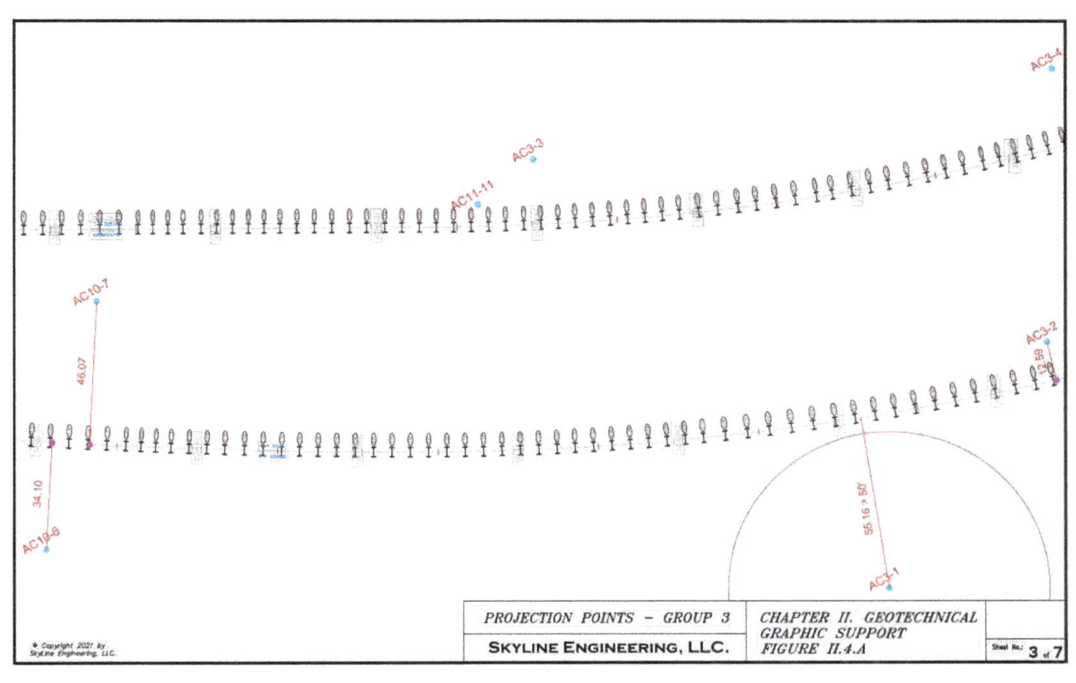
AC3-4
AC3-3
AC11-11
AC10-7
46.07
AC3-2
12.59
34.10
AC10-6
55.16 > 50'
AC3-1
PROJECTION POINTS – GROUP 3
SKYLINE ENGINEERING, LLC.
CHAPTER II. GEOTECHNICAL
GRAPHIC SUPPORT
FIGURE II.4.A
Sheet No: 3 of 7
© Copyright 2021 by Skyline Engineering, LLC.

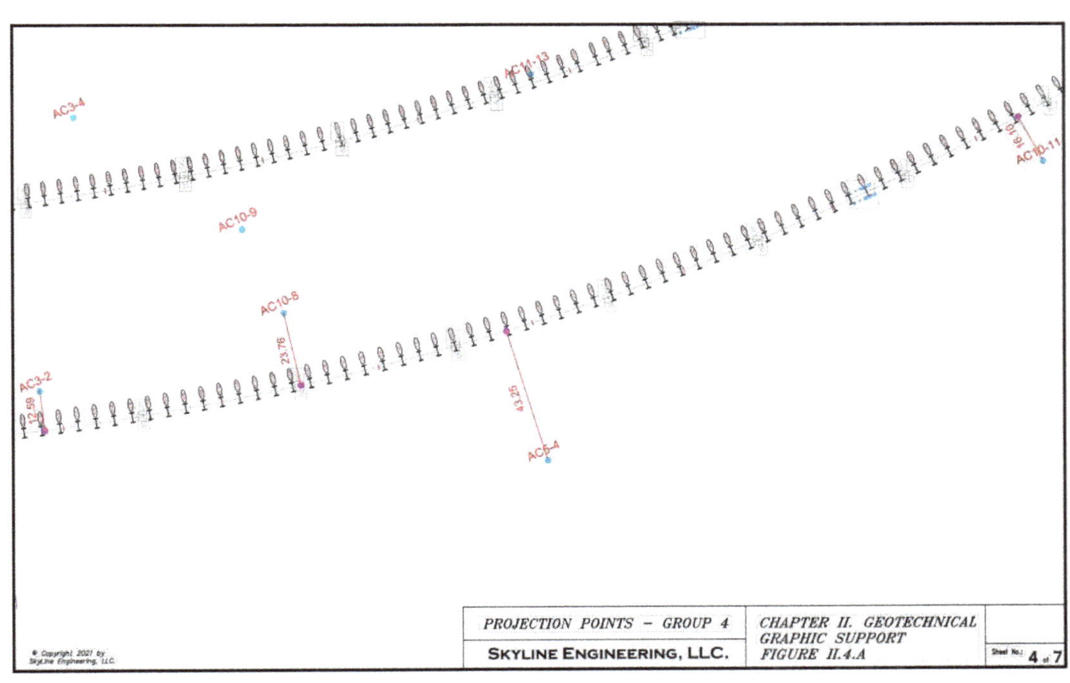
AC3-4
AC11-13
AC10-9
AC10-11
16.10
AC10-8
23.76
AC3-2
12.59
43.25
AC5-4
PROJECTION POINTS – GROUP 4
SKYLINE ENGINEERING, LLC.
CHAPTER II. GEOTECHNICAL
GRAPHIC SUPPORT
FIGURE II.4.A
Sheet No: 4 of 7
© Copyright 2021 by Skyline Engineering, LLC.

AC10-13

AC10-12

AC5-6

AC11-14

30.17

16.10

AC10-11

© Copyright 2021 by SkyLine Engineering, LLC.

PROJECTION POINTS – GROUP 5	CHAPTER II. GEOTECHNICAL GRAPHIC SUPPORT FIGURE II.4.A	Sheet No.: 5 of 7
SKYLINE ENGINEERING, LLC.		

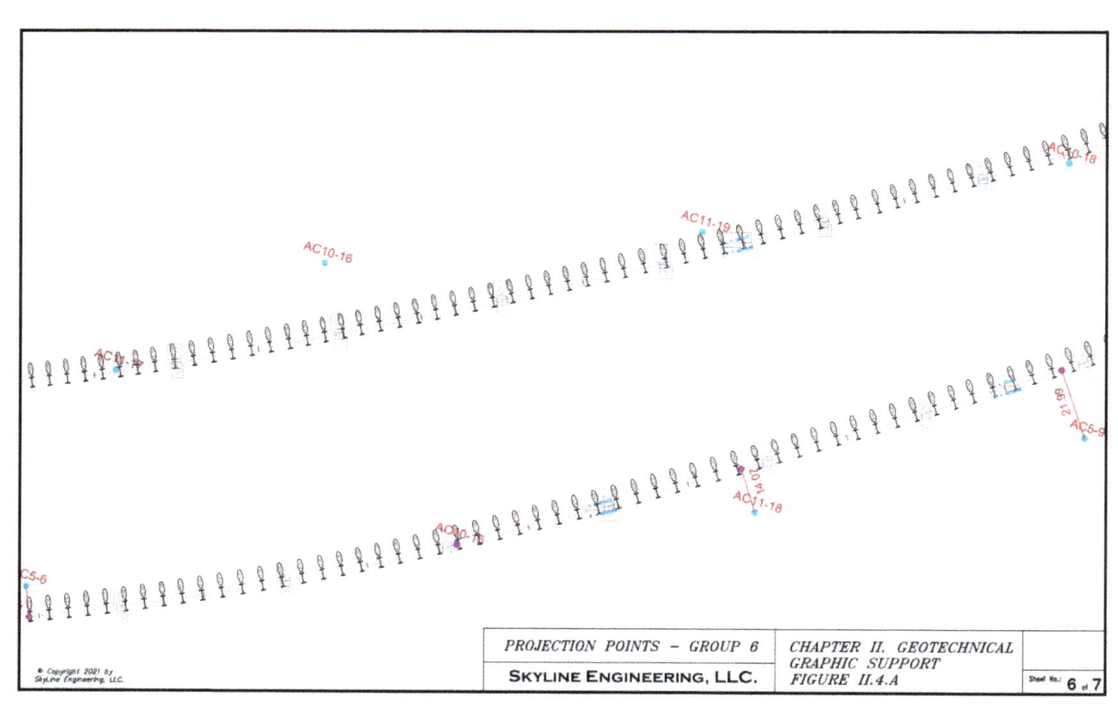

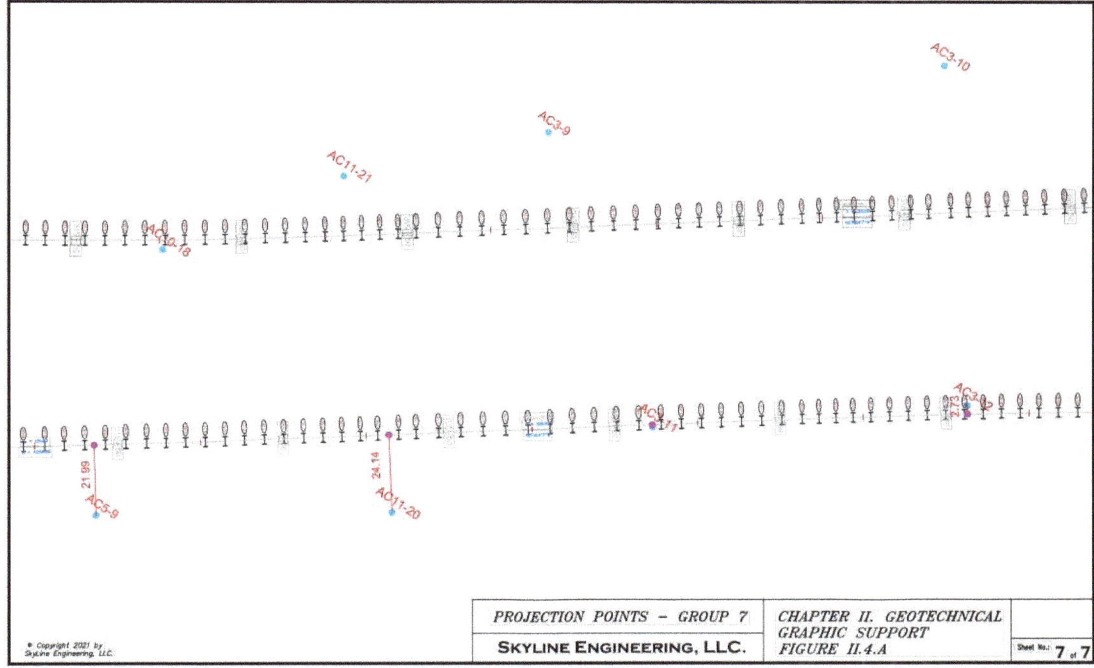

The Modeling Program has the input option for each soil layer – either the Soil Layer Depth from the Surface Elevation or the Soil Layer Elevation:

As an output of the Soil Profile Program, the Attached Figure II.4.B (Drawings 1-7) shows Boring Holes and continuous Soil Profile Segments through East Slurry Wall Baseline Segment.

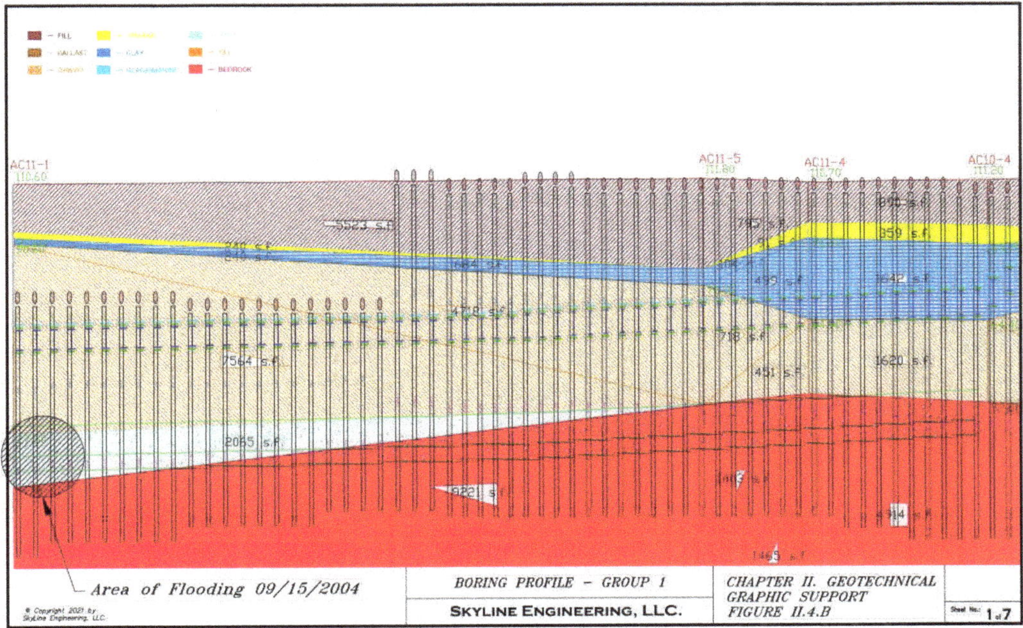

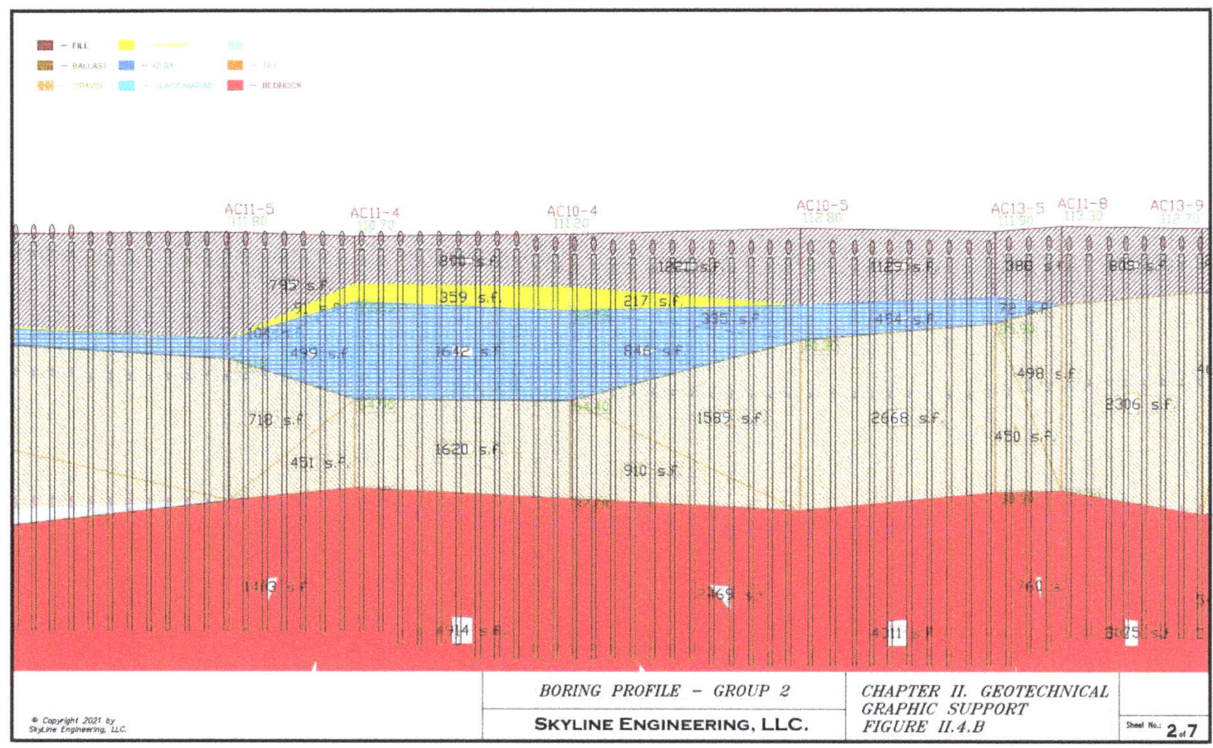
FILL
BALLAST
GRAVEL
CLAY
BEDROCK
AC11-5
AC11-4
AC10-4
AC10-5
AC13-5
AC11-8
AC13-9
BORING PROFILE - GROUP 2
SKYLINE ENGINEERING, LLC.
CHAPTER II. GEOTECHNICAL GRAPHIC SUPPORT FIGURE II.4.B
Sheet No.: 2 of 7
© Copyright 2021 by SkyLine Engineering, LLC.

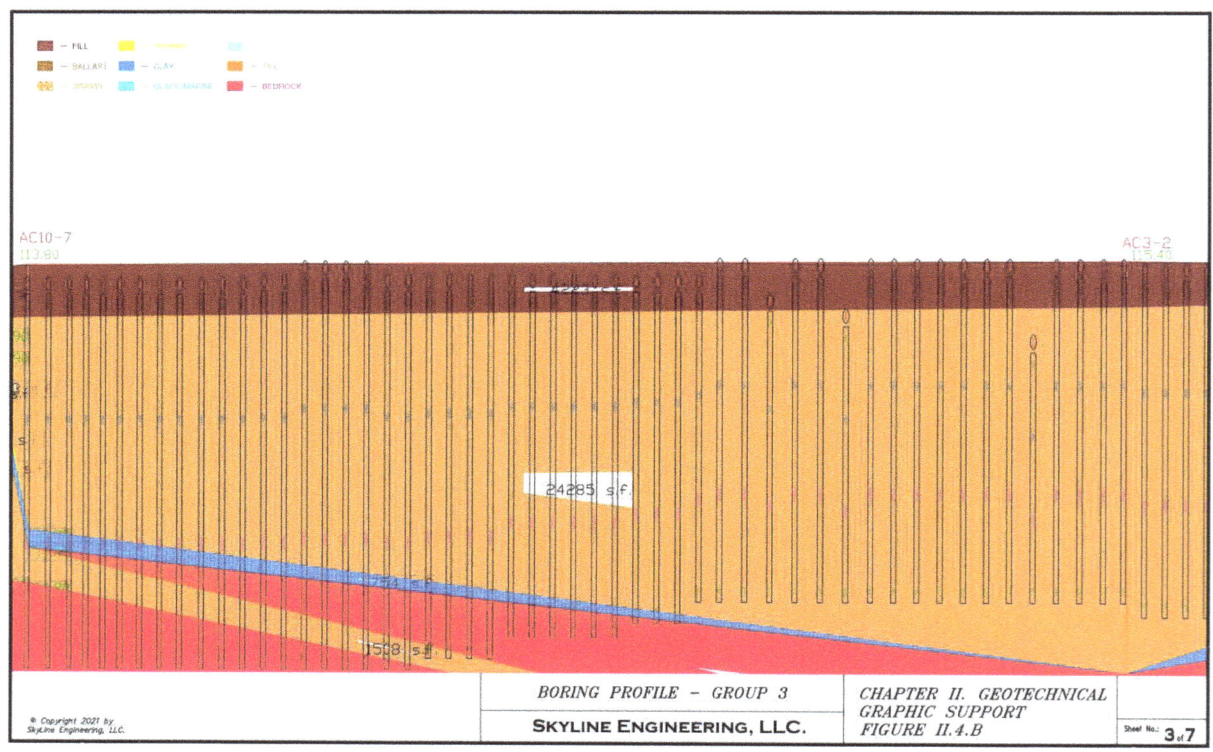
FILL
BALLAST
GRAVEL
CLAY
BEDROCK
AC10-7
AC3-2
24285 s.f.
BORING PROFILE - GROUP 3
SKYLINE ENGINEERING, LLC.
CHAPTER II. GEOTECHNICAL GRAPHIC SUPPORT FIGURE II.4.B
Sheet No.: 3 of 7
© Copyright 2021 by SkyLine Engineering, LLC.

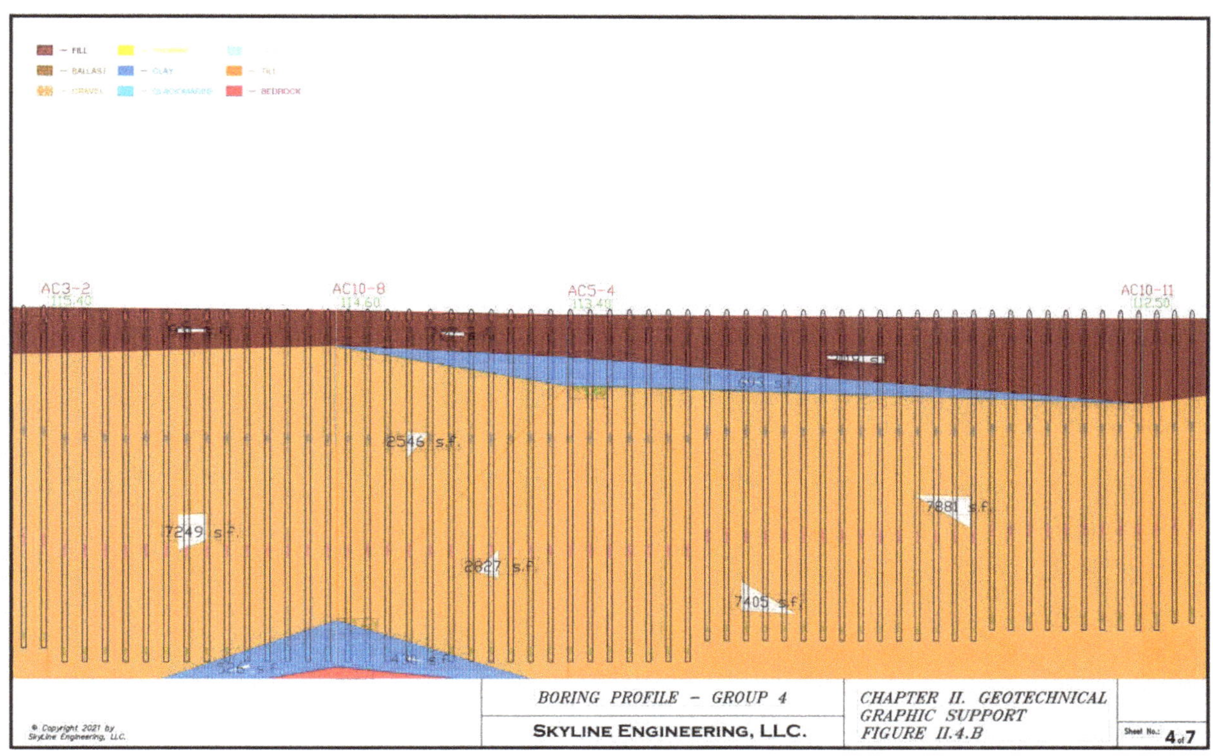

FILL
BALLAST
GRAVEL
CLAY
TILL
BEDROCK
AC3-2
AC10-8
AC5-4
AC10-11
2546 s.f.
7249 s.f.
2827 s.f.
7881 s.f.
7405 s.f.
BORING PROFILE - GROUP 4
SKYLINE ENGINEERING, LLC.
CHAPTER II. GEOTECHNICAL
GRAPHIC SUPPORT
FIGURE II.4.B
Sheet No.: 4 of 7
© Copyright 2021 by
SkyLine Engineering, LLC

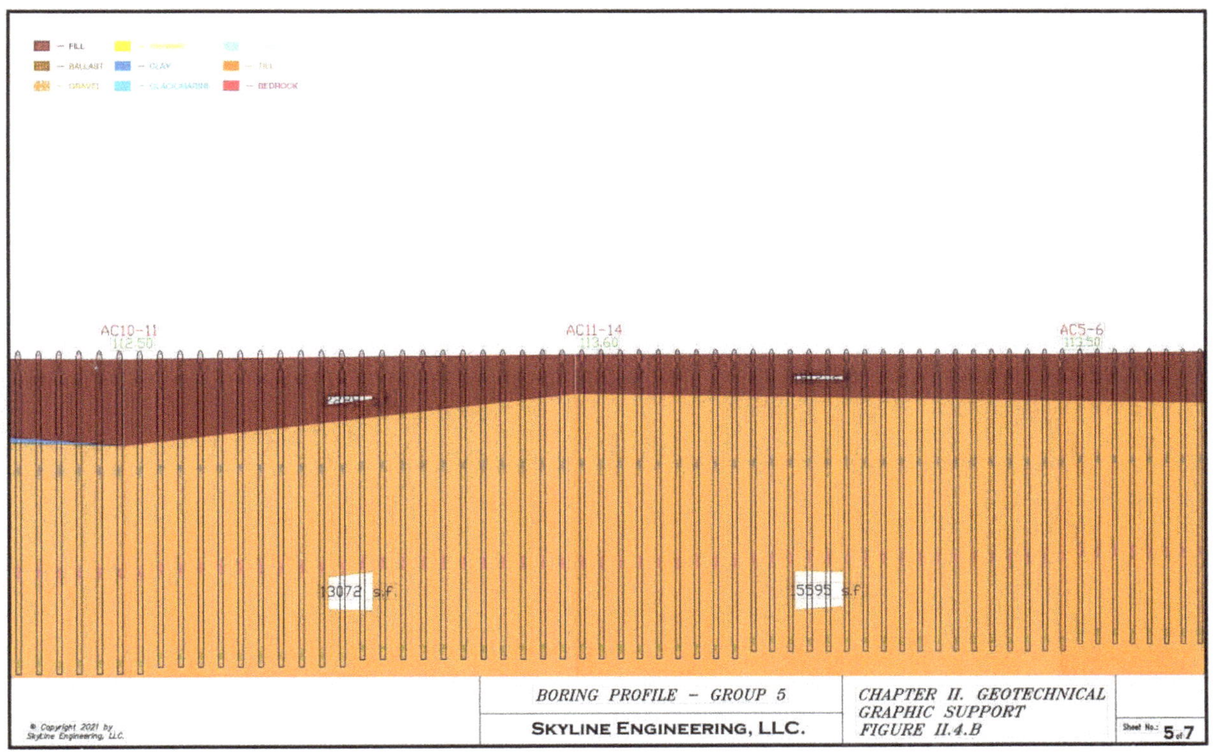

FILL
BALLAST
GRAVEL
CLAY
TILL
BEDROCK
AC10-11
AC11-14
AC5-6
13072 s.f.
15595 s.f.
BORING PROFILE - GROUP 5
SKYLINE ENGINEERING, LLC.
CHAPTER II. GEOTECHNICAL
GRAPHIC SUPPORT
FIGURE II.4.B
Sheet No.: 5 of 7
© Copyright 2021 by
SkyLine Engineering, LLC

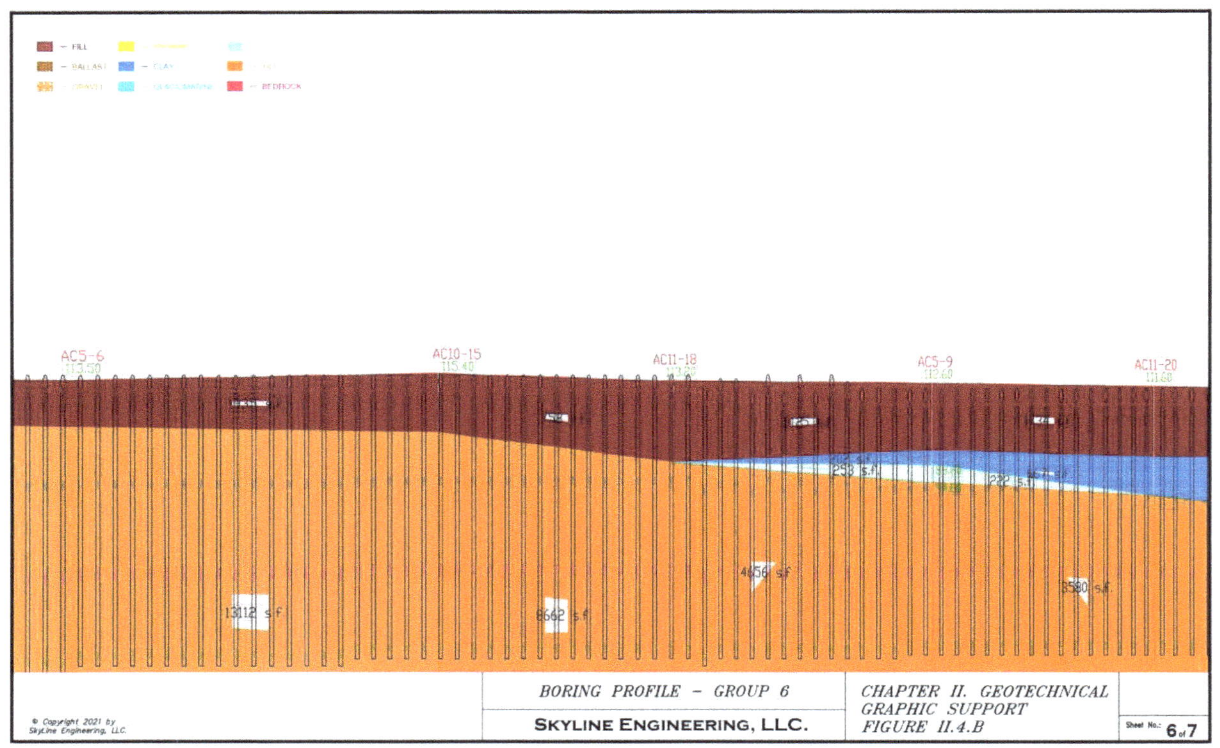

FILL
BALLAST
CLAY
BEDROCK
AC5-6
AC10-15
AC11-18
AC5-9
AC11-20
258 s.f
222 s.f
4656 s.f
3580 s.f
13112 s.f
8662 s.f
BORING PROFILE – GROUP 6
SKYLINE ENGINEERING, LLC.
CHAPTER II. GEOTECHNICAL GRAPHIC SUPPORT FIGURE II.4.B
Sheet No.: 6 of 7
© Copyright 2021 by SkyLine Engineering, LLC.

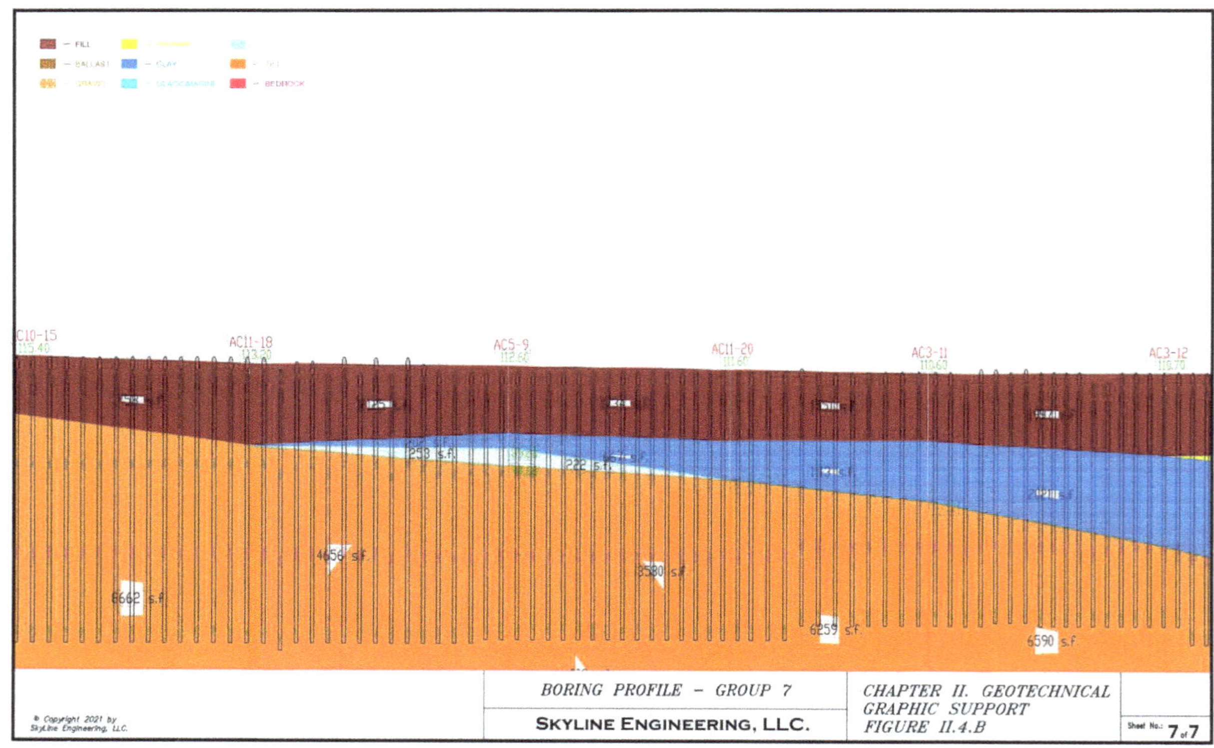

FILL
BALLAST
CLAY
BEDROCK
C10-15
115.40
AC11-18
AC5-9
AC11-20
AC3-11
AC3-12
258 s.f
222 s.f
4656 s.f
3580 s.f
8662 s.f
6259 s.f
6590 s.f
BORING PROFILE – GROUP 7
SKYLINE ENGINEERING, LLC.
CHAPTER II. GEOTECHNICAL GRAPHIC SUPPORT FIGURE II.4.B
Sheet No.: 7 of 7
© Copyright 2021 by SkyLine Engineering, LLC.

Figure II.4.C below illustrates the East Slurry Wall Profile Calculation Summary:

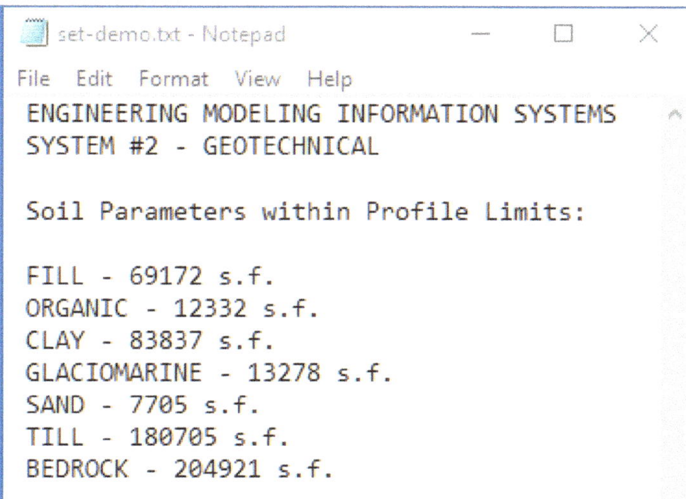

ENGINEERING MODELING INFORMATION SYSTEMS
SYSTEM #2 - GEOTECHNICAL

Soil Parameters within Profile Limits:

FILL - 69172 s.f.
ORGANIC - 12332 s.f.
CLAY - 83837 s.f.
GLACIOMARINE - 13278 s.f.
SAND - 7705 s.f.
TILL - 180705 s.f.
BEDROCK - 204921 s.f.

On September 15, 2004, the Central Artery North Bound was flooded. The East Slurry Wall Profile based on Boring Data showed a significant sand segment at the Harborside of the flooded area location – right against the base slab elevation-wise (shown as the circle mark on the Attached Figure II.4.B – Drawing 1)

CHAPTER III: STRUCTURAL

III.1 Deep Foundations & Slurry Walls

The Figure III.1.A below shows the Project Slurry Walls File Structure Scheme:

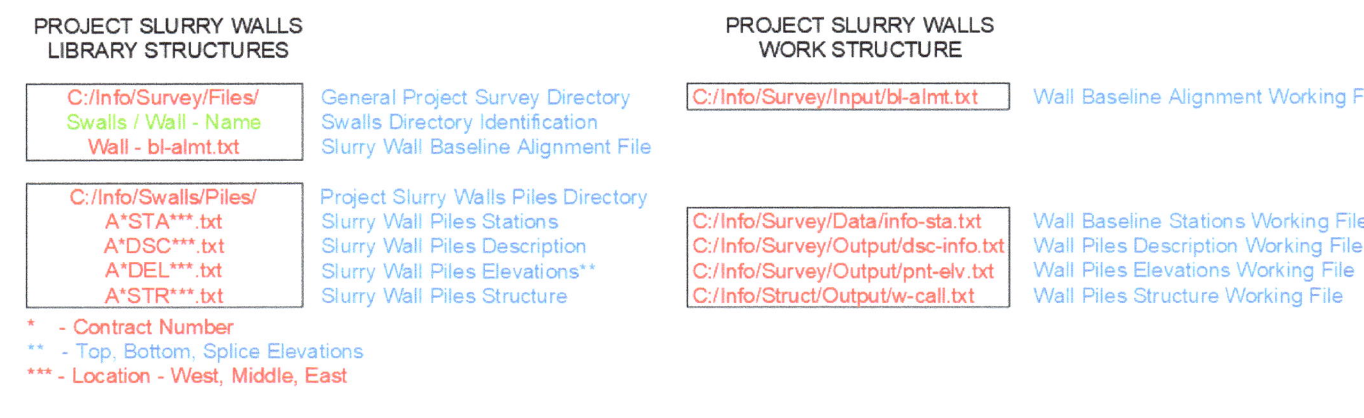

The Deep Foundations/Slurry Walls Original Database for each Wall includes:

- Survey Information - Baseline Alignment [1], Stations [2], Top and Bottom Elevations [4]
- Description Information – Piles or Columns Description [3]
- Structural Information – Piles or Columns Designation or Structural Size [5]

Figure III.1.B below illustrates the Input Information for the East Slurry Wall of the Central Artery Project

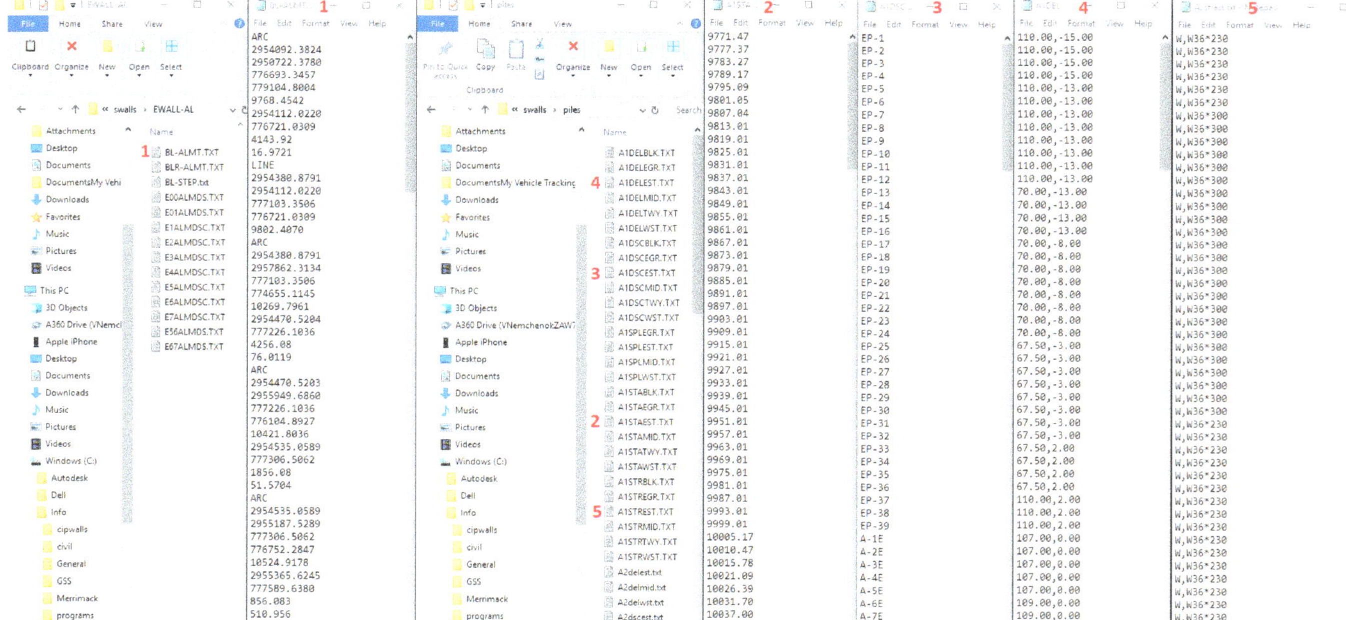

The logical steps to develop the Project Slurry Walls Real Space Modeling are as follows:

1. Choosing Slurry Wall Database Survey information [1,2]
2. Copying Selected Alignment and Station files info Generic Survey Input [bl-almt, info-sta]
3. Derive Coordinate File for each Pile on Slurry Wall using BL-COORD program

Figure III.1.C – Slurry Wall Piles Coordinate File (see Chapter I, Paragraph 2, Example 3)

bl-almt....	info-sta....	line-occ.txt - Notepad
ARC	9771.47	2954094.1394,776695.7968,N35d32'40"W,97+71.47
2954092.3824	9777.37	2954097.5658,776700.5999,N35d27'46"W,97+77.37
2950722.3780	9783.27	2954100.9854,776705.4078,N35d22'53"W,97+83.27
776693.3457	9789.17	2954104.3982,776710.2206,N35d17'59"W,97+89.17
779104.8004	9795.09	2954107.8157,776715.0546,N35d13'4"W,97+95.09
9768.4542	9801.05	2954111.2492,776719.9262,N35d8'8"W,98+01.05
2954112.0220	9807.04	2954114.6870,776724.8206,N54d53'3"E,98+07.04
776721.0309	9813.01	2954118.1212,776729.7041,N54d53'3"E,98+13.01
4143.92	9819.01	2954121.5726,776734.6120,N54d53'3"E,98+19.01
16.9721	9825.01	2954125.0240,776739.5199,N54d53'3"E,98+25.01
LINE	9831.01	2954128.4754,776744.4279,N54d53'3"E,98+31.01
2954380.8791	9837.01	2954131.9268,776749.3358,N54d53'3"E,98+37.01
2954112.0220	9843.01	2954135.3781,776754.2438,N54d53'3"E,98+43.01
777103.3506	9849.01	2954138.8295,776759.1517,N54d53'3"E,98+49.01
776721.0309	9855.01	2954142.2809,776764.0596,N54d53'3"E,98+55.01
9802.4070	9861.01	2954145.7323,776768.9676,N54d53'3"E,98+61.01
ARC	9867.01	2954149.1837,776773.8755,N54d53'3"E,98+67.01
2954380.8791	9873.01	2954152.6351,776778.7835,N54d53'3"E,98+73.01
2957862.3134	9879.01	2954156.0865,776783.6914,N54d53'3"E,98+79.01
777103.3506	9885.01	2954159.5379,776788.5994,N54d53'3"E,98+85.01
774655.1145	9891.01	2954162.9893,776793.5073,N54d53'3"E,98+91.01
10269.7961	9897.01	2954166.4407,776798.4152,N54d53'3"E,98+97.01
2954470.5204	9903.01	2954169.8921,776803.3232,N54d53'3"E,99+03.01
777226.1036	9909.01	2954173.3435,776808.2311,N54d53'3"E,99+09.01
4256.08	9915.01	2954176.7948,776813.1391,N54d53'3"E,99+15.01
76.0119	9921.01	2954180.2462,776818.0470,N54d53'3"E,99+21.01
ARC	9927.01	2954183.6976,776822.9550,N54d53'3"E,99+27.01
2954470.5203	9933.01	2954187.1490,776827.8629,N54d53'3"E,99+33.01
2955949.6860	9939.01	2954190.6004,776832.7708,N54d53'3"E,99+39.01
777226.1036	9945.01	2954194.0518,776837.6788,N54d53'3"E,99+45.01
776104.8927	9951.01	2954197.5032,776842.5867,N54d53'3"E,99+51.01
10421.8036	9957.01	2954200.9546,776847.4947,N54d53'3"E,99+57.01
2954535.0589	9963.01	2954204.4060,776852.4026,N54d53'3"E,99+63.01
777306.5062	9969.01	2954207.8574,776857.3105,N54d53'3"E,99+69.01
1856.08	9975.01	2954211.3088,776862.2185,N54d53'3"E,99+75.01
51.5704	9981.01	2954214.7602,776867.1264,N54d53'3"E,99+81.01
ARC	9987.01	2954218.2115,776872.0344,N54d53'3"E,99+87.01
2954535.0589	9993.01	2954221.6629,776876.9423,N54d53'3"E,99+93.01
2955187.5289	9999.01	2954225.1143,776881.8503,N54d53'3"E,99+99.01
777306.5062	10005.17	2954228.6578,776886.8891,N54d53'3"E,100+05.17
776752.2847	10010.47	2954231.7065,776891.2244,N54d53'3"E,100+10.47
10524.9178	10015.78	2954234.7610,776895.5680,N54d53'3"E,100+15.78
2955365.6245	10021.09	2954237.8155,776899.9115,N54d53'3"E,100+21.09
777589.6380	10026.39	2954240.8642,776904.2468,N54d53'3"E,100+26.39
856.083	10031.70	2954243.9187,776908.5904,N54d53'3"E,100+31.70
510.956	10037.00	2954246.9674,776912.9257,N54d53'3"E,100+37.00
ARC	10042.31	2954250.0219,776917.2692,N54d53'3"E,100+42.31

4. For Slurry Wall Piles Modeling (Layout, Elevations. Sections, 3D-Views), there is sufficient input information – Description, Coordinates, Elevation, Structural Designation – Generic input Files - see Figure III.1.D below.

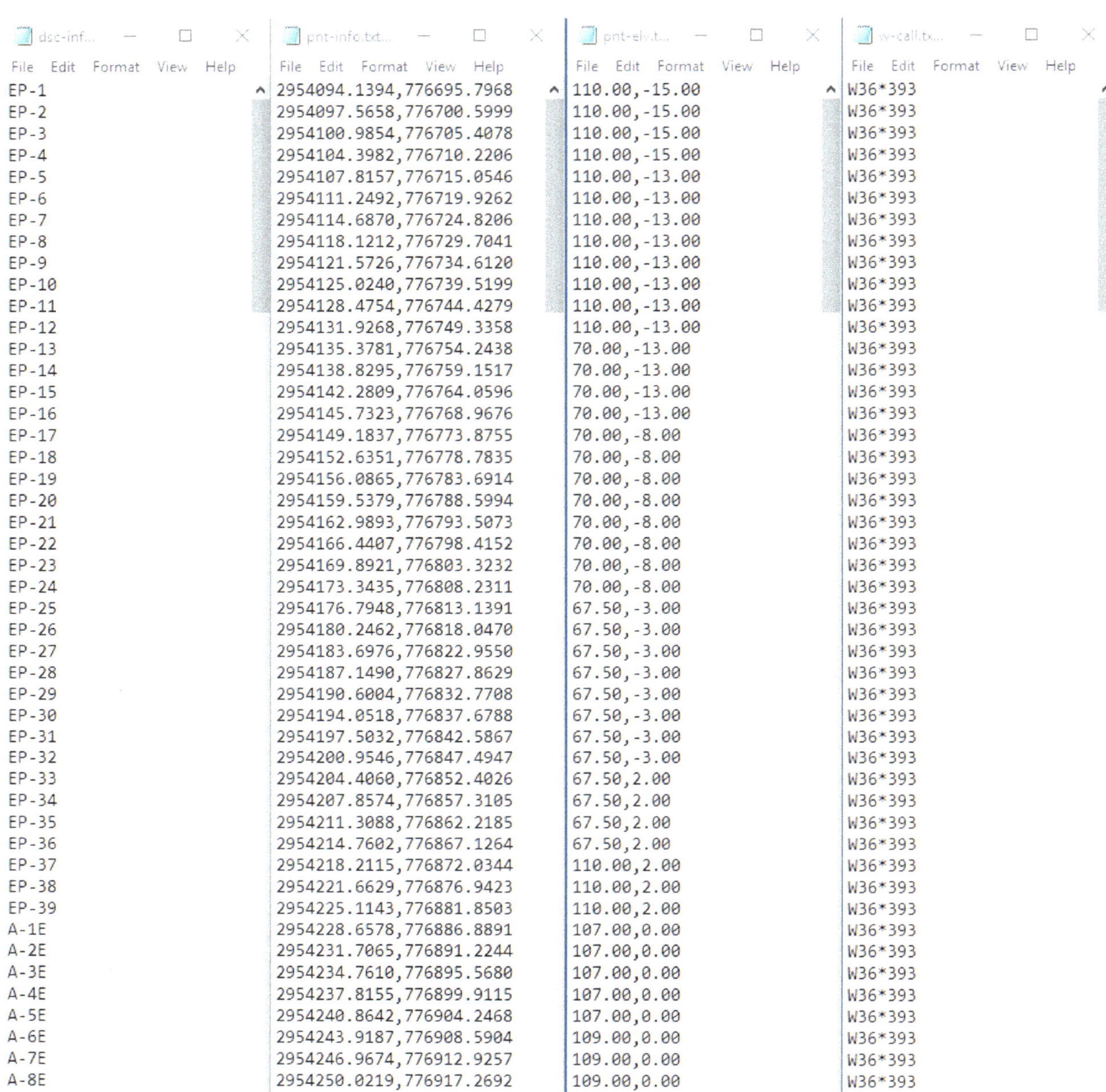

dsc-inf...	pnt-info.txt...	pnt-elv.t...	w-call.tx...
EP-1	2954094.1394,776695.7968	110.00,-15.00	W36*393
EP-2	2954097.5658,776700.5999	110.00,-15.00	W36*393
EP-3	2954100.9854,776705.4078	110.00,-15.00	W36*393
EP-4	2954104.3982,776710.2206	110.00,-15.00	W36*393
EP-5	2954107.8157,776715.0546	110.00,-13.00	W36*393
EP-6	2954111.2492,776719.9262	110.00,-13.00	W36*393
EP-7	2954114.6870,776724.8206	110.00,-13.00	W36*393
EP-8	2954118.1212,776729.7041	110.00,-13.00	W36*393
EP-9	2954121.5726,776734.6120	110.00,-13.00	W36*393
EP-10	2954125.0240,776739.5199	110.00,-13.00	W36*393
EP-11	2954128.4754,776744.4279	110.00,-13.00	W36*393
EP-12	2954131.9268,776749.3358	110.00,-13.00	W36*393
EP-13	2954135.3781,776754.2438	70.00,-13.00	W36*393
EP-14	2954138.8295,776759.1517	70.00,-13.00	W36*393
EP-15	2954142.2809,776764.0596	70.00,-13.00	W36*393
EP-16	2954145.7323,776768.9676	70.00,-13.00	W36*393
EP-17	2954149.1837,776773.8755	70.00,-8.00	W36*393
EP-18	2954152.6351,776778.7835	70.00,-8.00	W36*393
EP-19	2954156.0865,776783.6914	70.00,-8.00	W36*393
EP-20	2954159.5379,776788.5994	70.00,-8.00	W36*393
EP-21	2954162.9893,776793.5073	70.00,-8.00	W36*393
EP-22	2954166.4407,776798.4152	70.00,-8.00	W36*393
EP-23	2954169.8921,776803.3232	70.00,-8.00	W36*393
EP-24	2954173.3435,776808.2311	70.00,-8.00	W36*393
EP-25	2954176.7948,776813.1391	67.50,-3.00	W36*393
EP-26	2954180.2462,776818.0470	67.50,-3.00	W36*393
EP-27	2954183.6976,776822.9550	67.50,-3.00	W36*393
EP-28	2954187.1490,776827.8629	67.50,-3.00	W36*393
EP-29	2954190.6004,776832.7708	67.50,-3.00	W36*393
EP-30	2954194.0518,776837.6788	67.50,-3.00	W36*393
EP-31	2954197.5032,776842.5867	67.50,-3.00	W36*393
EP-32	2954200.9546,776847.4947	67.50,-3.00	W36*393
EP-33	2954204.4060,776852.4026	67.50,2.00	W36*393
EP-34	2954207.8574,776857.3105	67.50,2.00	W36*393
EP-35	2954211.3088,776862.2185	67.50,2.00	W36*393
EP-36	2954214.7602,776867.1264	67.50,2.00	W36*393
EP-37	2954218.2115,776872.0344	110.00,2.00	W36*393
EP-38	2954221.6629,776876.9423	110.00,2.00	W36*393
EP-39	2954225.1143,776881.8503	110.00,2.00	W36*393
A-1E	2954228.6578,776886.8891	107.00,0.00	W36*393
A-2E	2954231.7065,776891.2244	107.00,0.00	W36*393
A-3E	2954234.7610,776895.5680	107.00,0.00	W36*393
A-4E	2954237.8155,776899.9115	107.00,0.00	W36*393
A-5E	2954240.8642,776904.2468	107.00,0.00	W36*393
A-6E	2954243.9187,776908.5904	109.00,0.00	W36*393
A-7E	2954246.9674,776912.9257	109.00,0.00	W36*393
A-8E	2954250.0219,776917.2692	109.00,0.00	W36*393

5. Slurry Wall Piles Program Block Scheme for Plan, Elevation, 3D View, & Section Mode Options is illustrated on the next Page – Figure III.1.E.

The following Figures III.1.F & III.1.G show Program Developed Plan Views of Middle Slurry Wall Piles - Section MP and East Slurry Wall Piles – Section EP – respectively.

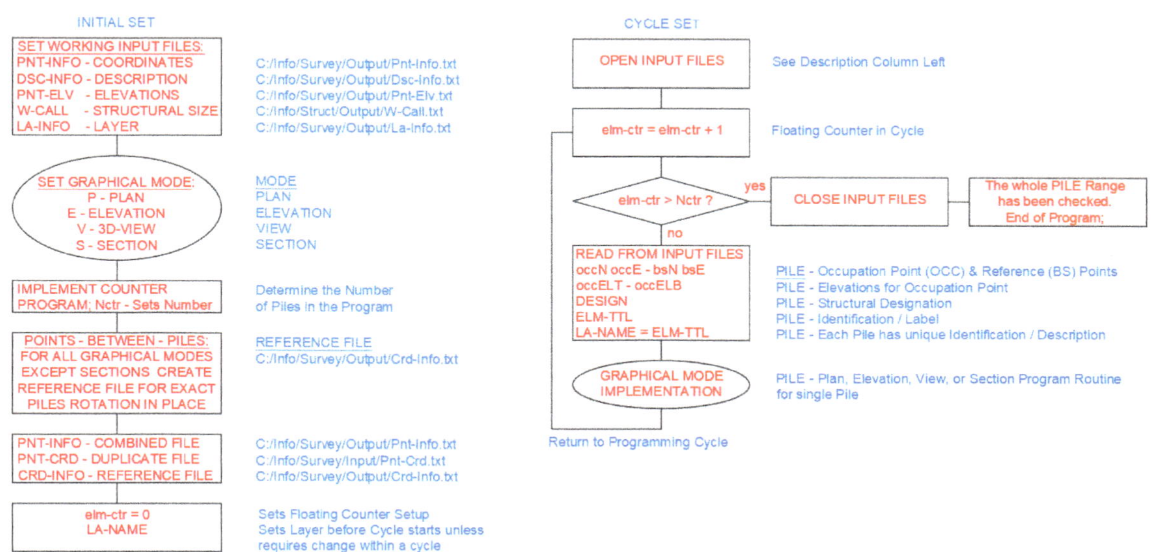

Figure III.1.E – Slurry Wall Piles Program Block Scheme.

Figure III.1.F – Middle Slurry Wall Partial Segment “MP” Plan View.

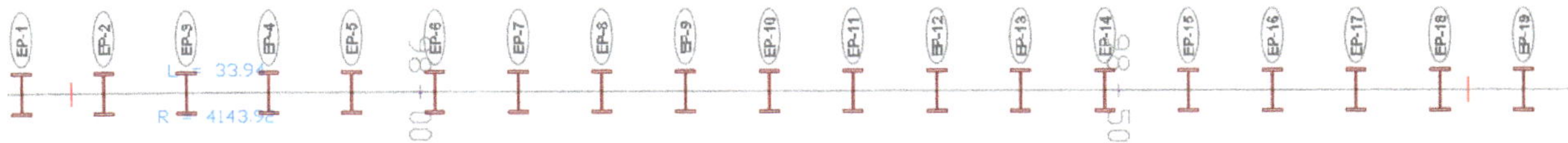

Figure III.1.G – East Slurry Wall Partial Segment “EP” Plan View.

Corresponding East Slurry Wall Partial Profile Segment with overlayed Soil Block is shown in Figure III.1.H. The enlarged profile views reflect the thickness of soil strata vs. the pile depth between Boring Holes AC 11-5 & AC 13-5, as illustrated in Figure III.1.I below. Figure III.1.J. demonstrates the East Slurry Wall Partial Profile Segment detailed view with Pile designation and elevations, followed by Section and Object Views. Graphically, each Pile has its own separate Layers for contour (layout), description, and takeoffs – Length and Weight. The program sets graphical mode, calculates Length and Weight for each Pile, and creates Output Chart - see Figure III.1.K.

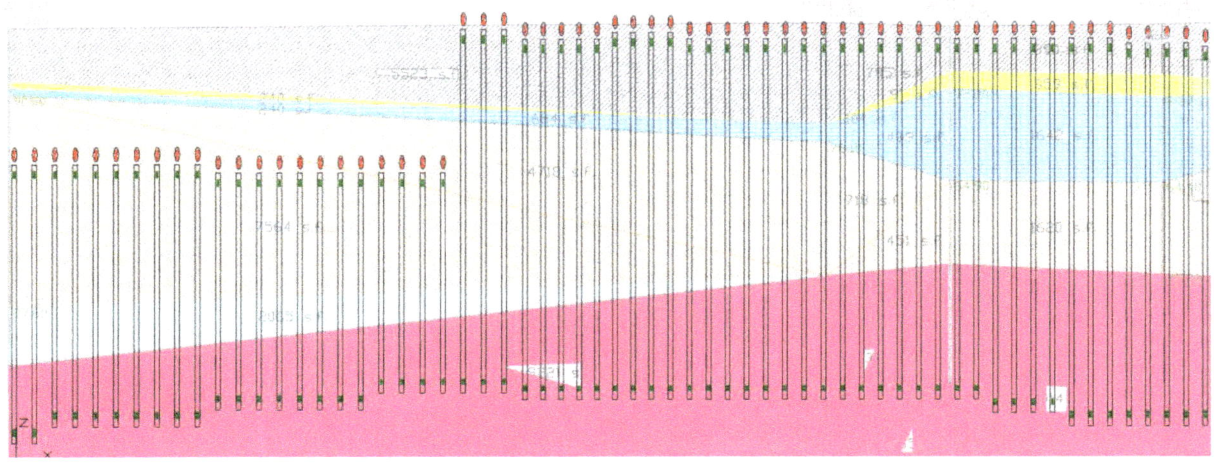

Figure III.1.H.

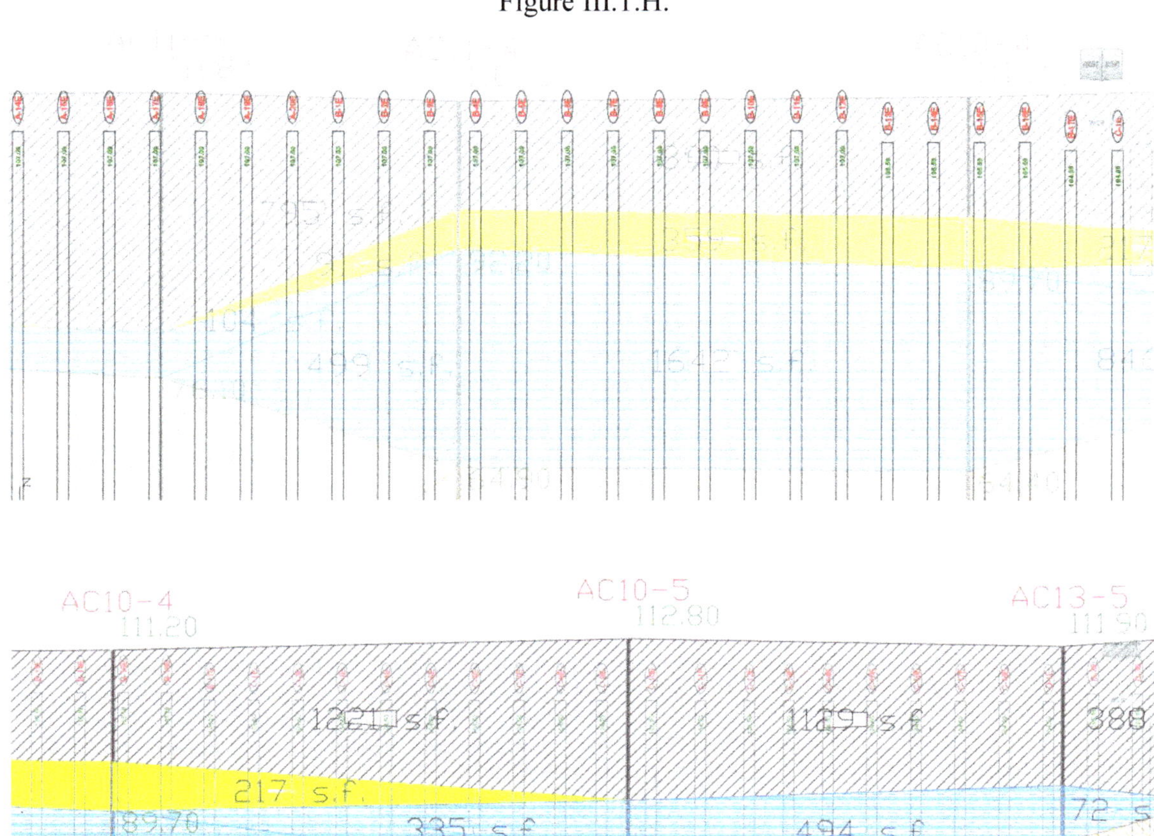

Figure III.1.I.

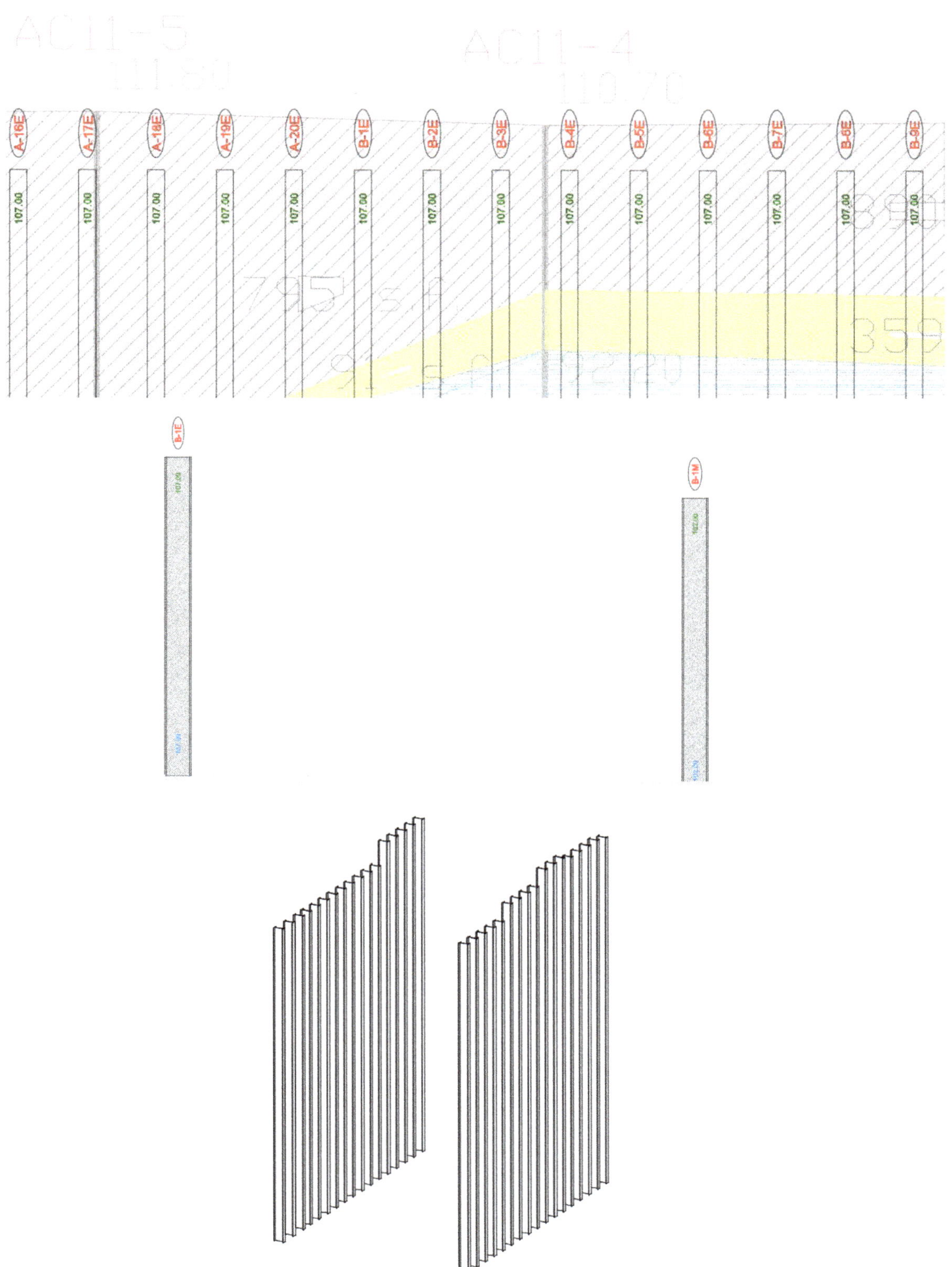

Figure III.1.J.

East Slurry Wall - Takeoffs.txt - Notepad

File Edit Format View Help

```
ENGINEERING MODELING INFORMATION SYSTEMS

SYSTEM #3 - STRUCTURAL

EAST SLURRY WALL PILES - DESIGNATION, LENGTH, WEIGHT
----------------------------------------------------
EP-1,125.00,49125.00
EP-2,125.00,49125.00
EP-3,125.00,49125.00
EP-4,125.00,49125.00
EP-5,123.00,48339.00
EP-6,123.00,48339.00
EP-7,123.00,48339.00
EP-8,123.00,48339.00
EP-9,123.00,48339.00
EP-10,123.00,48339.00
EP-11,123.00,48339.00
EP-12,123.00,48339.00
EP-13,83.00,32619.00
EP-14,83.00,32619.00
EP-15,83.00,32619.00
EP-16,83.00,32619.00
EP-17,78.00,30654.00
EP-18,78.00,30654.00
EP-19,78.00,30654.00
EP-20,78.00,30654.00
EP-21,78.00,30654.00
EP-22,78.00,30654.00
EP-23,78.00,30654.00
EP-24,78.00,30654.00
EP-25,70.50,27706.50
EP-26,70.50,27706.50
EP-27,70.50,27706.50
EP-28,70.50,27706.50
EP-29,70.50,27706.50
EP-30,70.50,27706.50
EP-31,70.50,27706.50
```

Middle Slurry Wall - Takeoffs.txt - Notepad

File Edit Format View Help

```
ENGINEERING MODELING INFORMATION SYSTEMS

SYSTEM #3 - STRUCTURAL

NIDDLE SLURRY WALL PILES - DESIGNATION, LENGHT, WEIGHT
------------------------------------------------------
MP-1,128.00,50304.00
MP-2,128.00,50304.00
MP-3,128.00,50304.00
MP-4,114.00,44802.00
MP-5,114.00,44802.00
MP-6,114.00,44802.00
MP-7,114.00,44802.00
MP-8,114.00,44802.00
MP-9,128.00,50304.00
MP-10,128.00,50304.00
MP-11,128.00,50304.00
MP-12,128.00,50304.00
MP-13,128.00,50304.00
MP-22,122.00,47946.00
MP-23,122.00,47946.00
MP-24,122.00,47946.00
MP-25,122.00,47946.00
MP-26,122.00,47946.00
MP-27,122.00,47946.00
MP-28,122.00,47946.00
MP-29,122.00,47946.00
MP-30,122.00,47946.00
MP-31,122.00,47946.00
MP-32,122.00,47946.00
MP-33,122.00,47946.00
MP-34,122.00,47946.00
MP-35,122.00,47946.00
MP-36,122.00,47946.00
MP-37,122.00,47946.00
MP-38,122.00,47946.00
MP-39,122.00,47946.00
```

Figure III.1.K.

III.2 Excavation Support

The following chart - Figure III.2.A - represents excavation structural support members used in programming, calculations, and modeling.

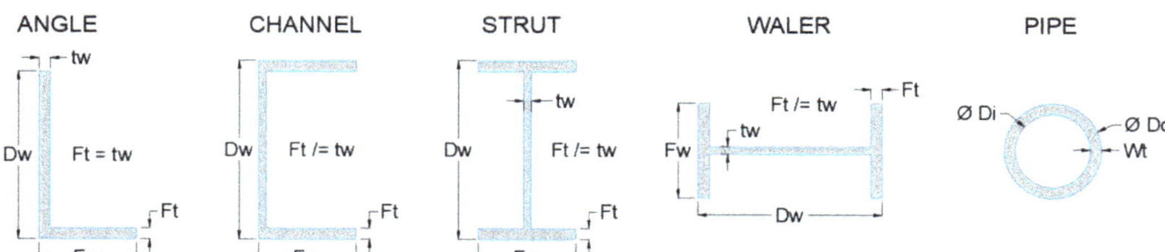

Figure III.2.B – below illustrates Excavation Support Structural Members Program Block Scheme.

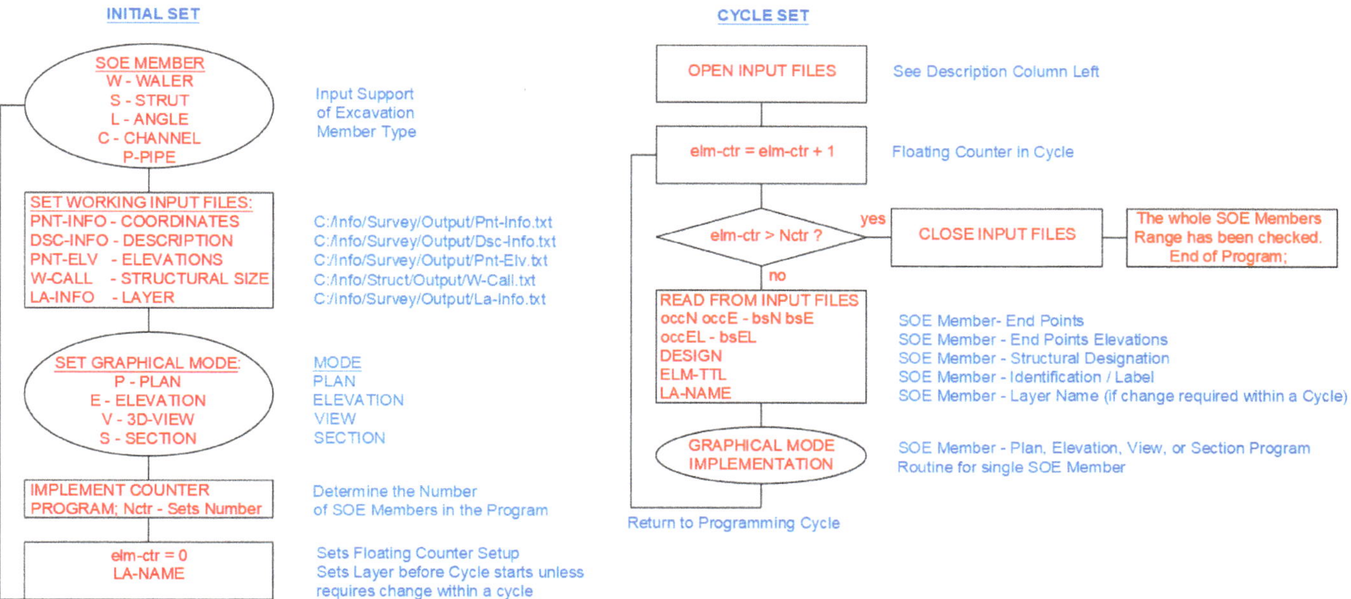

Figure III. 2. C below shows Excavation Support Members – Input & Output Program Files

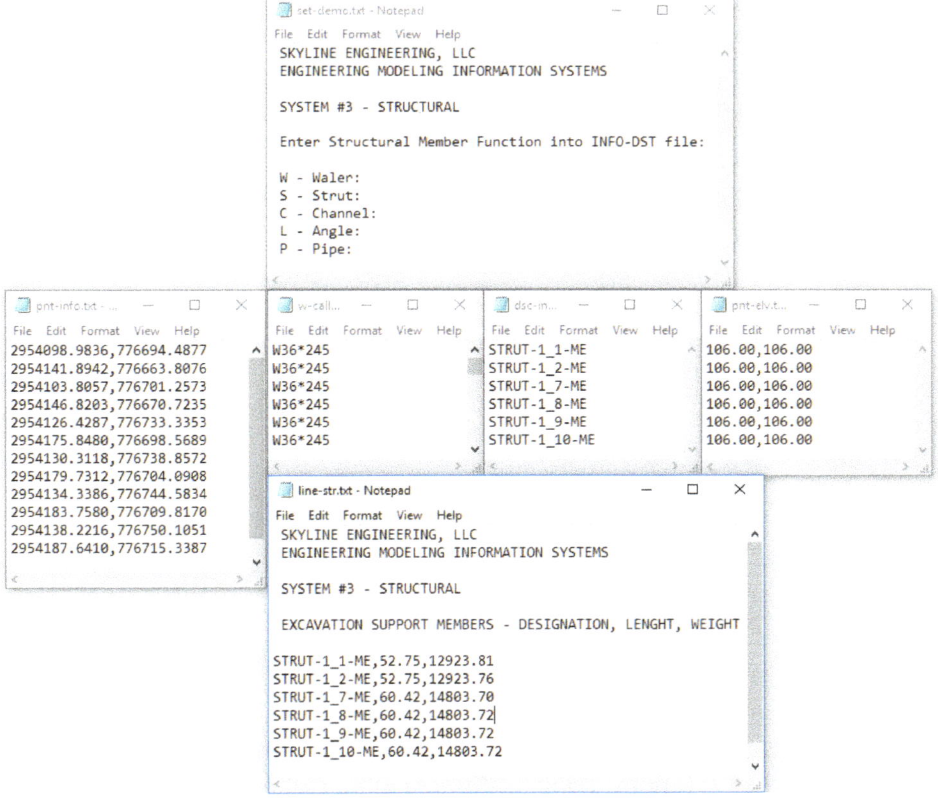

Figure III. 2.D – Program Output - Excavation Support Plan – Top Level – showing Pipes & Struts

Figures III.2.E & III.2.F show corresponding Support of Excavation Upper Levels 1 & 2 Profile views of Middle (Looking West) and East (Looking East) Slurry Walls. Note that the Profile Views include, besides the Designations, the Elevations, Lengths, Structural Sizes, and Diameters information for corresponding SOE members.

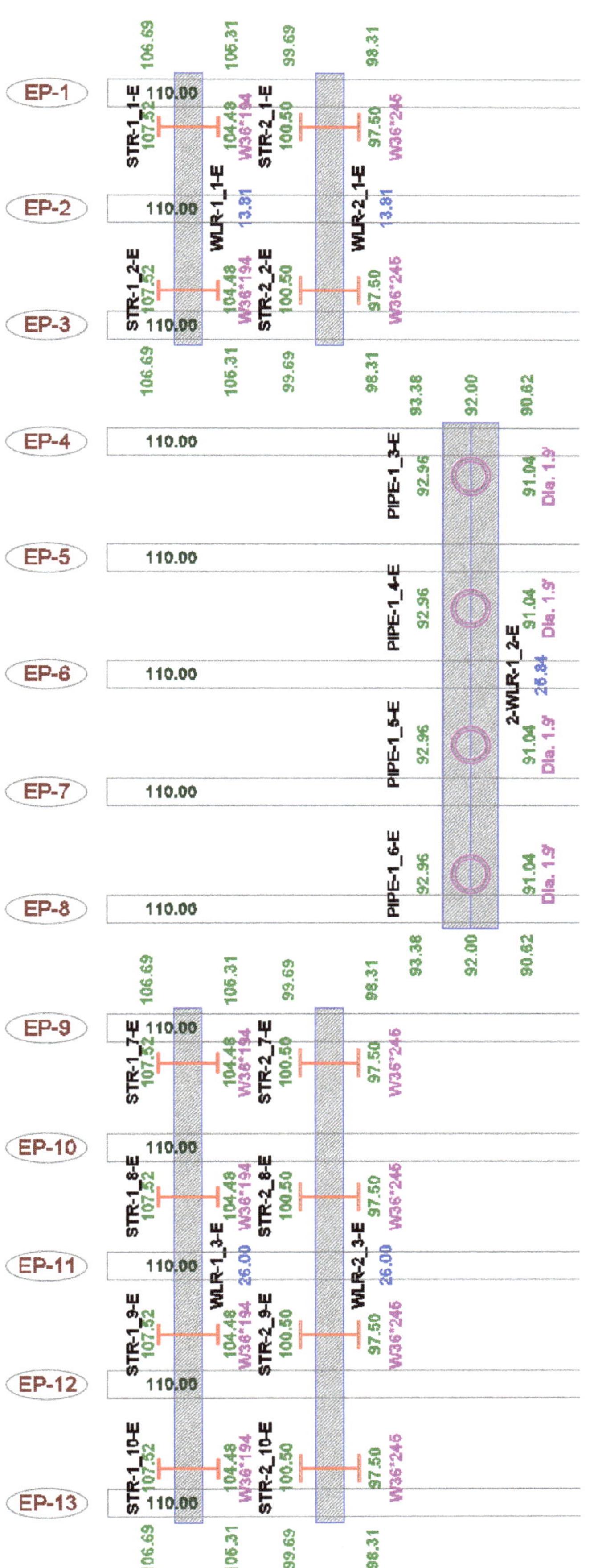

SUPPORT OF EXCAVATION. LEVELS 1 & 2. LOOKING EAST

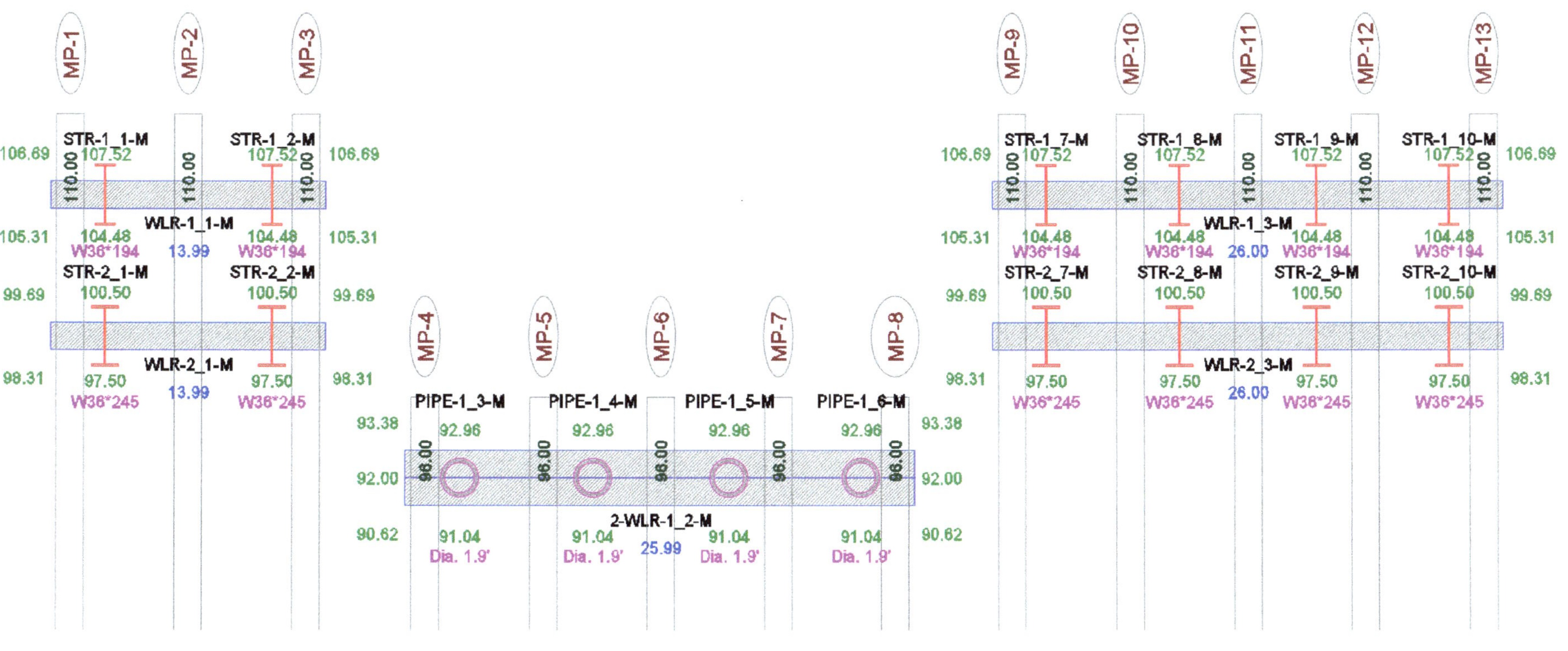

SUPPORT OF EXCAVATION. LEVELS 1 & 2. LOOKING WEST

As it already was emphasized, every view of the Support of Excavation System shows corresponding structural members in exact coordinate geometry. As a verification, Figures III.2.G and III.2.H illustrate corner points coordinates of Waler SOE members on plan and profile views for East and Middle Slurry Walls.

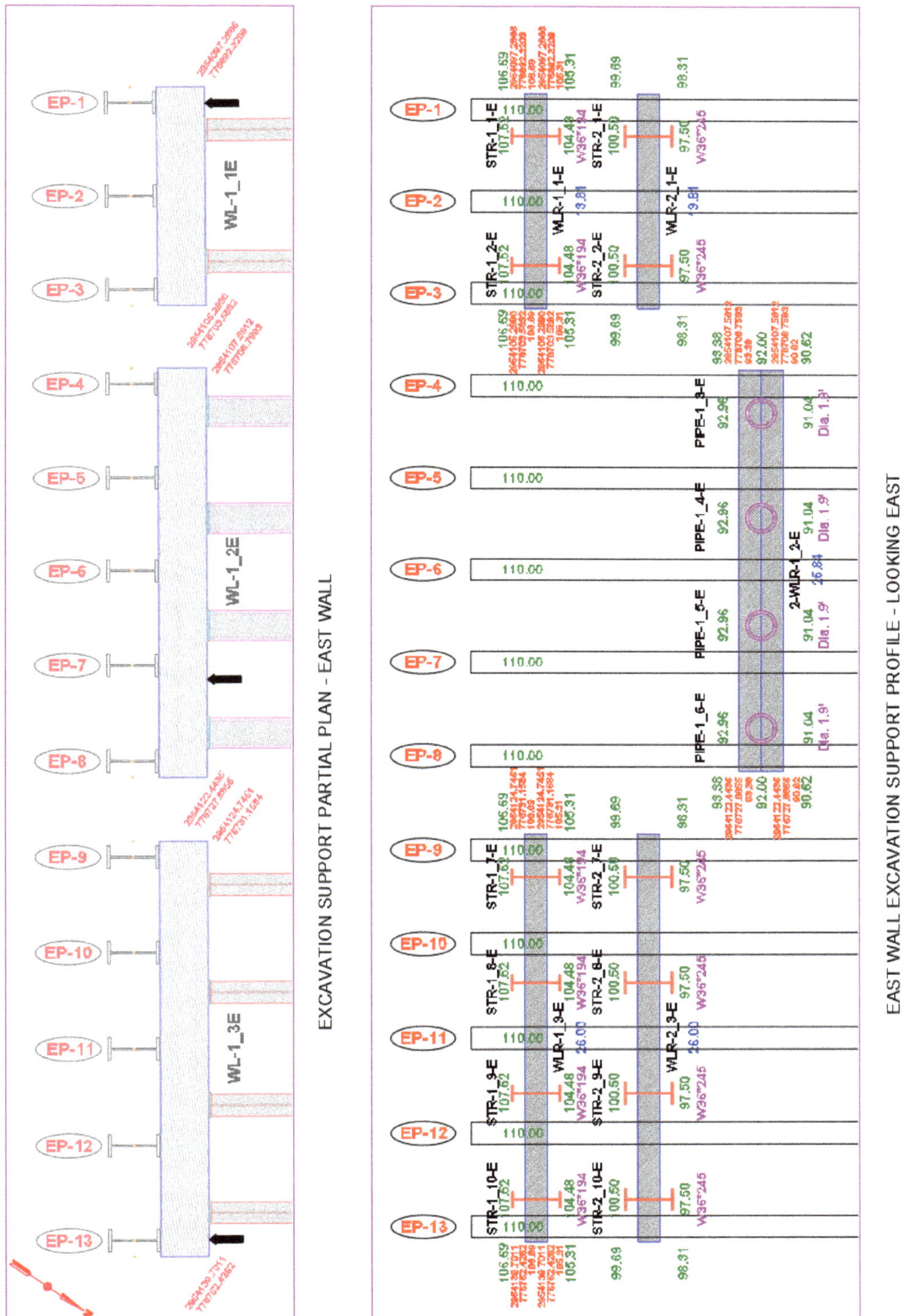

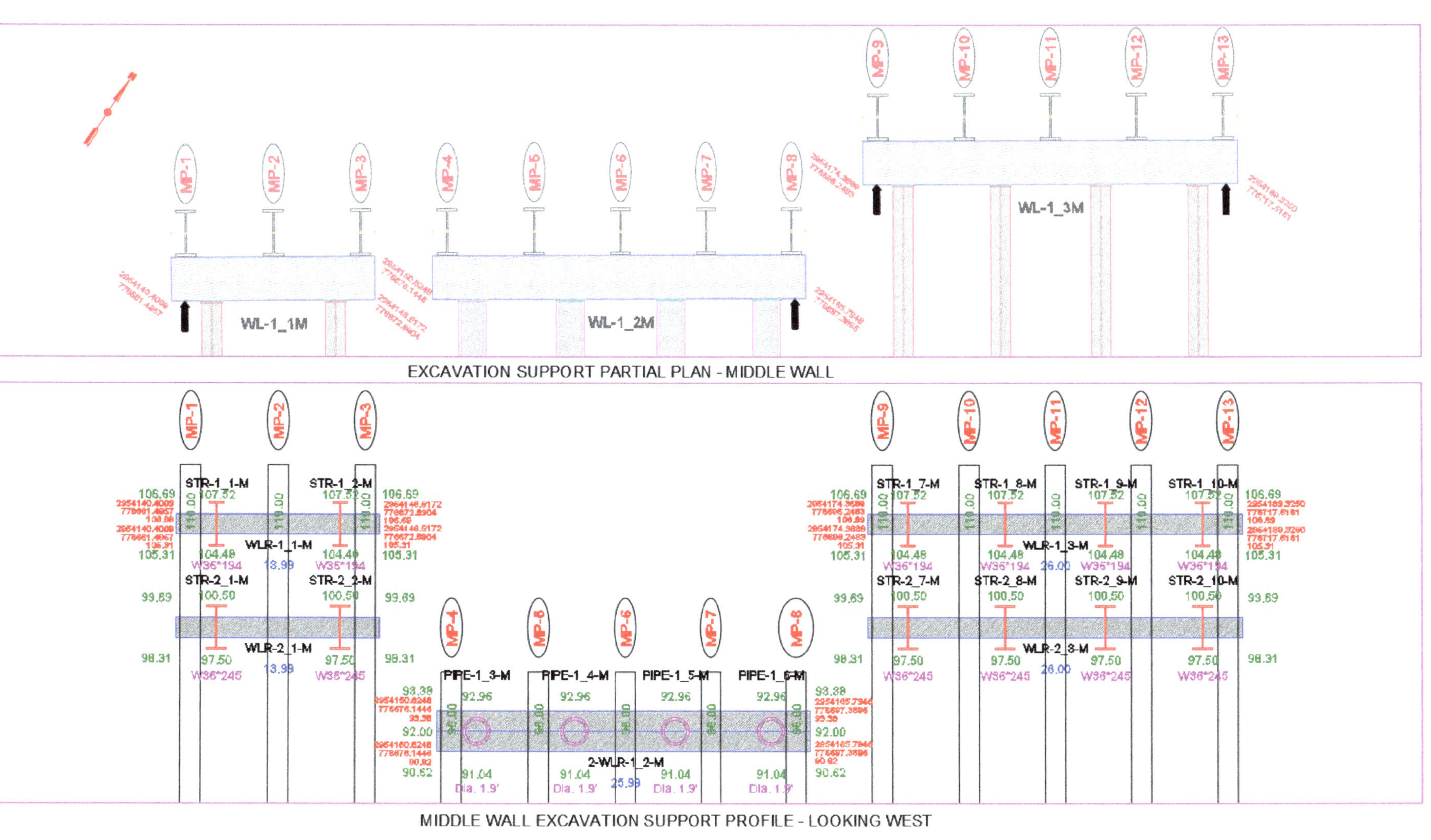
WL-1_1M
WL-1_2M
WL-1_3M
EXCAVATION SUPPORT PARTIAL PLAN - MIDDLE WALL
STR-1_1-M
STR-1_2-M
STR-1_7-M
STR-1_8-M
STR-1_9-M
STR-1_10-M
WLR-1_1-M
WLR-1_3-M
STR-2_1-M
STR-2_2-M
STR-2_7-M
STR-2_8-M
STR-2_9-M
STR-2_10-M
WLR-2_1-M
WLR-2_3-M
PIPE-1_3-M
PIPE-1_4-M
PIPE-1_5-M
PIPE-1_6-M
2-WLR-1_2-M
MIDDLE WALL EXCAVATION SUPPORT PROFILE - LOOKING WEST

Figures III.2.I and III.2.J show the Excavation Support full depth Elevation Views for Middle and East Walls.

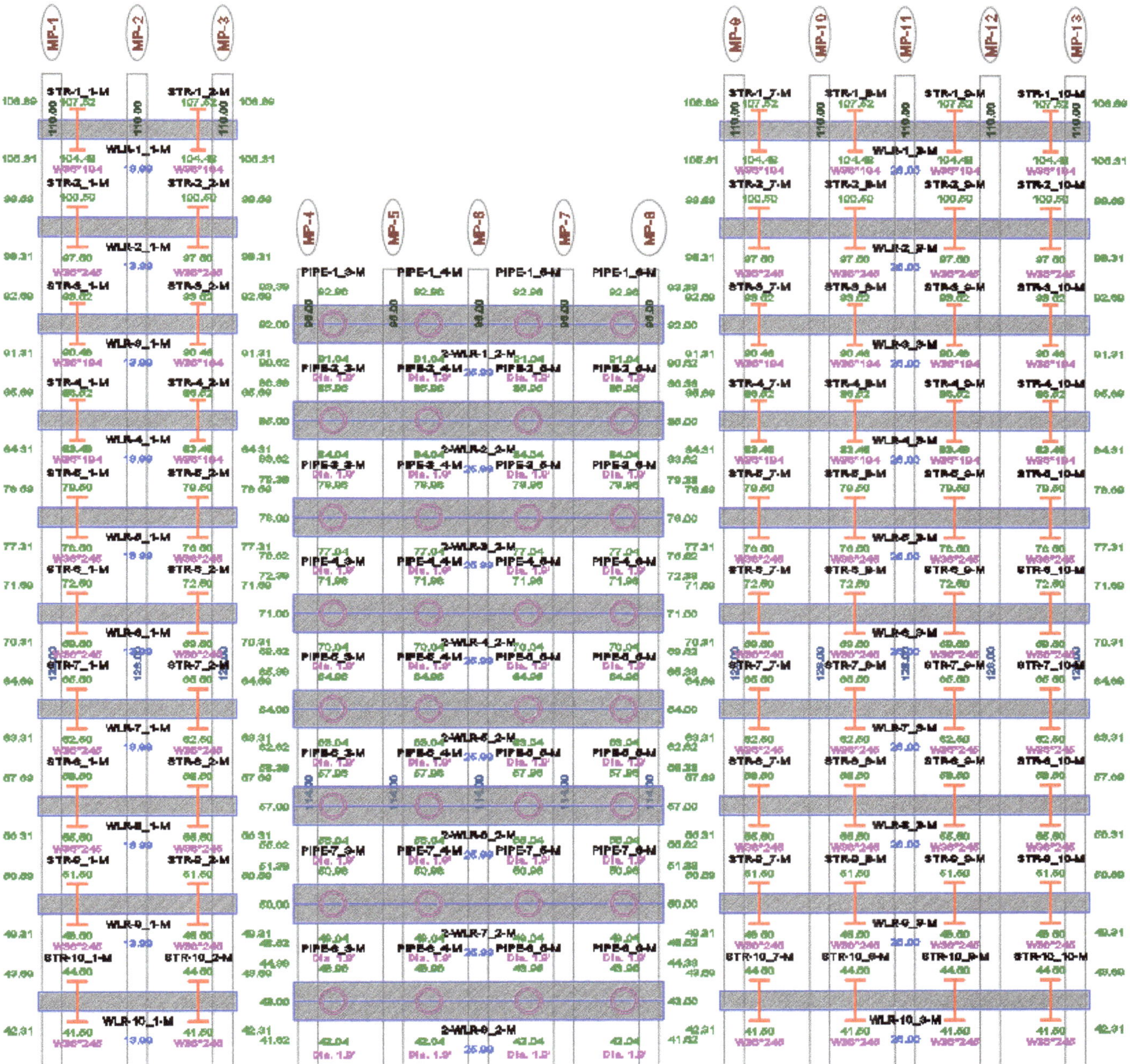

The Figures III.2.I Middle Wall. Excavation Support. Full Depth Elevation View.

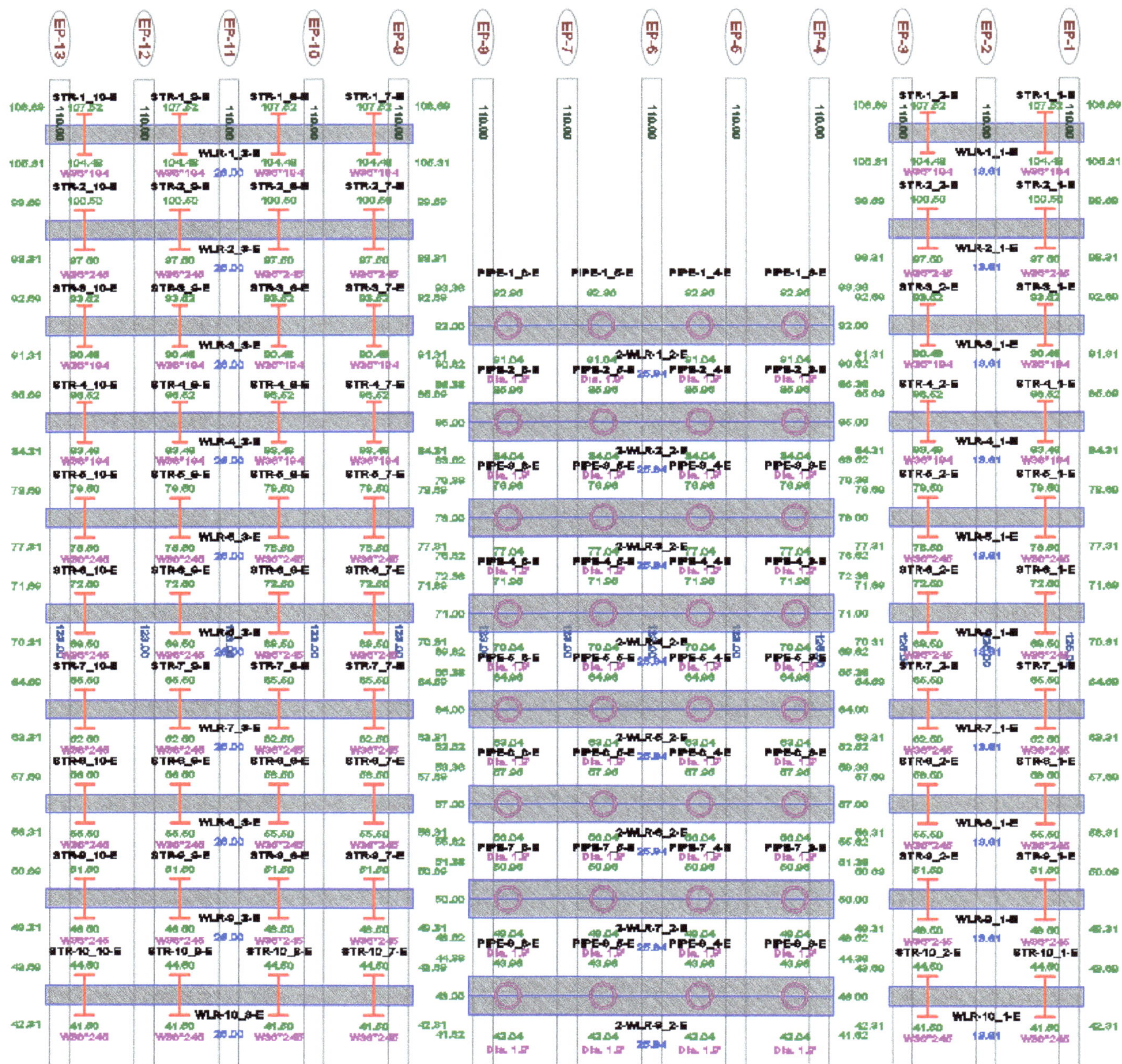

The Figures III.2.J East Wall. Excavation Support. Full Depth Elevation View.

Figures III.2.K, III.2.L, and III.2.M demonstrate Coordinates, Data Input Files, Full Depth Section Views, and Output (Takeoff) Information for Excavation Support Groups 1 & 7 (Walers & Struts), and Excavation Support Group 3 (Double Walers & Pipes).

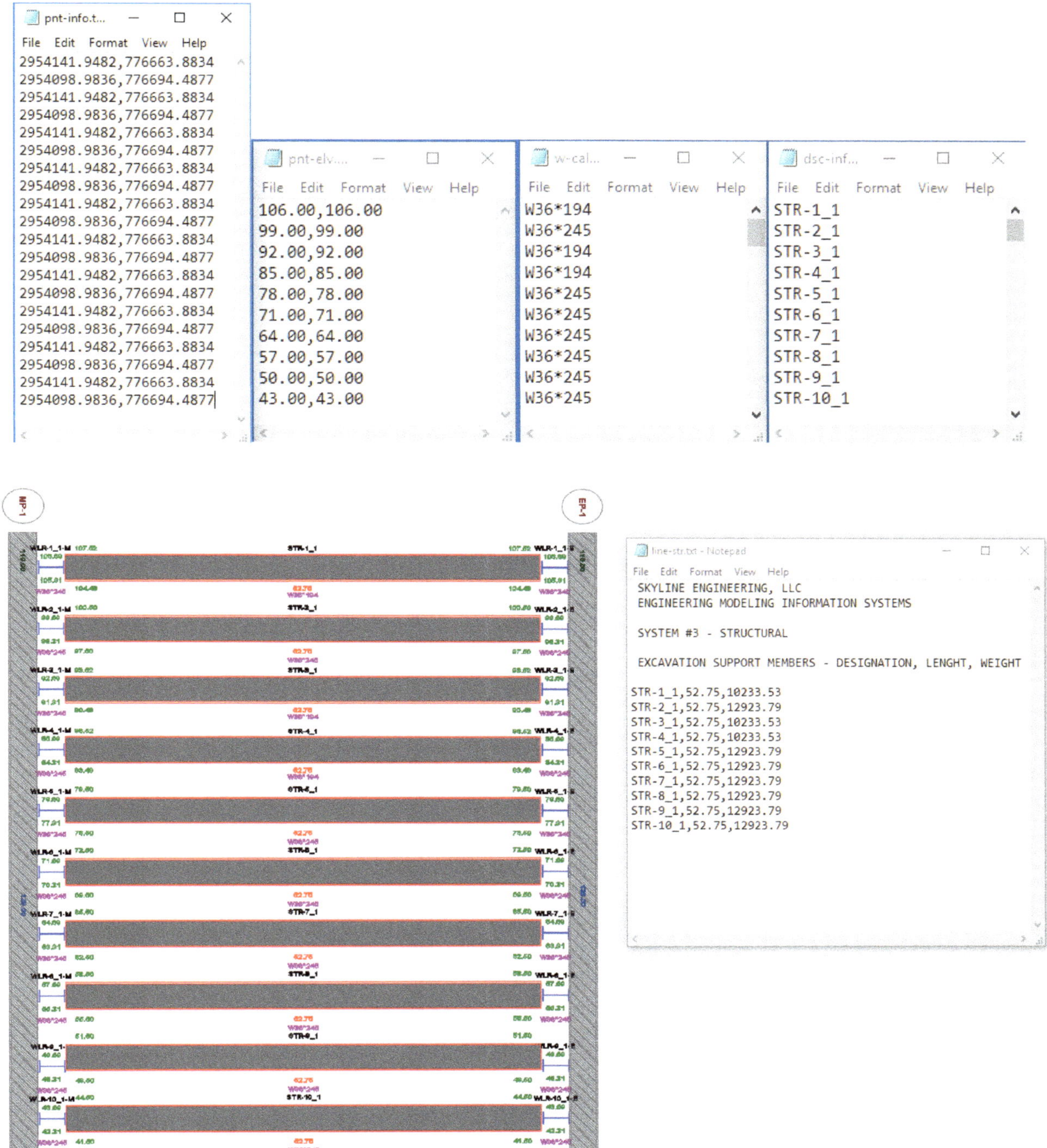

The Figure III.2.K. Excavation Support. Struts - Group 1 – Section View, Input & Takeoff Data.

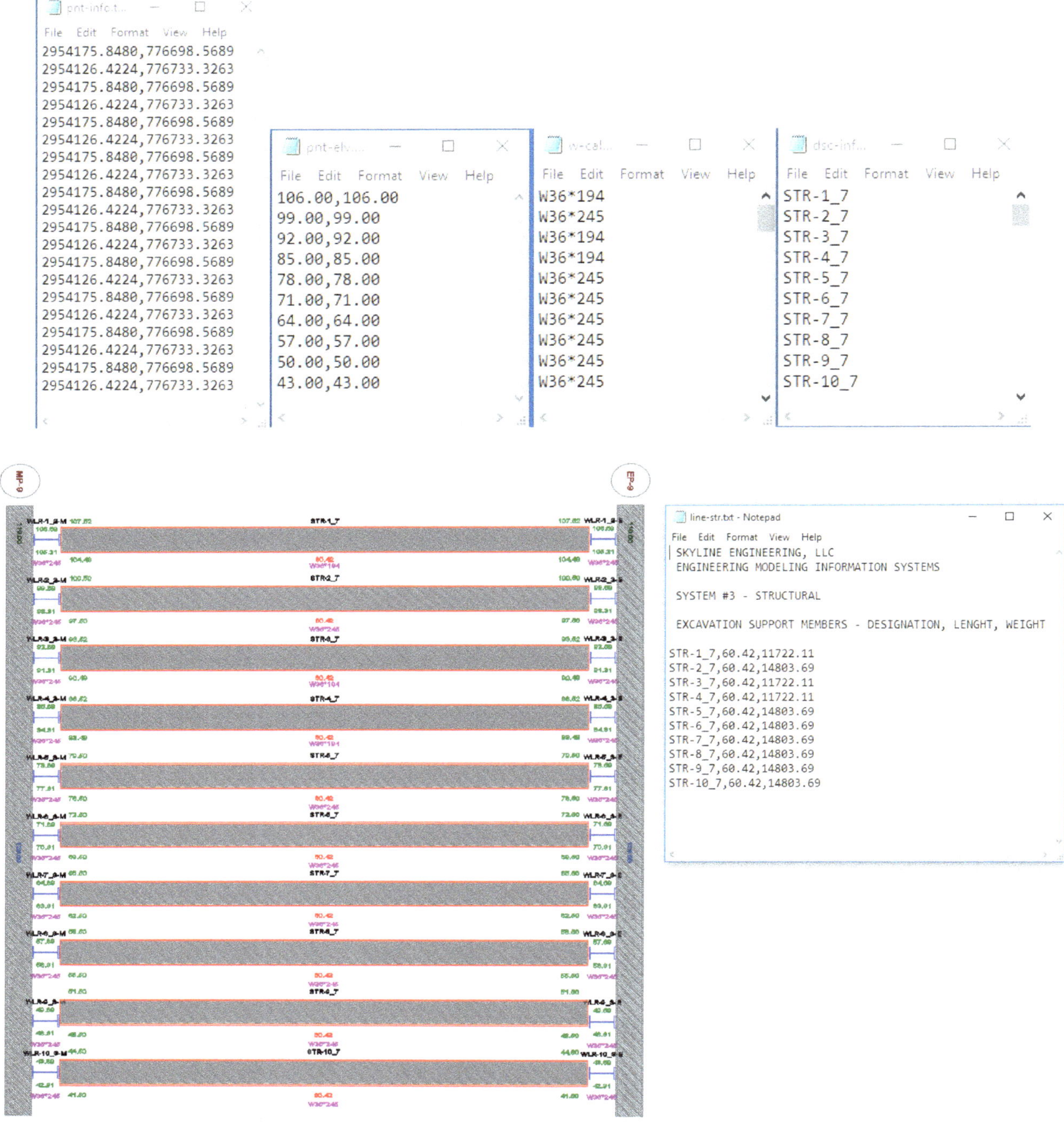

The Figure III.2.L. Excavation Support. Strut Group 7 – Section View, Input & Takeoff Data.

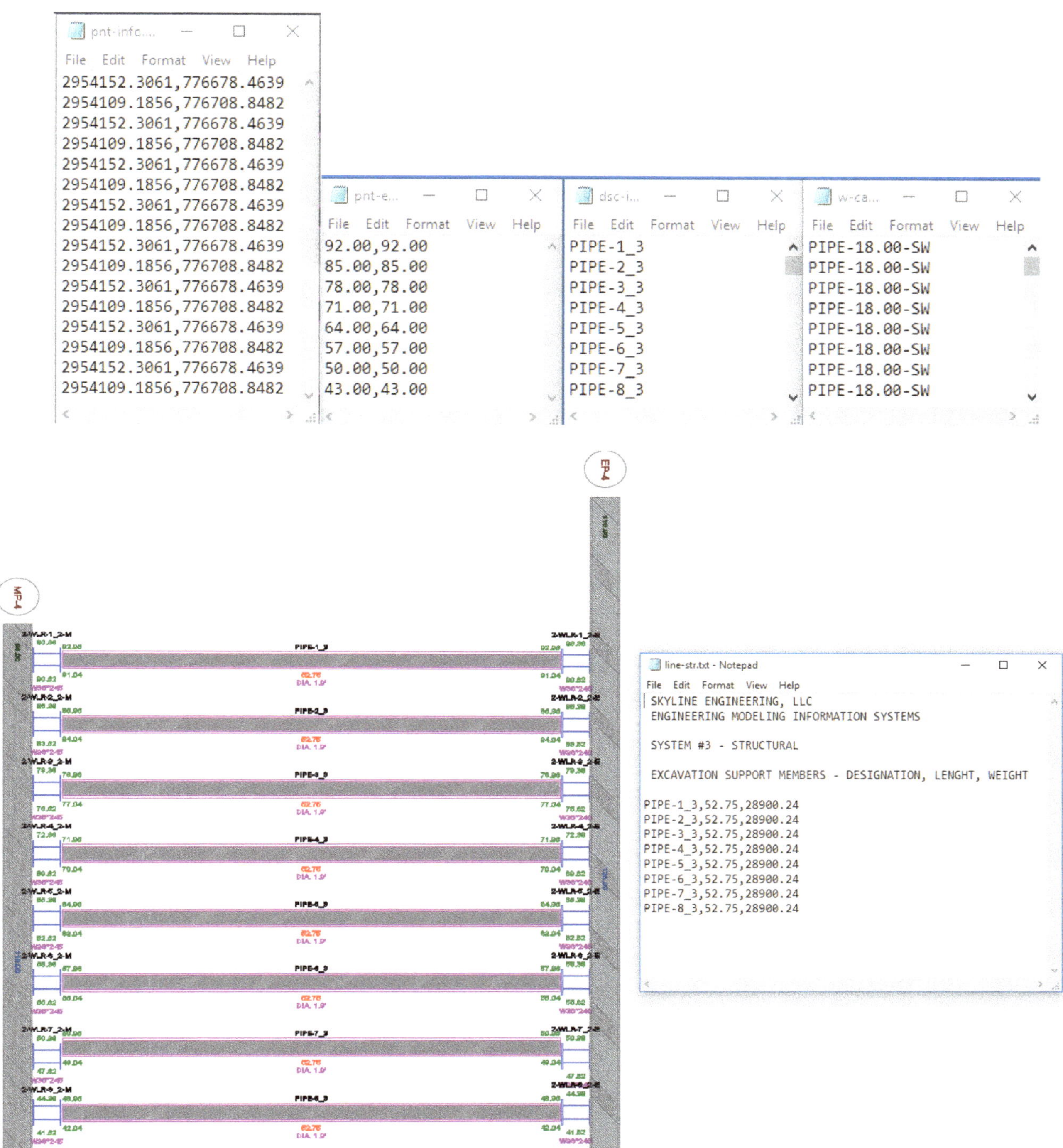

Figure III.2.M. Excavation Support. Strut Group 3 - Section View, Input & Takeoff Data.

3D Modeling aspect in Excavation Support helps to visualize the project. It is logical to present the information in separate groups (Figure III.2.N)

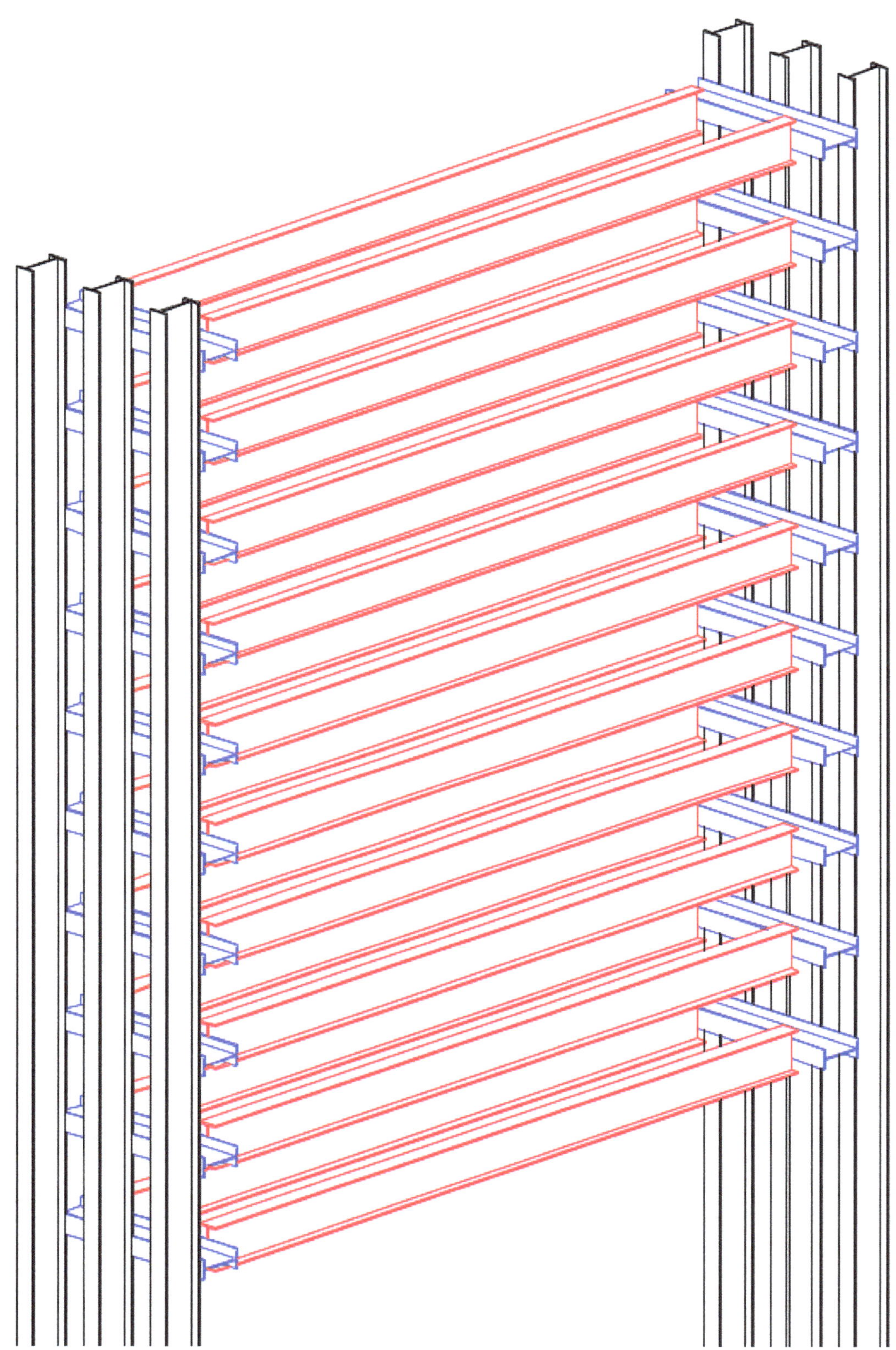

Figure III.2.N.a. Excavation Support – Group 1.

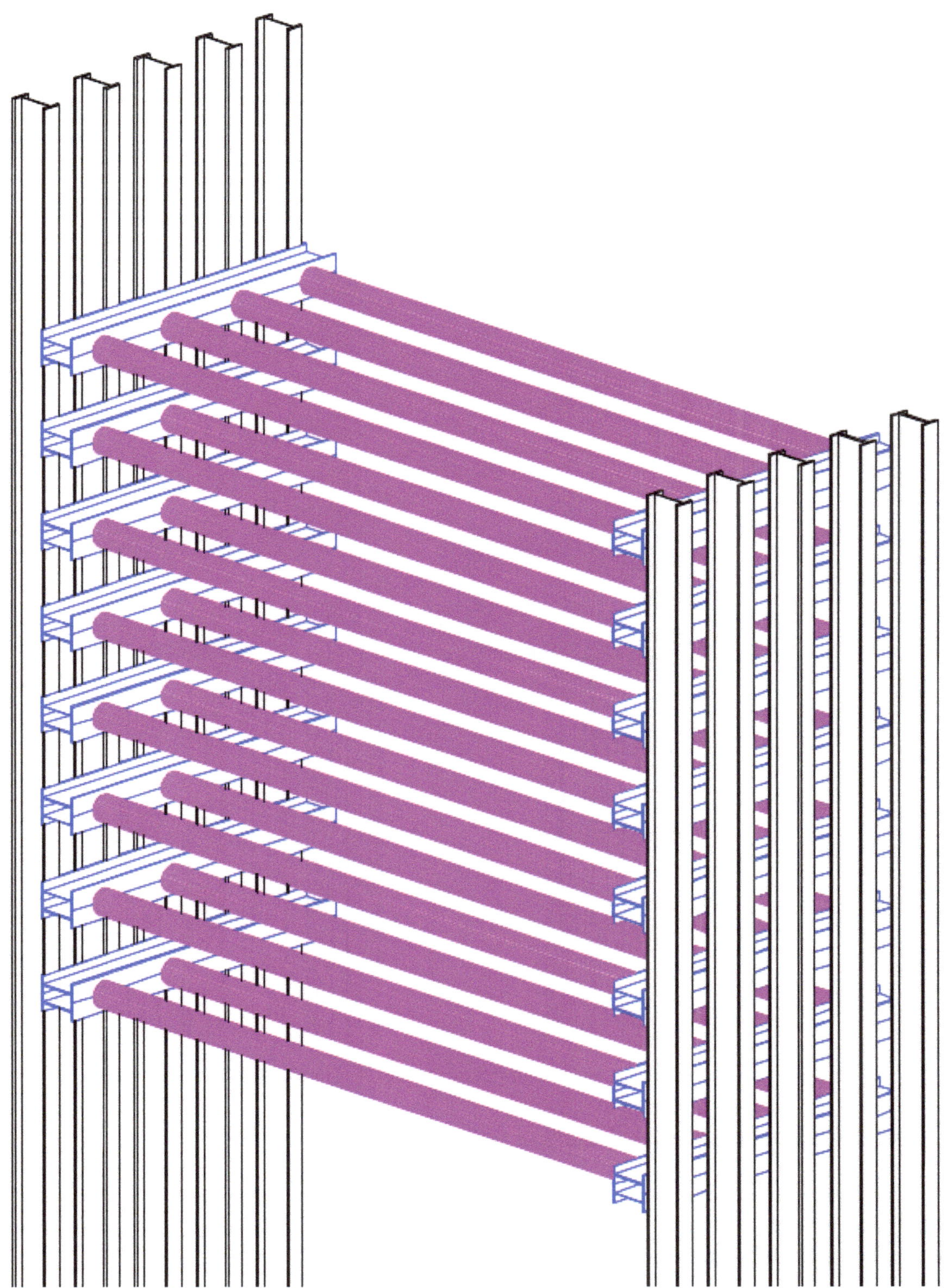

Figure III.2.N.b. Excavation Support – Group 2.

Each Excavation Support Member has its own unique identification by Layer. Using this feature, it is practical to combine and modify the developed model groups by turning some layers off and showing work progress. Figure III.2.P shows the sequential installation of Walers & Struts in Excavation Support Groups 1 and 2. The schedule example complementing the graphical model is shown in Chapter 5.

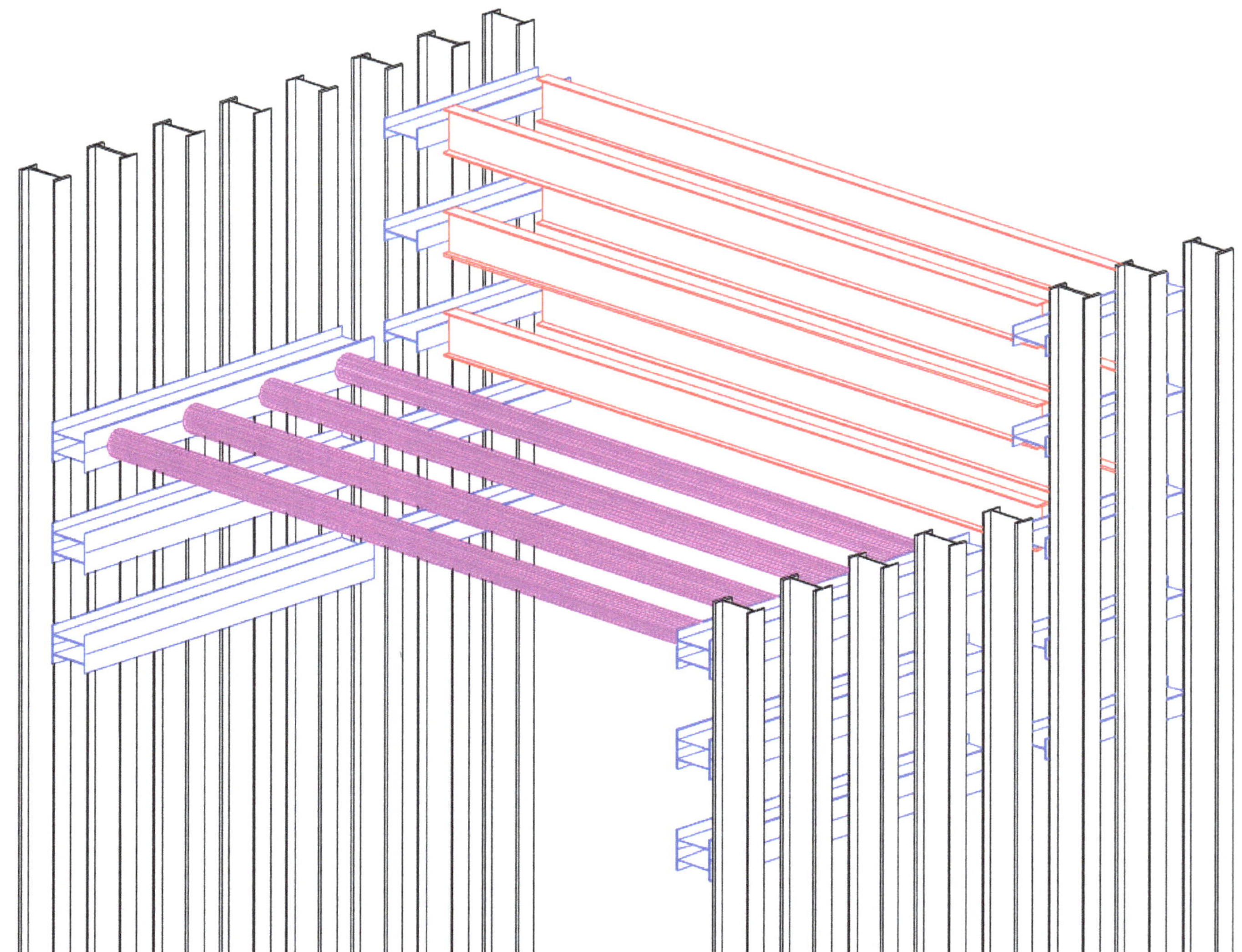

Figure III.2.P. Excavation Support Members – Sequential Installation.

III.3. Concrete Structures. Part A. Layout & Calculation.

The structural modeling of concrete objects in this application is based on initially developed cross-sections in exact project geometry. As it was mentioned in Chapter I.5, the current modeling instrument considers two methods of creating cross-sections:

1) Using the Project-provided templates (blocks) – adjust (and scale) the block per the result of the baseline correlation program and move it into real space by known baselines' coordinates.
2) Create the new cross-section using coordinates derived from Baselines Correlation and Offset Programs.

In this chapter, we consider only the second method. The first method was described in detail in Chapter I - Surveying Module I.5. For the second method of the concrete modeling, we will look at the Central Artery Tunnel South Bound - Design Section "G". The task approach is as follows:

1) The project provided S-Bound Baseline 25' Increment Stations and Corresponding Elevations - (See Chart Figure III.3.B)

2) The Baseline Correlations Programs (paragraph I.4) will show the complement Stations and Elevations for Correlated Baselines – see Attached Figure III.3.A (Plan).

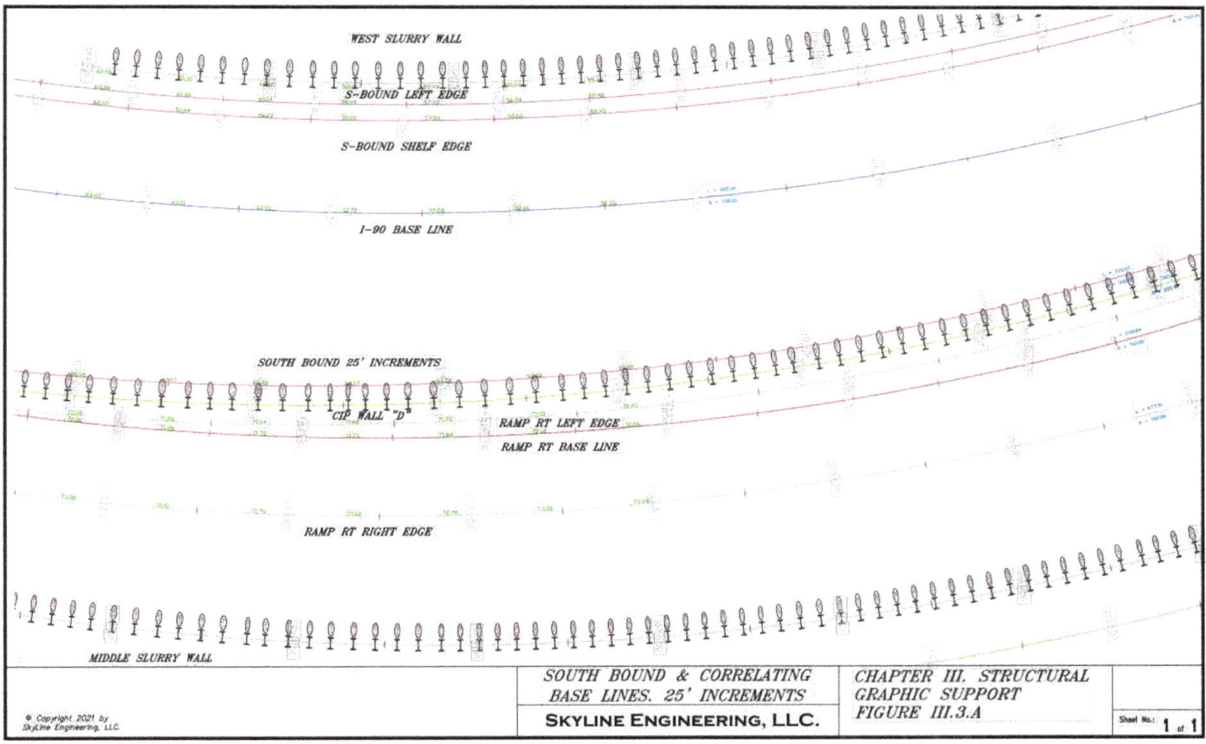

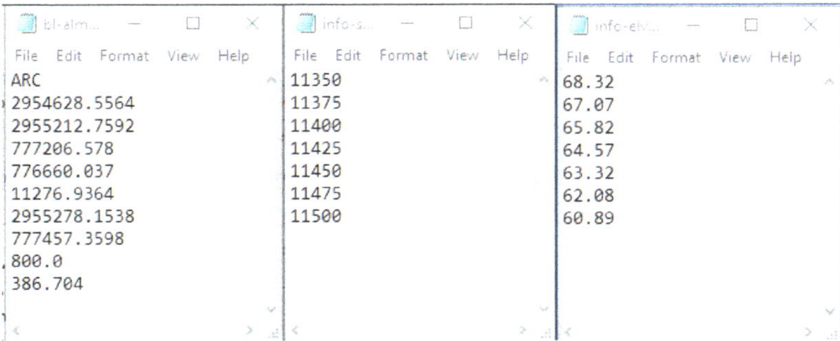

bl-alm...	info-s...	info-elv...
ARC	11350	68.32
2954628.5564	11375	67.07
2955212.7592	11400	65.82
777206.578	11425	64.57
776660.037	11450	63.32
11276.9364	11475	62.08
2955278.1538	11500	60.89
777457.3598		
800.0		
386.704		

Figure III.3.B.

3) From there, establishing Construction Joint (CJ) Stations – see Attached Figure III.3.C.

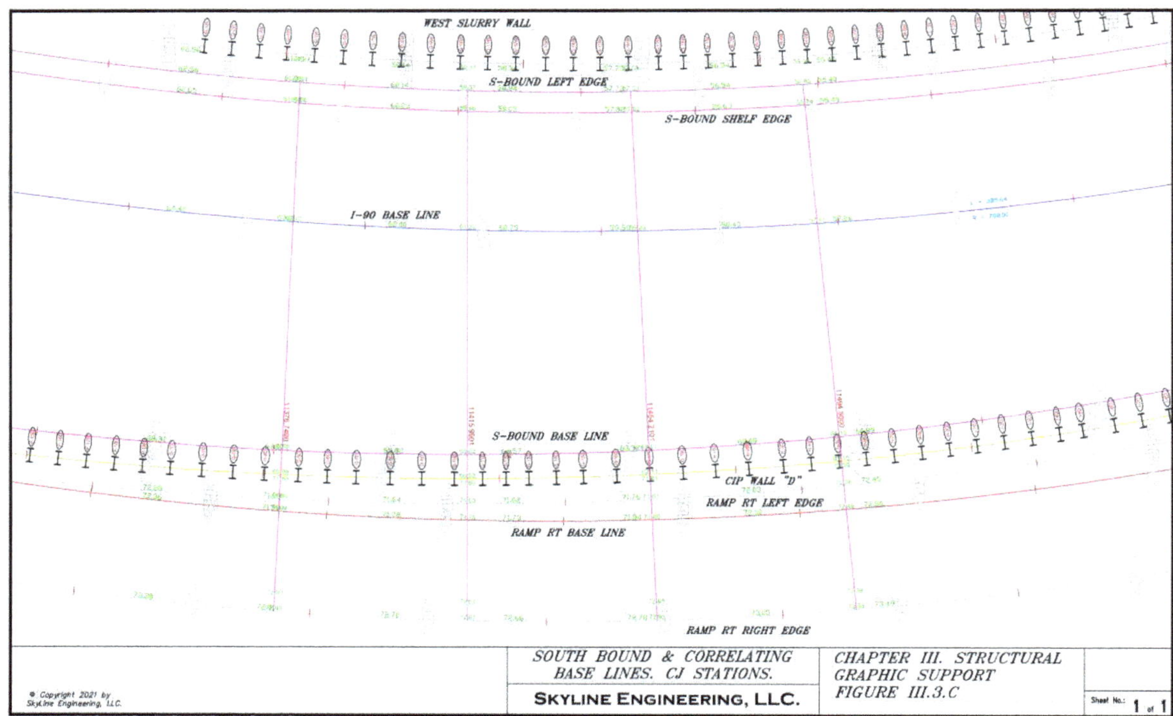

4) The following Attached Figure III.3.D provides the Detail Layout for Concrete Base Slab Lift Pours.

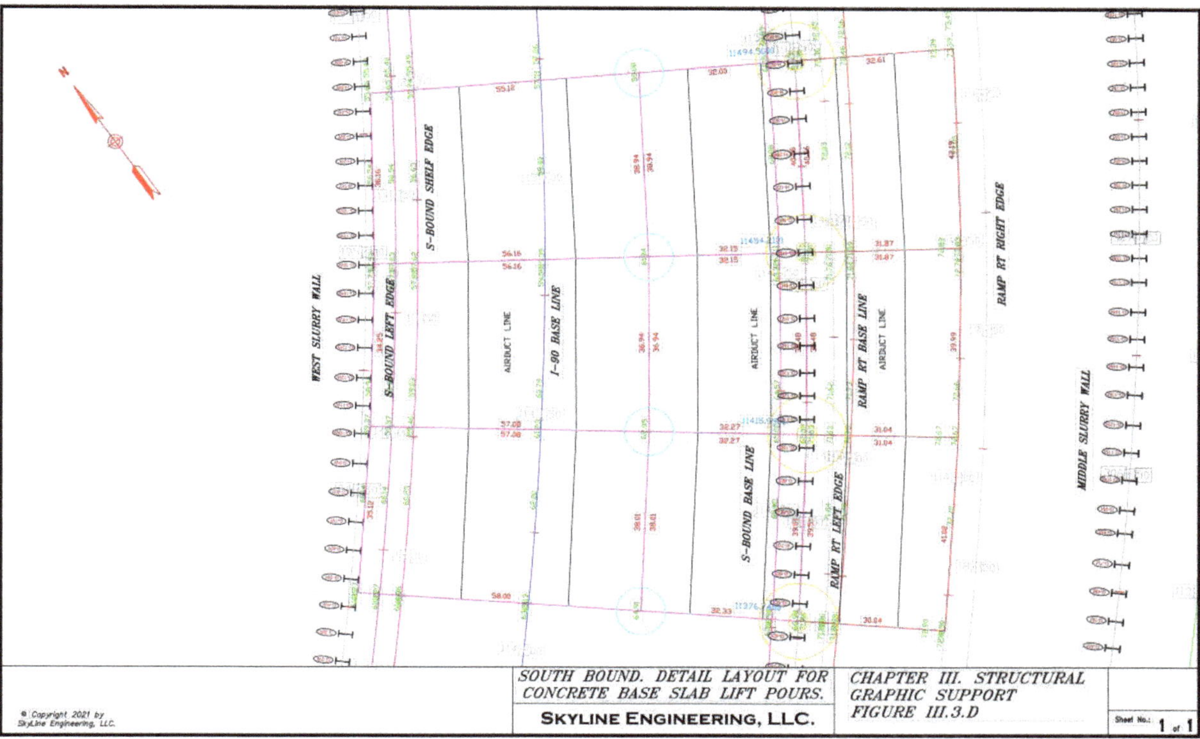

5) The Bottom Pour Height is 5'. The Top Pour Minimum Height (West Side) is 7'.

6) The Bottom Lift Pour CJ Location is 5' West of the Top Lift Pour CJ shown in Figure above (see cyan & yellow circles).

7) The Airduct Height is 5'. The West S-Bound Airduct is 22' wide; The East S-Bound Airduct is 17' wide; The Ramp R-T Airduct is 12' wide.

Figure III.3.E below shows the Block–Scheme for Intermediate Elevations Interpolation Program.

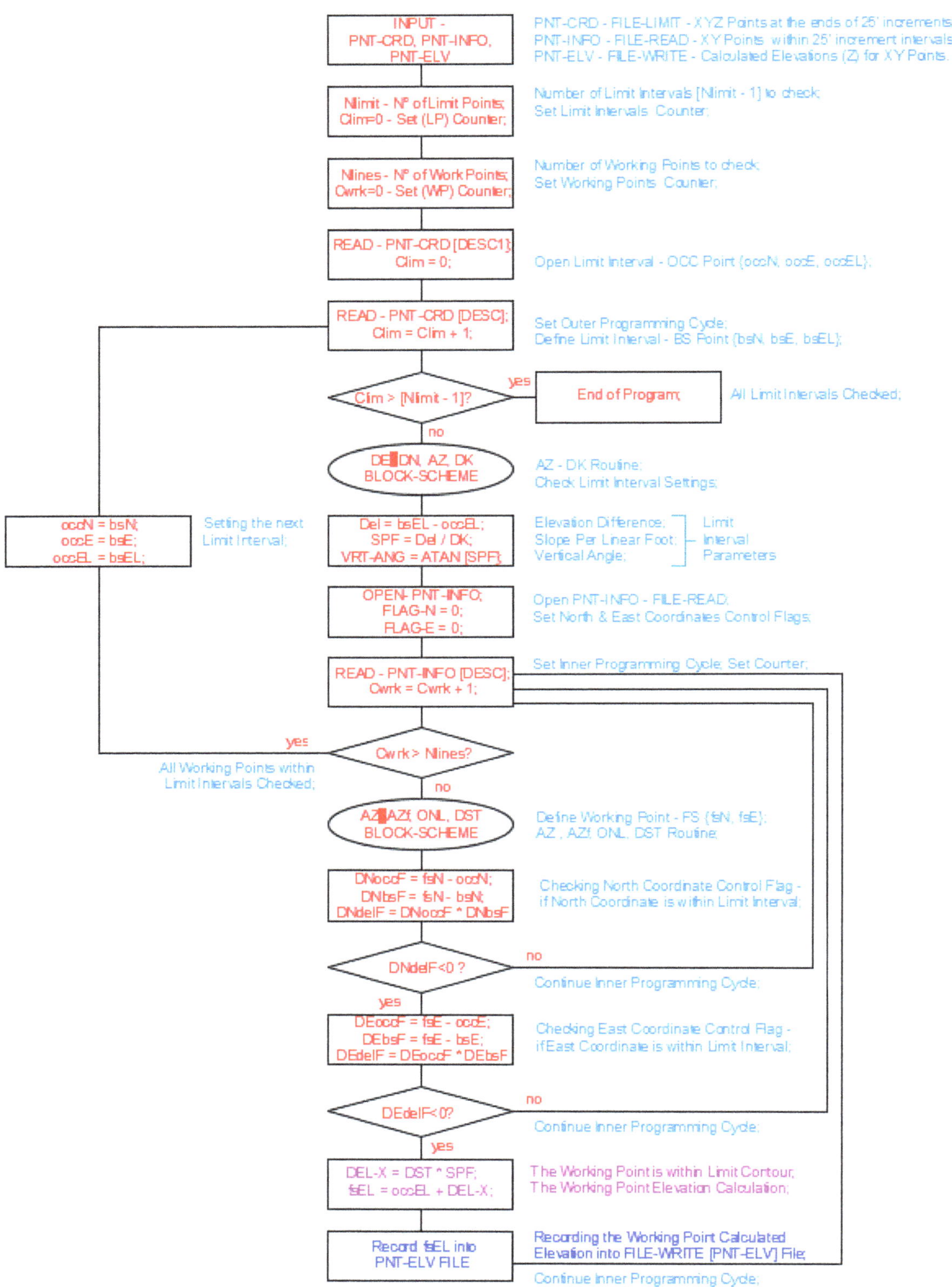

Now, when elevations are calculated, the next step is to create a chart with all CJ Bottom & Top Section/Contour Elevations - Figure III.3.F below:

```
inforsta.txt - Notepad                  info-elv.txt - Notepad
File Edit Format View Help              File Edit Format View Help
11376.74    BOTTOM LIFT POUR - EAST & WEST - 49.27,54.27,54.27,49.27
-           TOP LIFT POUR WEST - 54.27,61.27,61.27,61.36,63.13,64.91,54.27,54.27,59.27,59.27,54.27
-           TOP LIFT POUR EAST - 54.27,64.91,66.98,66.98,54.27,54.27,59.27,59.27,54.27
-           RAMP R-T BOTTOM - 57.86,64.86,64.86,61.86,61.86,57.86
-           RAMP R-T TOP - 64.86,71.86,71.86,71.98,72.90,72.90,64.86,64.86,69.86,69.86,64.86

11415.99    BOTTOM LIFT POUR - EAST & WEST - 47.37,52.37,52.37,47.37
-           TOP LIFT POUR WEST - 52.37,59.37,59.37,59.46,61.23,62.95,52.37,52.37,57.37,57.37,52.37
-           TOP LIFT POUR EAST - 52.37,62.95,65.02,65.02,52.37,52.37,57.37,57.37,52.37
-           RAMP R-T BOTTOM - 57.63,64.63,64.63,61.63,61.63,57.63
-           RAMP R-T TOP - 64.63,71.63,71.63,71.75,72.67,72.67,64.63,64.63,69.63,69.63,64.63

11454.21    BOTTOM LIFT POUR - EAST & WEST - 45.53,50.53,50.53,45.53
-           TOP LIFT POUR WEST - 50.53,57.53,57.53,57.62,59.39,61.04,50.53,50.53,55.53,55.53,50.53
-           TOP LIFT POUR EAST - 50.53,61.04,63.11,63.11,50.53,50.53,55.53,55.53,50.53
-           RAMP R-T BOTTOM - 57.81,64.81,64.81,61.81,61.81,57.81
-           RAMP R-T TOP - 64.81,71.81,71.81,71.89,72.83,72.83,64.81,64.81,69.81,69.81,64.81

11494.50    BOTTOM LIFT POUR - EAST & WEST - 43.65,48.65,48.65,43.65
-           TOP LIFT POUR WEST - 48.65,55.65,55.65,55.74,57.51,59.08,48.65,48.65,53.65,53.65,48.65
-           TOP LIFT POUR EAST - 48.65,59.08,61.15,61.15,48.65,48.65,53.65,53.65,48.65
-           RAMP R-T BOTTOM - 58.36,65.36,65.36,62.36,62.36,58.36
-           RAMP R-T TOP - 65.36,72.36,72.36,72.46,73.39,73.39,65.36,65.36,70.36,70.36,65.36
```

8) With known CJ Position, Airduct Layout and Vertical Arrangement, it is time for calculating coordinates (paragraph I.2), and interpolating CJ Elevations for all corresponding Baselines.
The example below shows CJ Cross-Section Bottom Lift Pour Contour – S-Bound Station 113+76.74 –Chart III.1.G below:

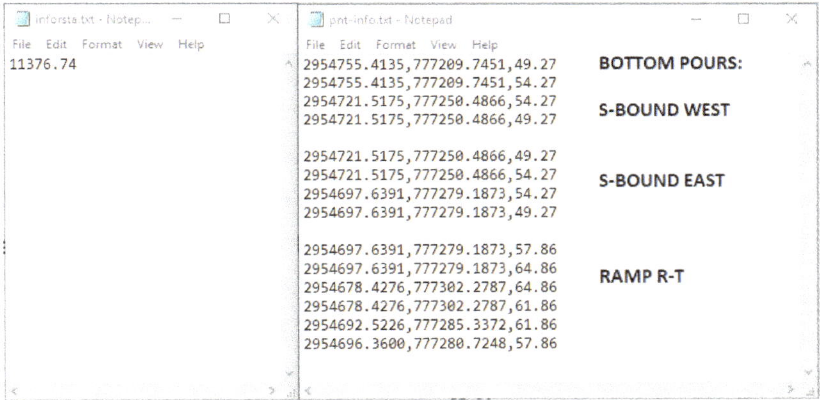

```
inforsta.txt - Notep...      pnt-info.txt - Notepad
File Edit Format View Help   File Edit Format View Help
11376.74                     2954755.4135,777209.7451,49.27     BOTTOM POURS:
                             2954755.4135,777209.7451,54.27
                             2954721.5175,777250.4866,54.27     S-BOUND WEST
                             2954721.5175,777250.4866,49.27

                             2954721.5175,777250.4866,49.27
                             2954721.5175,777250.4866,54.27     S-BOUND EAST
                             2954697.6391,777279.1873,54.27
                             2954697.6391,777279.1873,49.27

                             2954697.6391,777279.1873,57.86
                             2954697.6391,777279.1873,64.86     RAMP R-T
                             2954678.4276,777302.2787,64.86
                             2954678.4276,777302.2787,61.86
                             2954692.5226,777285.3372,61.86
                             2954696.3600,777280.7248,57.86
```

Figure III.3.H. demonstrates the Block Schemes for the Program, creating Cross Section / 3D Solid Membrane Contours. The Program works for any plane in 3D space, with an unlimited pre-defined number of points.

- Part 1. – Preparation Program setting the Number (Set) of Points per Contour, the Number of Working Sets (Contours), and each Proposed Section/Contour Orientation.
- Part 2. – Program Implementation – Drawing Set of Sections/Contours with pre-defined Type, Layer, and Number of Points for Each Contour with the calculating and recording of takeoff information – Area, Perimeter, Center of Inertia Coordinates.

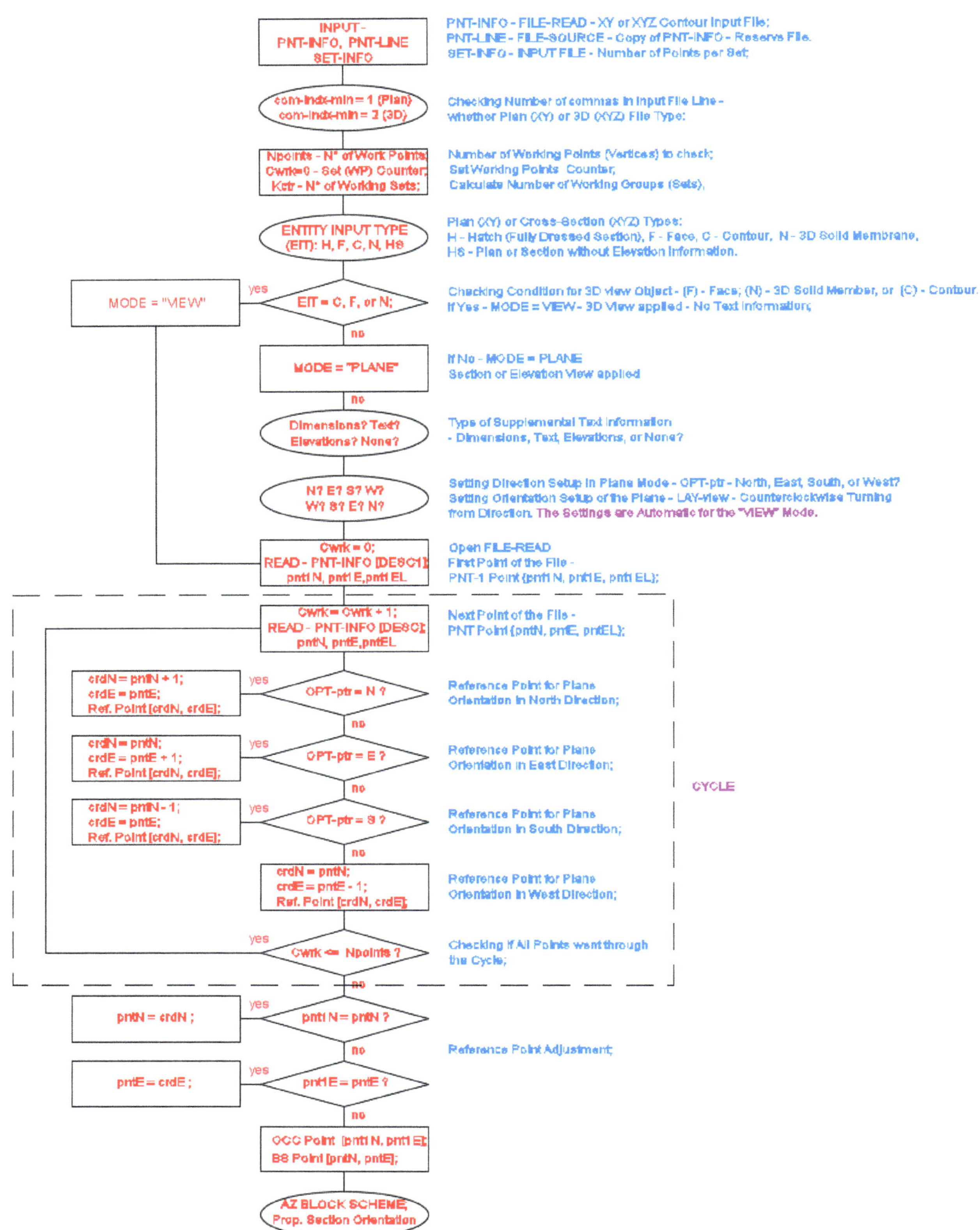

Figure III.3.H - Part 1 – Preparation Program Block-Scheme.

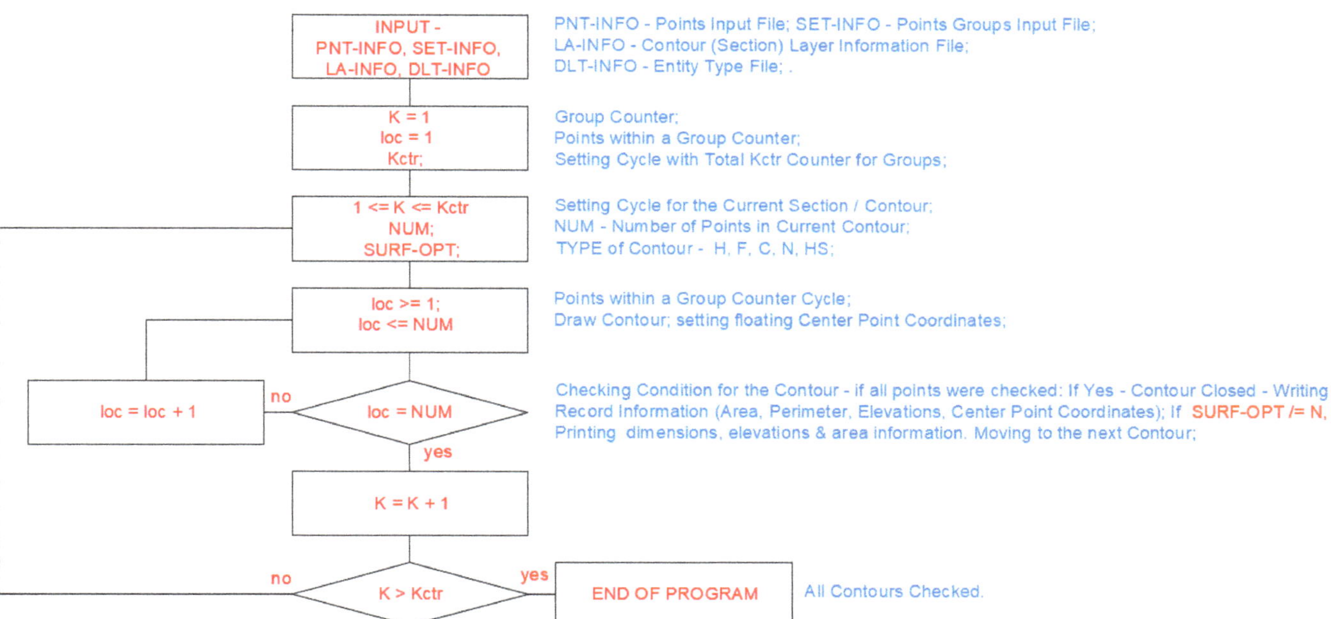

Figure III.3.H - Part 2 – Program Implementation Block-Scheme.

Figure III.3.J Below Demonstrates an Input Information for CJ Cross-Section Top Lift Pour Contour – S-Bound Station 114+54.21 – including XYZ coordinates, the Number of Points and the unique Layer Name for each Contour Part:

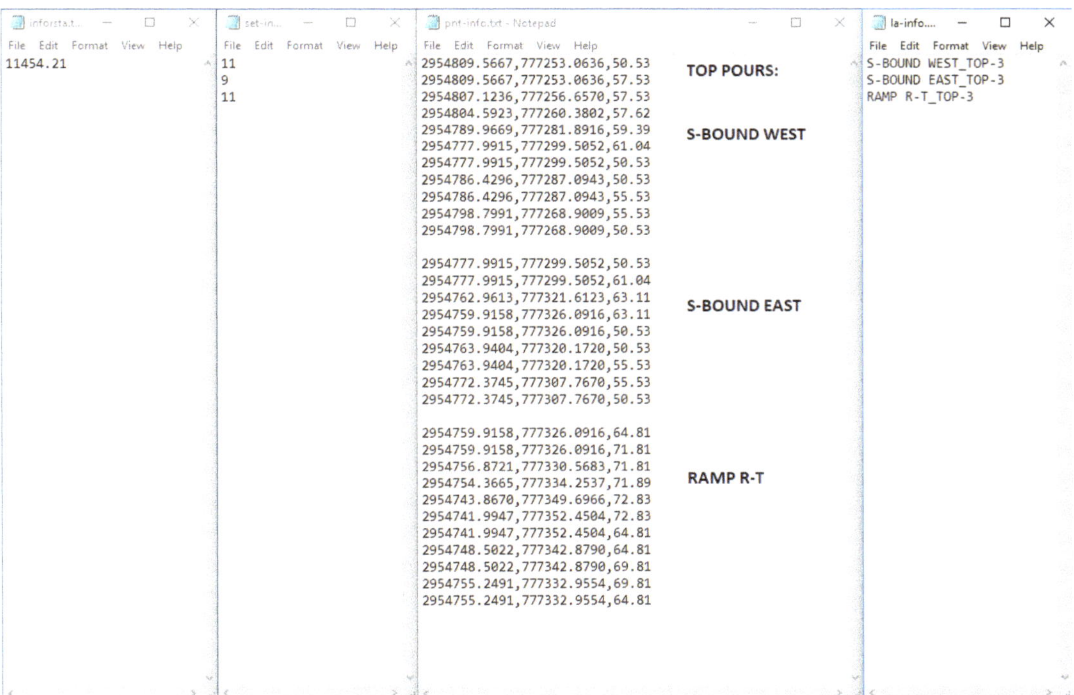

The next Figure III.3.K below demonstrates the Program Output – the Segment of South Bound – Ramp R-T Tunnel X-Sections, derived from the Detailed Layout shown in attached Figure III.3.D.

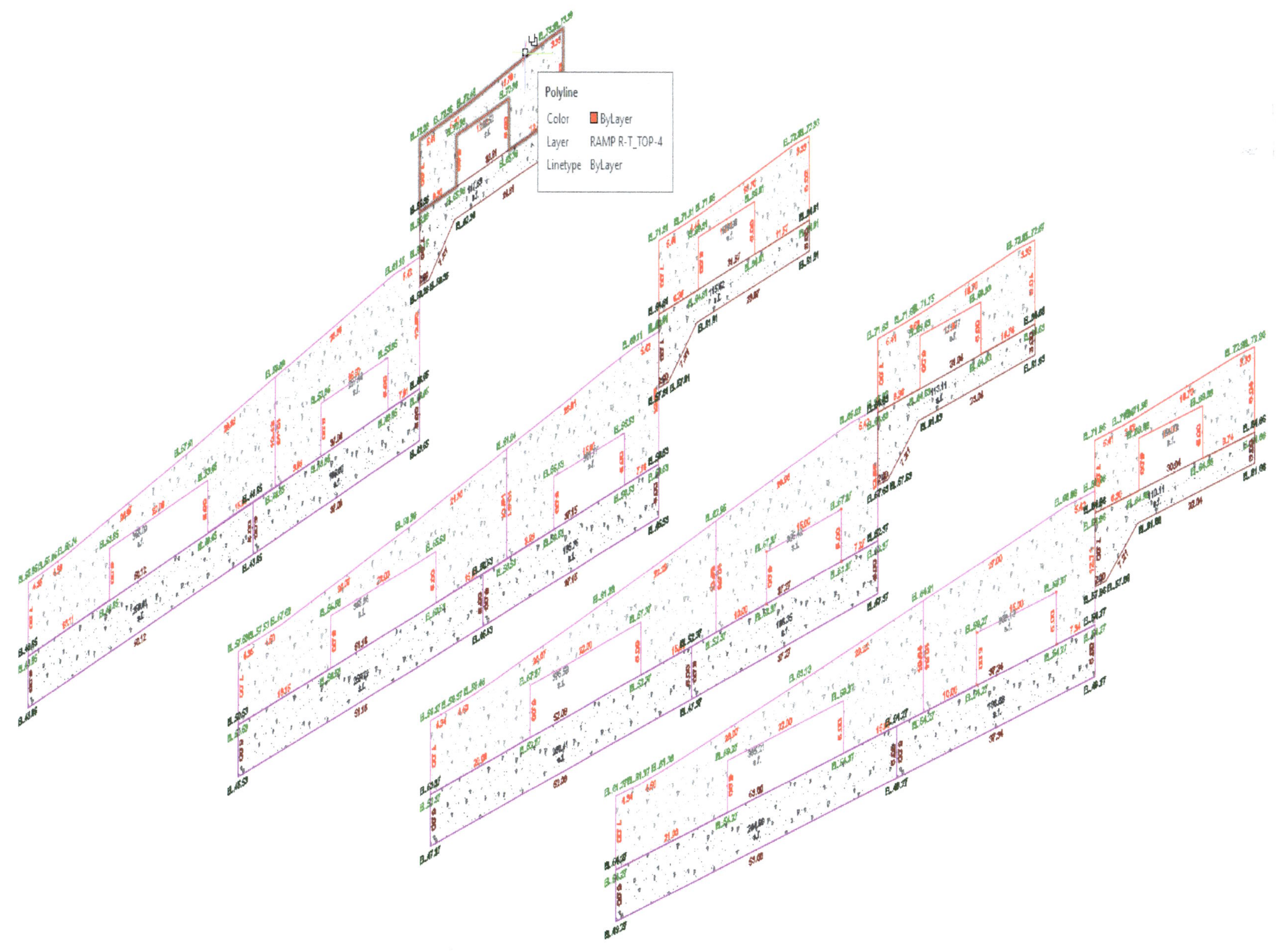
Polyline
Color ByLayer
Layer RAMP R-T_TOP-4
Linetype ByLayer

Note that each X-Section Component has its own layer, as demonstrated for X-Section #4. That gives the Model the flexibility to isolate and extract any Component, as needed. Also, every X-Section Component has the square footage area labeled. Figure III.3.L below shows the "dressed-up" X-Section after the separation sections layers, and applying the base-line station calculation program, block-scheme of which is shown in Figure I.5.C.

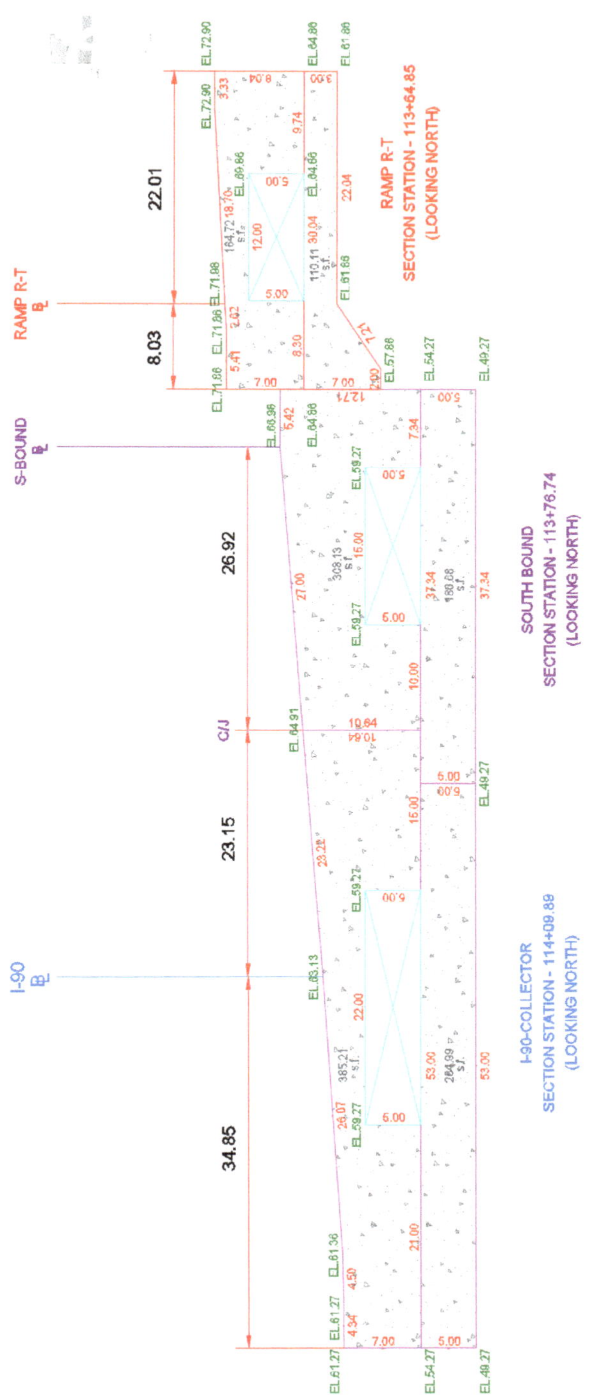

Next, working with 2 adjacent X-Sections, to determine distances between the bottom and top pours at the edges (blue) and CJ (magenta) locations – Figure III.3.M. Note that the Layout from Figure III.3.D reflects only Top Pour Distances.

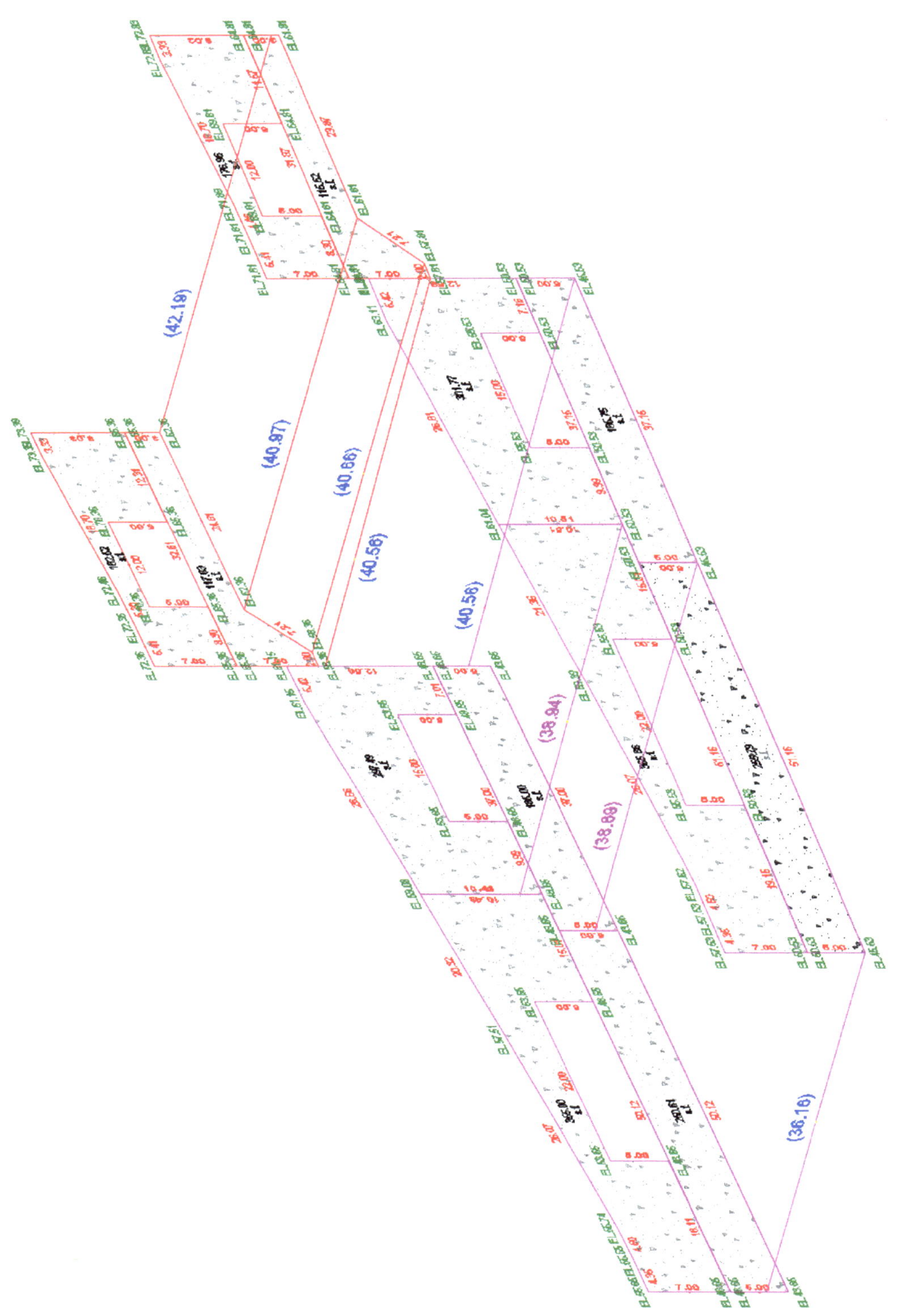

Considering any part of Lift Pour Geometry as a Truncated Pyramid, the Volume is calculated as follows:

$$V = H * [F1 + F2 + \sqrt{(F1 * F2)}] / 3;$$

Where F1 and F2 – areas of corresponding sections, H – average normal distance between them.

Figures III.3.N and III.3.P below demonstrate the Input Chart with correlating Lift Pour Segments Areas and normal Distances, prepared for Volume Calculation, and Resulting Output Chart

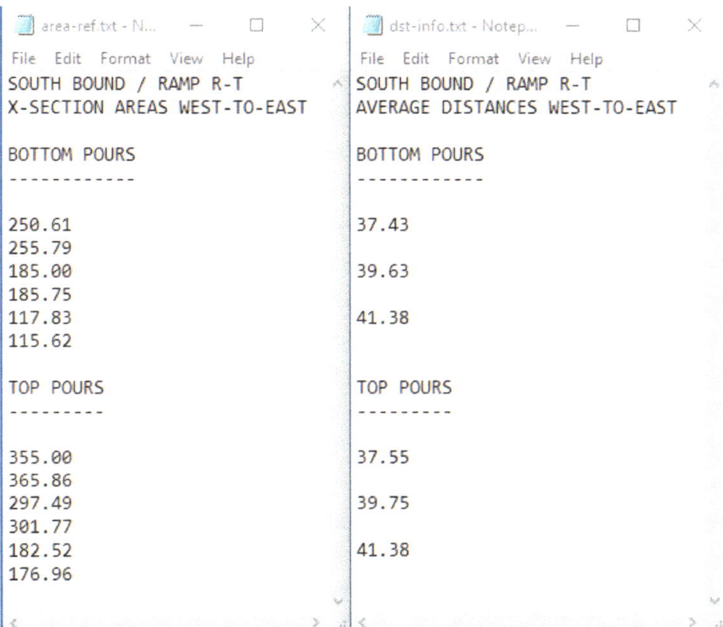

```
area-ref.txt
SOUTH BOUND / RAMP R-T
X-SECTION AREAS WEST-TO-EAST

BOTTOM POURS
------------

250.61
255.79
185.00
185.75
117.83
115.62

TOP POURS
---------

355.00
365.86
297.49
301.77
182.52
176.96
```

```
dst-info.txt
SOUTH BOUND / RAMP R-T
AVERAGE DISTANCES WEST-TO-EAST

BOTTOM POURS
------------

37.43

39.63

41.38

TOP POURS
---------

37.55

39.75

41.38
```

Figure III.3.N – Input Chart

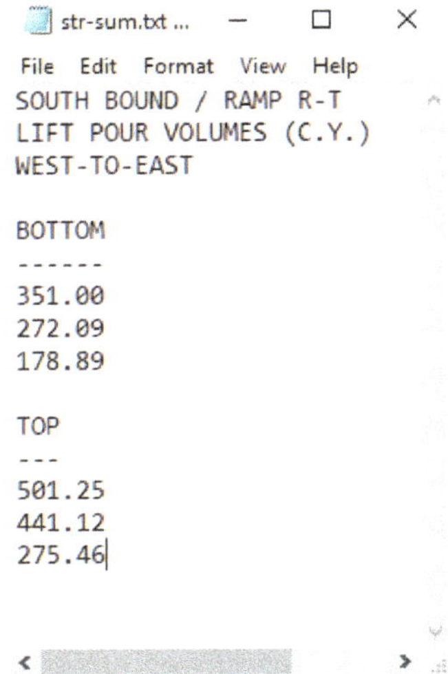

```
str-sum.txt
SOUTH BOUND / RAMP R-T
LIFT POUR VOLUMES (C.Y.)
WEST-TO-EAST

BOTTOM
------
351.00
272.09
178.89

TOP
---
501.25
441.12
275.46
```

Figure III.3.P– Output Chart

Figure III.3.R below demonstrates Lift Pours Volume Calculations Block-Scheme

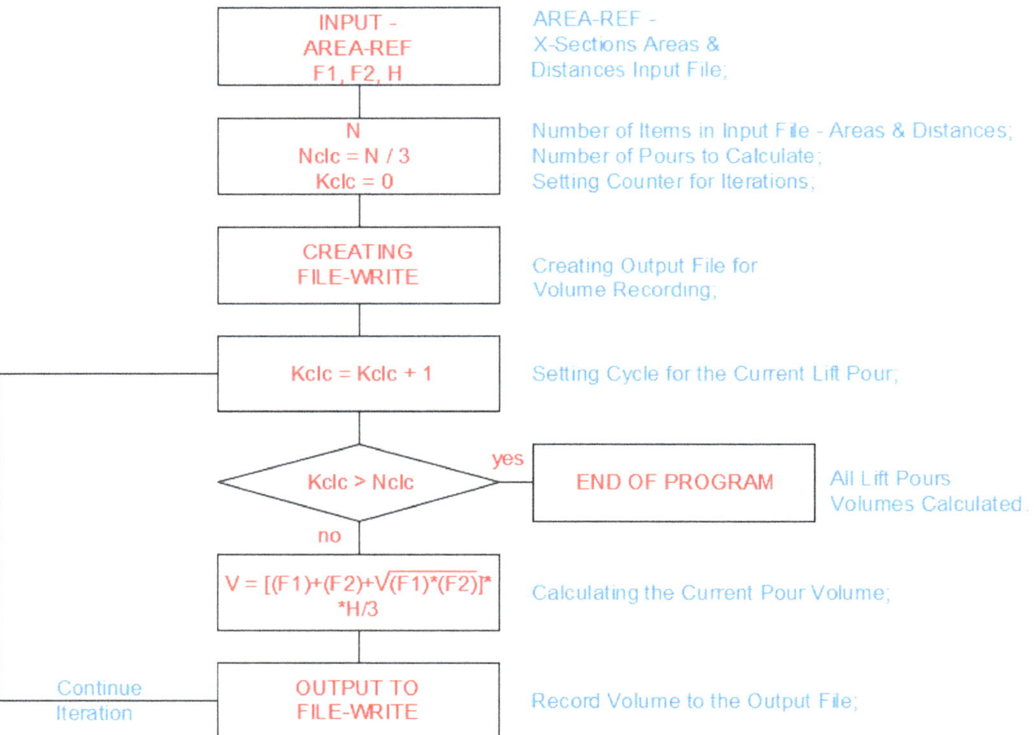

III.3. Concrete Structures. Part B. 3D Modeling.

The approach for 3D Modeling of Concrete Lift Pours from developed X-Sections is shown below in 3 steps in Figures III.3.S.a through III.3.S.c.

Step 1 – X-Section Corner Input Points Designation:

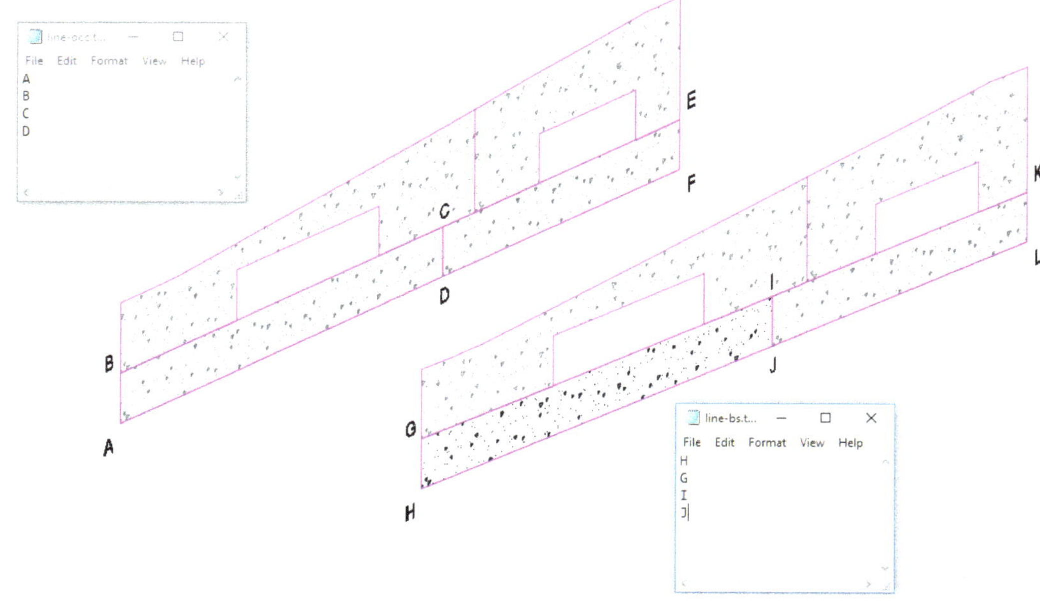

Step 2 – X-Section Corner Input Points Setting (Duplication) & Arrangement:

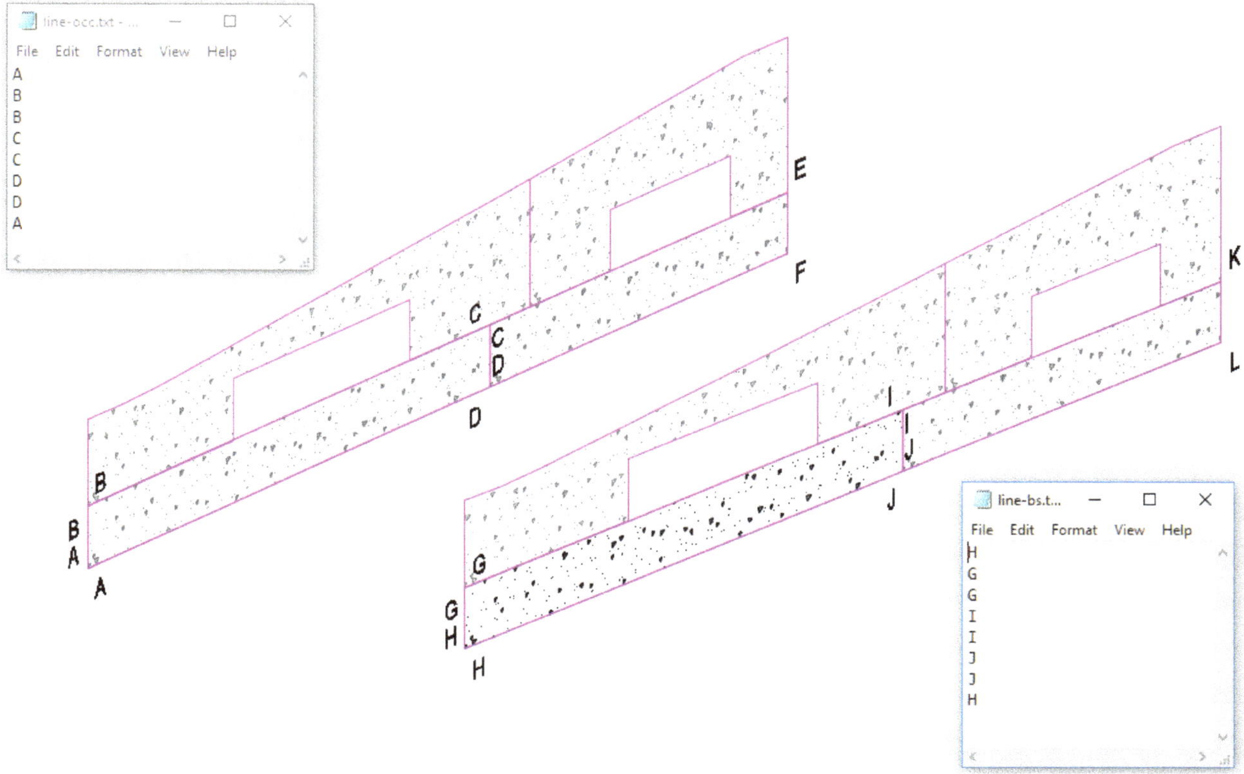

Step 3 – X-Section Corner Input Points Distribution in Groups:

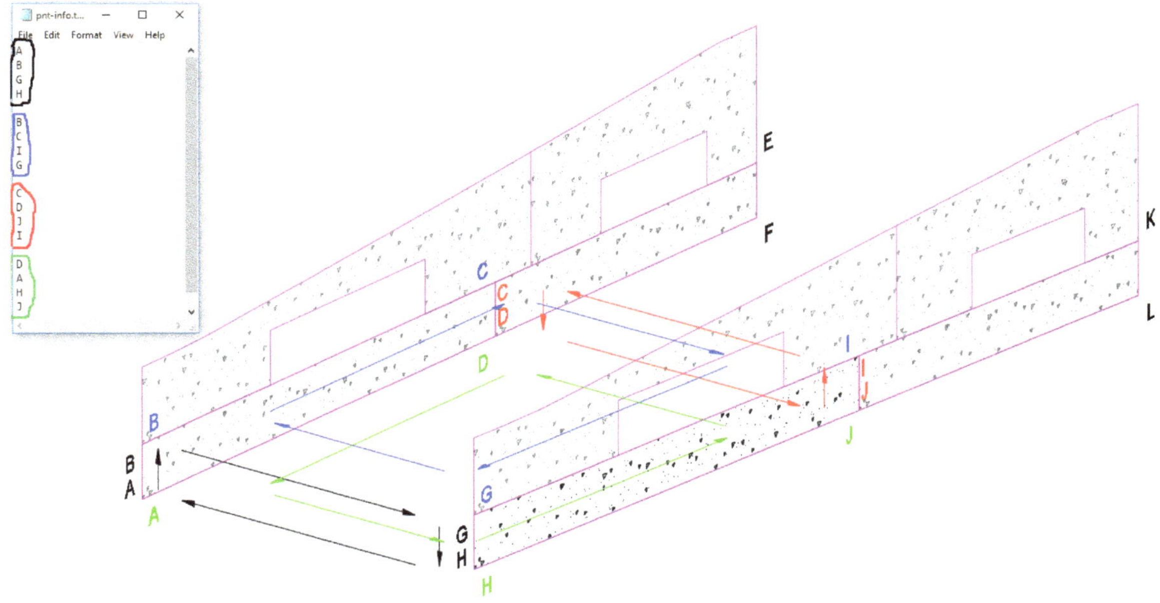

The actual calculation steps following the approach scheme are as follows:

1) Points Designation:

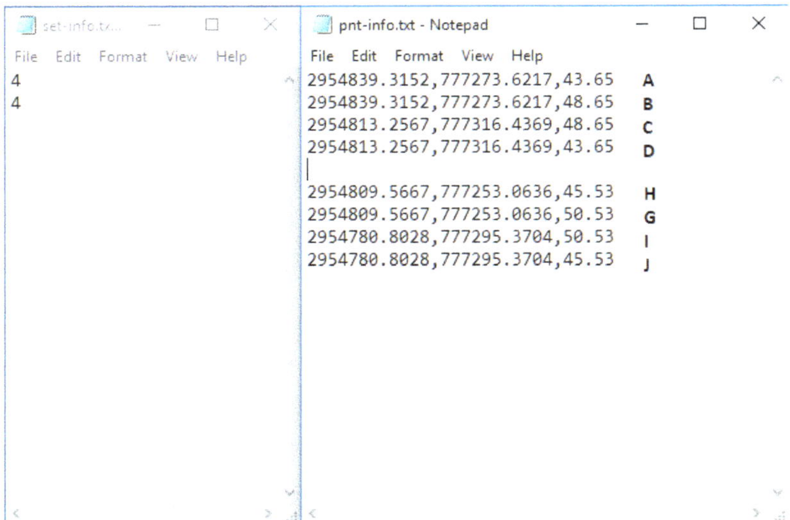

set-info.txt

```
4
4
```

pnt-info.txt - Notepad

```
2954839.3152,777273.6217,43.65    A
2954839.3152,777273.6217,48.65    B
2954813.2567,777316.4369,48.65    C
2954813.2567,777316.4369,43.65    D

2954809.5667,777253.0636,45.53    H
2954809.5667,777253.0636,50.53    G
2954780.8028,777295.3704,50.53    I
2954780.8028,777295.3704,45.53    J
```

2) Points Duplication & Arrangement:

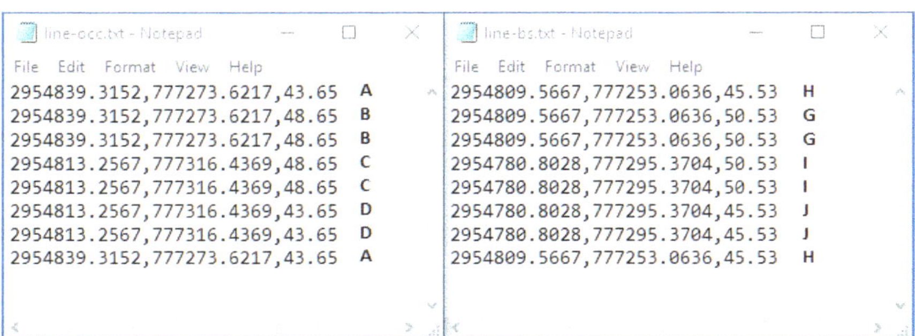

line-occ.txt - Notepad

```
2954839.3152,777273.6217,43.65   A
2954839.3152,777273.6217,48.65   B
2954839.3152,777273.6217,48.65   B
2954813.2567,777316.4369,48.65   C
2954813.2567,777316.4369,48.65   C
2954813.2567,777316.4369,43.65   D
2954813.2567,777316.4369,43.65   D
2954839.3152,777273.6217,43.65   A
```

line-bs.txt - Notepad

```
2954809.5667,777253.0636,45.53   H
2954809.5667,777253.0636,50.53   G
2954809.5667,777253.0636,50.53   G
2954780.8028,777295.3704,50.53   I
2954780.8028,777295.3704,50.53   I
2954780.8028,777295.3704,45.53   J
2954780.8028,777295.3704,45.53   J
2954809.5667,777253.0636,45.53   H
```

3) Points Distribution in Groups:

set-inf...

```
4
4
4
4
```

pnt-info.txt - Notepad

```
2954839.3152,777273.6217,43.65    A
2954839.3152,777273.6217,48.65    B
2954809.5667,777253.0636,50.53    G
2954809.5667,777253.0636,45.53    H

2954839.3152,777273.6217,48.65    B
2954813.2567,777316.4369,48.65    C
2954780.8028,777295.3704,50.53    I
2954809.5667,777253.0636,50.53    G

2954813.2567,777316.4369,48.65    C
2954813.2567,777316.4369,43.65    D
2954780.8028,777295.3704,45.53    J
2954780.8028,777295.3704,50.53    I

2954813.2567,777316.4369,43.65    D
2954839.3152,777273.6217,43.65    A
2954809.5667,777253.0636,45.53    H
2954780.8028,777295.3704,45.53    J
```

4) Typical Point File – Ready for Program Input:

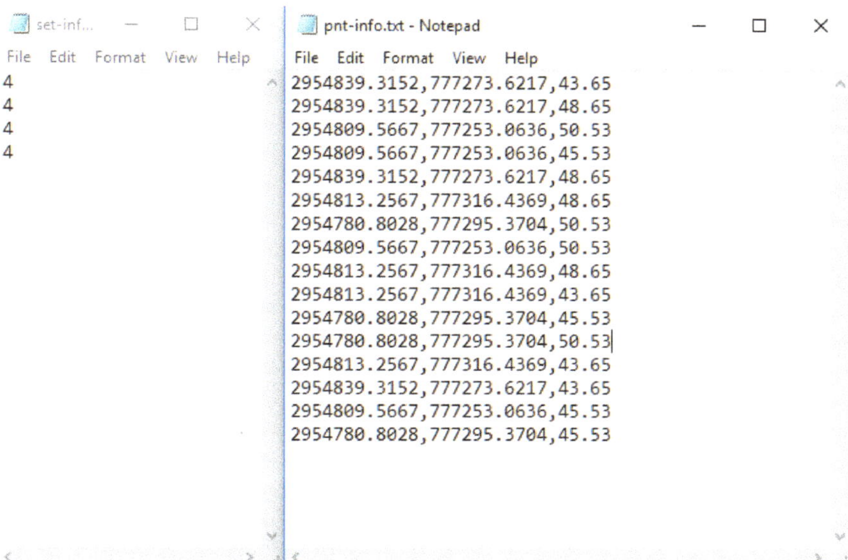


```
2954839.3152,777273.6217,43.65
2954839.3152,777273.6217,48.65
2954809.5667,777253.0636,50.53
2954809.5667,777253.0636,45.53
2954839.3152,777273.6217,48.65
2954813.2567,777316.4369,48.65
2954780.8028,777295.3704,50.53
2954809.5667,777253.0636,50.53
2954813.2567,777316.4369,48.65
2954813.2567,777316.4369,43.65
2954780.8028,777295.3704,45.53
2954780.8028,777295.3704,50.53
2954813.2567,777316.4369,43.65
2954839.3152,777273.6217,43.65
2954809.5667,777253.0636,45.53
2954780.8028,777295.3704,45.53
```

The Figure III.3.T below shows the Program result example for South Bound & Ramp R-T Bottom & Top Lift Pours. The Cover has been partially removed to view Airduct Segments.

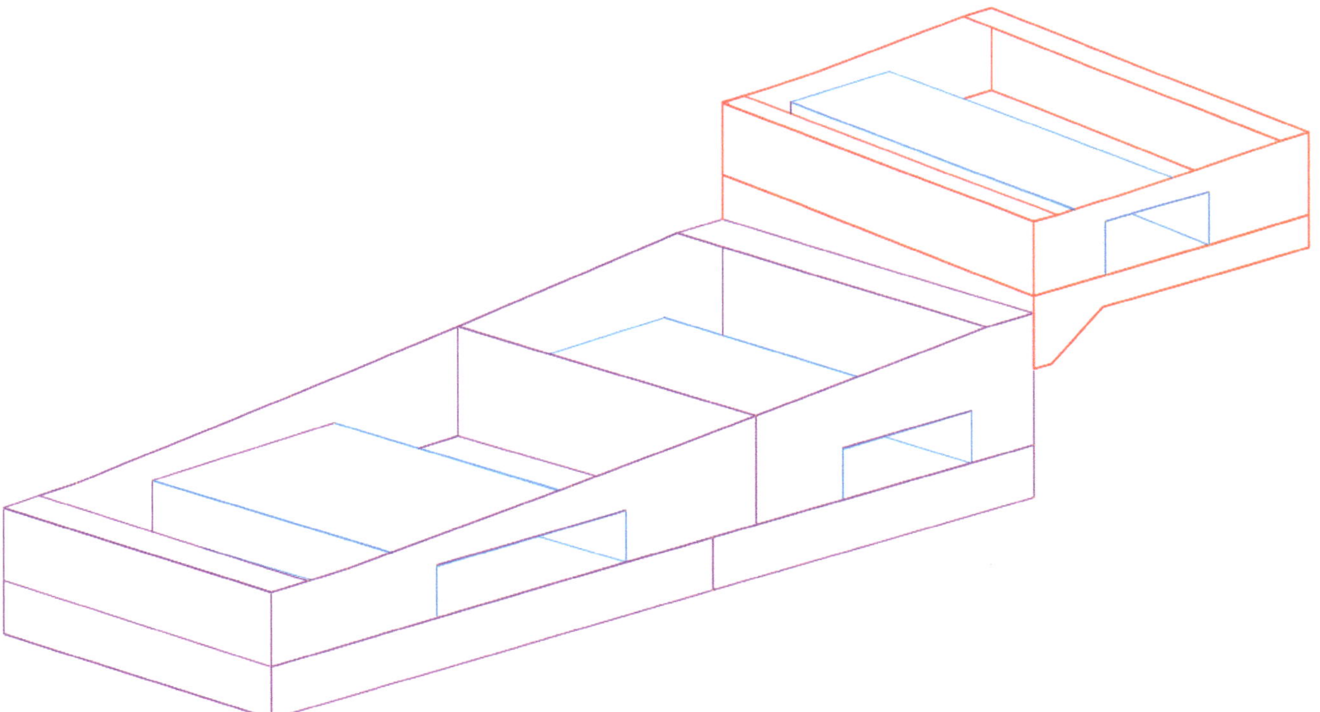

The next set of the affiliated program allows to cut & remove the portion of the concrete structure wall or top cover to view rebar, electrical, or mechanical inserts with the takeoff recording - see Figure III.3.U below:

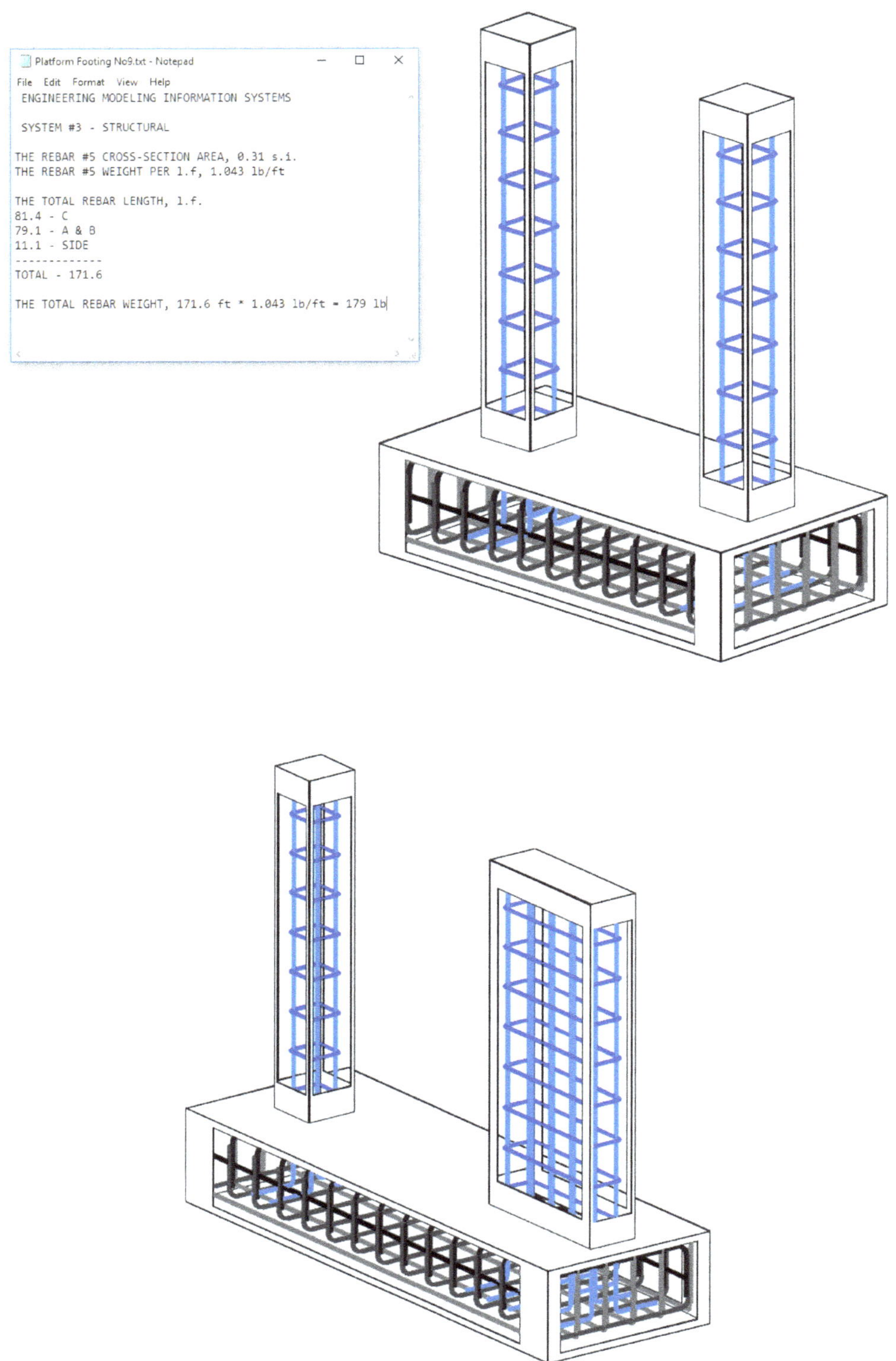

Figure
III.3.V below illustrates the Block-Scheme of Creating Openings Program:

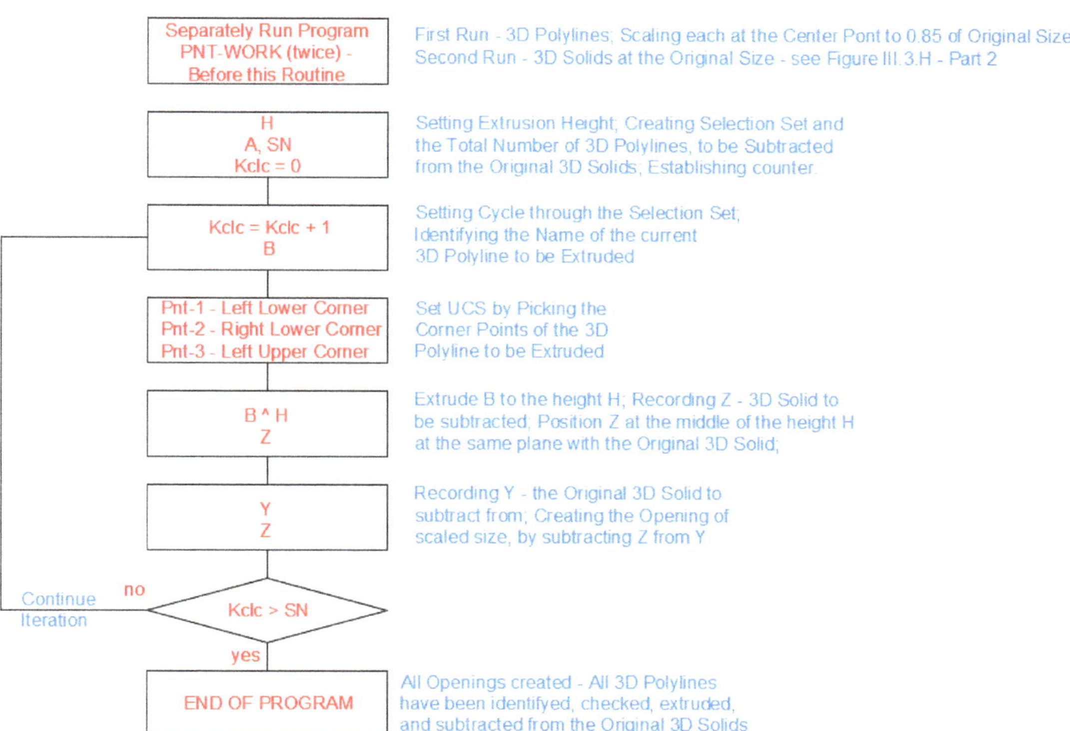

The Takeoff Recording Program (Figure III.3.W below) is common for Structural, Utility, and Transportation Applications. It works for Structural Members, Rebar, Rails, Piping, and Electrical Conduits.

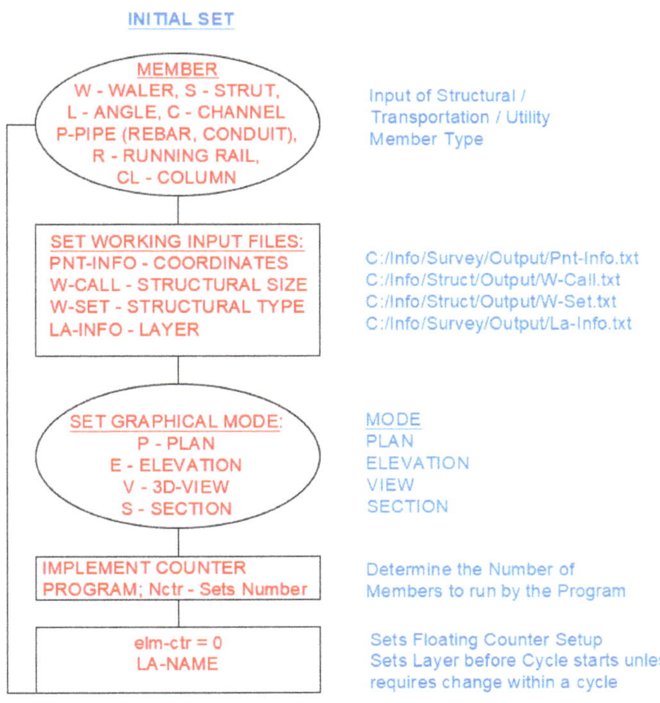

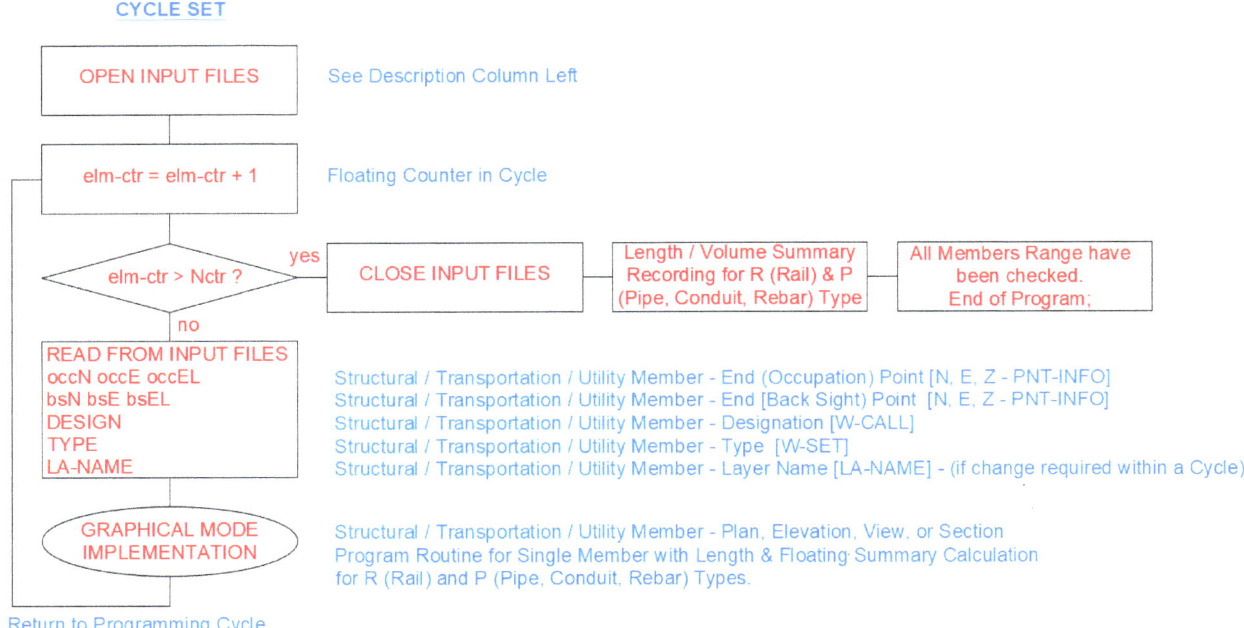

III.4. Subsequent Steel Applications – Columns for Cast-in-Place Walls & Roof Girders

Figures III.4.A, III.4.B & III.4.C below show the Wall "D" Columns Layout, Combined 3D View - Profile Parameters and 3D Modeling added to South Bound – Ramp RT Tunnel segment. The Layout, Input Organizational Structure, and Programming Block-Scheme are similar to those for Slurry Wall Piles illustrated in Figures III.1.C, III.1.D, & III.1.E.

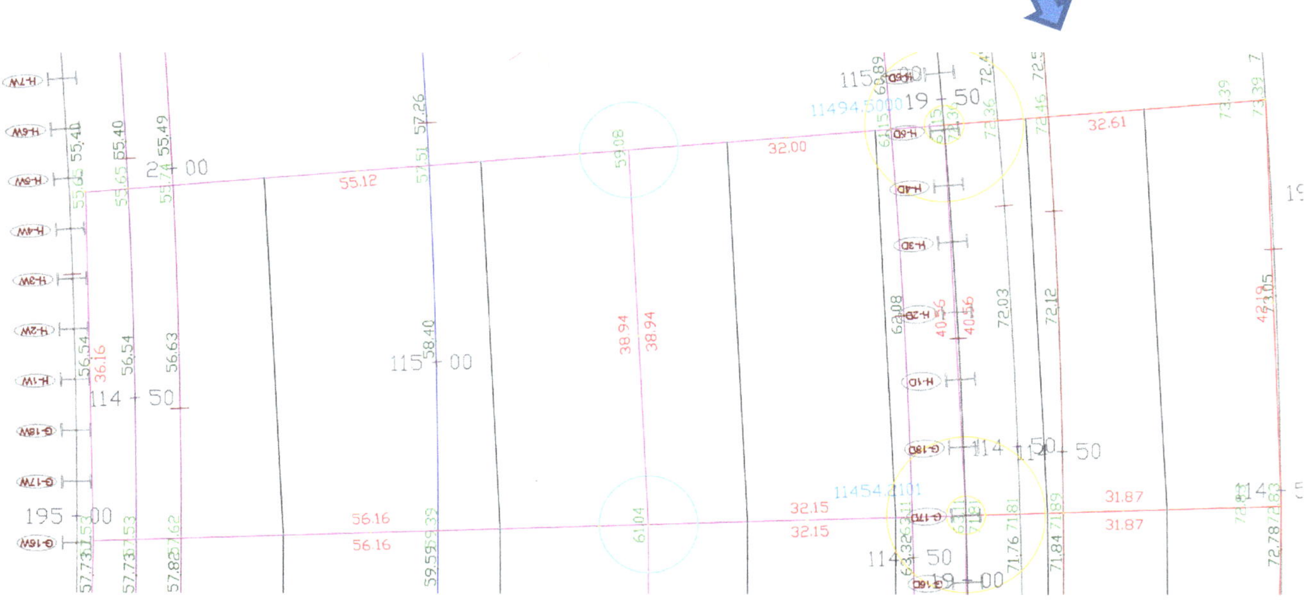

Figure III.4.A. Wall "D" Column Layout, added to Tunnel Segment.

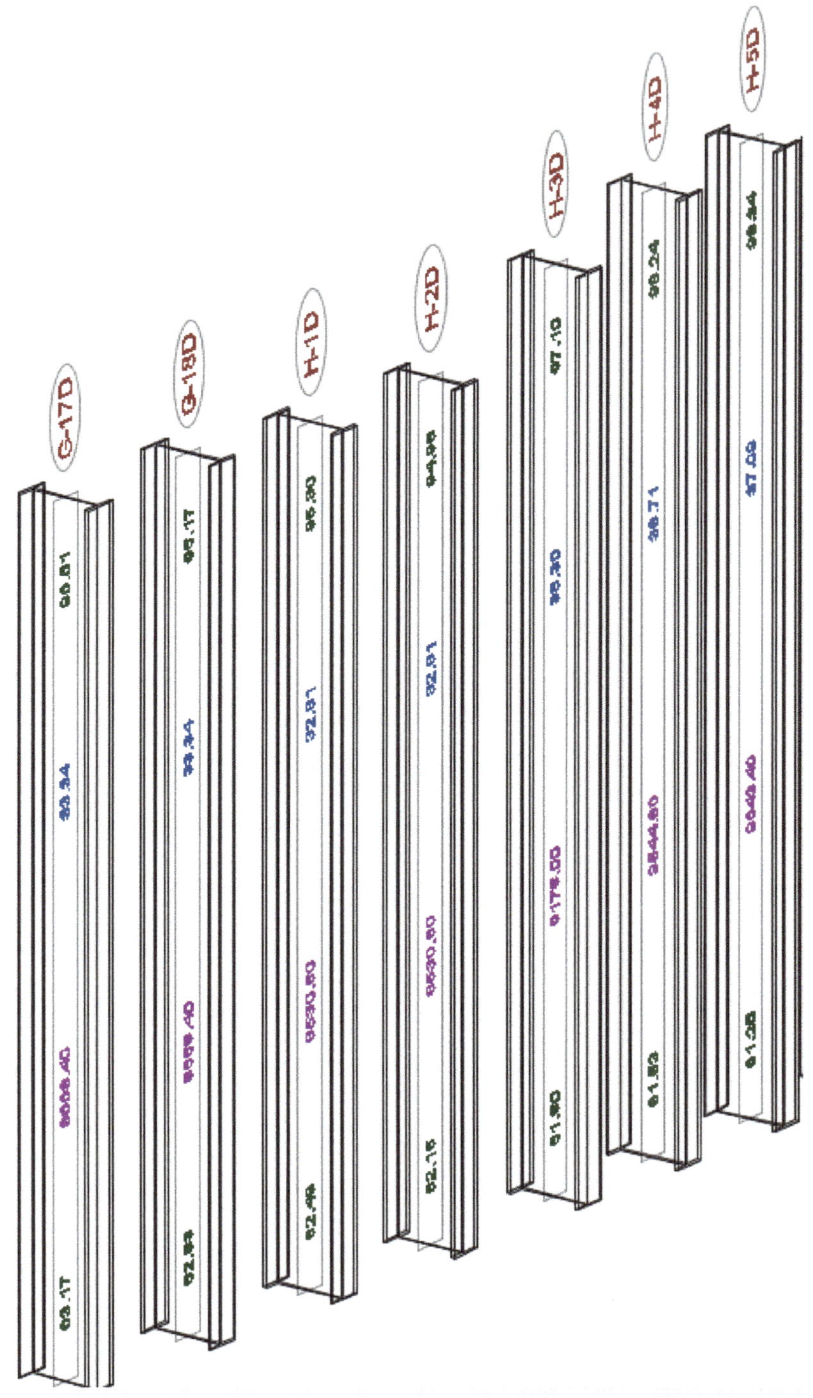

Figure III.4.B. Wall “D” Columns - Combined 3D View/Profile Parameters.

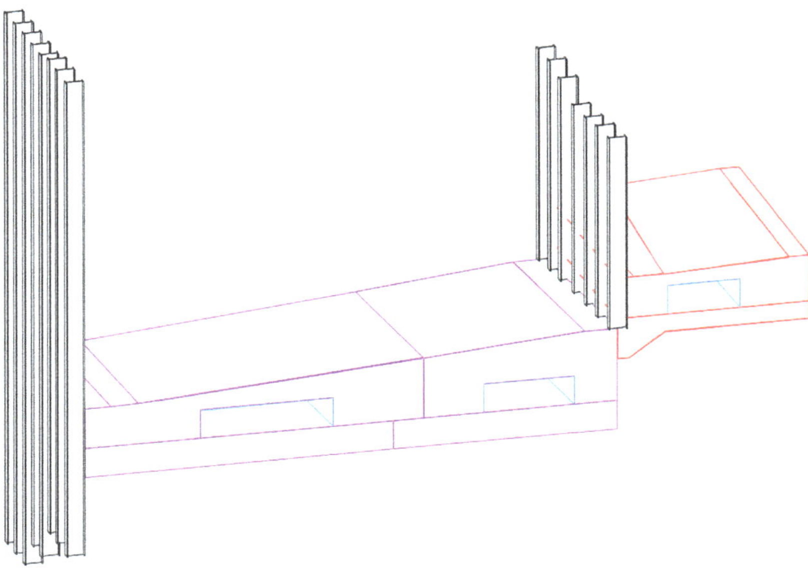

Figure III.4.C. West Slurry Wall Piles & Wall "D" Columns 3D Modeling - added to South Bound – Ramp RT Tunnel segment.

For Roof Girders Modeling, the Input Information is based on Slurry Wall Piles and Cast-In-Place Wall Columns Location and Structural Information – see Figures III.4.D and III.4.E below:

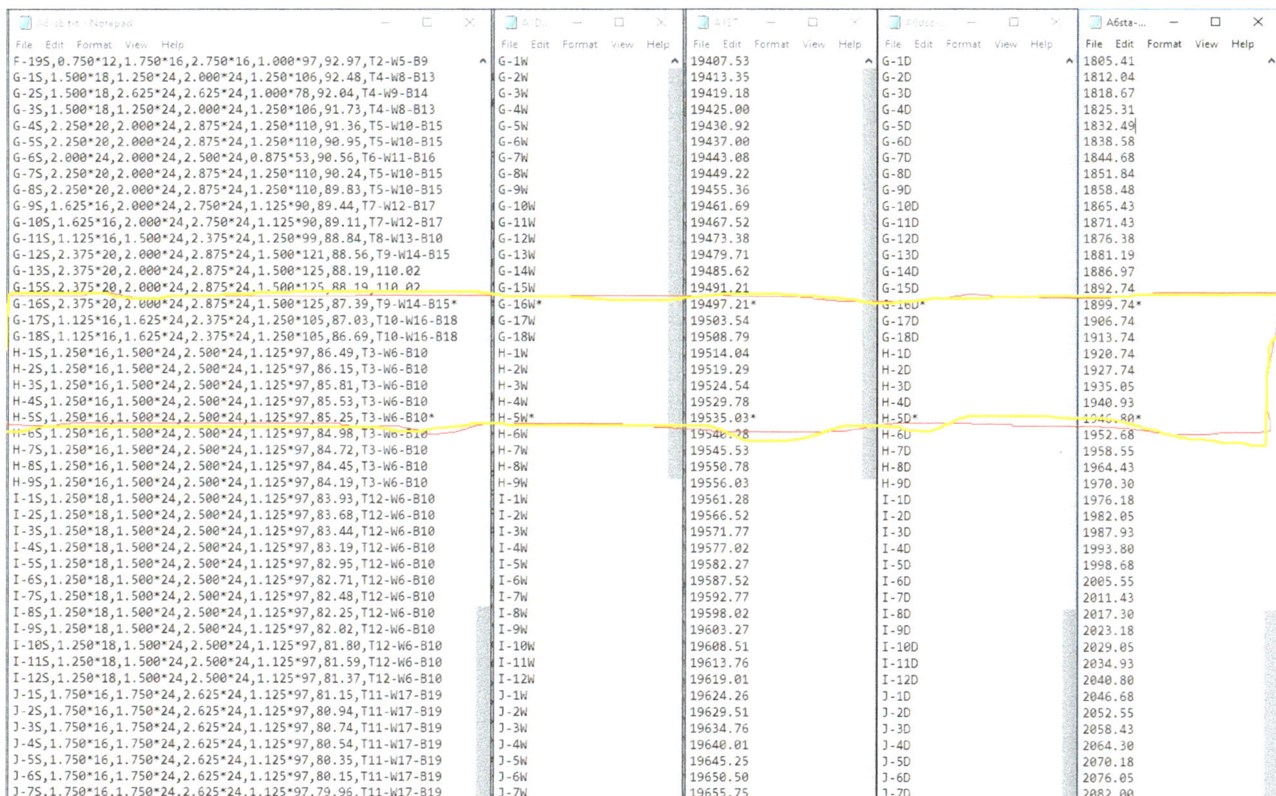

				A6sta-...
F-19S,0.750*12,1.750*16,2.750*16,1.000*97,92.97,T2-W5-B9	G-1W	19407.53	G-1D	1805.41
G-1S,1.500*18,1.250*24,2.000*24,1.250*106,92.48,T4-W8-B13	G-2W	19413.35	G-2D	1812.04
G-2S,1.500*18,2.625*24,2.625*24,1.000*78,92.04,T4-W9-B14	G-3W	19419.18	G-3D	1818.67
G-3S,1.500*18,1.250*24,2.000*24,1.250*106,91.73,T4-W8-B13	G-4W	19425.00	G-4D	1825.31
G-4S,2.250*20,2.000*24,2.875*24,1.250*110,91.36,T5-W10-B15	G-5W	19430.92	G-5D	1832.49
G-5S,2.250*20,2.000*24,2.875*24,1.250*110,90.95,T5-W10-B15	G-6W	19437.00	G-6D	1838.58
G-6S,2.000*24,2.000*24,2.500*24,0.875*53,90.56,T6-W11-B16	G-7W	19443.08	G-7D	1844.68
G-7S,2.250*20,2.000*24,2.875*24,1.250*110,90.24,T5-W10-B15	G-8W	19449.22	G-8D	1851.84
G-8S,2.250*20,2.000*24,2.875*24,1.250*110,89.83,T5-W10-B15	G-9W	19455.36	G-9D	1858.48
G-9S,1.625*16,2.000*24,2.750*24,1.125*90,89.44,T7-W12-B17	G-10W	19461.69	G-10D	1865.43
G-10S,1.625*16,2.000*24,2.750*24,1.125*90,89.11,T7-W12-B17	G-11W	19467.52	G-11D	1871.43
G-11S,1.125*16,1.500*24,2.375*24,1.250*99,88.84,T8-W13-B10	G-12W	19473.38	G-12D	1876.38
G-12S,2.375*20,2.000*24,2.875*24,1.500*121,88.56,T9-W14-B15	G-13W	19479.71	G-13D	1881.19
G-13S,2.375*20,2.000*24,2.875*24,1.500*125,88.19,110.02	G-14W	19485.62	G-14D	1886.97
G-15S,2.375*20,2.000*24,2.875*24,1.500*125,88.19,110.02	G-15W	19491.21	G-15D	1892.74
G-16S,2.375*20,2.000*24,2.875*24,1.500*125,87.39,T9-W14-B15*	G-16W*	19497.21*	G-16D*	1899.74*
G-17S,1.125*16,1.625*24,2.375*24,1.250*105,87.03,T10-W16-B18	G-17W	19503.54	G-17D	1906.74
G-18S,1.125*16,1.625*24,2.375*24,1.250*105,86.69,T10-W16-B18	G-18W	19508.79	G-18D	1913.74
H-1S,1.250*16,1.500*24,2.500*24,1.125*97,86.49,T3-W6-B10	H-1W	19514.04	H-1D	1920.74
H-2S,1.250*16,1.500*24,2.500*24,1.125*97,86.15,T3-W6-B10	H-2W	19519.29	H-2D	1927.74
H-3S,1.250*16,1.500*24,2.500*24,1.125*97,85.81,T3-W6-B10	H-3W	19524.54	H-3D	1935.05
H-4S,1.250*16,1.500*24,2.500*24,1.125*97,85.53,T3-W6-B10	H-4W	19529.78	H-4D	1940.93
H-5S,1.250*16,1.500*24,2.500*24,1.125*97,85.25,T3-W6-B10*	H-5W*	19535.03*	H-5D*	1946.80*
H-6S,1.250*16,1.500*24,2.500*24,1.125*97,84.98,T3-W6-B10	H-6W	[illegible]	H-6D	1952.68
H-7S,1.250*16,1.500*24,2.500*24,1.125*97,84.72,T3-W6-B10	H-7W	19545.53	H-7D	1958.55
H-8S,1.250*16,1.500*24,2.500*24,1.125*97,84.45,T3-W6-B10	H-8W	19550.78	H-8D	1964.43
H-9S,1.250*16,1.500*24,2.500*24,1.125*97,84.19,T3-W6-B10	H-9W	19556.03	H-9D	1970.30
I-1S,1.250*18,1.500*24,2.500*24,1.125*97,83.93,T12-W6-B10	I-1W	19561.28	I-1D	1976.18
I-2S,1.250*18,1.500*24,2.500*24,1.125*97,83.68,T12-W6-B10	I-2W	19566.52	I-2D	1982.05
I-3S,1.250*18,1.500*24,2.500*24,1.125*97,83.44,T12-W6-B10	I-3W	19571.77	I-3D	1987.93
I-4S,1.250*18,1.500*24,2.500*24,1.125*97,83.19,T12-W6-B10	I-4W	19577.02	I-4D	1993.80
I-5S,1.250*18,1.500*24,2.500*24,1.125*97,82.95,T12-W6-B10	I-5W	19582.27	I-5D	1998.68
I-6S,1.250*18,1.500*24,2.500*24,1.125*97,82.71,T12-W6-B10	I-6W	19587.52	I-6D	2005.55
I-7S,1.250*18,1.500*24,2.500*24,1.125*97,82.48,T12-W6-B10	I-7W	19592.77	I-7D	2011.43
I-8S,1.250*18,1.500*24,2.500*24,1.125*97,82.25,T12-W6-B10	I-8W	19598.02	I-8D	2017.30
I-9S,1.250*18,1.500*24,2.500*24,1.125*97,82.02,T12-W6-B10	I-9W	19603.27	I-9D	2023.18
I-10S,1.250*18,1.500*24,2.500*24,1.125*97,81.80,T12-W6-B10	I-10W	19608.51	I-10D	2029.05
I-11S,1.250*18,1.500*24,2.500*24,1.125*97,81.59,T12-W6-B10	I-11W	19613.76	I-11D	2034.93
I-12S,1.250*18,1.500*24,2.500*24,1.125*97,81.37,T12-W6-B10	I-12W	19619.01	I-12D	2040.80
J-1S,1.750*16,1.750*24,2.625*24,1.125*97,81.15,T11-W17-B19	J-1W	19624.26	J-1D	2046.68
J-2S,1.750*16,1.750*24,2.625*24,1.125*97,80.94,T11-W17-B19	J-2W	19629.51	J-2D	2052.55
J-3S,1.750*16,1.750*24,2.625*24,1.125*97,80.74,T11-W17-B19	J-3W	19634.76	J-3D	2058.43
J-4S,1.750*16,1.750*24,2.625*24,1.125*97,80.54,T11-W17-B19	J-4W	19640.01	J-4D	2064.30
J-5S,1.750*16,1.750*24,2.625*24,1.125*97,80.35,T11-W17-B19	J-5W	19645.25	J-5D	2070.18
J-6S,1.750*16,1.750*24,2.625*24,1.125*97,80.15,T11-W17-B19	J-6W	19650.50	J-6D	2076.05
J-7S,1.750*16,1.750*24,2.625*24,1.125*97,79.96,T11-W17-B19	J-7W	19655.75	J-7D	2082.00

Figure III.4.D – Roof Girder & Pile/Column Designation and Stations.

The Pile/Column Structural Size determines the Offset Distance from the Wall Center Line & the Roof Girder Connection Point Coordinates:

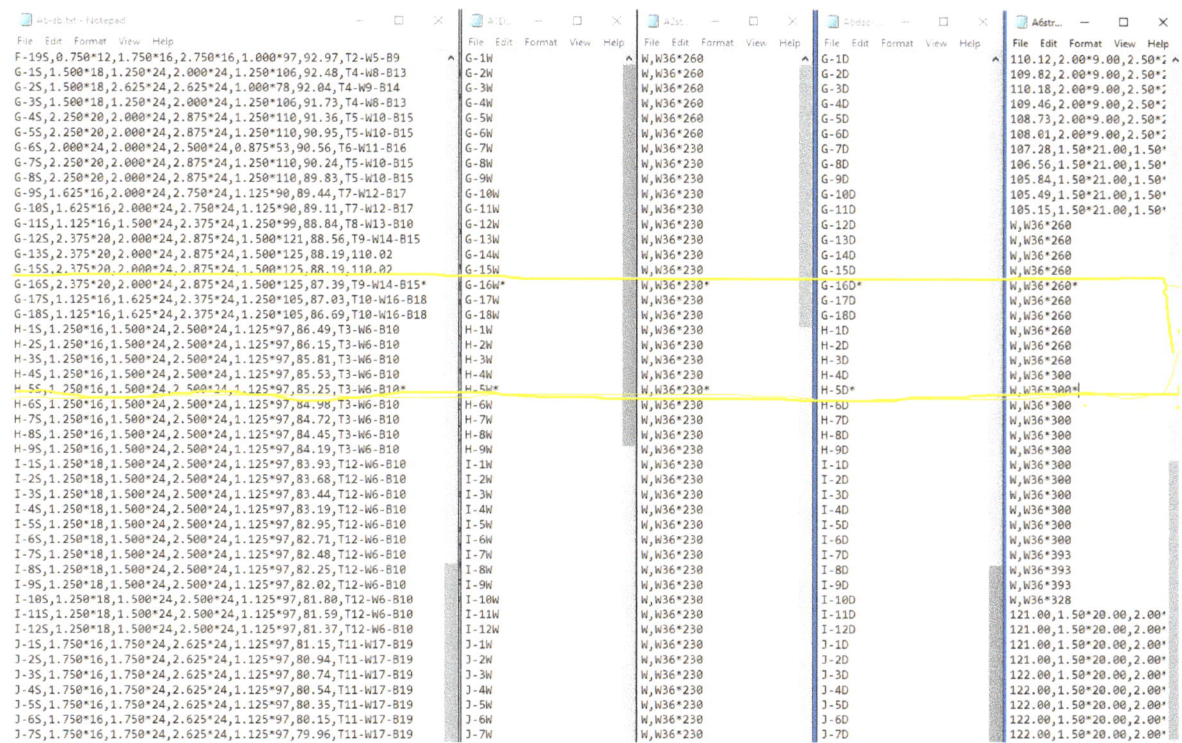

```
F-19S,0.750*12,1.750*16,2.750*16,1.000*97,92.97,T2-W5-B9
G-1S,1.500*18,1.250*24,2.000*24,1.250*106,92.48,T4-W8-B13
G-2S,1.500*18,2.625*24,2.625*24,1.000*78,92.04,T4-W9-B14
G-3S,1.500*18,1.250*24,2.000*24,1.250*106,91.73,T4-W8-B13
G-4S,2.250*20,2.000*24,2.875*24,1.250*110,91.36,T5-W10-B15
G-5S,2.250*20,2.000*24,2.875*24,1.250*110,90.95,T5-W10-B15
G-6S,2.000*24,2.000*24,2.500*24,0.875*53,90.56,T6-W11-B16
G-7S,2.250*20,2.000*24,2.875*24,1.250*110,90.24,T5-W10-B15
G-8S,2.250*20,2.000*24,2.875*24,1.250*110,89.83,T5-W10-B15
G-9S,1.625*16,2.000*24,2.750*24,1.125*90,89.44,T7-W12-B17
G-10S,1.625*16,2.000*24,2.750*24,1.125*90,89.11,T7-W12-B17
G-11S,1.125*16,1.500*24,2.375*24,1.250*99,88.84,T8-W13-B18
G-12S,2.375*20,2.000*24,2.875*24,1.500*121,88.56,T9-W14-B15
G-13S,2.375*20,2.000*24,2.875*24,1.500*125,88.19,110.02
G-15S,2.375*20,2.000*24,2.875*24,1.500*125,88.19,110.02
G-16S,2.375*20,2.000*24,2.875*24,1.500*125,87.39,T9-W14-B15*
G-17S,1.125*16,1.625*24,2.375*24,1.250*105,87.03,T10-W16-B18
G-18S,1.125*16,1.625*24,2.375*24,1.250*105,86.69,T10-W16-B18
H-1S,1.250*16,1.500*24,2.500*24,1.125*97,86.49,T3-W6-B10
H-2S,1.250*16,1.500*24,2.500*24,1.125*97,86.15,T3-W6-B10
H-3S,1.250*16,1.500*24,2.500*24,1.125*97,85.81,T3-W6-B10
H-4S,1.250*16,1.500*24,2.500*24,1.125*97,85.53,T3-W6-B10
H-5S,1.250*16,1.500*24,2.500*24,1.125*97,85.25,T3-W6-B10*
H-6S,1.250*16,1.500*24,2.500*24,1.125*97,84.98,T3-W6-B10
H-7S,1.250*16,1.500*24,2.500*24,1.125*97,84.72,T3-W6-B10
H-8S,1.250*16,1.500*24,2.500*24,1.125*97,84.45,T3-W6-B10
H-9S,1.250*16,1.500*24,2.500*24,1.125*97,84.19,T3-W6-B10
I-1S,1.250*18,1.500*24,2.500*24,1.125*97,83.93,T12-W6-B10
I-2S,1.250*18,1.500*24,2.500*24,1.125*97,83.68,T12-W6-B10
I-3S,1.250*18,1.500*24,2.500*24,1.125*97,83.44,T12-W6-B10
I-4S,1.250*18,1.500*24,2.500*24,1.125*97,83.19,T12-W6-B10
I-5S,1.250*18,1.500*24,2.500*24,1.125*97,82.95,T12-W6-B10
I-6S,1.250*18,1.500*24,2.500*24,1.125*97,82.71,T12-W6-B10
I-7S,1.250*18,1.500*24,2.500*24,1.125*97,82.48,T12-W6-B10
I-8S,1.250*18,1.500*24,2.500*24,1.125*97,82.25,T12-W6-B10
I-9S,1.250*18,1.500*24,2.500*24,1.125*97,82.02,T12-W6-B10
I-10S,1.250*18,1.500*24,2.500*24,1.125*97,81.80,T12-W6-B10
I-11S,1.250*18,1.500*24,2.500*24,1.125*97,81.59,T12-W6-B10
I-12S,1.250*18,1.500*24,2.500*24,1.125*97,81.37,T12-W6-B10
J-1S,1.750*16,1.750*24,2.625*24,1.125*97,81.15,T11-W17-B19
J-2S,1.750*16,1.750*24,2.625*24,1.125*97,80.94,T11-W17-B19
J-3S,1.750*16,1.750*24,2.625*24,1.125*97,80.74,T11-W17-B19
J-4S,1.750*16,1.750*24,2.625*24,1.125*97,80.54,T11-W17-B19
J-5S,1.750*16,1.750*24,2.625*24,1.125*97,80.35,T11-W17-B19
J-6S,1.750*16,1.750*24,2.625*24,1.125*97,80.15,T11-W17-B19
J-7S,1.750*16,1.750*24,2.625*24,1.125*97,79.96,T11-W17-B19
```

```
G-1W
G-2W
G-3W
G-4W
G-5W
G-6W
G-7W
G-8W
G-9W
G-10W
G-11W
G-12W
G-13W
G-14W
G-15W
G-16W*
G-17W
G-18W
H-1W
H-2W
H-3W
H-4W
H-5W*
H-6W
H-7W
H-8W
H-9W
I-1W
I-2W
I-3W
I-4W
I-5W
I-6W
I-7W
I-8W
I-9W
I-10W
I-11W
I-12W
J-1W
J-2W
J-3W
J-4W
J-5W
J-6W
J-7W
```

```
W,W36*260
W,W36*260
W,W36*260
W,W36*260
W,W36*260
W,W36*260
W,W36*230
W,W36*230
W,W36*230
W,W36*230
W,W36*230
W,W36*230
W,W36*230
W,W36*230
W,W36*230
W,W36*230*
W,W36*230
W,W36*230
W,W36*230
W,W36*230
W,W36*230
W,W36*230
W,W36*230*
W,W36*230
W,W36*230
W,W36*230
W,W36*230
W,W36*230
W,W36*230
W,W36*230
W,W36*230
W,W36*230
W,W36*230
W,W36*230
W,W36*230
W,W36*230
W,W36*230
W,W36*230
W,W36*230
W,W36*230
W,W36*230
W,W36*230
W,W36*230
W,W36*230
W,W36*230
W,W36*230
```

```
G-1D
G-2D
G-3D
G-4D
G-5D
G-6D
G-7D
G-8D
G-9D
G-10D
G-11D
G-12D
G-13D
G-14D
G-15D
G-16D*
G-17D
G-18D
H-1D
H-2D
H-3D
H-4D
H-5D*
H-6D
H-7D
H-8D
H-9D
I-1D
I-2D
I-3D
I-4D
I-5D
I-6D
I-7D
I-8D
I-9D
I-10D
I-11D
I-12D
J-1D
J-2D
J-3D
J-4D
J-5D
J-6D
J-7D
```

```
110.12,2.00*9.00,2.50*
109.82,2.00*9.00,2.50*
110.18,2.00*9.00,2.50*
109.46,2.00*9.00,2.50*
108.73,2.00*9.00,2.50*
108.01,2.00*9.00,2.50*
107.28,1.50*21.00,1.50*
106.56,1.50*21.00,1.50*
105.84,1.50*21.00,1.50*
105.49,1.50*21.00,1.50*
105.15,1.50*21.00,1.50*
W,W36*260
W,W36*260
W,W36*260
W,W36*260
W,W36*260*
W,W36*260
W,W36*260
W,W36*260
W,W36*260
W,W36*260
W,W36*300
W,W36*300*
W,W36*300
W,W36*300
W,W36*300
W,W36*300
W,W36*300
W,W36*300
W,W36*300
W,W36*300
W,W36*300
W,W36*300
W,W36*393
W,W36*393
W,W36*393
W,W36*328
121.00,1.50*20.00,2.00*
121.00,1.50*20.00,2.00*
121.00,1.50*20.00,2.00*
121.00,1.50*20.00,2.00*
122.00,1.50*20.00,2.00*
122.00,1.50*20.00,2.00*
122.00,1.50*20.00,2.00*
122.00,1.50*20.00,2.00*
122.00,1.50*20.00,2.00*
```

Figure III.4.E – Roof Girder & Pile/Column Structural Size.

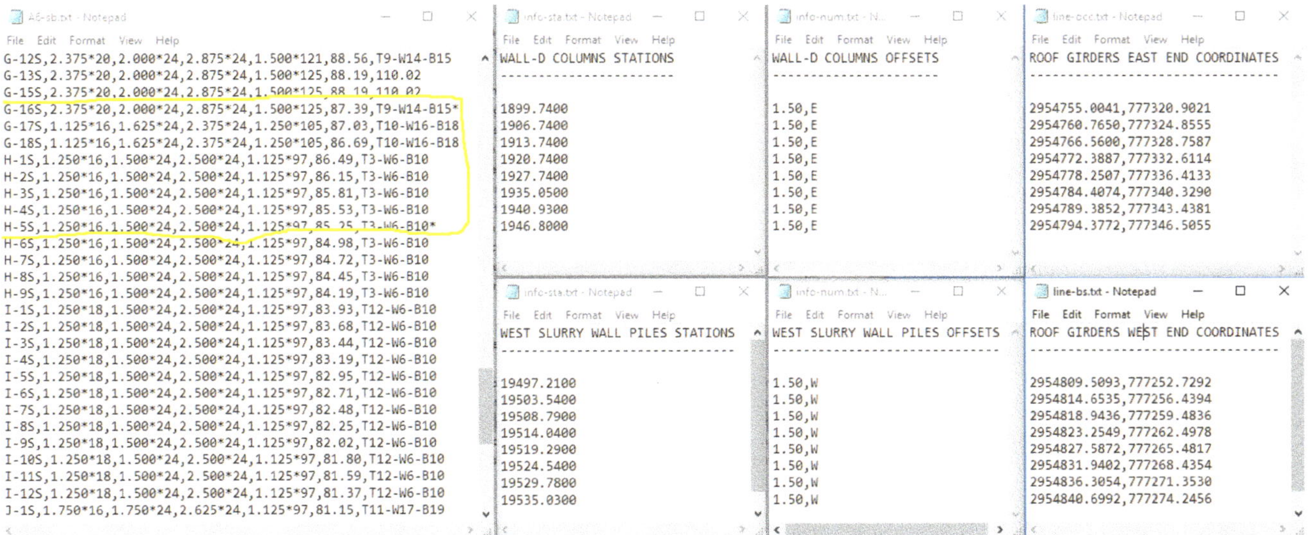

```
G-12S,2.375*20,2.000*24,2.875*24,1.500*121,88.56,T9-W14-B15
G-13S,2.375*20,2.000*24,2.875*24,1.500*125,88.19,110.02
G-15S,2.375*20,2.000*24,2.875*24,1.500*125,88.19,110.02
G-16S,2.375*20,2.000*24,2.875*24,1.500*125,87.39,T9-W14-B15*
G-17S,1.125*16,1.625*24,2.375*24,1.250*105,87.03,T10-W16-B18
G-18S,1.125*16,1.625*24,2.375*24,1.250*105,86.69,T10-W16-B18
H-1S,1.250*16,1.500*24,2.500*24,1.125*97,86.49,T3-W6-B10
H-2S,1.250*16,1.500*24,2.500*24,1.125*97,86.15,T3-W6-B10
H-3S,1.250*16,1.500*24,2.500*24,1.125*97,85.81,T3-W6-B10
H-4S,1.250*16,1.500*24,2.500*24,1.125*97,85.53,T3-W6-B10
H-5S,1.250*16,1.500*24,2.500*24,1.125*97,85.25,T3-W6-B10*
H-6S,1.250*16,1.500*24,2.500*24,1.125*97,84.98,T3-W6-B10
H-7S,1.250*16,1.500*24,2.500*24,1.125*97,84.72,T3-W6-B10
H-8S,1.250*16,1.500*24,2.500*24,1.125*97,84.45,T3-W6-B10
H-9S,1.250*16,1.500*24,2.500*24,1.125*97,84.19,T3-W6-B10
I-1S,1.250*18,1.500*24,2.500*24,1.125*97,83.93,T12-W6-B10
I-2S,1.250*18,1.500*24,2.500*24,1.125*97,83.68,T12-W6-B10
I-3S,1.250*18,1.500*24,2.500*24,1.125*97,83.44,T12-W6-B10
I-4S,1.250*18,1.500*24,2.500*24,1.125*97,83.19,T12-W6-B10
I-5S,1.250*18,1.500*24,2.500*24,1.125*97,82.95,T12-W6-B10
I-6S,1.250*18,1.500*24,2.500*24,1.125*97,82.71,T12-W6-B10
I-7S,1.250*18,1.500*24,2.500*24,1.125*97,82.48,T12-W6-B10
I-8S,1.250*18,1.500*24,2.500*24,1.125*97,82.25,T12-W6-B10
I-9S,1.250*18,1.500*24,2.500*24,1.125*97,82.02,T12-W6-B10
I-10S,1.250*18,1.500*24,2.500*24,1.125*97,81.80,T12-W6-B10
I-11S,1.250*18,1.500*24,2.500*24,1.125*97,81.59,T12-W6-B10
I-12S,1.250*18,1.500*24,2.500*24,1.125*97,81.37,T12-W6-B10
J-1S,1.750*16,1.750*24,2.625*24,1.125*97,81.15,T11-W17-B19
```

```
WALL-D COLUMNS STATIONS
-----------------------

1899.7400
1906.7400
1913.7400
1920.7400
1927.7400
1935.0500
1940.9300
1946.8000
```

```
WALL-D COLUMNS OFFSETS
----------------------

1.50,E
1.50,E
1.50,E
1.50,E
1.50,E
1.50,E
1.50,E
1.50,E
```

```
ROOF GIRDERS EAST END COORDINATES
---------------------------------

2954755.0041,777320.9021
2954760.7650,777324.8555
2954766.5600,777328.7587
2954772.3887,777332.6114
2954778.2507,777336.4133
2954784.4074,777340.3290
2954789.3852,777343.4381
2954794.3772,777346.5055
```

```
WEST SLURRY WALL PILES STATIONS
-------------------------------

19497.2100
19503.5400
19508.7900
19514.0400
19519.2900
19524.5400
19529.7800
19535.0300
```

```
WEST SLURRY WALL PILES OFFSETS
------------------------------

1.50,W
1.50,W
1.50,W
1.50,W
1.50,W
1.50,W
1.50,W
1.50,W
```

```
ROOF GIRDERS WEST END COORDINATES
---------------------------------

2954809.5093,777252.7292
2954814.6535,777256.4394
2954818.9436,777259.4836
2954823.2549,777262.4978
2954827.5872,777265.4817
2954831.9402,777268.4354
2954836.3054,777271.3530
2954840.6992,777274.2456
```

Figure III.4.E – Roof Girder End Points Coordinates.

With known coordinates, the next step is getting the Roof Girder Segment Plan View, West Wall and Wall "D" Elevation Views – see Figures III.4.F, III.4.G, III.4.H respectively - below:

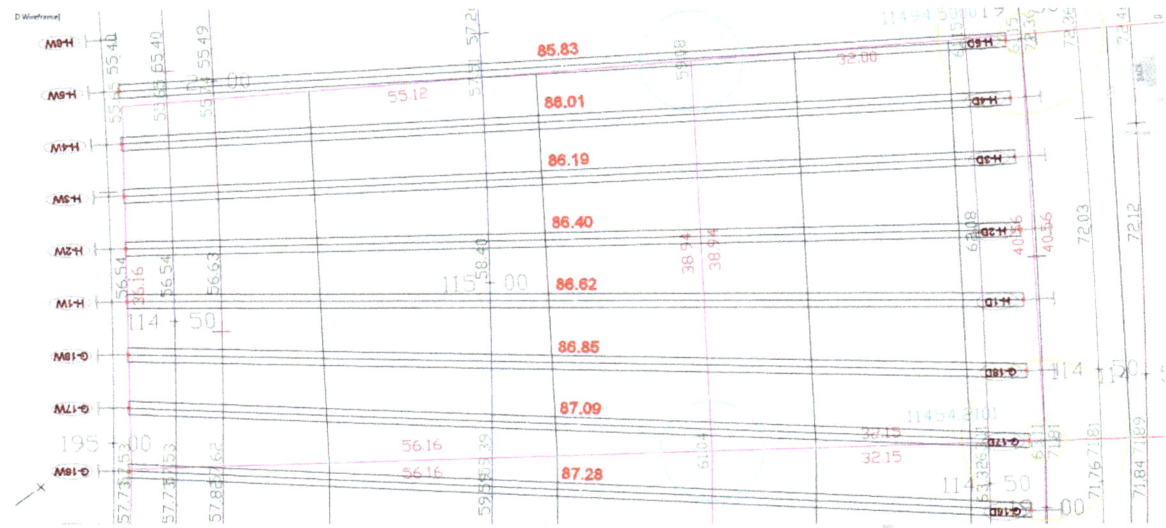

Figure III.4.F – Roof Girders Segment Plan View.

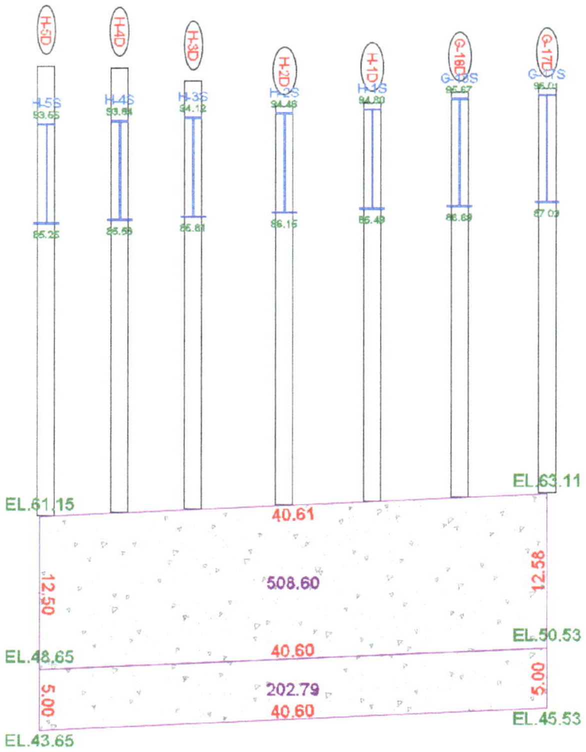

Figure III.4.G – Roof Girders Segment Wall "D" - Elevation View - (Looking East).

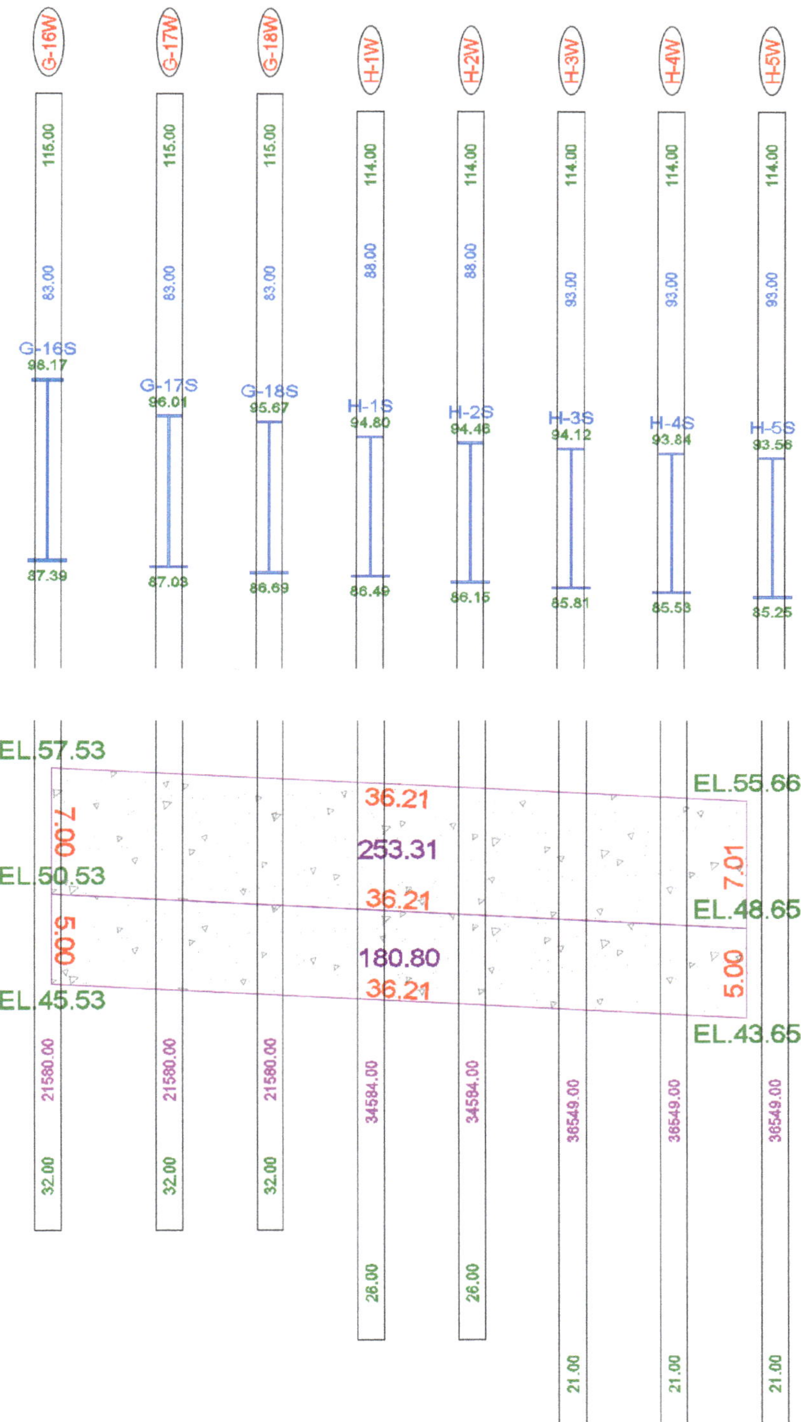

Figure III.4.H – Roof Girders Segment West Slurry Wall - Elevation View - (Looking West).

Next, modifying the "Dressed Up" Tunnel X-Section from Figure III.3.L by adding Section View of West Slurry Wall Pile G-5W, Cast-in-Place Wall "D" Column G-5D, and Roof Girder G-5S:

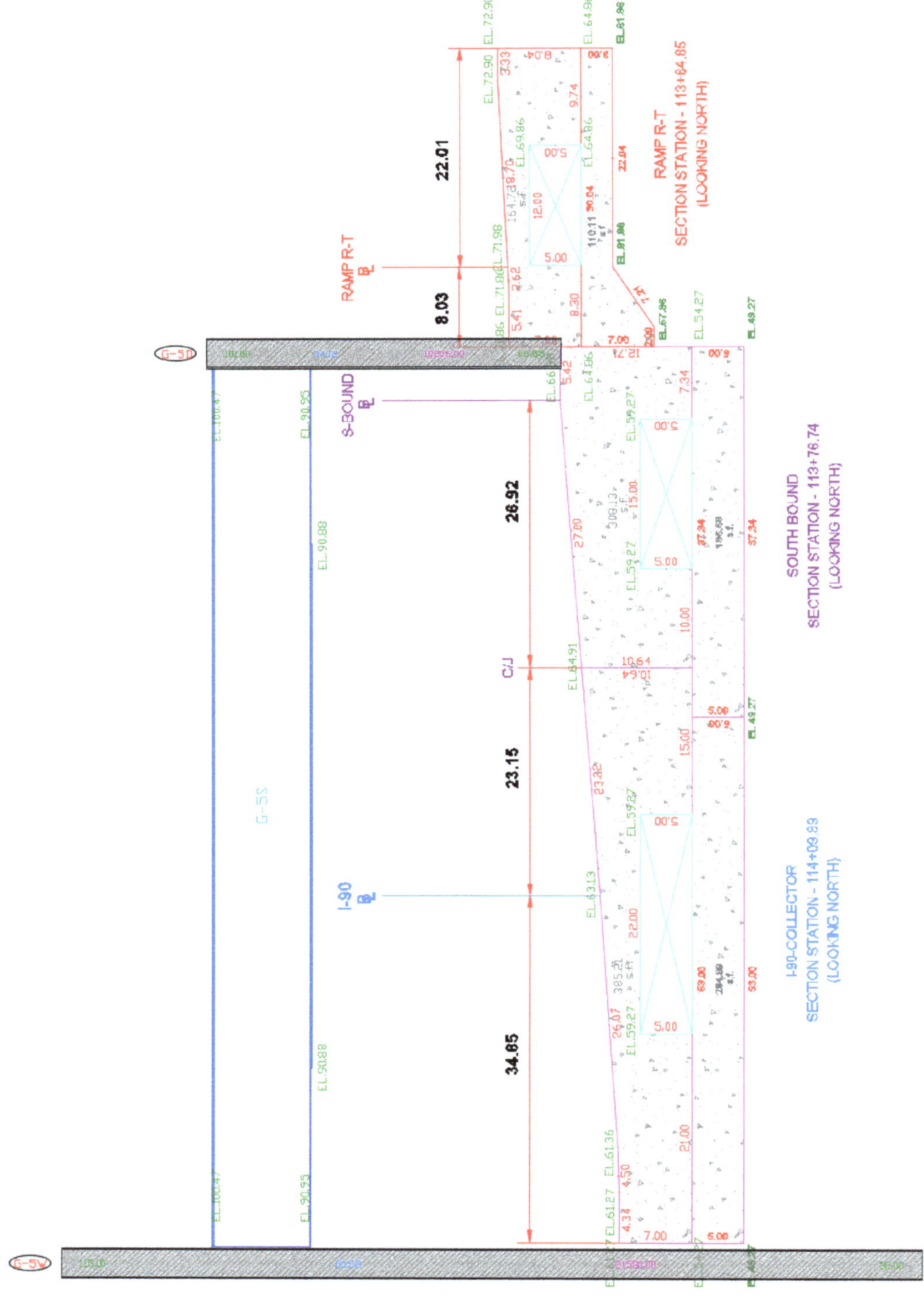

Figure III.4.J. Modified Tunnel X-Section with added Pile, Column and Roof Girder Sections.

Figure III.4.K demonstrates the Tunnel Segment 3D Model with the corresponding Chart of Roof Girders' End Point Coordinates and Takeoff Calculations for the Length and Weight.

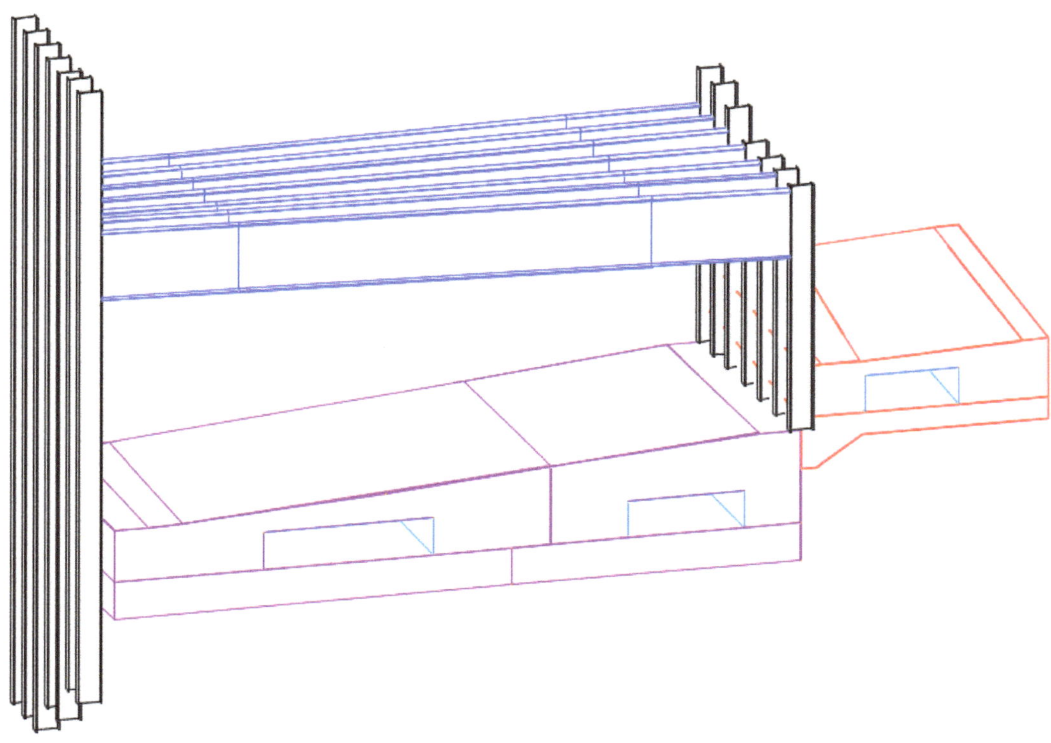

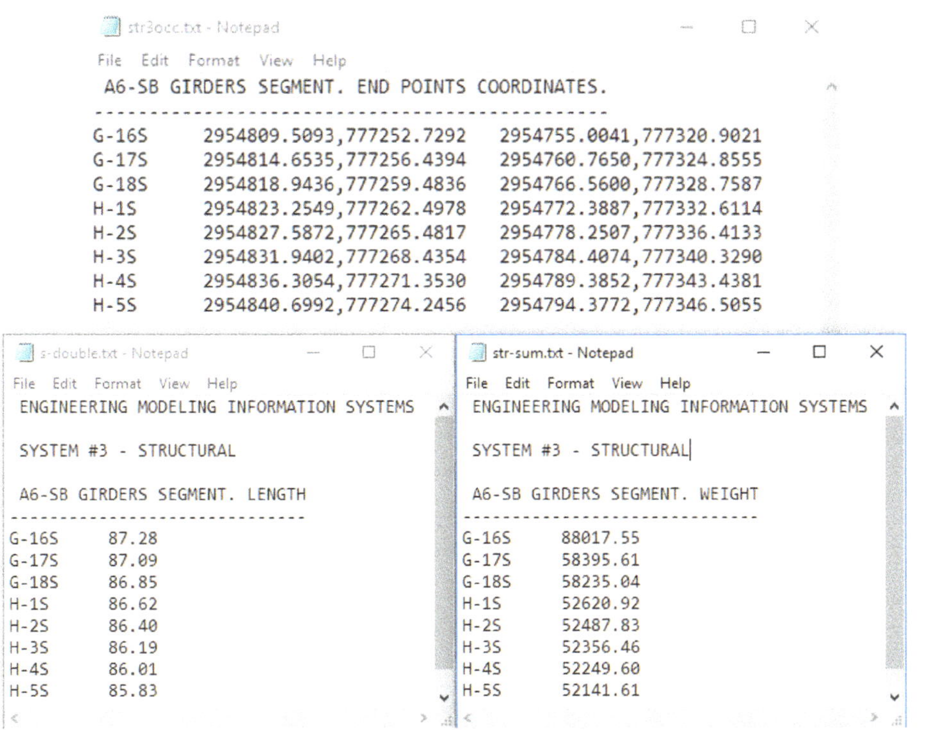

str3occ.txt - Notepad

File Edit Format View Help

```
A6-SB GIRDERS SEGMENT. END POINTS COORDINATES.
-----------------------------------------------------
G-16S     2954809.5093,777252.7292   2954755.0041,777320.9021
G-17S     2954814.6535,777256.4394   2954760.7650,777324.8555
G-18S     2954818.9436,777259.4836   2954766.5600,777328.7587
H-1S      2954823.2549,777262.4978   2954772.3887,777332.6114
H-2S      2954827.5872,777265.4817   2954778.2507,777336.4133
H-3S      2954831.9402,777268.4354   2954784.4074,777340.3290
H-4S      2954836.3054,777271.3530   2954789.3852,777343.4381
H-5S      2954840.6992,777274.2456   2954794.3772,777346.5055
```

s-double.txt - Notepad

File Edit Format View Help

```
ENGINEERING MODELING INFORMATION SYSTEMS

SYSTEM #3 - STRUCTURAL

A6-SB GIRDERS SEGMENT. LENGTH
------------------------------
G-16S     87.28
G-17S     87.09
G-18S     86.85
H-1S      86.62
H-2S      86.40
H-3S      86.19
H-4S      86.01
H-5S      85.83
```

str-sum.txt - Notepad

File Edit Format View Help

```
ENGINEERING MODELING INFORMATION SYSTEMS

SYSTEM #3 - STRUCTURAL

A6-SB GIRDERS SEGMENT. WEIGHT
------------------------------
G-16S     88017.55
G-17S     58395.61
G-18S     58235.04
H-1S      52620.92
H-2S      52487.83
H-3S      52356.46
H-4S      52249.60
H-5S      52141.61
```

III.5. Curved Shape Structures.

Figure III.5.A. below shows a Partial Model of Ventilation Building for North & South Bound of Central Artery Tunnel.

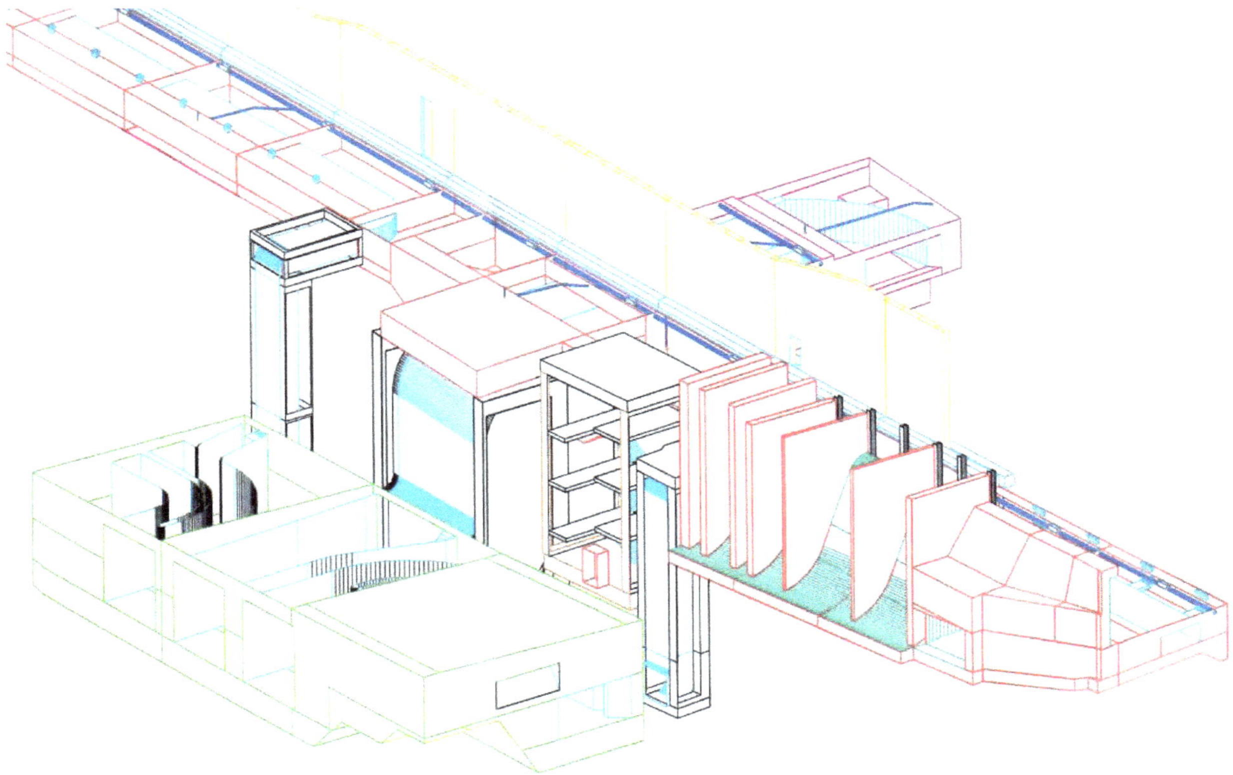

As it can be seen from Figure III.5.A, the Ventilation Building Structure has numerous horizontal and vertical connection ducts containing curved segments. To model 3D structure with Curved Shapes accurately, it has to be evaluated as a justified number of chord segments.

Figure III.5.B below illustrates the setting up and justifying the size of chord segment for the required Horizontal and Vertical Curved Structures.

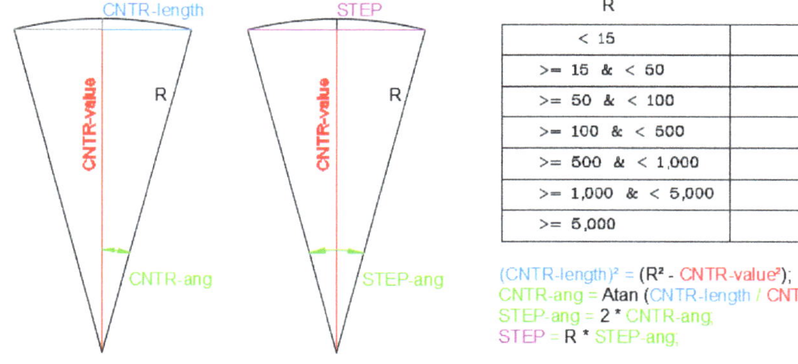

R	CNTR-value
< 15	0.9998
>= 15 & < 50	0.9999
>= 50 & < 100	0.99995
>= 100 & < 500	0.999995
>= 500 & < 1,000	0.9999984
>= 1,000 & < 5,000	0.99999988
>= 5,000	0.9999999

(CNTR-length)² = (R² - CNTR-value²);
CNTR-ang = Atan (CNTR-length / CNTR-value);
STEP-ang = 2 * CNTR-ang;
STEP = R * STEP-ang;

Horizontal Curve Structure.

The Block-Scheme for the required number of Chord Segments and Vertices' Coordinates Calculation Program is based on Curve Segment Definition [Paragraph 1.2.2] - Figure III.5.C:

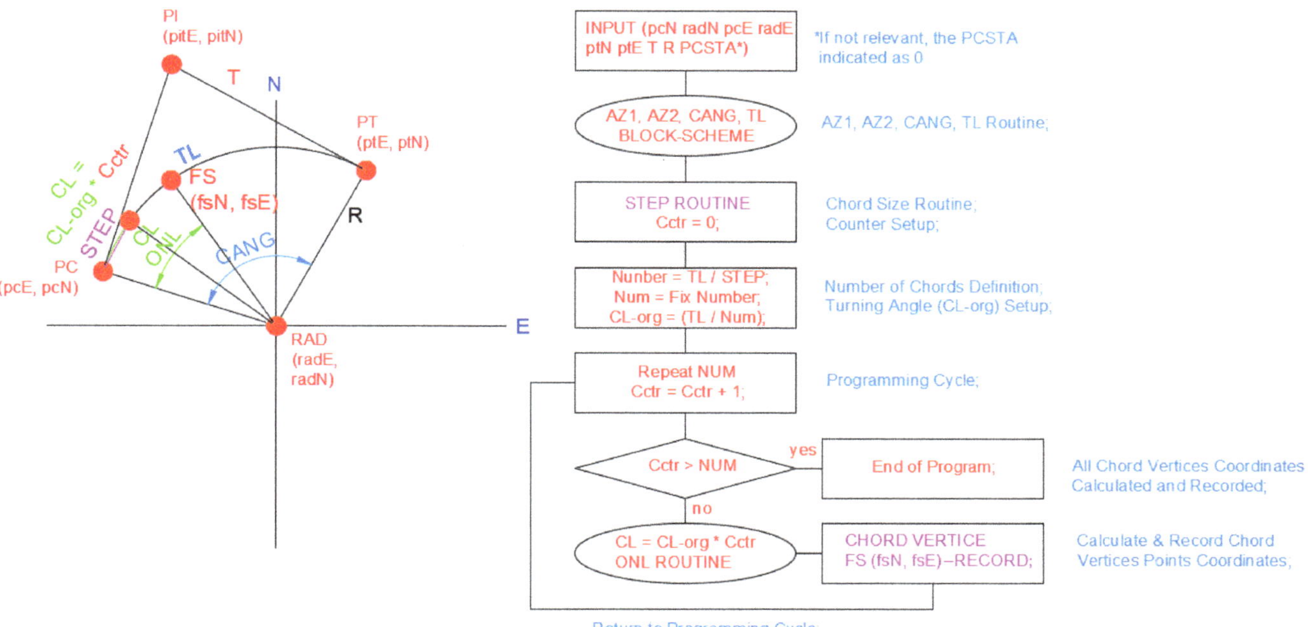

Vertical Curve Structure.

The Block-Scheme for the required number of Chord Segments and Vertices' Coordinates Calculation Program is shown in Figure III.5.D

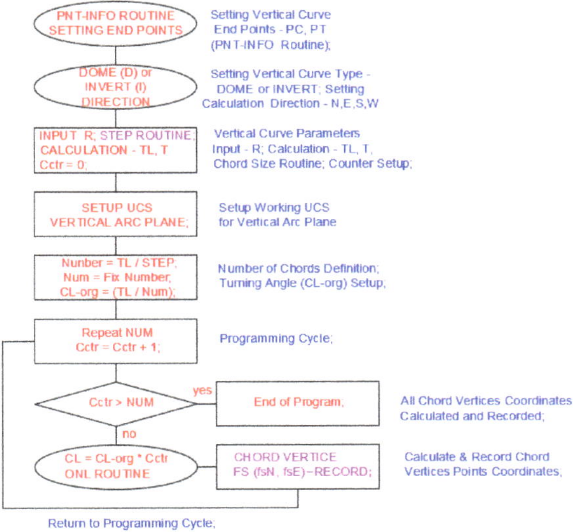

The types of Vertical Curves (Dome, Invert) and Chord Vertices' Coordinates Files are shown in Figures III.5.E and III.5.F below.

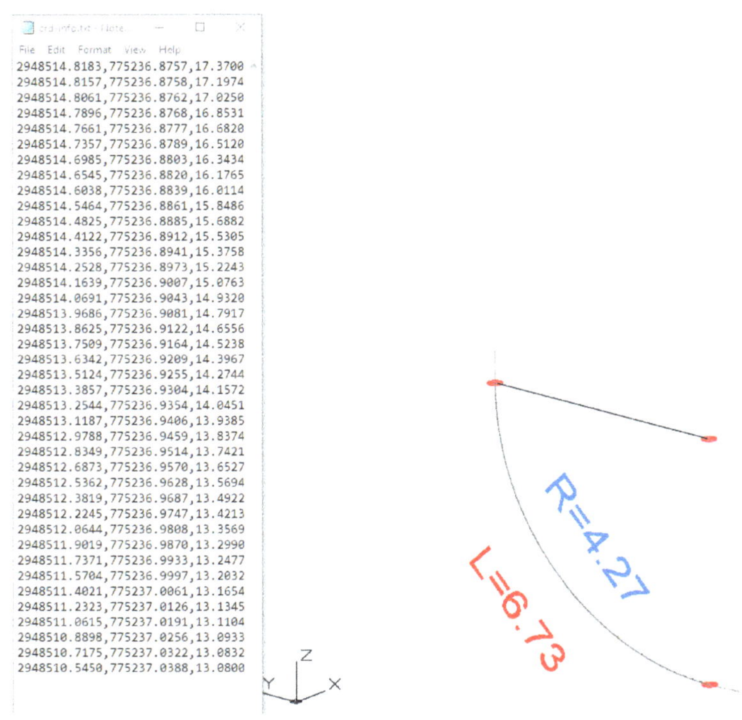

Figure III.5.E – Vertical Curve - Invert.

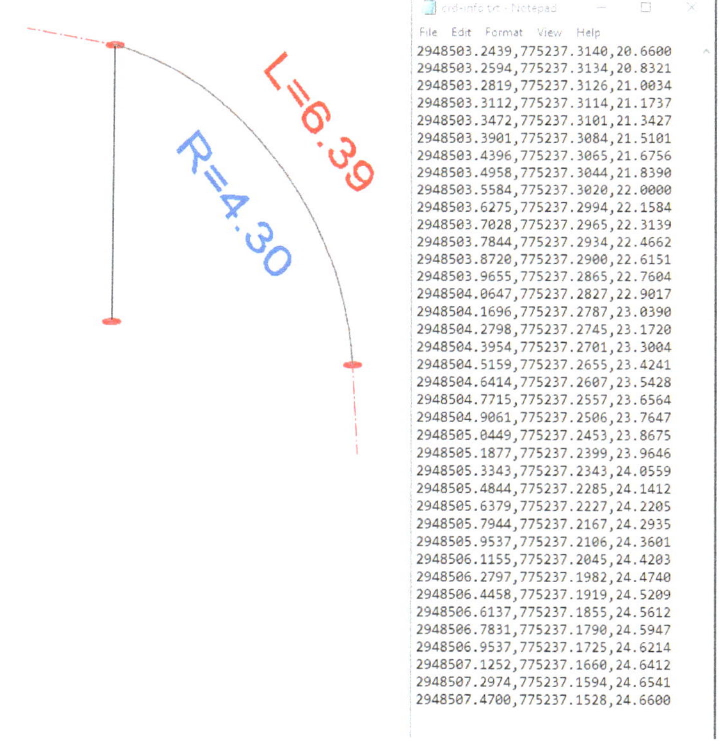

Figure III.5.F – Vertical Curve – Dome.

Note the Direction of Calculation of Vertices' Coordinates.
Invert Option - Coordinates - Northing Decrease, Easting Increase, Elevation Decrease.
Dom Option - Coordinates – Northing Increase, Easting Decrease, Elevation Increase.

Direction notification setup is important to keep consistency between curved surface edges while creating the Modeling Input File – see Block-Scheme on Figure III.5.D above.

An Example of Vertical Curve Structure – Modeling of Existing Aquarium Station Vestibule before Renovation – 2003 is shown below in Figure III.5.G:

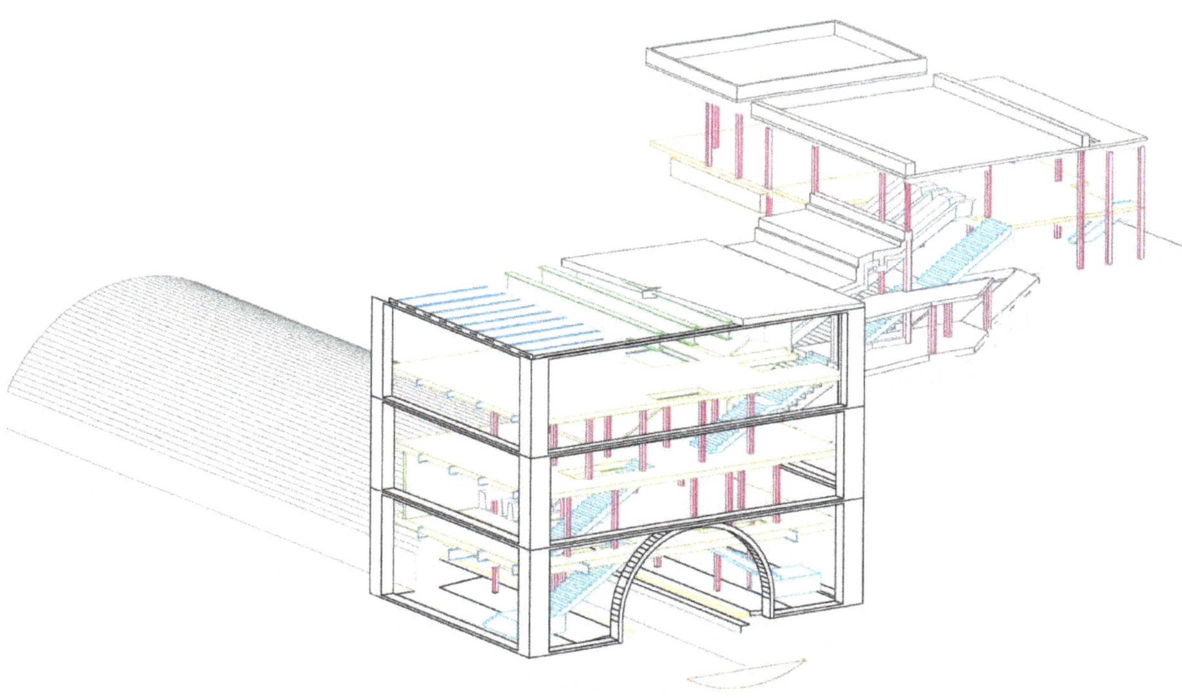

Figure III.5.G.

Inclined Curve Structures.

Figures III.5.H and III.5.J below show Paint Booth and Train Wash System Models for Cabot Yard Improvements Project. Both include Inclined Curved Structures. The corresponding programming Block-Scheme is shown in the following Figure III.5.K.

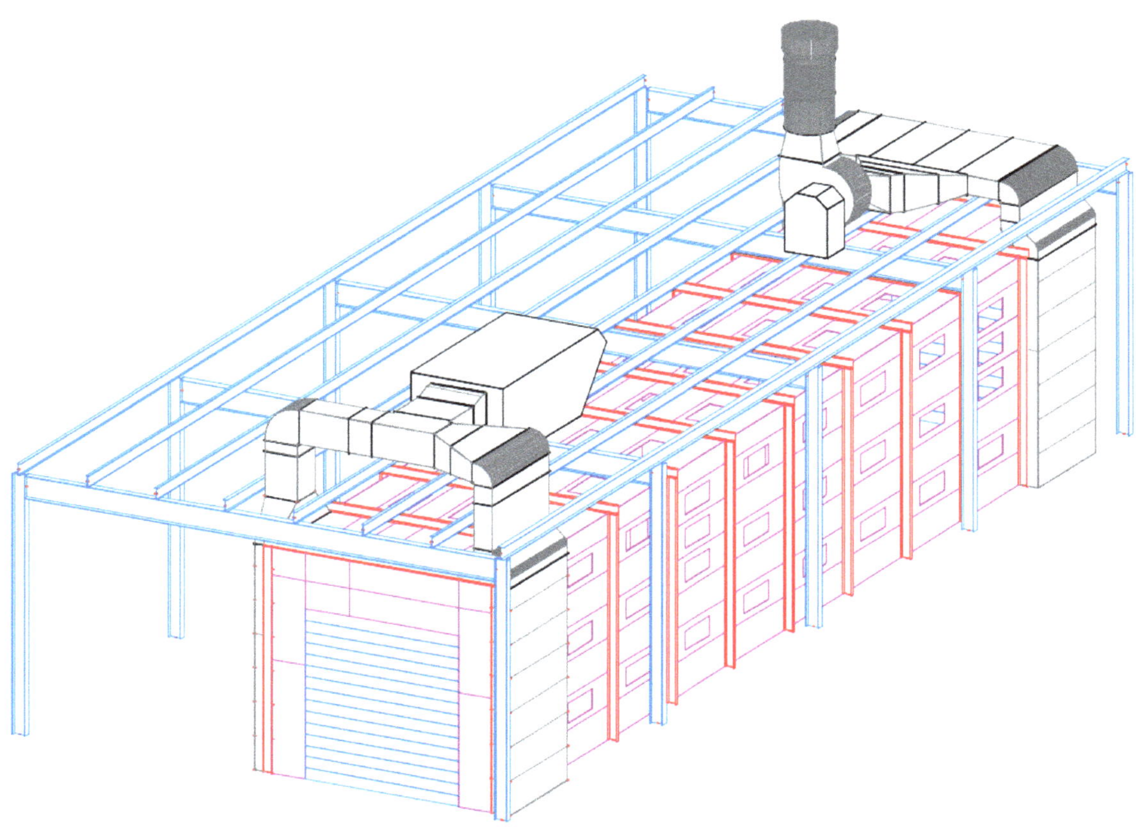

Figure III.5.H – Paint Booth Model.

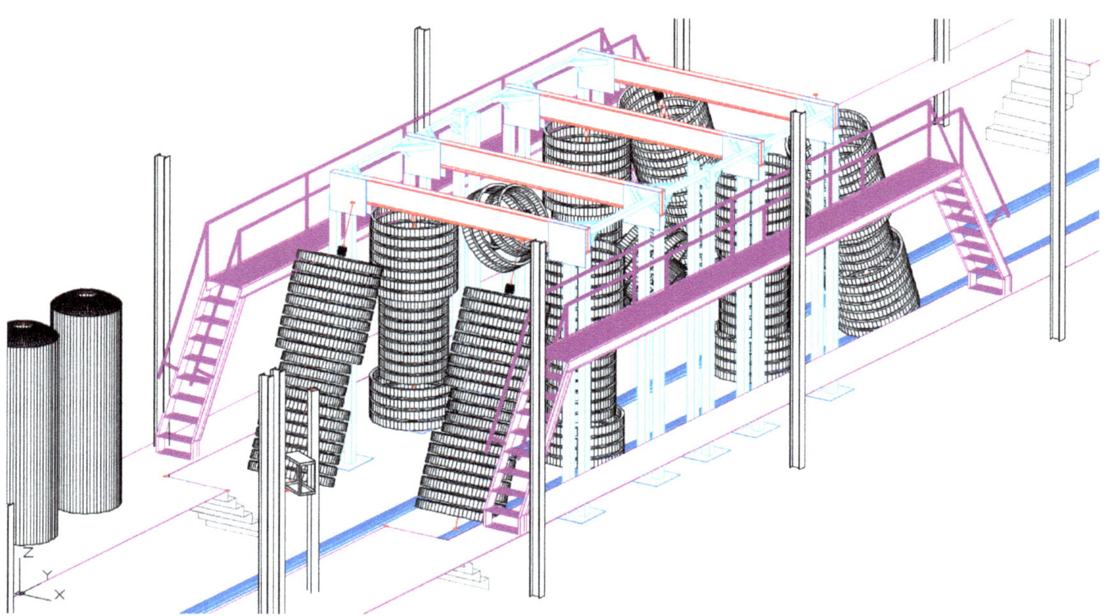

Figure III.5.J – Train Wash System Model.

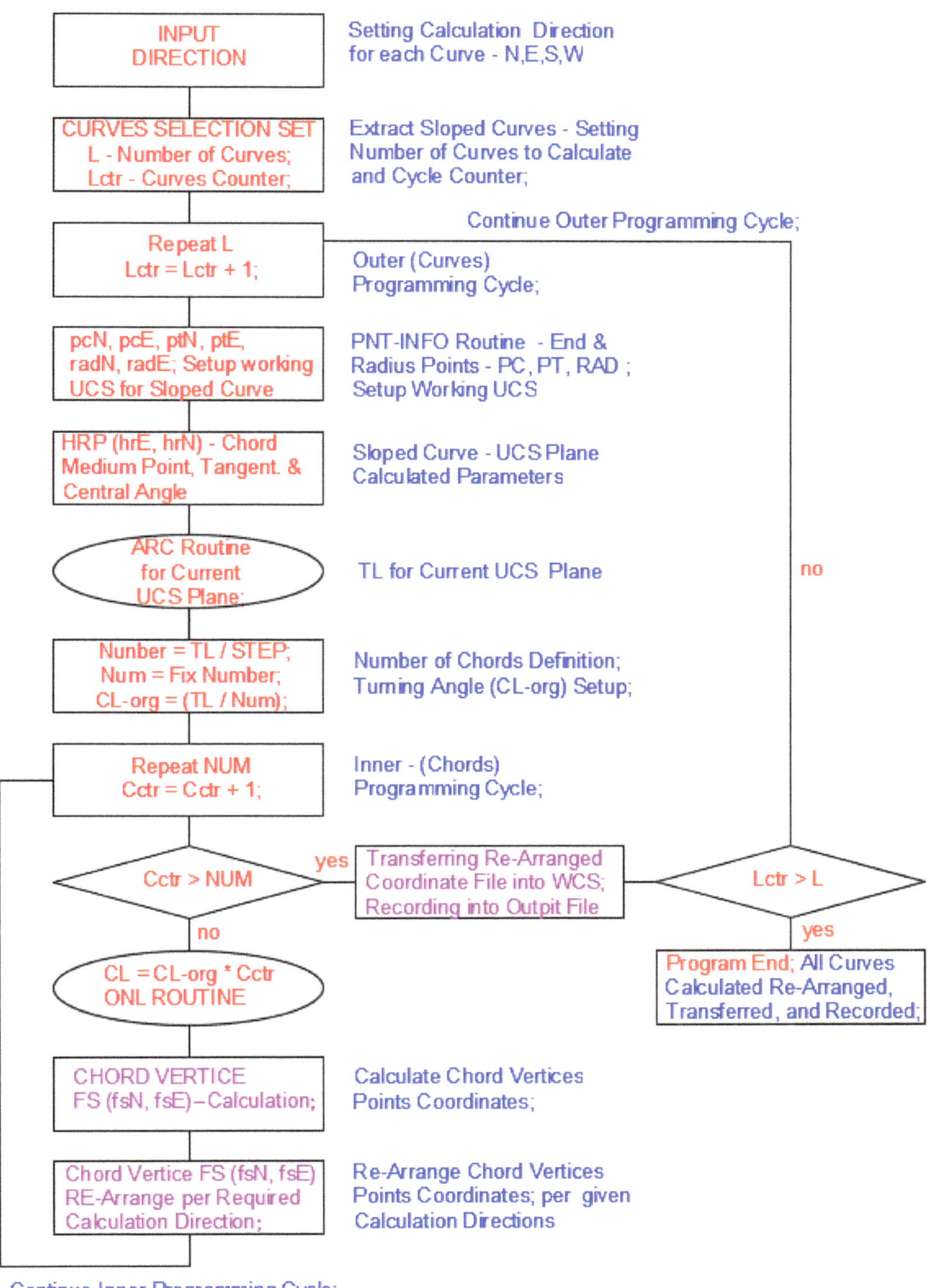

Figure III.5.K. Inclined Curved Model Block-Scheme.

The practical example of Inclined Curved Structure calculations - step by step - is shown below for Traction Power Duct Bank on Figure III.5.L.

Figure III.5.L. Step-by-Step Inclined Curve Calculation

```
swth-inf.txt - Notepad
File  Edit  Format  View  Help
Enter the Required Directions of Chord Points into This File!
```

```
swth-in...
File  Edit  Format  View  Help
N
N
```

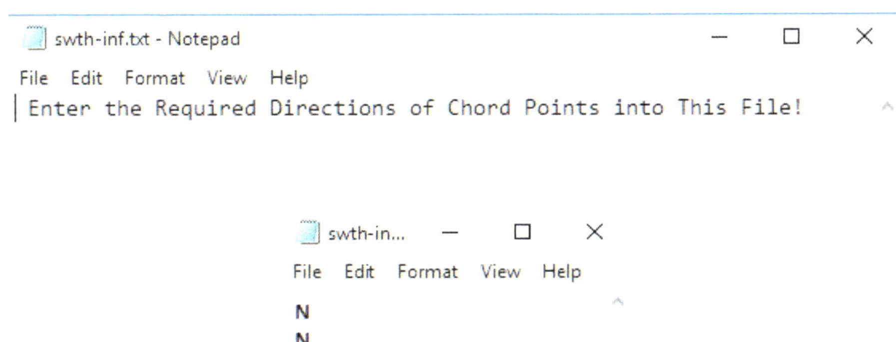

Both Curves Calculated in North Direction.

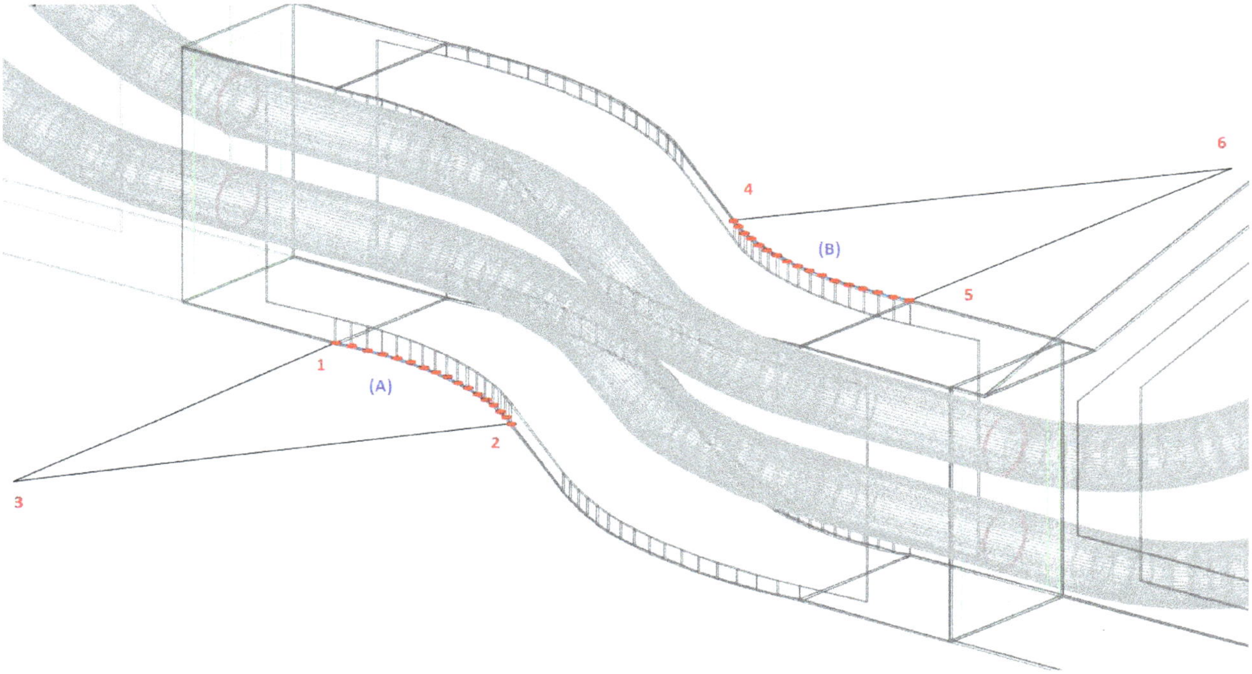

```
pnt-info.txt - Note...
File  Edit  Format  View  Help
2948685.3221,775256.3905,6.63 (1)
2948687.4472,775257.0912,6.53 (2)
2948687.3960,775253.6576,6.47 (3)
2948683.3282,775256.3307,8.60 (4)
2948681.1973,775255.6307,8.71 (5)
2948681.2532,775259.0619,8.71 (6)
```

End and Radius Points of Curves
(Note – all the points are on different elevations – confirming sloped position)

Calculation results – both curves have 17 chord points increasing in North Direction - see chart below. The modeled Traction Power Ductbank is shown in the following Figure III.5.M.

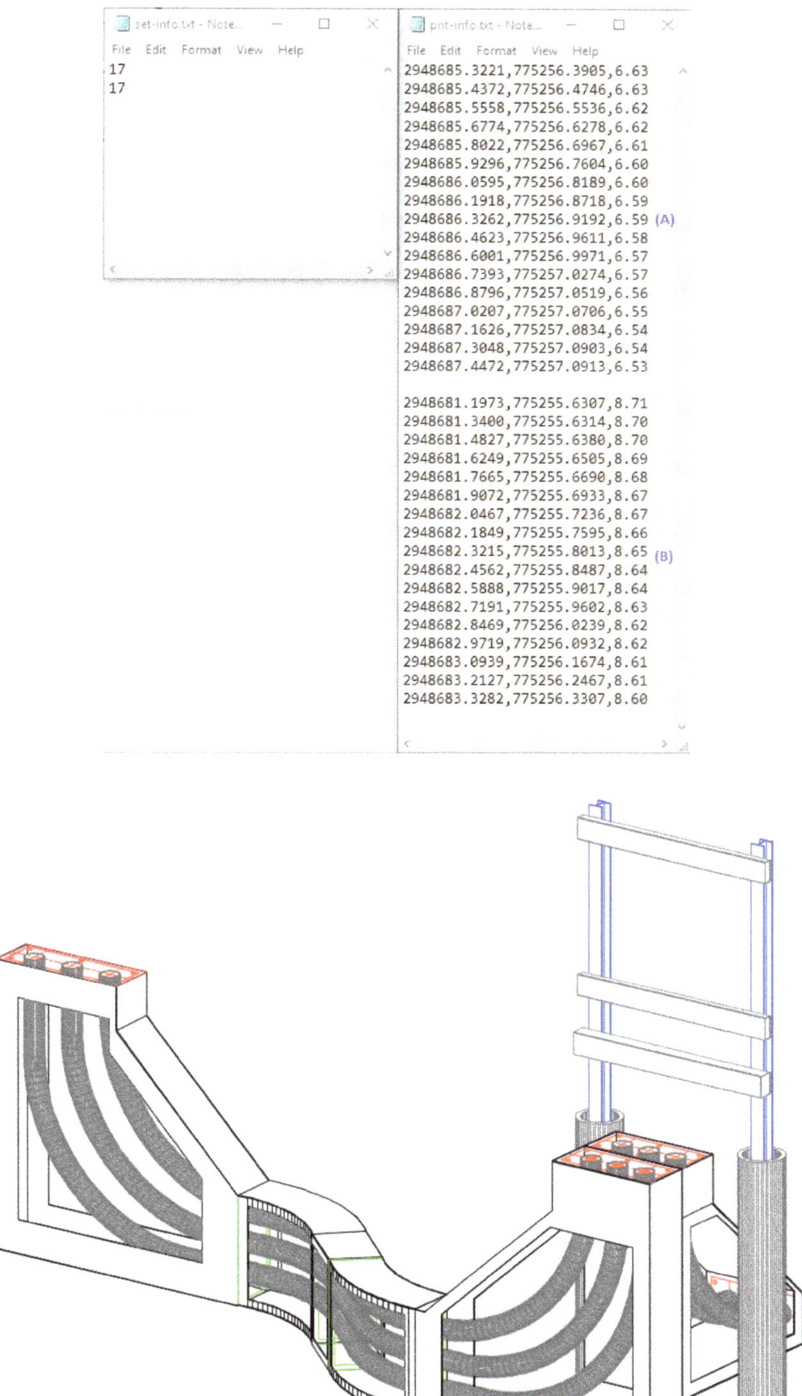

Figure III.5.M. The modeled Traction Power Ductbank.

CHAPTER IV: UTILITIES

IV.1. CONFLICT ANALYSIS.

Studying utility as-built records from the previous work at the construction site is a key element for accurate utilities placement per project design requirements. However, available as-built construction records are not always providing clear and complete information of existing utilities location on site. One of these modeling tools' goals is the ability to show graphically (either plan, profile, section, or 3D view) – the exact shape, location, and grade of existing utility line to analyze potential conflict with proposed utilities and foundations.

The Attached Figures IV.1.A. & IV.1.B illustrate existing utility–proposed track power duct bank conflicts. The second one also suggests potential Duct Bank modification with coordinates of the beginning of the revised Duct Bank segment.

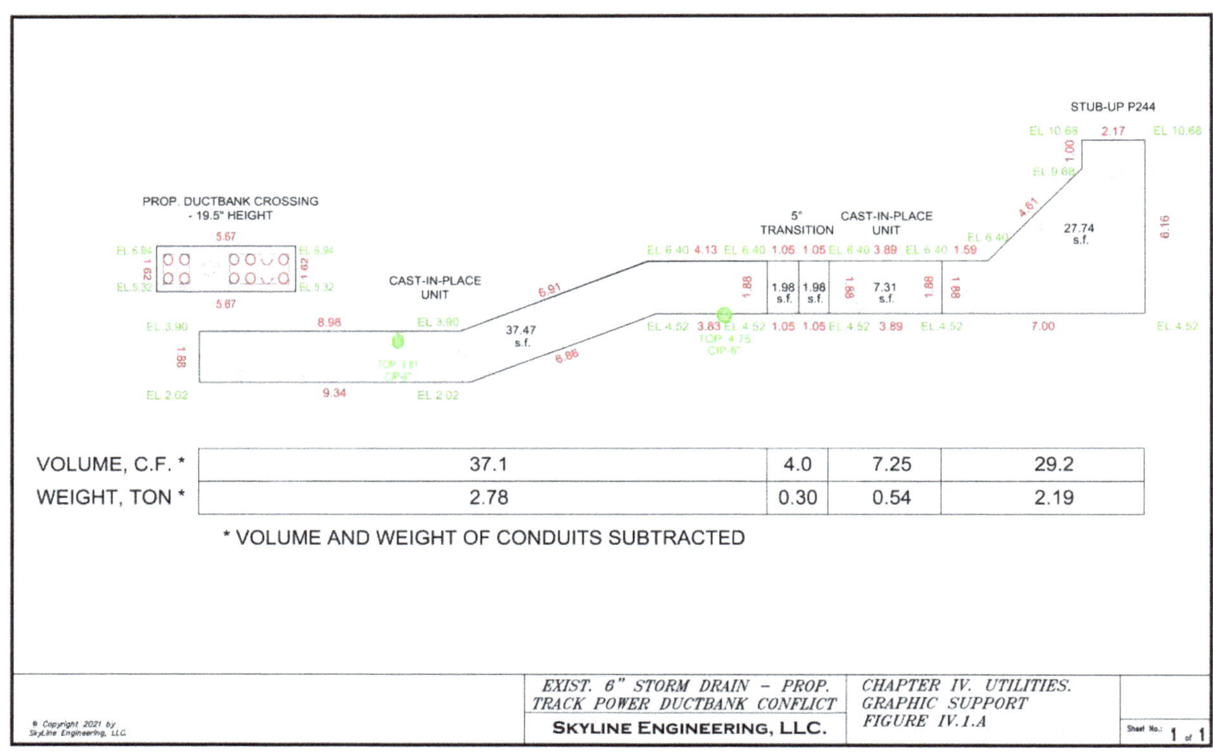

VOLUME, C.F. *	37.1	4.0	7.25	29.2
WEIGHT, TON *	2.78	0.30	0.54	2.19

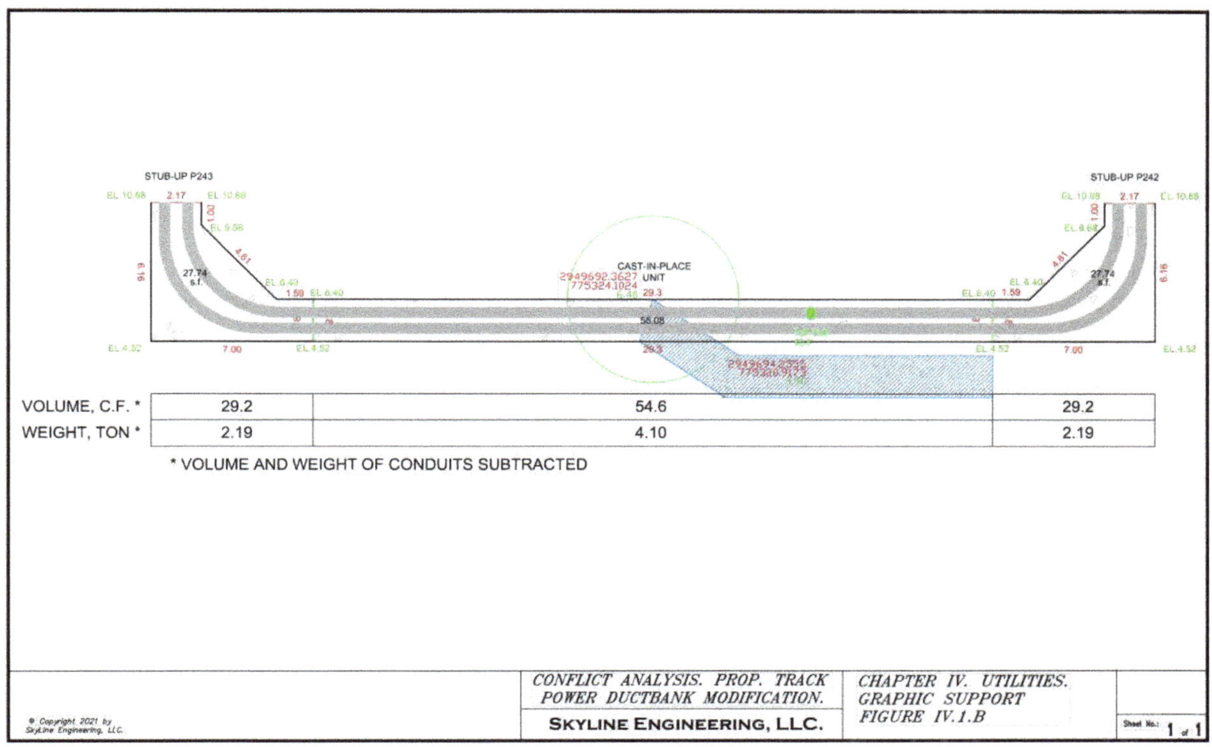

IV.2. CROSS-SECTION ANALYSIS – DESIGN CONSIDERATIONS

The cross-sections provided below reflect Substation Building and Power Track Duct Banks design modification considering adjacent utilities location. The attached Figures IV.2.A & IV.2.B show Substation Building Cross-Sections along Grid Lines A & B.

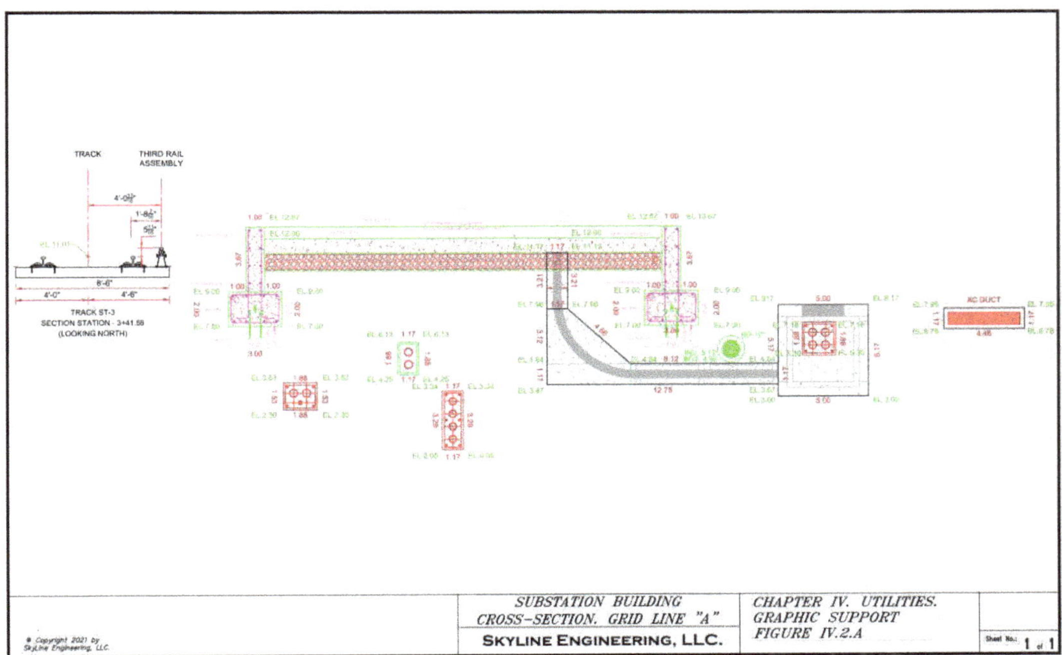

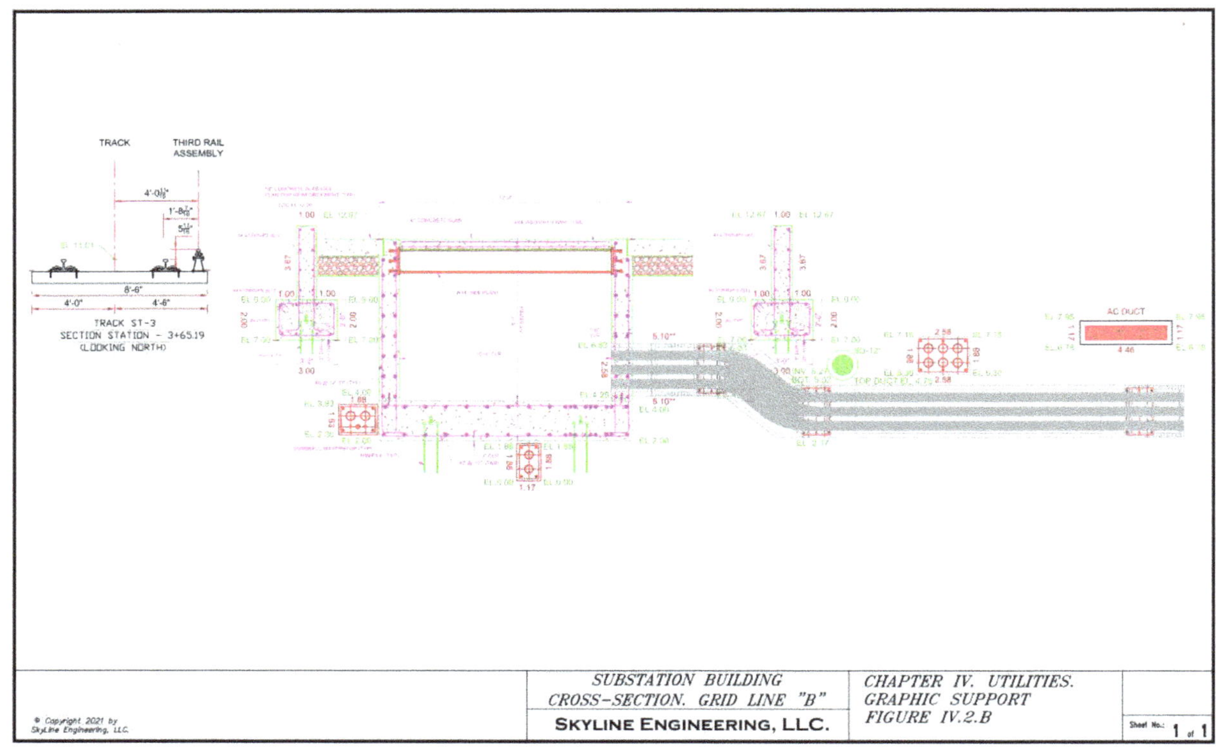

The Substation Building Foundation and Utilities 3D Modeling overview are shown in Figure IV.2.C:

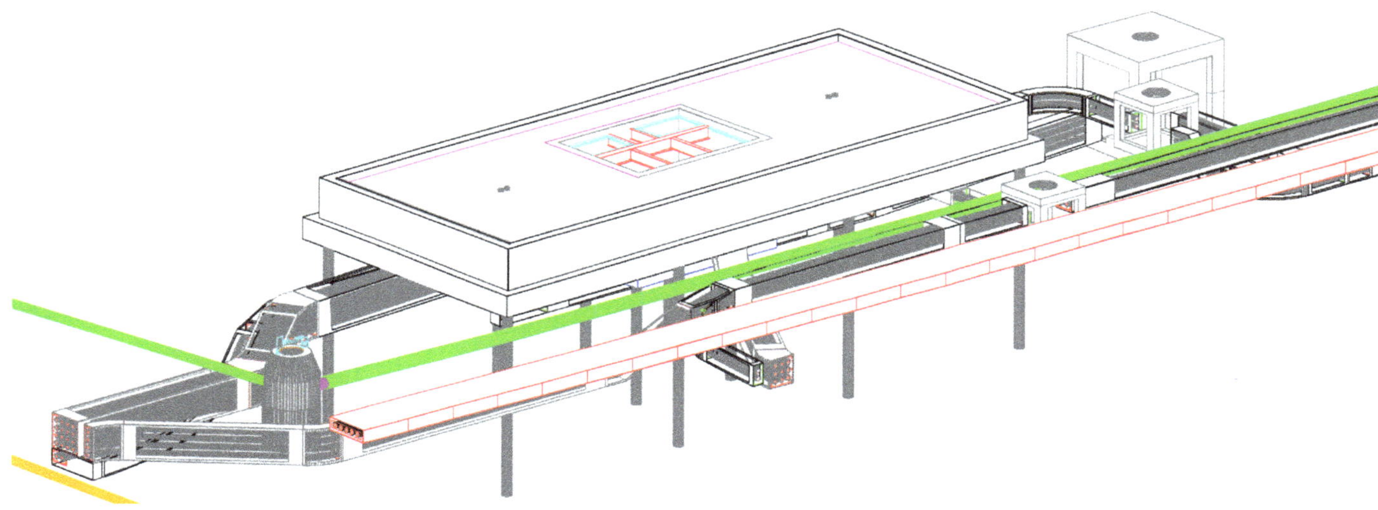

The Proposed Duct Bank to Switch House #1 has a few surrounding Structures and Utilities. The Figures IV.2.D, IV.2.E, and the Attached Figure IV.2.F illustrate the X-Sections of this Duct Bank with surrounding and connecting structures:

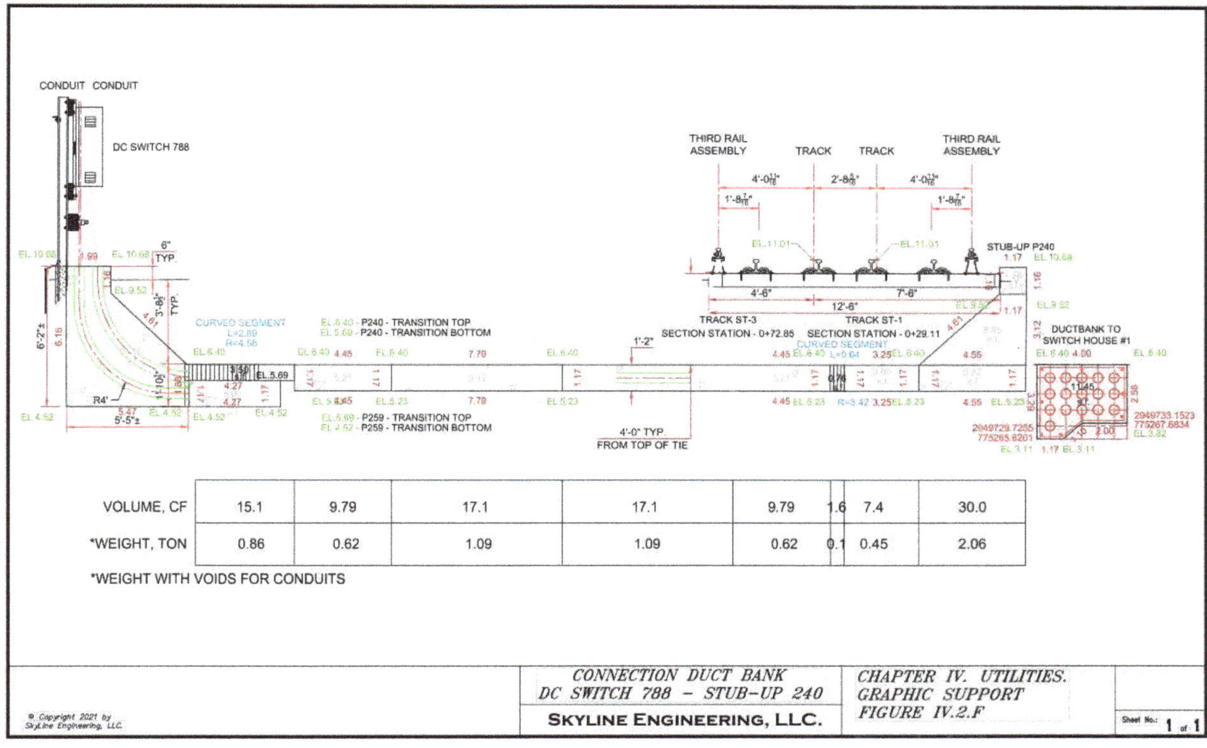

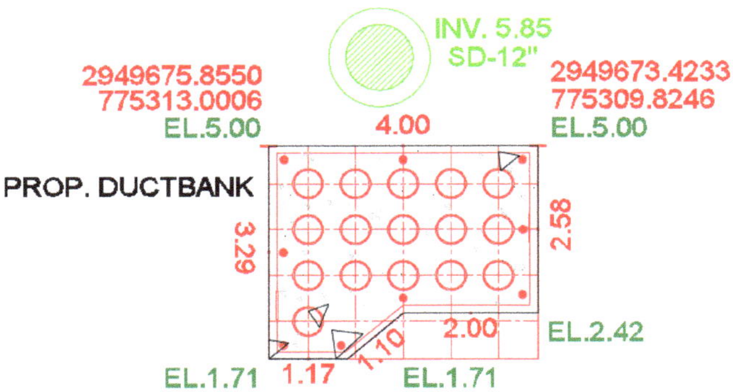

Figure IV.2.D. Duct Bank/12" Underdrain

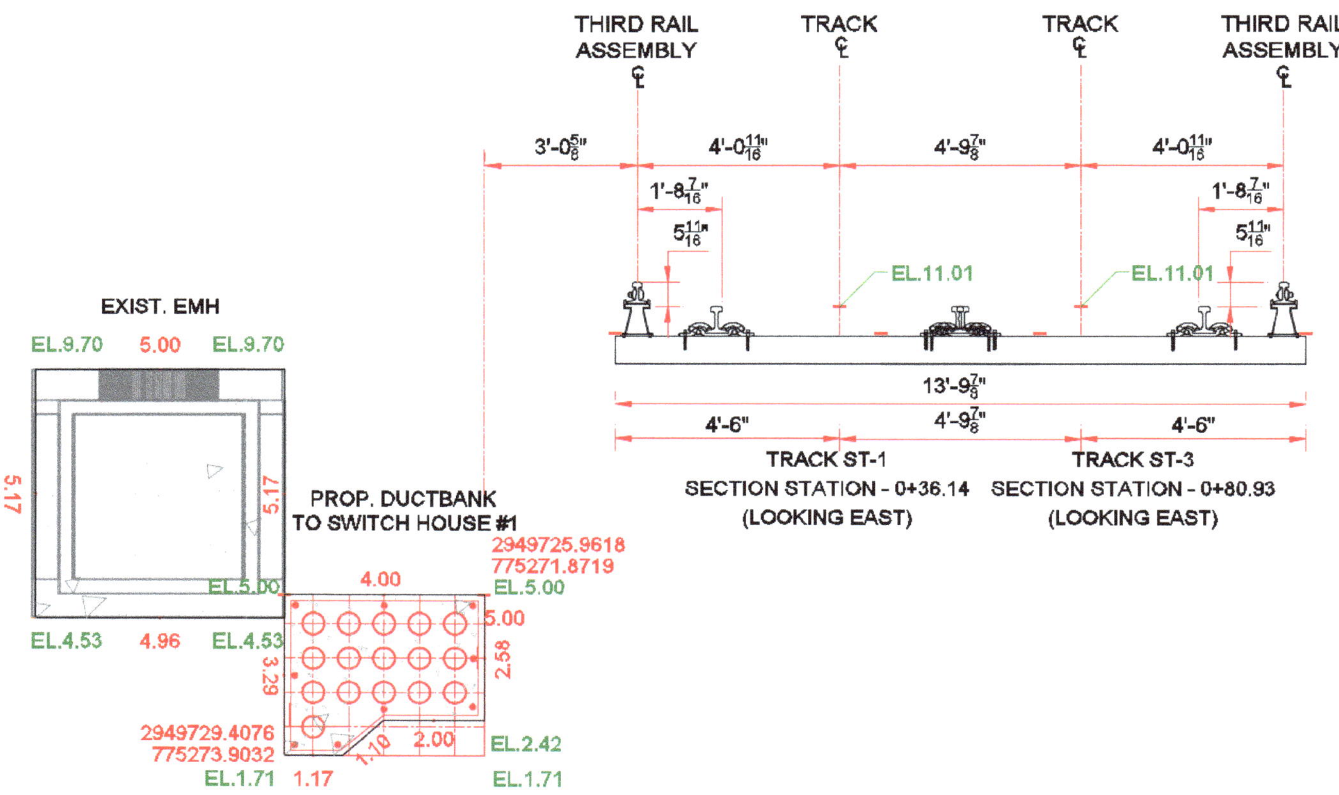

Figure IV.2.E. Existing Electric Manhole, adjacent to Proposed Ductbank

The attached Figure IV.2.F. demonstrates Connection Duct Bank from Disconnect Switch 788 to Stub-Up 240, adjacent to Proposed Ductbank to Switch House #1 – (See Disconnect Switch 788 Overall Plan – the Figure IV.3.B as a Map). Note that the blue color on the X-Section designates the Curved Segment of the Duct Bank, showing the Curve Length and Radius.

Attached Figure IV.2.G. shows Renovated Track, Proposed Negative Ductbank Return & Existing Steam Line.

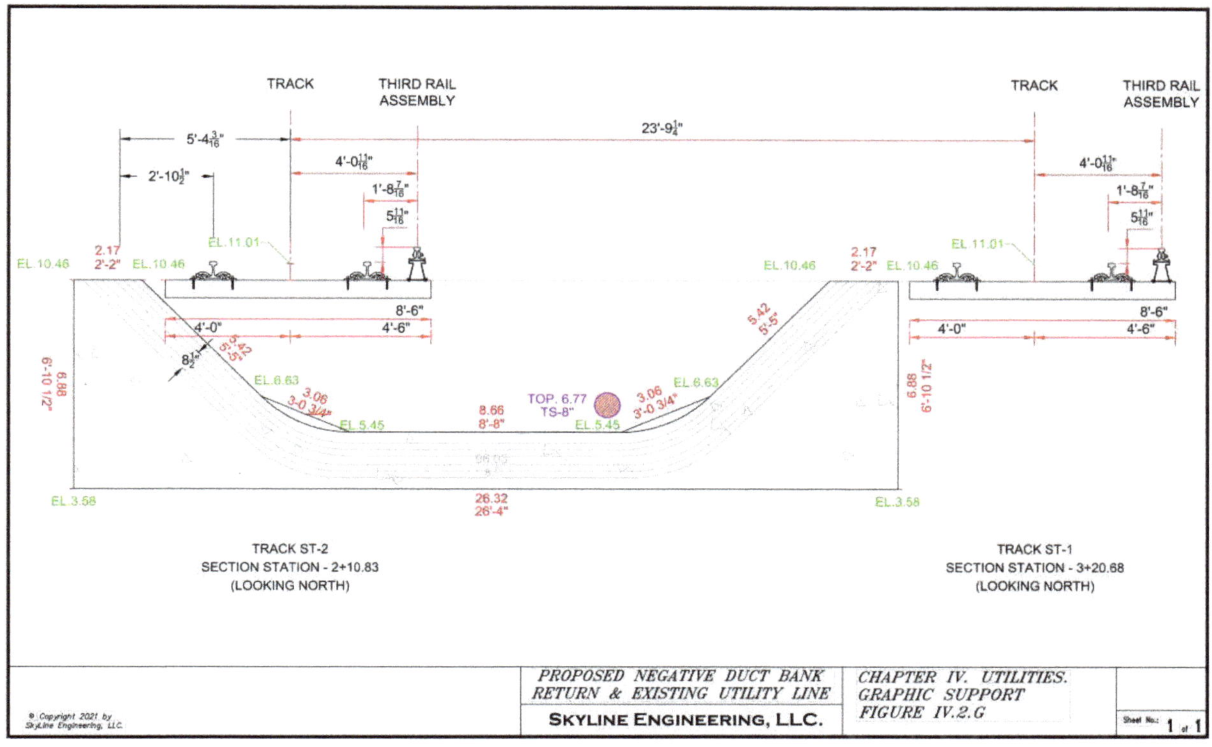

The Detailed Block-Scheme for Utility Cross-Section Analysis is shown below in the Figure IV.2.H.

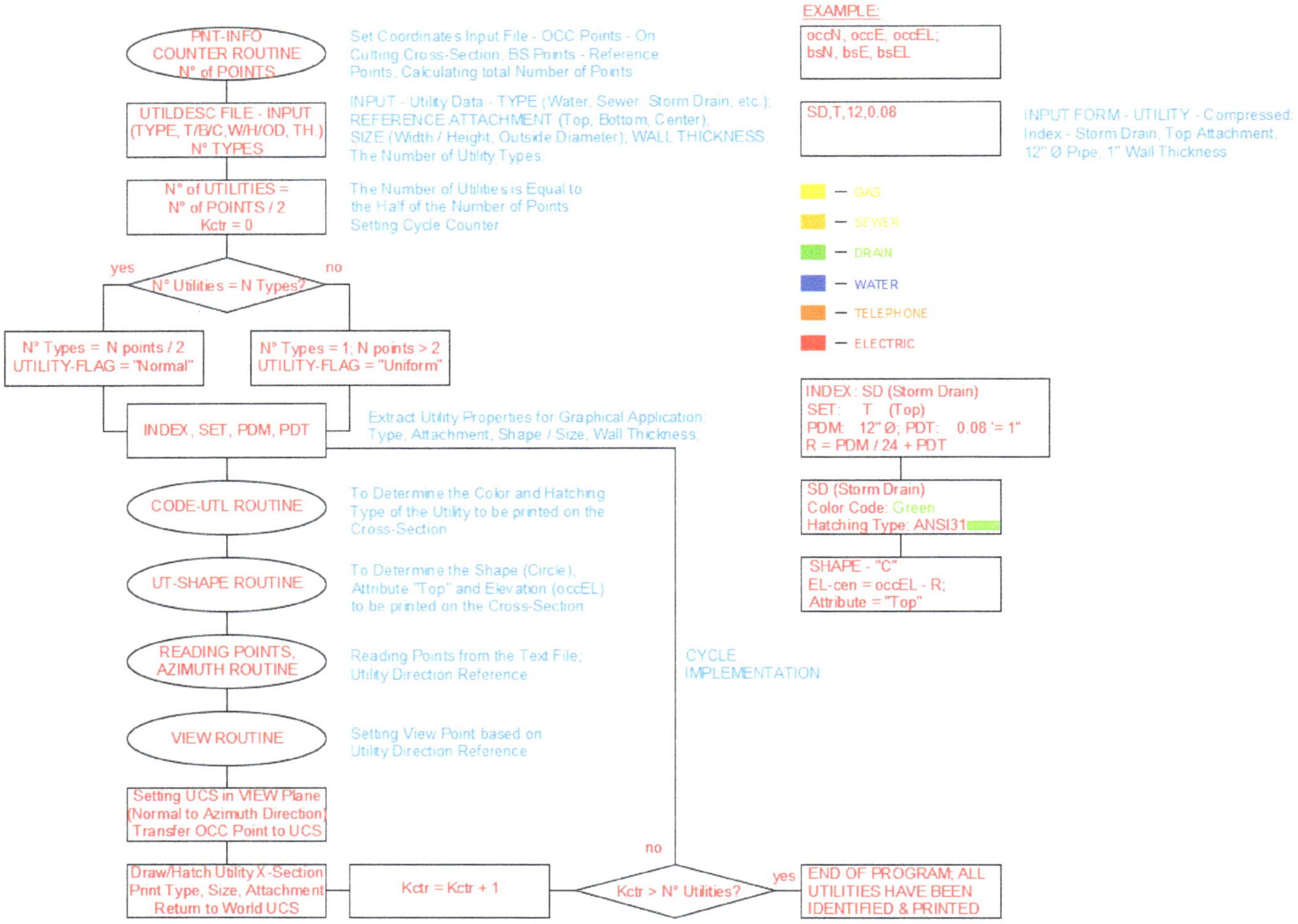

PNT-INFO COUNTER ROUTINE N° of POINTS
Set Coordinates Input File - OCC Points - On Cutting Cross-Section, BS Points - Reference Points, Calculating total Number of Points
UTILDESC FILE - INPUT (TYPE, T/B/C,W/H/OD, TH.) N° TYPES
INPUT - Utility Data - TYPE (Water, Sewer, Storm Drain, etc.); REFERENCE ATTACHMENT (Top, Bottom, Center); SIZE (Width / Height, Outside Diameter), WALL THICKNESS. The Number of Utility Types
N° of UTILITIES = N° of POINTS / 2 Kctr = 0
The Number of Utilities is Equal to the Half of the Number of Points Setting Cycle Counter
yes
no
N° Utilities = N Types?
N° Types = N points / 2 UTILITY-FLAG = "Normal"
N° Types = 1; N points > 2 UTILITY-FLAG = "Uniform"
INDEX, SET, PDM, PDT
Extract Utility Properties for Graphical Application: Type, Attachment, Shape / Size, Wall Thickness;
CODE-UTL ROUTINE
To Determine the Color and Hatching Type of the Utility to be printed on the Cross-Section
UT-SHAPE ROUTINE
To Determine the Shape (Circle), Attribute "Top" and Elevation (occEL) to be printed on the Cross-Section
READING POINTS, AZIMUTH ROUTINE
Reading Points from the Text File; Utility Direction Reference
VIEW ROUTINE
Setting View Point based on Utility Direction Reference
Setting UCS in VIEW Plane (Normal to Azimuth Direction) Transfer OCC Point to UCS
Draw/Hatch Utility X-Section Print Type, Size, Attachment Return to World UCS
Kctr = Kctr + 1
Kctr > N° Utilities?
no
yes
CYCLE IMPLEMENTATION
END OF PROGRAM; ALL UTILITIES HAVE BEEN IDENTIFIED & PRINTED
EXAMPLE:
occN, occE, occEL; bsN, bsE, bsEL
SD,T,12,0.08
INPUT FORM - UTILITY - Compressed: Index - Storm Drain, Top Attachment, 12" Ø Pipe, 1" Wall Thickness
— GAS
— SEWER
— DRAIN
— WATER
— TELEPHONE
— ELECTRIC
INDEX: SD (Storm Drain) SET: T (Top) PDM: 12" Ø; PDT: 0.08 '= 1" R = PDM / 24 + PDT
SD (Storm Drain) Color Code: Green Hatching Type: ANSI31
SHAPE - "C" EL-cen = occEL - R; Attribute = "Top"

The following Figure IV.2.J illustrates the Input Steps & the Result of X-Section Program Run

14649
east edge d_bank
14650
east edge d_bank
14653
"top cl 3" pvc cond"
14654
"top cl 3" pvc cond"
File Edit Format View Help
2947839.0570,775213.3480,23.23
2947837.0580,775213.4490,23.23

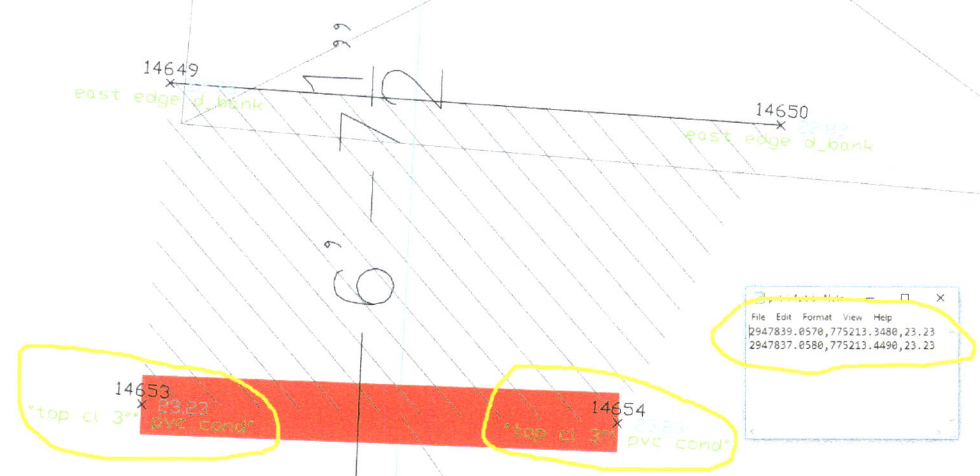

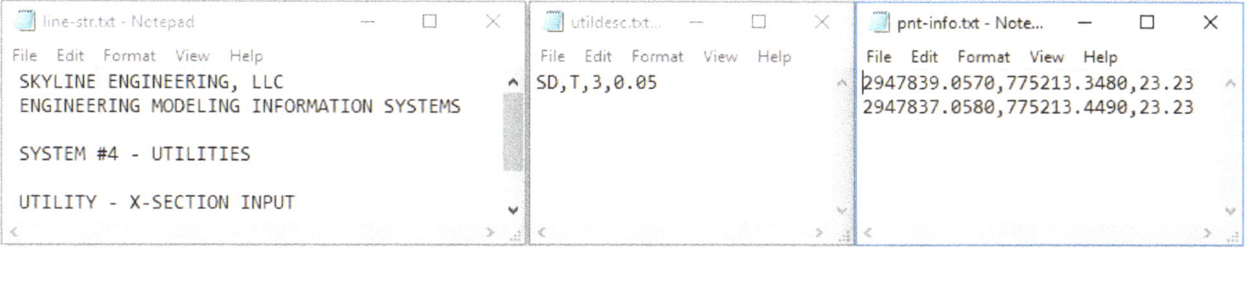

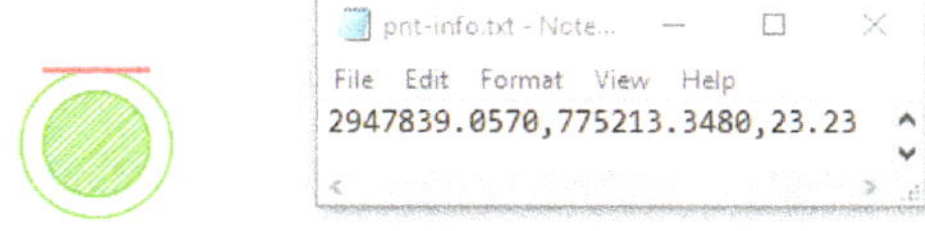

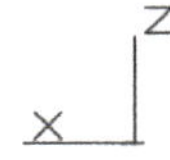

Note the UCS Icon in a "World" position, and the marked Top of the pipe X-section has exactly the same coordinates as the as-built point 14653 and an Occupation Point of the Input File PNT-INFO.

IV.3. MODELING APPROACH & OUTPUT PRESENTATION

The following chart - Figure IV.3.A - represents Utility Shapes used in programming, calculations, and modeling.

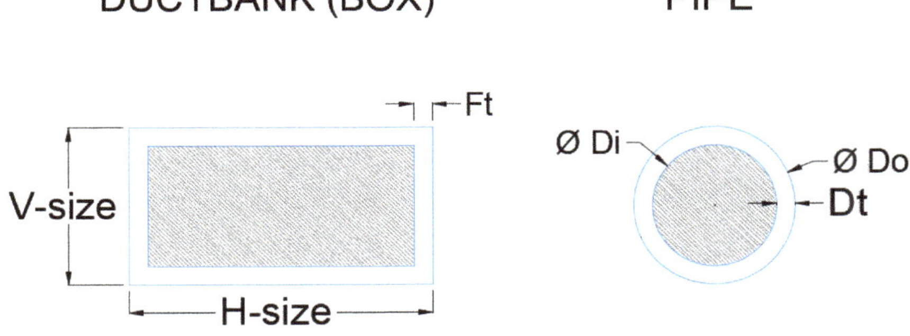

Figure IV.3.A. Utility Shapes.

The Modeling Approach includes Reference Plan, X-Sections, Elevations with Takeoffs, & a 3D Model.

This paragraph shows an example of modeling of the Cluster of Power Track Duct Banks, running from Disconnect Switch #788 – Figures IV.3.B. (Overall Plan) & IV.3.C (3D Model) below:

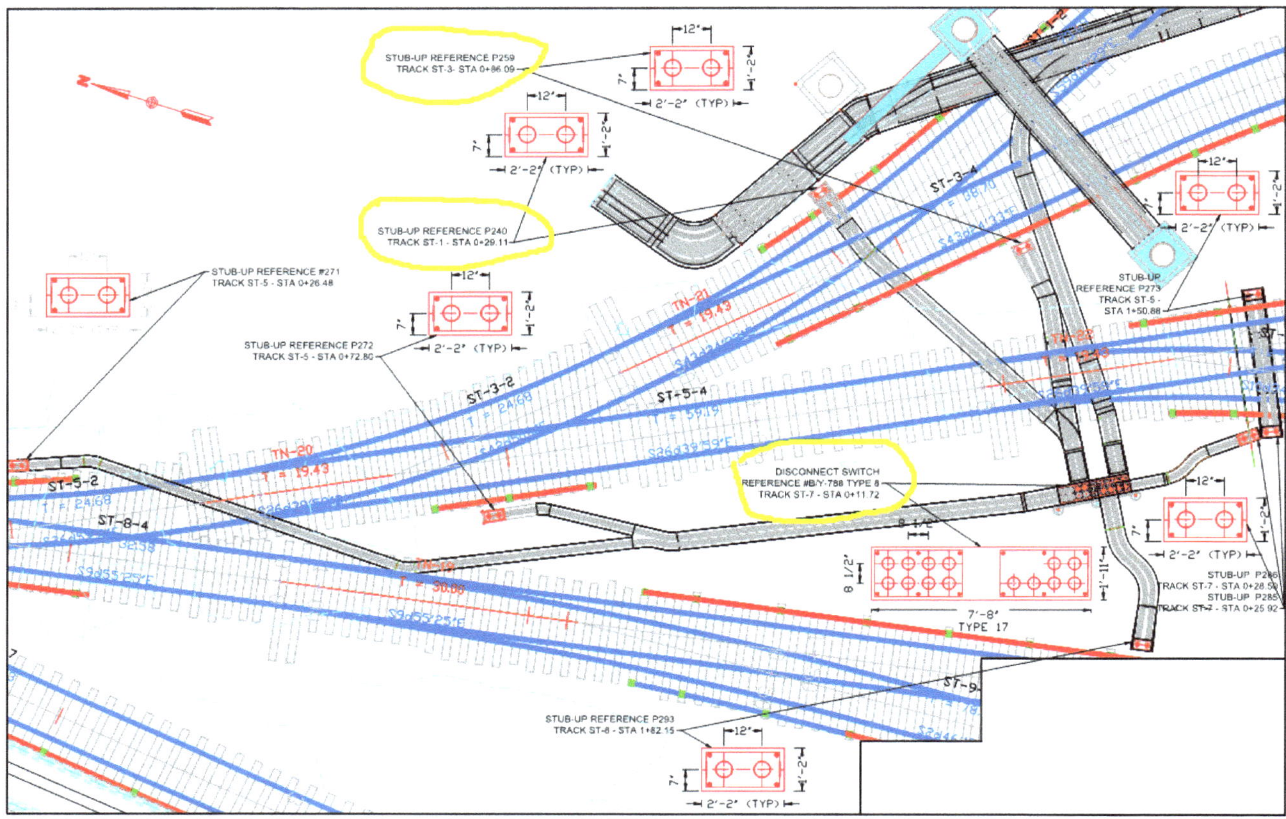

Figure IV.3.B – Overall Plan.

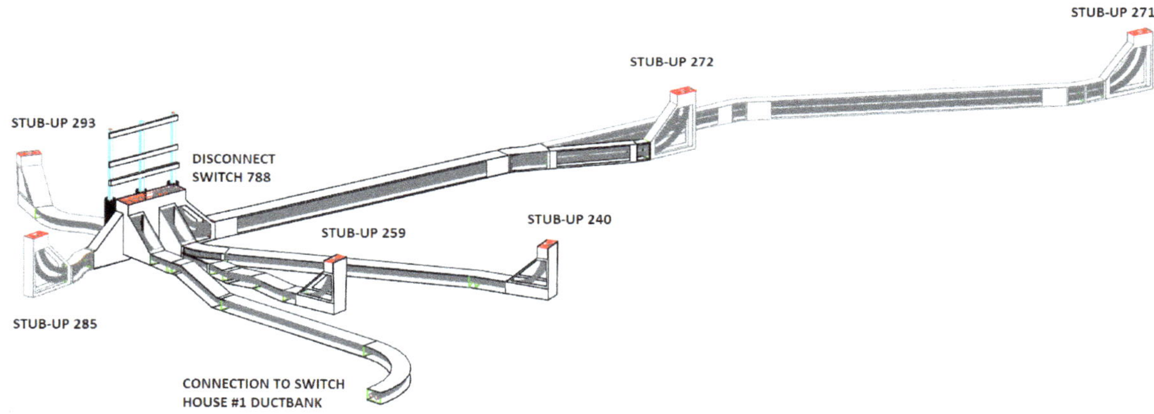

Figure IV.3.C. Disconnect Switch #788 – 3D Reference Model.

The Example of X-Sections/Elevations with Takeoffs has already been introduced in Paragraph IV.2 – Figure IV.2.F. The following Figures, IV.3.D. & IV.3.E., show partial plans for Duct Bank Stub-Ups 240 & 259 - detailed information regarding the curved segments' layout (Length, Radius).

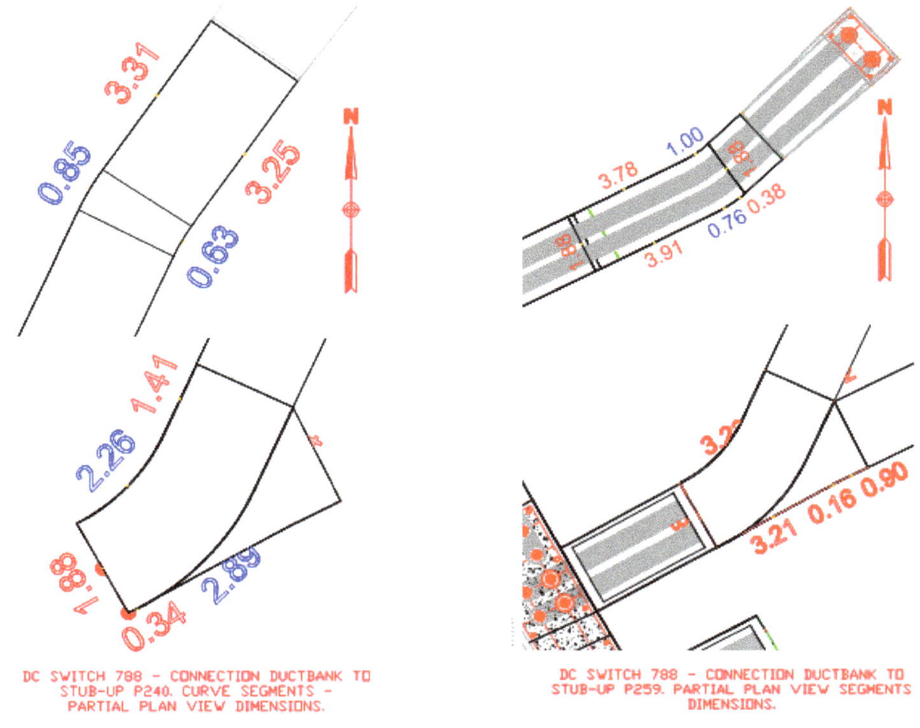

Figure IV.3.D. Partial Plan – Stub-Up 240. Figure IV.3.E. Partial Plan – Stub-Up 259

The Detailed Reference 3D Model Views for Duct Banks between DC Switch 788 and Stub-Ups 240 & 259 are shown in Figures IV.3.F and IV.3.G below.

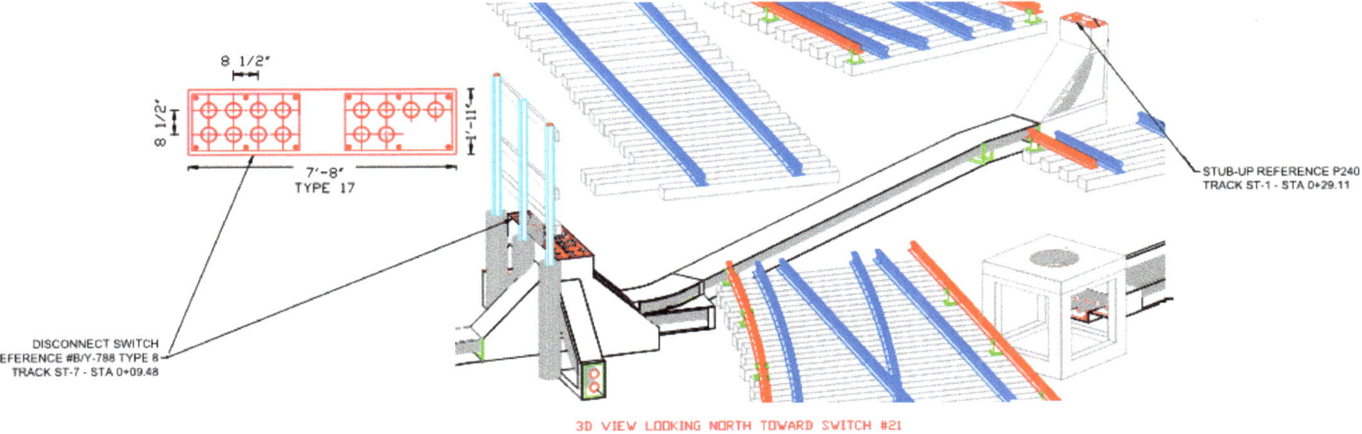

Figure IV.3.F. Ductbank between DC Switch 788 and Stub-Up 240. Detailed Reference 3D View.

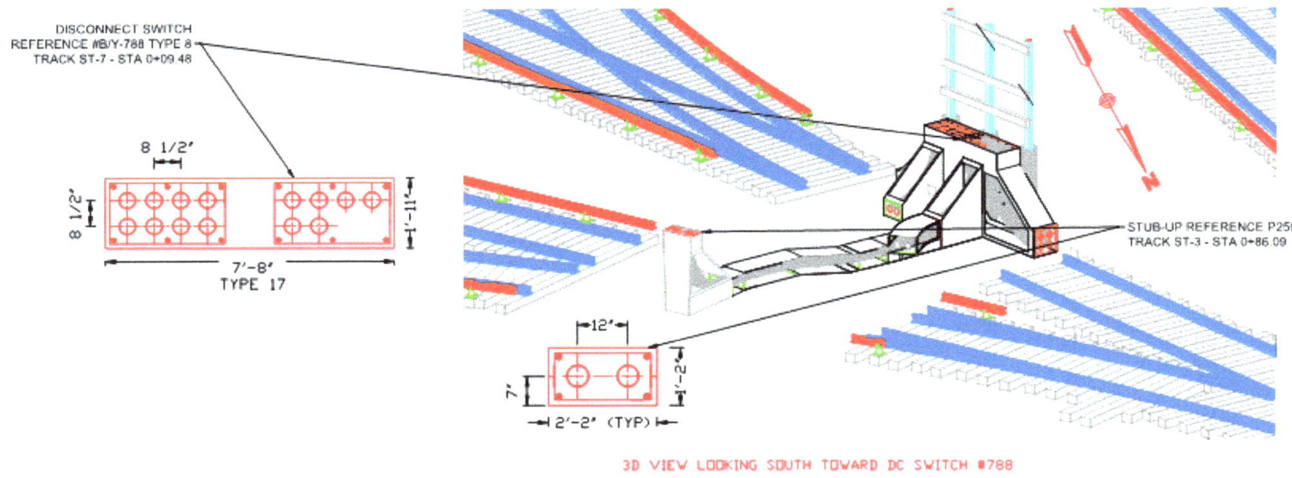

Figure IV.3.G. Ductbank between DC Switch 788 and Stub-Up 259. Detailed Reference 3D View.

The Block-Scheme for Utility Member Modeling (Plans, Elevations, 3D Views) is represented in Figure IV.3.H. below. The Section Mode has already been discussed in detail in Chapter IV.2 – see Figure IV.2.H.

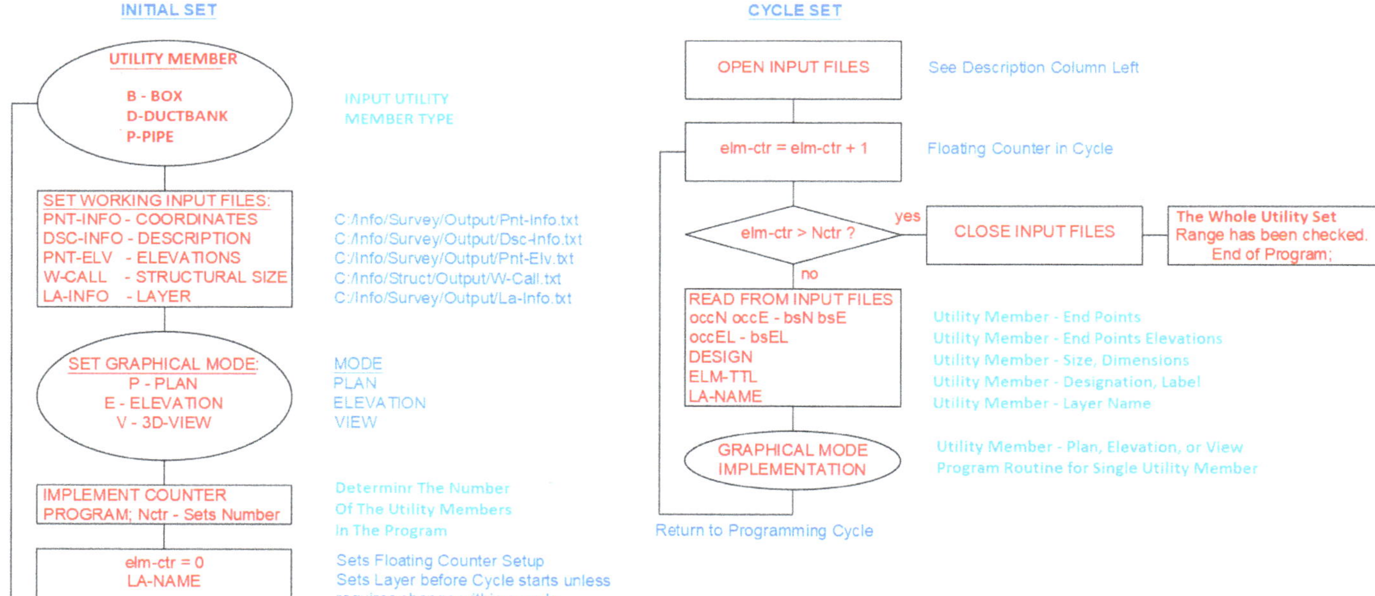

Figure IV.3.H. Utility Member Modeling Block-Scheme.

CHAPTER V: MANAGEMENT

The goal of this chapter is to connect the Working Schedule Output Information (EXCEL, PDF) and AutoCAD Environment to provide a clear & detailed correlation between the Project Working Schedule and Real-World Project Modeling, answering the question WHAT PART of the PROJECT to be built, WHERE, and WHEN.

The Examples shown below are from the Contract No. C17A9 Central Artery/Tunnel Project.

V.1 INPUT FILE STRUCTURE.

The Schedule File Structure for Programming Input includes Activity (Code), Title (Description), Duration, Start and Finish Dates Files, located in Schedule Output Directory – the Figure V.1.A. below.

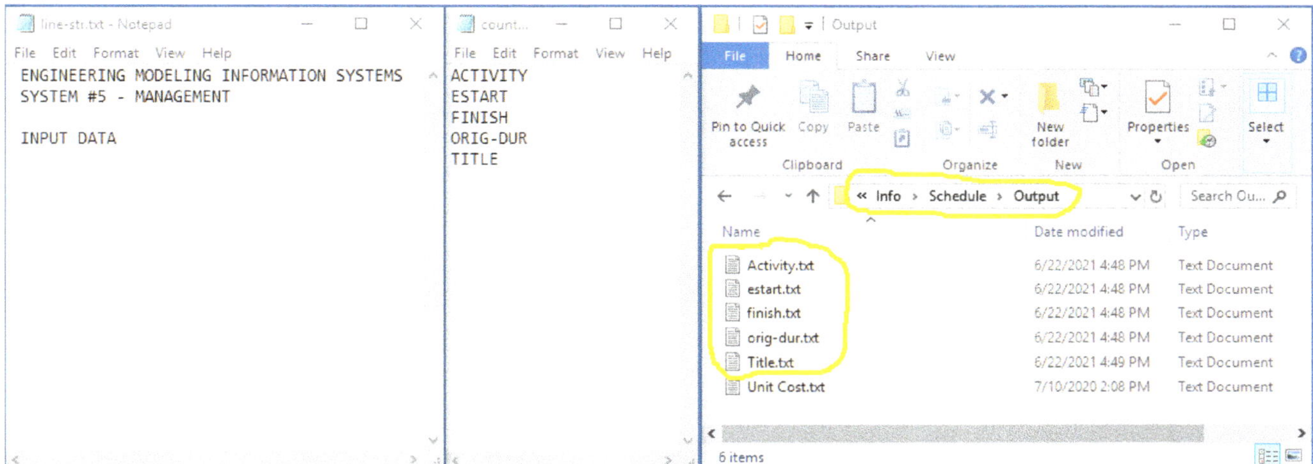

The Example of Input Files contents – Figure V.1.B.

ACT	TITLE	OD	ES	EF
B1002307	Pretrench & guide walls S bulkhead Z203	5	03-Oct-96	09-Oct-96
A9019000	Pre-trench & Constr MSW Guide Walls for Z203&208	15	09-Oct-96	30-Oct-96
B1080030	Constr. Slurry Wall panel MT-1 565.29 s.f. Z203	2	31-Oct-96	01-Nov-96
B1080040	Constr. Slurry Wall panel MT-3 532.33 s.f. Z203	2	04-Nov-96	05-Nov-96
B1080035	Constr. Slurry Wall panel MT-2 1633.53 s.f. Z203	4	06-Nov-96	12-Nov-96
B1080045	Constr. Slurry Wall panel MT-4 1465.19 s.f. Z203	3	13-Nov-96	15-Nov-96
A9099870	Constr. Slurry Wall panel M-74 1469.13 s.f.	3	18-Nov-96	20-Nov-96
B1080210	Constr. Slurry Wall panel TB-8 1460.00 s.f.	4	21-Nov-96	26-Nov-96
A9099875	Constr. Slurry Wall panel M-75 1258.47 s.f.	3	27-Nov-96	02-Dec-96
B1080215	Constr. Slurry Wall panel TB-9 1314.00 s.f.	4	03-Dec-96	06-Dec-96
B1080205	Constr. Slurry Wall panel TB-7 1340.28 s.f.	4	09-Dec-96	12-Dec-96
B1080230	Constr. Slurry Wall panel TB-12 1048.28 s.f.	3	13-Dec-96	17-Dec-96
B1080200	Constr. Slurry Wall panel TB-6 1340.28 s.f.	4	18-Dec-96	23-Dec-96
B1080225	Constr. Slurry Wall panel TB-11 1497.96 s.f.	4	24-Dec-96	30-Dec-96
B1080195	Constr. Slurry Wall panel TB-5 1340.28 s.f.	4	31-Dec-96	06-Jan-97
B1080235	Constr. Slurry Wall panel TB-13 1340.28 s.f.	4	07-Jan-97	10-Jan-97
B1080190	Constr. Slurry Wall panel TB-4 1340.28 s.f.	4	13-Jan-97	16-Jan-97
B1080240	Constr. Slurry Wall panel TB-14 1340.28 s.f.	4	17-Jan-97	22-Jan-97
B1080220	Constr. Slurry Wall panel TB-10 1340.28 s.f.	4	23-Jan-97	28-Jan-97
A9099820	Constr. Slurry Wall panel M-64 595.98 s.f.	2	30-Jan-97	31-Jan-97
A9099815	Constr. Slurry Wall panel M-63 1190.97 s.f.	3	03-Feb-97	05-Feb-97
A9099840	Constr. Slurry Wall panel M-68 571.47 s.f.	2	03-Feb-97	04-Feb-97
A9099855	Constr. Slurry Wall panel M-71 571.47 s.f.	2	05-Feb-97	06-Feb-97
A9099845	Constr. Slurry Wall panel M-69 1141.94 s.f.	3	07-Feb-97	11-Feb-97
A9099825	Constr. Slurry Wall panel M-65 1128.30 s.f.	3	12-Feb-97	14-Feb-97
A9099850	Constr. Slurry Wall panel M-70 1142.93 s.f.	3	18-Feb-97	20-Feb-97
A9099835	Constr. Slurry Wall panel M-67 1104.01 s.f.	3	21-Feb-97	25-Feb-97
A9099860	Constr. Slurry Wall panel M-72 1113.42 s.f.	3	26-Feb-97	28-Feb-97
B1002552	Remove MSW SPTC guide walls Z203	3	03-Mar-97	05-Mar-97

The Schedule Control Directory Contains Working Files, supporting all Programs' Phases Implementation – Figure V.1.C:

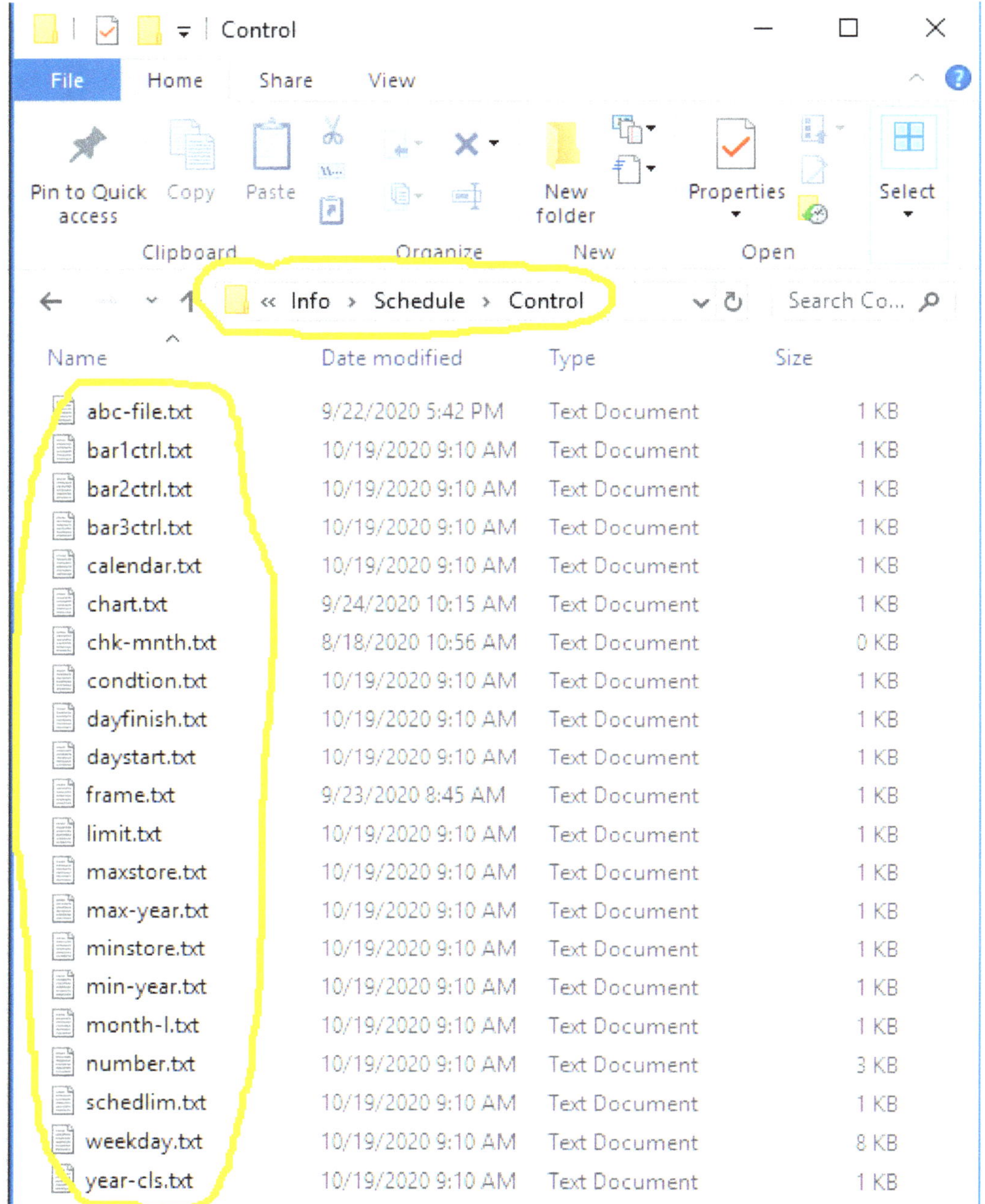

Figure V.1.C. Supporting Files – Schedule Control Directory.

The Programming Block-Scheme can be Logically separated into 2 groups – Setting & Description (Figure V.1.D) and Calendar & Drawing (Figure V.1.F). The First Group is responsible for setting the graphical size of the Chart and printing all Input Files Information from Figure V.1.B.

Figure V.1.D. Scheduling Block-Scheme I – Setting & Description.

The result of Scheduling Block-Scheme I Program Implementation – Chart – Progress in AutoCAD Environment is shown below in Figure V.1.E.

SCHEDULE_CHART

ACT	TITLE	OD	ES	EF
SM001465	P/S SPECIAL BARRIER TREATMENT DESIGN	2	18-APR-96	19-APR-96
SM002291	P/S TEMP HH EMERG EGRESS 1	10	18-APR-96	01-MAY-96
SM002294	P/S TEMP HH EMERG EGRESS 1A	10	18-APR-96	01-MAY-96
SMR01465	R/A SPECIAL BARRIER TREATMENT DESIGN	30	20-APR-96	19-MAY-96
SM002205	P/S TRAFFIC PLAN PHASE 2A1	20	25-APR-96	22-MAY-96
SMR02291	R/A TEMP HH EMERG EGRESS 1	30	02-MAY-96	31-MAY-96
SMR02294	R/A TEMP HH EMERG EGRESS 2	30	02-MAY-96	31-MAY-96
SM001490	P/S TEMP. LIGHTING & TRAFFIC SIGNAL. PHASE 2A1	20	23-MAY-96	20-JUN-96
SMR02205	R/A BP/B & CITY BOSTON TRAFFIC PLAN PHASE 2A1	30	23-MAY-96	21-JUN-96
A9000830	INST (1) INCL-55979 @ STA 130+40 CANB	1	03-JUN-96	03-JUN-96
A9450600	FABRICATE & DELIV BENT #48 UNDERPINNING STEEL	100	03-JUN-96	23-OCT-96
A9451600	FABRICATE & DELIV BENT #49 UNDERPINNING STEEL	100	03-JUN-96	23-OCT-96
A9000840	INST (1) INCL-55980 @ STA 130+25 CANB	1	04-JUN-96	04-JUN-96
SMR01490	R/A TEMP. LIGHTING & TRAFFIC SIGNAL. PHASE 2A1	30	21-JUN-96	20-JUL-96
UTM04112	INSTL 40 LF 4" STM @ 199 ON SURF ART	3	25-SEP-96	27-SEP-96
B1002295	SET UP WORK ZONE 203	2	01-OCT-96	02-OCT-96
B1002300	EXCAV & EARTH SUPPT EMERG EGRESS IN 1ST LOC Z203	10	03-OCT-96	17-OCT-96
B1002307	PRETRENCH & GUIDE WALLS S BULKHEAD Z203	5	03-OCT-96	09-OCT-96
A9019000	PRE-TRENCH & CONSTR MSW GUIDE WALLS FOR Z203&208	15	09-OCT-96	30-OCT-96
B1002301	FAB & DELIVER TEMP HEADHOUSE EMERG EGRESS	30	18-OCT-96	02-DEC-96
B1002305	CONSTR FNDT EMERG EGRESS 1ST LOCATION Z203	20	18-OCT-96	15-NOV-96
B1051257	ROUGH CARPENTRY EMERG EGRESS 1ST LOCATION	10	18-OCT-96	31-OCT-96
B1080030	CONSTR. SLURRY WALL PANEL MT-1 565.29 S.F. Z203	2	31-OCT-96	01-NOV-96
B1080040	CONSTR. SLURRY WALL PANEL MT-3 532.33 S.F. Z203	2	04-NOV-96	05-NOV-96
B1080035	CONSTR. SLURRY WALL PANEL MT-2 1633.53 S.F. Z203	4	06-NOV-96	12-NOV-96
B1080045	CONSTR. SLURRY WALL PANEL MT-4 1465.19 S.F. Z203	3	13-NOV-96	15-NOV-96
A9099870	CONSTR. SLURRY WALL PANEL M-74 1469.13 S.F.	3	18-NOV-96	20-NOV-96
B1080210	CONSTR. SLURRY WALL PANEL TB-8 1460.00 S.F.	4	21-NOV-96	26-NOV-96
A9099875	CONSTR. SLURRY WALL PANEL M-75 1258.47 S.F.	3	27-NOV-96	02-DEC-96
B1002308	INSTALL TEMP HEADHOUSE EMERG EGRESS 1ST LOC Z203	5	03-DEC-96	09-DEC-96
B1080215	CONSTR. SLURRY WALL PANEL TB-9 1314.00 S.F.	4	03-DEC-96	06-DEC-96
B1080205	CONSTR. SLURRY WALL PANEL TB-7 1340.28 S.F.	4	09-DEC-96	12-DEC-96
B1080230	CONSTR. SLURRY WALL PANEL TB-12 1048.28 S.F.	3	13-DEC-96	17-DEC-96
B1080200	CONSTR. SLURRY WALL PANEL TB-6 1340.28 S.F.	4	18-DEC-96	23-DEC-96
B1080225	CONSTR. SLURRY WALL PANEL TB-11 1497.96 S.F.	4	24-DEC-96	30-DEC-96
B1080195	CONSTR. SLURRY WALL PANEL TB-5 1340.28 S.F.	4	31-DEC-96	06-JAN-97
B1080235	CONSTR. SLURRY WALL PANEL TB-13 1340.28 S.F.	4	07-JAN-97	10-JAN-97
B1080190	CONSTR. SLURRY WALL PANEL TB-4 1340.28 S.F.	4	13-JAN-97	16-JAN-97
B1080240	CONSTR. SLURRY WALL PANEL TB-14 1340.28 S.F.	4	17-JAN-97	22-JAN-97
B1080220	CONSTR. SLURRY WALL PANEL TB-10 1340.28 S.F.	4	23-JAN-97	28-JAN-97
A9099820	CONSTR. SLURRY WALL PANEL M-64 595.98 S.F.	2	30-JAN-97	31-JAN-97
A9099815	CONSTR. SLURRY WALL PANEL M-63 1190.97 S.F.	3	03-FEB-97	05-FEB-97
A9099840	CONSTR. SLURRY WALL PANEL M-68 571.47 S.F.	2	03-FEB-97	04-FEB-97
A9099855	CONSTR. SLURRY WALL PANEL M-71 571.47 S.F.	2	05-FEB-97	06-FEB-97
A9099845	CONSTR. SLURRY WALL PANEL M-69 1141.94 S.F.	3	07-FEB-97	11-FEB-97
A9099825	CONSTR. SLURRY WALL PANEL M-65 1128.30 S.F.	3	12-FEB-97	14-FEB-97
A9099850	CONSTR. SLURRY WALL PANEL M-70 1142.93 S.F.	3	18-FEB-97	20-FEB-97
A9099835	CONSTR. SLURRY WALL PANEL M-67 1104.01 S.F.	3	21-FEB-97	25-FEB-97
A9099860	CONSTR. SLURRY WALL PANEL M-72 1113.42 S.F.	3	26-FEB-97	28-FEB-97
B1002552	REMOVE MSW SPTC GUIDE WALLS Z203	3	03-MAR-97	05-MAR-97

Figure V.1.E. Chart Progress after Programming implementation of Block-Scheme I

The Second Group is dealing with actual Time Information, setting up the Earliest Start and Latest Finish Dates to determine the Working Interval of the Chart graphically; determining the Number of Months and the Number of Days for each Month in the working Interval, considering Leap or Plain Year; also determines the Days of the Week at the beginning of each month depending on the working Interval Years; recording Start and Finish Dates for each Activity; laying out correlating points, inserts Pointers, and draws Bar Lines for each Activity – completing the Calendar Part of the Schedule Graphical Chart.

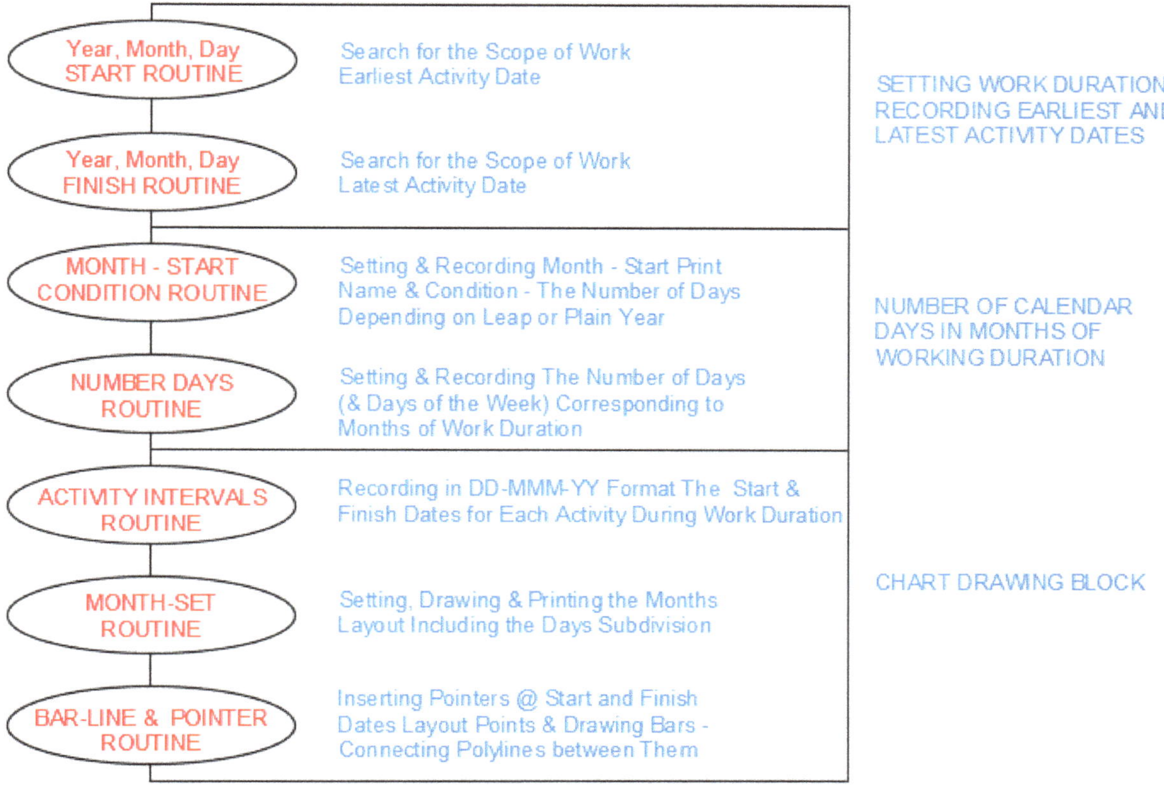

Figure V.1.F. Scheduling Block-Scheme II – Calendar & Drawing.

The result of Scheduling Block-Scheme II Program Run – Complete Schedule Chart in AutoCAD Environment is shown on the following Attached Figures V.1.G, V.1.H, and V.1.J.

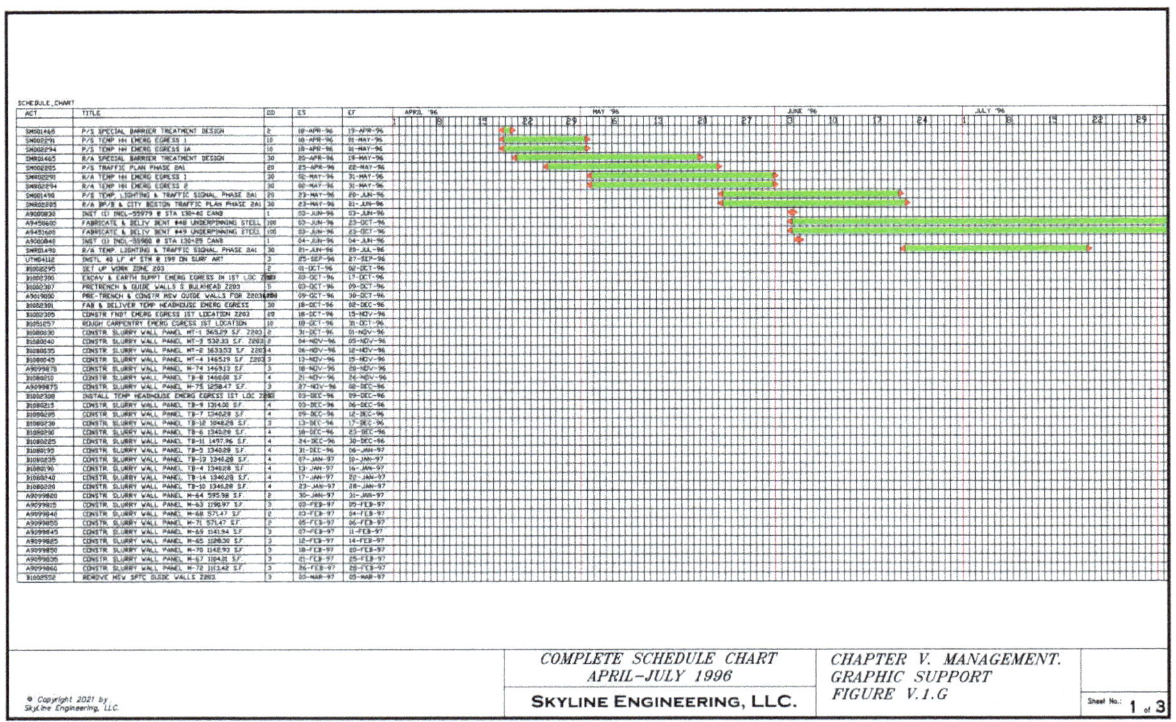

SCHEDULE_CHART

ACT	TITLE	DD	ES	EF
SM001465	P/S SPECIAL BARRIER TREATMENT DESIGN	2	18-APR-96	19-APR-96
SM002291	P/S TEMP HH EMERG EGRESS 1	10	18-APR-96	01-MAY-96
SM002294	P/S TEMP HH EMERG EGRESS 1A	10	18-APR-96	01-MAY-96
SMR01465	R/A SPECIAL BARRIER TREATMENT DESIGN	30	20-APR-96	19-MAY-96
SM002205	P/S TRAFFIC PLAN PHASE 2A1	20	25-APR-96	22-MAY-96
SMR02291	R/A TEMP HH EMERG EGRESS 1	30	02-MAY-96	31-MAY-96
SMR02294	R/A TEMP HH EMERG EGRESS 2	30	02-MAY-96	31-MAY-96
SM001490	P/S TEMP. LIGHTING & TRAFFIC SIGNAL PHASE 2A1	20	23-MAY-96	20-JUN-96
SMR02205	R/A BP/B & CITY BOSTON TRAFFIC PLAN PHASE 2A1	30	23-MAY-96	21-JUN-96
A9000830	INST (1) INCL-55979 @ STA 130+40 CANB	1	03-JUN-96	03-JUN-96
A9450600	FABRICATE & DELIV BENT #48 UNDERPINNING STEEL	100	03-JUN-96	23-OCT-96
A9451600	FABRICATE & DELIV BENT #49 UNDERPINNING STEEL	100	03-JUN-96	23-OCT-96
A9000840	INST (1) INCL-55980 @ STA 130+25 CANB	1	04-JUN-96	04-JUN-96
SMR01490	R/A TEMP. LIGHTING & TRAFFIC SIGNAL PHASE 2A1	30	21-JUN-96	20-JUL-96
UTN04112	INSTL 40 LF 4" STM @ 199 ON SURF ART	3	25-SEP-96	27-SEP-96
B1002295	SET UP WORK ZONE 203	2	01-OCT-96	02-OCT-96
B1002300	EXCAV & EARTH SUPPT EMERG EGRESS IN 1ST LOC 2203	[illegible]	03-OCT-96	17-OCT-96
B1002307	PRETRENCH & GUIDE WALLS & BULKHEAD 2203	5	03-OCT-96	09-OCT-96
A9019000	PRE-TRENCH & CONSTR MSW GUIDE WALLS FOR 2203	[illegible]	09-OCT-96	30-OCT-96
B1002301	FAB & DELIVER TEMP HEADHOUSE EMERG EGRESS	30	18-OCT-96	02-DEC-96
B1002305	CONSTR FNDT EMERG EGRESS 1ST LOCATION 2203	20	18-OCT-96	15-NOV-96
B1051257	ROUGH CARPENTRY EMERG EGRESS 1ST LOCATION	10	18-OCT-96	31-OCT-96
B1080030	CONSTR. SLURRY WALL PANEL MT-1 565.29 S.F. 2203	2	31-OCT-96	01-NOV-96
B1080040	CONSTR. SLURRY WALL PANEL MT-3 532.33 S.F. 2203	2	04-NOV-96	05-NOV-96
B1080035	CONSTR. SLURRY WALL PANEL MT-2 1633.53 S.F. 2203	4	06-NOV-96	12-NOV-96
B1080045	CONSTR. SLURRY WALL PANEL MT-4 1465.19 S.F. 2203	3	13-NOV-96	15-NOV-96
A9099870	CONSTR. SLURRY WALL PANEL M-74 1469.13 S.F.	3	18-NOV-96	20-NOV-96
B1080210	CONSTR. SLURRY WALL PANEL TB-8 1460.00 S.F.	4	21-NOV-96	26-NOV-96
A9099875	CONSTR. SLURRY WALL PANEL M-75 1258.47 S.F.	3	27-NOV-96	02-DEC-96
B1002308	INSTALL TEMP HEADHOUSE EMERG EGRESS 1ST LOC 2203	[illegible]	03-DEC-96	09-DEC-96
B1080215	CONSTR. SLURRY WALL PANEL TB-9 1314.00 S.F.	4	03-DEC-96	06-DEC-96
B1080205	CONSTR. SLURRY WALL PANEL TB-7 1340.28 S.F.	4	09-DEC-96	12-DEC-96
B1080230	CONSTR. SLURRY WALL PANEL TB-12 1048.28 S.F.	3	13-DEC-96	17-DEC-96
B1080200	CONSTR. SLURRY WALL PANEL TB-6 1340.28 S.F.	4	18-DEC-96	23-DEC-96
B1080225	CONSTR. SLURRY WALL PANEL TB-11 1497.96 S.F.	4	24-DEC-96	30-DEC-96
B1080195	CONSTR. SLURRY WALL PANEL TB-5 1340.28 S.F.	4	31-DEC-96	06-JAN-97
B1080235	CONSTR. SLURRY WALL PANEL TB-13 1340.28 S.F.	4	07-JAN-97	10-JAN-97
B1080190	CONSTR. SLURRY WALL PANEL TB-4 1340.28 S.F.	4	13-JAN-97	16-JAN-97
B1080240	CONSTR. SLURRY WALL PANEL TB-14 1340.28 S.F.	4	17-JAN-97	22-JAN-97
B1080220	CONSTR. SLURRY WALL PANEL TB-10 1340.28 S.F.	4	23-JAN-97	28-JAN-97
A9099820	CONSTR. SLURRY WALL PANEL M-64 595.98 S.F.	2	30-JAN-97	31-JAN-97
A9099815	CONSTR. SLURRY WALL PANEL M-63 1190.97 S.F.	3	03-FEB-97	05-FEB-97
A9099840	CONSTR. SLURRY WALL PANEL M-68 571.47 S.F.	2	03-FEB-97	04-FEB-97
A9099855	CONSTR. SLURRY WALL PANEL M-71 571.47 S.F.	2	05-FEB-97	06-FEB-97
A9099845	CONSTR. SLURRY WALL PANEL M-69 1141.94 S.F.	3	07-FEB-97	11-FEB-97
A9099825	CONSTR. SLURRY WALL PANEL M-65 1128.30 S.F.	3	12-FEB-97	14-FEB-97
A9099850	CONSTR. SLURRY WALL PANEL M-70 1142.93 S.F.	3	18-FEB-97	20-FEB-97
A9099835	CONSTR. SLURRY WALL PANEL M-67 1104.81 S.F.	3	21-FEB-97	25-FEB-97
A9099860	CONSTR. SLURRY WALL PANEL M-72 1113.42 S.F.	3	26-FEB-97	28-FEB-97
B1002552	REMOVE MSW SPTC GUIDE WALLS 2203	3	03-MAR-97	05-MAR-97

COMPLETE SCHEDULE CHART
APRIL–JULY 1996

SKYLINE ENGINEERING, LLC.

CHAPTER V. MANAGEMENT.
GRAPHIC SUPPORT
FIGURE V.1.G

Sheet No.: 1 of 3

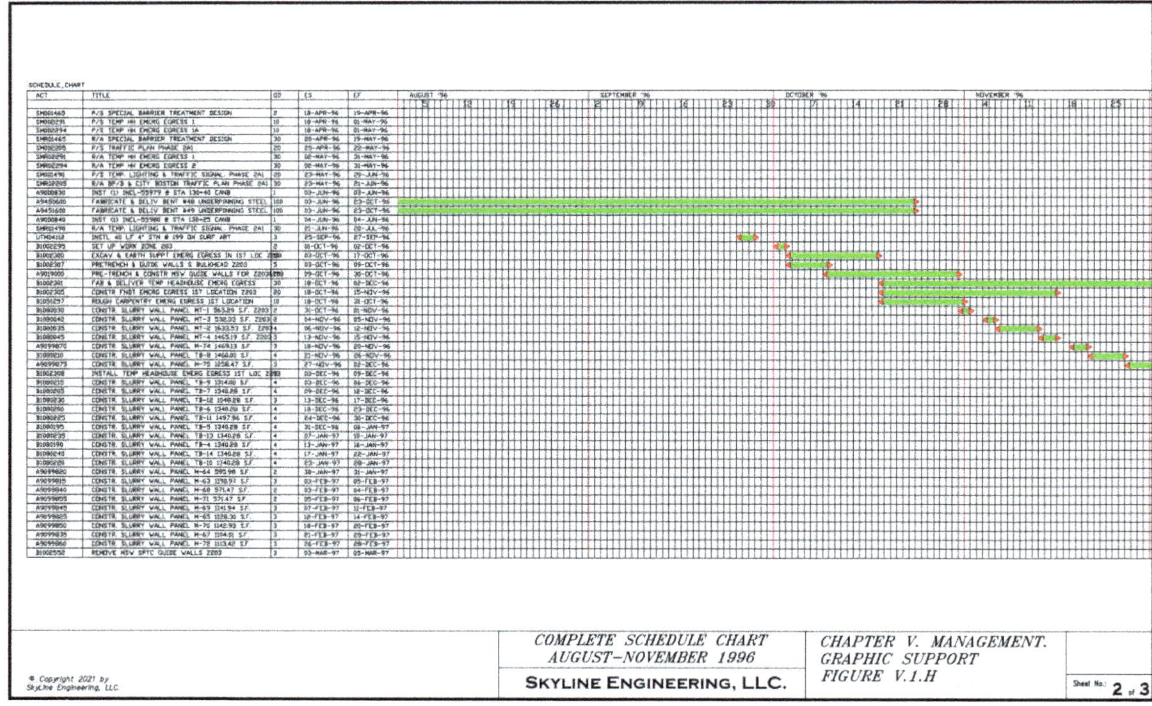

SCHEDULE_CHART

ACT	TITLE	DD	ES	EF
SM001465	P/S SPECIAL BARRIER TREATMENT DESIGN	2	18-APR-96	19-APR-96
SM002291	P/S TEMP HH EMERG EGRESS 1	10	18-APR-96	01-MAY-96
SM002294	P/S TEMP HH EMERG EGRESS 1A	10	18-APR-96	01-MAY-96
SMR01465	R/A SPECIAL BARRIER TREATMENT DESIGN	30	20-APR-96	19-MAY-96
SM002205	P/S TRAFFIC PLAN PHASE 2A1	20	25-APR-96	22-MAY-96
SMR02291	R/A TEMP HH EMERG EGRESS 1	30	02-MAY-96	31-MAY-96
SMR02294	R/A TEMP HH EMERG EGRESS 2	30	02-MAY-96	31-MAY-96
SM001490	P/S TEMP. LIGHTING & TRAFFIC SIGNAL PHASE 2A1	20	23-MAY-96	20-JUN-96
SMR02205	R/A BP/B & CITY BOSTON TRAFFIC PLAN PHASE 2A1	30	23-MAY-96	21-JUN-96
A9000830	INST (1) INCL-55979 @ STA 130+40 CANB	1	03-JUN-96	03-JUN-96
A9450600	FABRICATE & DELIV BENT #48 UNDERPINNING STEEL	100	03-JUN-96	23-OCT-96
A9451600	FABRICATE & DELIV BENT #49 UNDERPINNING STEEL	100	03-JUN-96	23-OCT-96
A9000840	INST (1) INCL-55980 @ STA 130+25 CANB	1	04-JUN-96	04-JUN-96
SMR01490	R/A TEMP. LIGHTING & TRAFFIC SIGNAL PHASE 2A1	30	21-JUN-96	20-JUL-96
UTN04112	INSTL 40 LF 4" STM @ 199 ON SURF ART	3	25-SEP-96	27-SEP-96
B1002295	SET UP WORK ZONE 203	2	01-OCT-96	02-OCT-96
B1002300	EXCAV & EARTH SUPPT EMERG EGRESS IN 1ST LOC 2203	[illegible]	03-OCT-96	17-OCT-96
B1002307	PRETRENCH & GUIDE WALLS & BULKHEAD 2203	5	03-OCT-96	09-OCT-96
A9019000	PRE-TRENCH & CONSTR MSW GUIDE WALLS FOR 2203	[illegible]	09-OCT-96	30-OCT-96
B1002301	FAB & DELIVER TEMP HEADHOUSE EMERG EGRESS	30	18-OCT-96	02-DEC-96
B1002305	CONSTR FNDT EMERG EGRESS 1ST LOCATION 2203	20	18-OCT-96	15-NOV-96
B1051257	ROUGH CARPENTRY EMERG EGRESS 1ST LOCATION	10	18-OCT-96	31-OCT-96
B1080030	CONSTR. SLURRY WALL PANEL MT-1 565.29 S.F. 2203	2	31-OCT-96	01-NOV-96
B1080040	CONSTR. SLURRY WALL PANEL MT-3 532.33 S.F. 2203	2	04-NOV-96	05-NOV-96
B1080035	CONSTR. SLURRY WALL PANEL MT-2 1633.53 S.F. 2203	4	06-NOV-96	12-NOV-96
B1080045	CONSTR. SLURRY WALL PANEL MT-4 1465.19 S.F. 2203	3	13-NOV-96	15-NOV-96
A9099870	CONSTR. SLURRY WALL PANEL M-74 1469.13 S.F.	3	18-NOV-96	20-NOV-96
B1080210	CONSTR. SLURRY WALL PANEL TB-8 1460.00 S.F.	4	21-NOV-96	26-NOV-96
A9099875	CONSTR. SLURRY WALL PANEL M-75 1258.47 S.F.	3	27-NOV-96	02-DEC-96
B1002308	INSTALL TEMP HEADHOUSE EMERG EGRESS 1ST LOC 2203	[illegible]	03-DEC-96	09-DEC-96
B1080215	CONSTR. SLURRY WALL PANEL TB-9 1314.00 S.F.	4	03-DEC-96	06-DEC-96
B1080205	CONSTR. SLURRY WALL PANEL TB-7 1340.28 S.F.	4	09-DEC-96	12-DEC-96
B1080230	CONSTR. SLURRY WALL PANEL TB-12 1048.28 S.F.	3	13-DEC-96	17-DEC-96
B1080200	CONSTR. SLURRY WALL PANEL TB-6 1340.28 S.F.	4	18-DEC-96	23-DEC-96
B1080225	CONSTR. SLURRY WALL PANEL TB-11 1497.96 S.F.	4	24-DEC-96	30-DEC-96
B1080195	CONSTR. SLURRY WALL PANEL TB-5 1340.28 S.F.	4	31-DEC-96	06-JAN-97
B1080235	CONSTR. SLURRY WALL PANEL TB-13 1340.28 S.F.	4	07-JAN-97	10-JAN-97
B1080190	CONSTR. SLURRY WALL PANEL TB-4 1340.28 S.F.	4	13-JAN-97	16-JAN-97
B1080240	CONSTR. SLURRY WALL PANEL TB-14 1340.28 S.F.	4	17-JAN-97	22-JAN-97
B1080220	CONSTR. SLURRY WALL PANEL TB-10 1340.28 S.F.	4	23-JAN-97	28-JAN-97
A9099820	CONSTR. SLURRY WALL PANEL M-64 595.98 S.F.	2	30-JAN-97	31-JAN-97
A9099815	CONSTR. SLURRY WALL PANEL M-63 1190.97 S.F.	3	03-FEB-97	05-FEB-97
A9099840	CONSTR. SLURRY WALL PANEL M-68 571.47 S.F.	2	03-FEB-97	04-FEB-97
A9099855	CONSTR. SLURRY WALL PANEL M-71 571.47 S.F.	2	05-FEB-97	06-FEB-97
A9099845	CONSTR. SLURRY WALL PANEL M-69 1141.94 S.F.	3	07-FEB-97	11-FEB-97
A9099825	CONSTR. SLURRY WALL PANEL M-65 1128.30 S.F.	3	12-FEB-97	14-FEB-97
A9099850	CONSTR. SLURRY WALL PANEL M-70 1142.93 S.F.	3	18-FEB-97	20-FEB-97
A9099835	CONSTR. SLURRY WALL PANEL M-67 1104.81 S.F.	3	21-FEB-97	25-FEB-97
A9099860	CONSTR. SLURRY WALL PANEL M-72 1113.42 S.F.	3	26-FEB-97	28-FEB-97
B1002552	REMOVE MSW SPTC GUIDE WALLS 2203	3	03-MAR-97	05-MAR-97

COMPLETE SCHEDULE CHART
AUGUST–NOVEMBER 1996

SKYLINE ENGINEERING, LLC.

CHAPTER V. MANAGEMENT.
GRAPHIC SUPPORT
FIGURE V.1.H

Sheet No.: 2 of 3

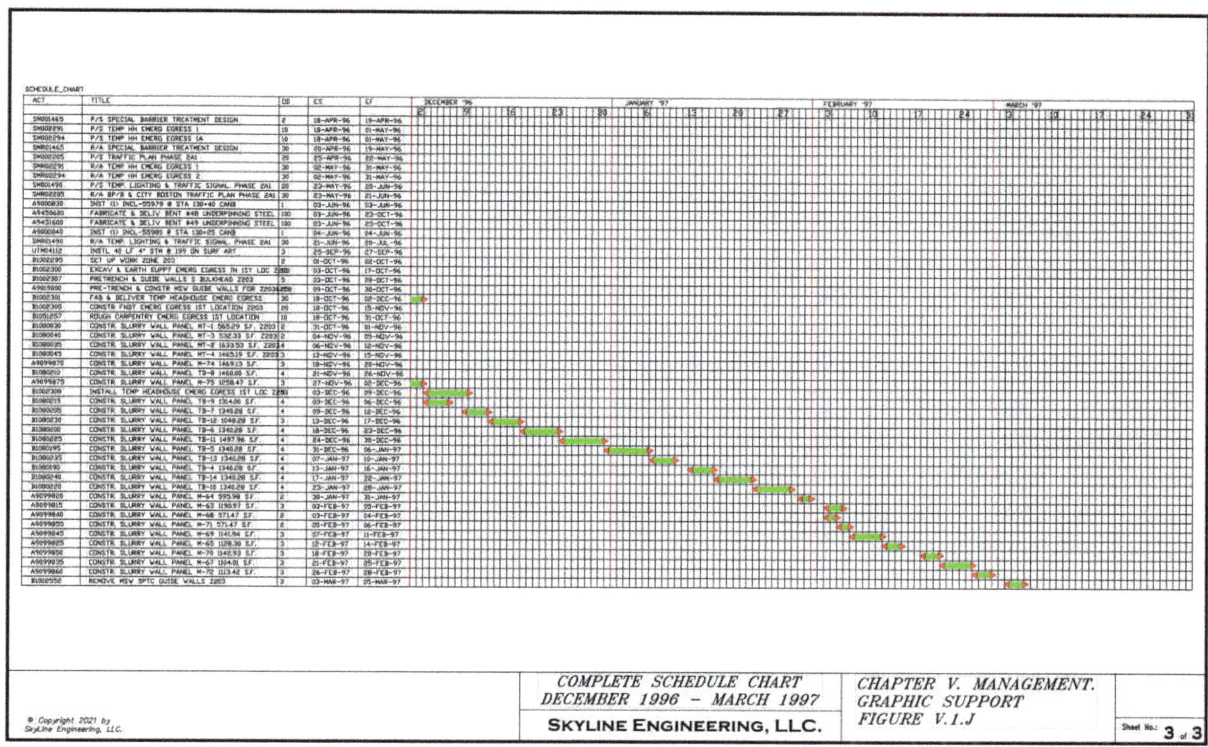

SCHEDULE_CHART

ACT	TITLE	OD	ES	EF
SM001465	P/S SPECIAL BARRIER TREATMENT DESIGN	2	18-APR-96	19-APR-96
SM002291	P/S TEMP HH EMERG EGRESS 1	10	18-APR-96	01-MAY-96
SM002294	P/S TEMP HH EMERG EGRESS 1A	10	18-APR-96	01-MAY-96
SMR01465	R/A SPECIAL BARRIER TREATMENT DESIGN	30	20-APR-96	19-MAY-96
SM002205	P/S TRAFFIC PLAN PHASE 2A1	20	25-APR-96	22-MAY-96
SMR02291	R/A TEMP HH EMERG EGRESS 1	30	02-MAY-96	31-MAY-96
SMR02294	R/A TEMP HH EMERG EGRESS 2	30	02-MAY-96	31-MAY-96
SM001490	P/S TEMP. LIGHTING & TRAFFIC SIGNAL PHASE 2A1	20	23-MAY-96	20-JUN-96
SMR02205	R/A BP/B & CITY BOSTON TRAFFIC PLAN PHASE 2A1	30	23-MAY-96	21-JUN-96
A9000830	INST (1) INCL-55979 @ STA 130+40 CANB	1	03-JUN-96	03-JUN-96
A9450600	FABRICATE & DELIV BENT #48 UNDERPINNING STEEL	100	03-JUN-96	23-OCT-96
A9451600	FABRICATE & DELIV BENT #49 UNDERPINNING STEEL	100	03-JUN-96	23-OCT-96
A9000840	INST (1) INCL-55980 @ STA 130+25 CANB	1	04-JUN-96	04-JUN-96
SMR01490	R/A TEMP. LIGHTING & TRAFFIC SIGNAL PHASE 2A1	30	21-JUN-96	29-JUL-96
UTM04112	INSTL 40 LF 4" STM @ 199 ON SURF ART	3	25-SEP-96	27-SEP-96
B1002295	SET UP WORK ZONE 203	2	01-OCT-96	02-OCT-96
B1002300	EXCAV & EARTH SUPPT EMERG EGRESS IN 1ST LOC Z203	[illegible]	03-OCT-96	17-OCT-96
B1002307	PRETRENCH & GUIDE WALLS S BULKHEAD Z203	5	03-OCT-96	09-OCT-96
A9019000	PRE-TRENCH & CONSTR MSW GUIDE WALLS FOR Z203&208	[illegible]	09-OCT-96	30-OCT-96
B1002301	FAB & DELIVER TEMP HEADHOUSE EMERG EGRESS	30	18-OCT-96	02-DEC-96
B1002305	CONSTR FNDT EMERG EGRESS 1ST LOCATION Z203	20	18-OCT-96	15-NOV-96
B1051257	ROUGH CARPENTRY EMERG EGRESS 1ST LOCATION	10	18-OCT-96	31-OCT-96
B1080030	CONSTR. SLURRY WALL PANEL MT-1 565.29 S.F. Z203	2	31-OCT-96	01-NOV-96
B1080040	CONSTR. SLURRY WALL PANEL MT-3 532.33 S.F. Z203	2	04-NOV-96	05-NOV-96
B1080035	CONSTR. SLURRY WALL PANEL MT-2 1633.53 S.F. Z203	4	06-NOV-96	12-NOV-96
B1080045	CONSTR. SLURRY WALL PANEL MT-4 1465.19 S.F. Z203	3	13-NOV-96	15-NOV-96
A9099870	CONSTR. SLURRY WALL PANEL M-74 1469.13 S.F.	3	18-NOV-96	20-NOV-96
B1080210	CONSTR. SLURRY WALL PANEL TB-8 1460.00 S.F.	4	21-NOV-96	26-NOV-96
A9099875	CONSTR. SLURRY WALL PANEL M-75 1258.47 S.F.	3	27-NOV-96	02-DEC-96
B1002309	INSTALL TEMP HEADHOUSE EMERG EGRESS 1ST LOC Z203	[illegible]	03-DEC-96	09-DEC-96
B1080215	CONSTR. SLURRY WALL PANEL TB-9 1314.00 S.F.	4	03-DEC-96	06-DEC-96
B1080205	CONSTR. SLURRY WALL PANEL TB-7 1340.28 S.F.	4	09-DEC-96	12-DEC-96
B1080230	CONSTR. SLURRY WALL PANEL TB-12 1040.28 S.F.	3	13-DEC-96	17-DEC-96
B1080200	CONSTR. SLURRY WALL PANEL TB-6 1340.28 S.F.	4	18-DEC-96	23-DEC-96
B1080225	CONSTR. SLURRY WALL PANEL TB-11 1497.96 S.F.	4	24-DEC-96	30-DEC-96
B1080195	CONSTR. SLURRY WALL PANEL TB-5 1340.28 S.F.	4	31-DEC-96	06-JAN-97
B1080235	CONSTR. SLURRY WALL PANEL TB-13 1340.28 S.F.	4	07-JAN-97	10-JAN-97
B1080190	CONSTR. SLURRY WALL PANEL TB-4 1340.28 S.F.	4	13-JAN-97	16-JAN-97
B1080240	CONSTR. SLURRY WALL PANEL TB-14 1340.28 S.F.	4	17-JAN-97	22-JAN-97
B1080220	CONSTR. SLURRY WALL PANEL TB-10 1340.28 S.F.	4	23-JAN-97	28-JAN-97
A9099820	CONSTR. SLURRY WALL PANEL M-64 595.98 S.F.	2	30-JAN-97	31-JAN-97
A9099815	CONSTR. SLURRY WALL PANEL M-63 1190.97 S.F.	3	03-FEB-97	05-FEB-97
A9099840	CONSTR. SLURRY WALL PANEL M-68 571.47 S.F.	2	03-FEB-97	04-FEB-97
A9099855	CONSTR. SLURRY WALL PANEL M-71 571.47 S.F.	2	05-FEB-97	06-FEB-97
A9099845	CONSTR. SLURRY WALL PANEL M-69 1141.94 S.F.	3	07-FEB-97	11-FEB-97
A9099825	CONSTR. SLURRY WALL PANEL M-65 1128.30 S.F.	3	12-FEB-97	14-FEB-97
A9099850	CONSTR. SLURRY WALL PANEL M-70 1142.93 S.F.	3	18-FEB-97	20-FEB-97
A9099835	CONSTR. SLURRY WALL PANEL M-67 1104.01 S.F.	3	21-FEB-97	25-FEB-97
A9099860	CONSTR. SLURRY WALL PANEL M-72 1113.42 S.F.	3	26-FEB-97	28-FEB-97
B1002552	REMOVE MSW SPTC GUIDE WALLS Z203	3	03-MAR-97	05-MAR-97

V.2 SCHEDULE – GRAPHICAL MODEL DETAILED CORRELATION.

In order to establish the clear connection between scheduling activities and graphical objects, the Complete Schedule Chart has to be broken into the smaller Detailed Charts, uniformed either by the type of Activity or limited working period. Figures V.2.A, V.2.B, and V.2.C. represent the Detail Charts for the Middle Slurry Wall installation operations during the time periods of October-November 1996, December 1996 - January 1997, and February-March 1997. Each of the Activity Items from these charts has the Graphical Object correlation. Each object has its own unique layer, which gives the flexibility to represent particular objects corresponding to activities in Schedule Sequence.

Figure V.2.A – Middle Slurry Wall Construction - Schedule Chart – October – November 1996

SCHEDULE_CHART

ACT	TITLE	OD	ES	EF
B1002307	PRETRENCH & GUIDE WALLS S BULKHEAD Z203	5	03-OCT-96	09-OCT-96
A9019000	PRE-TRENCH & CONSTR MSW GUIDE WALLS FOR Z203&208	15	09-OCT-96	30-OCT-96
B1080030	CONSTR. SLURRY WALL PANEL MT-1 565.29 S.F. Z203	2	31-OCT-96	01-NOV-96
B1080040	CONSTR. SLURRY WALL PANEL MT-3 532.33 S.F. Z203	2	04-NOV-96	05-NOV-96
B1080035	CONSTR. SLURRY WALL PANEL MT-2 1633.53 S.F. Z203	4	06-NOV-96	12-NOV-96
B1080045	CONSTR. SLURRY WALL PANEL MT-4 1465.19 S.F. Z203	3	13-NOV-96	15-NOV-96
A9099870	CONSTR. SLURRY WALL PANEL M-74 1469.13 S.F.	3	18-NOV-96	20-NOV-96
B1080210	CONSTR. SLURRY WALL PANEL TB-8 1460.00 S.F.	4	21-NOV-96	26-NOV-96
A9099875	CONSTR. SLURRY WALL PANEL M-75 1258.47 S.F.	3	27-NOV-96	02-DEC-96
B1080215	CONSTR. SLURRY WALL PANEL TB-9 1314.00 S.F.	4	03-DEC-96	06-DEC-96

OCTOBER '96 — 7, 14, 21, 28; NOVEMBER '96 — 4, 11, 18, 25; DECEMBER '96 — 2, 9

Figure V.2.B – Middle Slurry Wall Construction - Schedule Chart – December 1996–January 1997

SCHEDULE_CHART

ACT	TITLE	OD	ES	EF
B1080205	CONSTR. SLURRY WALL PANEL TB-7 1340.28 S.F.	4	09-DEC-96	12-DEC-96
B1080230	CONSTR. SLURRY WALL PANEL TB-12 1048.28 S.F.	3	13-DEC-96	17-DEC-96
B1080200	CONSTR. SLURRY WALL PANEL TB-6 1340.28 S.F.	4	18-DEC-96	23-DEC-96
B1080225	CONSTR. SLURRY WALL PANEL TB-11 1497.96 S.F.	4	24-DEC-96	30-DEC-96
B1080195	CONSTR. SLURRY WALL PANEL TB-5 1340.28 S.F.	4	31-DEC-96	06-JAN-97
B1080235	CONSTR. SLURRY WALL PANEL TB-13 1340.28 S.F.	4	07-JAN-97	10-JAN-97
B1080190	CONSTR. SLURRY WALL PANEL TB-4 1340.28 S.F.	4	13-JAN-97	16-JAN-97
B1080240	CONSTR. SLURRY WALL PANEL TB-14 1340.28 S.F.	4	17-JAN-97	22-JAN-97
B1080220	CONSTR. SLURRY WALL PANEL TB-10 1340.28 S.F.	4	23-JAN-97	28-JAN-97
A9099820	CONSTR. SLURRY WALL PANEL M-64 595.98 S.F.	2	30-JAN-97	31-JAN-97

Figure V.2.C – Middle Slurry Wall Construction - Schedule Chart – February– March 1997

SCHEDULE_CHART

ACT	TITLE	OD	ES	EF
A9099815	CONSTR. SLURRY WALL PANEL M-63 1190.97 S.F.	3	03-FEB-97	05-FEB-97
A9099840	CONSTR. SLURRY WALL PANEL M-68 571.47 S.F.	2	03-FEB-97	04-FEB-97
A9099855	CONSTR. SLURRY WALL PANEL M-71 571.47 S.F.	2	05-FEB-97	06-FEB-97
A9099845	CONSTR. SLURRY WALL PANEL M-69 1141.94 S.F.	3	07-FEB-97	11-FEB-97
A9099825	CONSTR. SLURRY WALL PANEL M-65 1128.30 S.F.	3	12-FEB-97	14-FEB-97
A9099850	CONSTR. SLURRY WALL PANEL M-70 1142.93 S.F.	3	18-FEB-97	20-FEB-97
A9099835	CONSTR. SLURRY WALL PANEL M-67 1104.01 S.F.	3	21-FEB-97	25-FEB-97
A9099860	CONSTR. SLURRY WALL PANEL M-72 1113.42 S.F.	3	26-FEB-97	28-FEB-97
B1002552	REMOVE MSW SPTC GUIDE WALLS Z203	3	03-MAR-97	05-MAR-97

Figure V.2.D. Middle Slurry Wall Panels Profile Fragment - Primary (Blue), Secondary (Magenta), & Follow-Up (Black) – with Installation Dates from Schedule Charts and Areas (Yellow Circles).

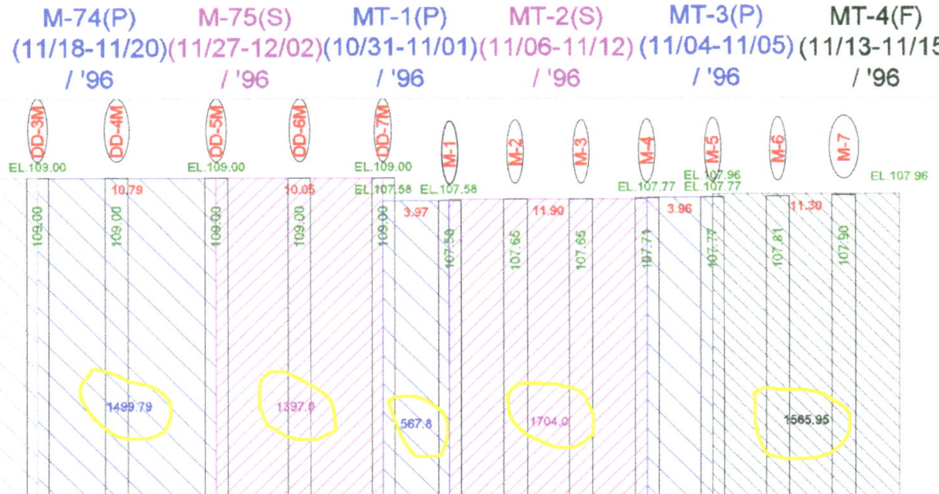

The Attached Figure V.2.E. illustrates a combined view of Schedule Charts for October & November 1996 and February 1997 for Middle Slurry Wall Installation with the Corresponding Wall Real-World Segment Layout – Panels Designation with Installation Dates.

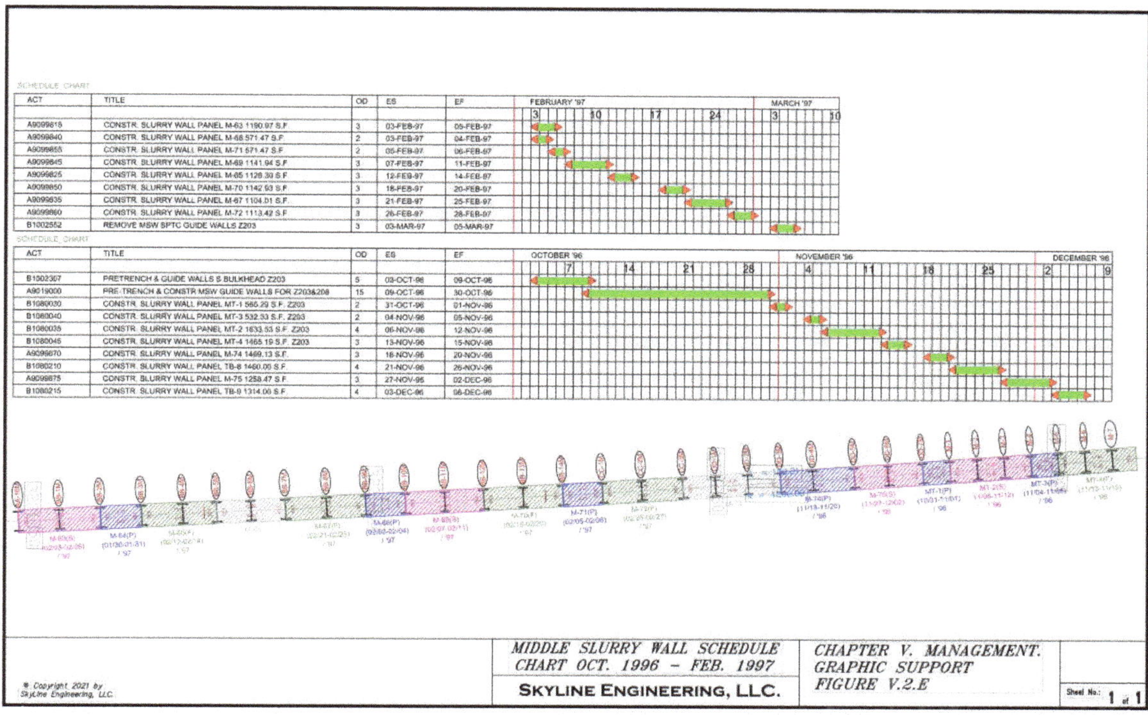

Figure V.2.F. Slurry Walls Panel Output Overall

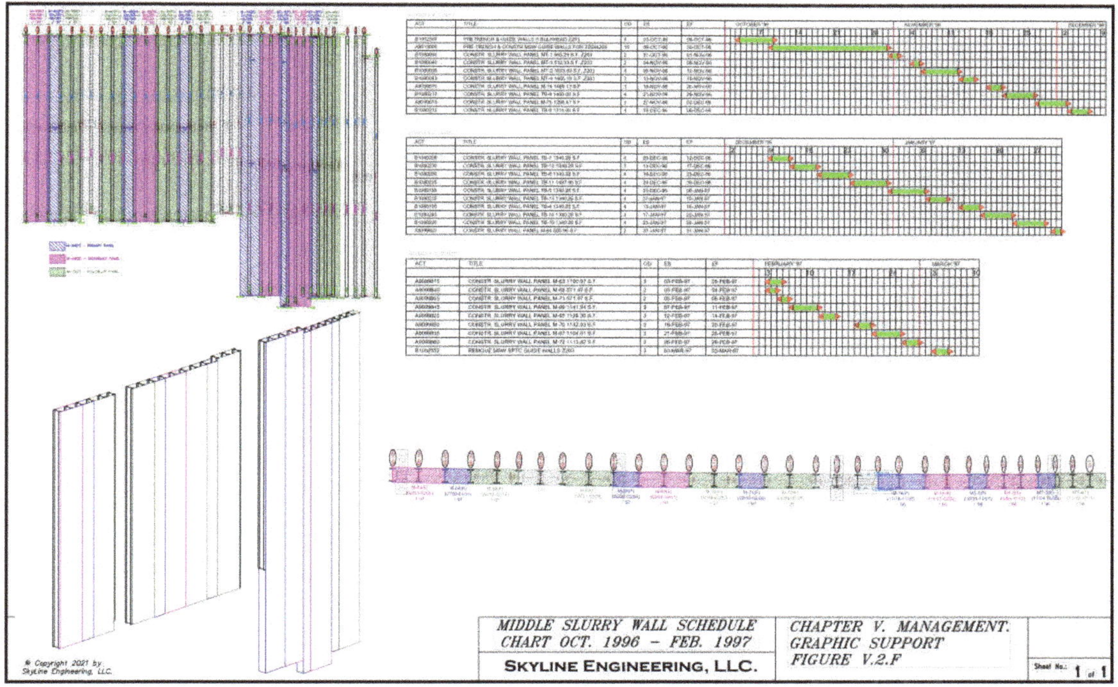

V.3 SCHEDULE – GRAPHICAL MODEL INSTALLATION SEQUENCE.

The Developed Correlation gives the possibility to show the installation sequence according to Schedule Dates. The Figures V.3.A – V.3.G below show the Installation Sequence with Dates for the above-mentioned Middle Slurry Wall Segment.

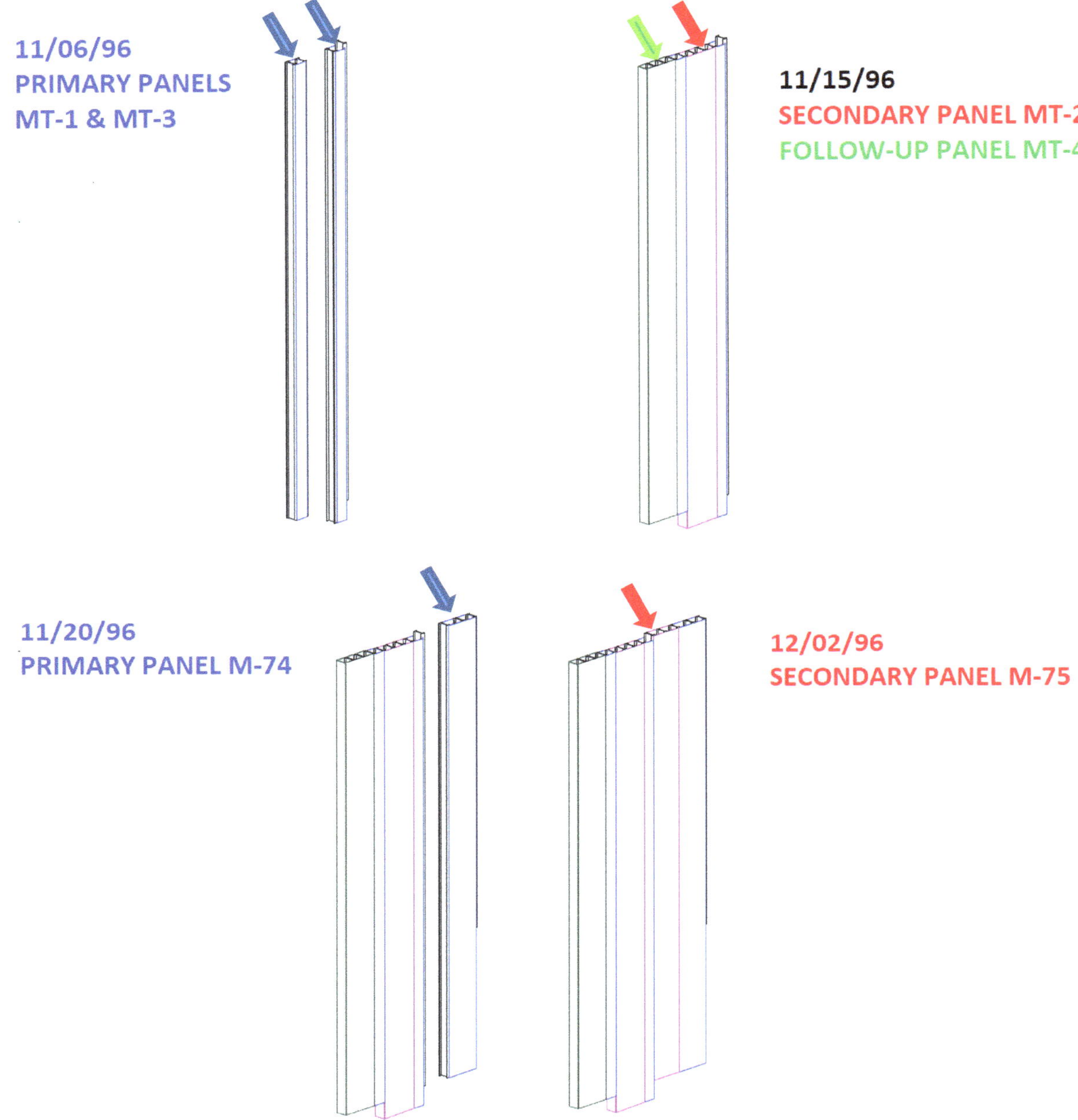

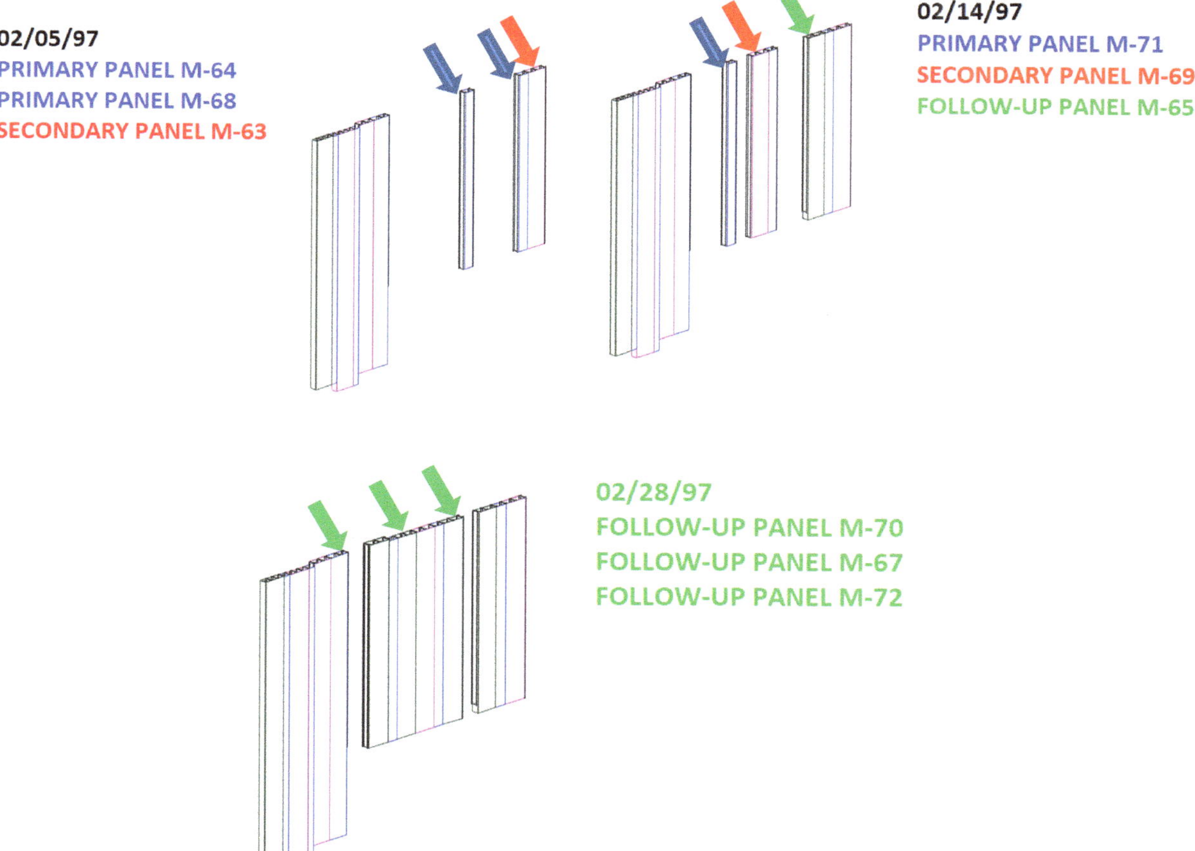

The Figures V.3.A – V.3.G. Middle Slurry Wall Panels Installation Sequence.

V.4. PDF IMPORT INTO AUTOCAD. FILES CONVERSION ROUTINE & ORGANIZATIONAL STRUCTURE.

The newer versions of AutoCAD (2021 & up) have a great option of importing PDF Files into the AutoCAD environment. Since the communication between Authority, Designer, and Contractor is set up mostly via PDF Files, this feature gets a critical role in the process of Project Revision Updates in a timely manner, as well as accurate and up-to-date presentation of As-Built Drawings.

This Paragraph describes the Conversion Routine and Organizational Structure of incoming PDF Files and resulting AutoCAD Drawings. The Figure V.4.A below gives an example of PDFS and DWGS Directories Placement.

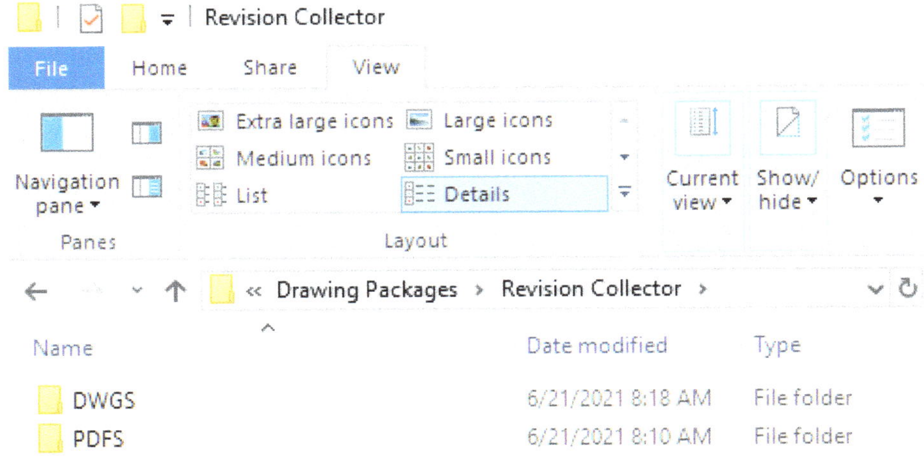

Figure V.4.B demonstrates the Sub-Directories Setup Routine.

```
(setq PDF-DATA-PATH "C:/                    /Drawing Packages/Revision Collector/PDFS/")

(setq PDF-DATA-PATH_VOLUME-1 (strcat PDF-DATA-PATH "Volume 1/"))
(setq PDF-DATA-PATH_VOLUME-2 (strcat PDF-DATA-PATH "Volume 2/"))
(setq PDF-DATA-PATH_VOLUME-3 (strcat PDF-DATA-PATH "Volume 3/"))
(setq PDF-DATA-PATH_VOLUME-4 (strcat PDF-DATA-PATH "Volume 4/"))
(setq PDF-DATA-PATH_VOLUME-5 (strcat PDF-DATA-PATH "Volume 5/"))
(setq PDF-DATA-PATH_VOLUME-6 (strcat PDF-DATA-PATH "Volume 6/"))

(setq DWG-DATA-PATH "C:/                    /Drawing Packages/Revision Collector/DWGS/")

(setq DWG-DATA-PATH_VOLUME-1 (strcat DWG-DATA-PATH "Volume 1/"))
(setq DWG-DATA-PATH_VOLUME-2 (strcat DWG-DATA-PATH "Volume 2/"))
(setq DWG-DATA-PATH_VOLUME-3 (strcat DWG-DATA-PATH "Volume 3/"))
(setq DWG-DATA-PATH_VOLUME-4 (strcat DWG-DATA-PATH "Volume 4/"))
(setq DWG-DATA-PATH_VOLUME-5 (strcat DWG-DATA-PATH "Volume 5/"))
(setq DWG-DATA-PATH_VOLUME-6 (strcat DWG-DATA-PATH "Volume 6/"))
```

Figure V.4.C. shows the Sub-Directories Placement.

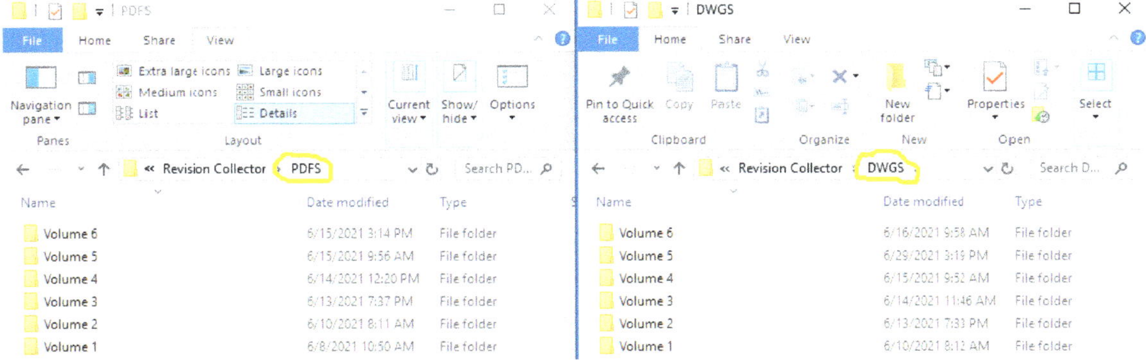

Figure V.4.D illustrates the Files Setup, Import, and Saving Routine.

```
(if (= dir_ctr 1)
(progn
(setq PDF-DATA-DIR (strcat PDF-DATA-PATH_VOLUME-1 FILE-NAME))
(setq DWG-DATA-DIR (strcat DWG-DATA-PATH_VOLUME-1 FILE-NAME))
)
)
(if (= dir_ctr 2)
(progn
(setq PDF-DATA-DIR (strcat PDF-DATA-PATH_VOLUME-2 FILE-NAME))
(setq DWG-DATA-DIR (strcat DWG-DATA-PATH_VOLUME-2 FILE-NAME))
)
)
(if (= dir_ctr 3)
(progn
(setq PDF-DATA-DIR (strcat PDF-DATA-PATH_VOLUME-3 FILE-NAME))
(setq DWG-DATA-DIR (strcat DWG-DATA-PATH_VOLUME-3 FILE-NAME))
)
)
(if (= dir_ctr 4)
(progn
(setq PDF-DATA-DIR (strcat PDF-DATA-PATH_VOLUME-4 FILE-NAME))
(setq DWG-DATA-DIR (strcat DWG-DATA-PATH_VOLUME-4 FILE-NAME))
)
)
(if (= dir_ctr 5)
(progn
(setq PDF-DATA-DIR (strcat PDF-DATA-PATH_VOLUME-5 FILE-NAME))
(setq DWG-DATA-DIR (strcat DWG-DATA-PATH_VOLUME-5 FILE-NAME))
)
)
(if (= dir_ctr 6)
(progn
(setq PDF-DATA-DIR (strcat PDF-DATA-PATH_VOLUME-6 FILE-NAME))
(setq DWG-DATA-DIR (strcat DWG-DATA-PATH_VOLUME-6 FILE-NAME))
)
)

(setq PDF-DATA-FILE (strcat PDF-DATA-DIR PDFWORD))
(setq DWG-DATA-FILE (strcat DWG-DATA-DIR DWGWORD))

(command "IMPORT" PDF-DATA-FILE "1" "0,0,0" "1" "0")
(command "SAVE" DWG-DATA-FILE)
```

The Resulting Organizational File Structure is shown on Figure V.4.E.

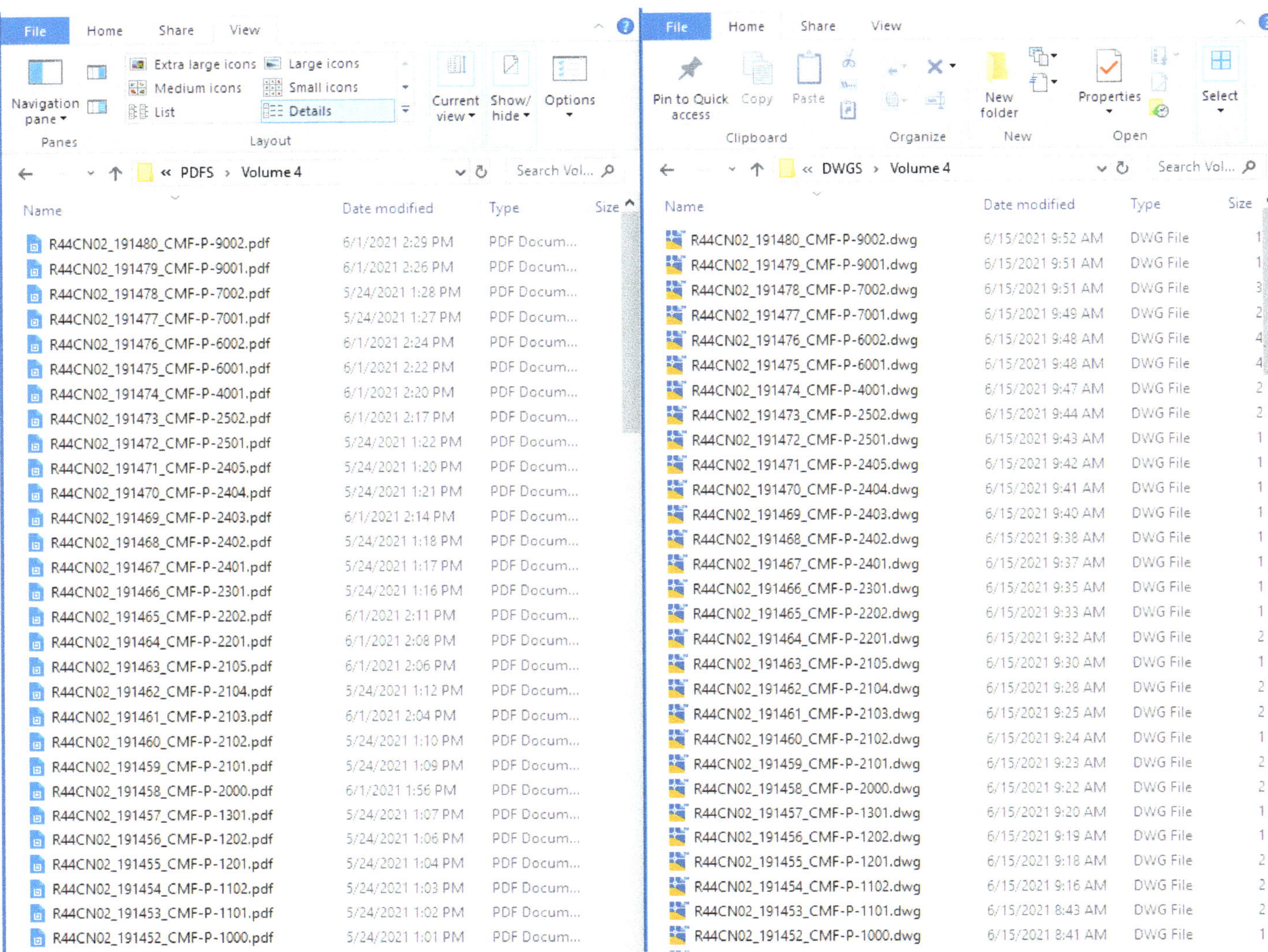
File
Home
Share
View
Navigation pane
Extra large icons
Large icons
Medium icons
Small icons
List
Details
Panes
Layout
Current view
Show/hide
Options
« PDFS › Volume 4
Search Vol...
Name
Date modified
Type
Size
R44CN02_191480_CMF-P-9002.pdf 6/1/2021 2:29 PM PDF Docum...
R44CN02_191479_CMF-P-9001.pdf 6/1/2021 2:26 PM PDF Docum...
R44CN02_191478_CMF-P-7002.pdf 5/24/2021 1:28 PM PDF Docum...
R44CN02_191477_CMF-P-7001.pdf 5/24/2021 1:27 PM PDF Docum...
R44CN02_191476_CMF-P-6002.pdf 6/1/2021 2:24 PM PDF Docum...
R44CN02_191475_CMF-P-6001.pdf 6/1/2021 2:22 PM PDF Docum...
R44CN02_191474_CMF-P-4001.pdf 6/1/2021 2:20 PM PDF Docum...
R44CN02_191473_CMF-P-2502.pdf 6/1/2021 2:17 PM PDF Docum...
R44CN02_191472_CMF-P-2501.pdf 5/24/2021 1:22 PM PDF Docum...
R44CN02_191471_CMF-P-2405.pdf 5/24/2021 1:20 PM PDF Docum...
R44CN02_191470_CMF-P-2404.pdf 5/24/2021 1:21 PM PDF Docum...
R44CN02_191469_CMF-P-2403.pdf 6/1/2021 2:14 PM PDF Docum...
R44CN02_191468_CMF-P-2402.pdf 5/24/2021 1:18 PM PDF Docum...
R44CN02_191467_CMF-P-2401.pdf 5/24/2021 1:17 PM PDF Docum...
R44CN02_191466_CMF-P-2301.pdf 5/24/2021 1:16 PM PDF Docum...
R44CN02_191465_CMF-P-2202.pdf 6/1/2021 2:11 PM PDF Docum...
R44CN02_191464_CMF-P-2201.pdf 6/1/2021 2:08 PM PDF Docum...
R44CN02_191463_CMF-P-2105.pdf 6/1/2021 2:06 PM PDF Docum...
R44CN02_191462_CMF-P-2104.pdf 5/24/2021 1:12 PM PDF Docum...
R44CN02_191461_CMF-P-2103.pdf 6/1/2021 2:04 PM PDF Docum...
R44CN02_191460_CMF-P-2102.pdf 5/24/2021 1:10 PM PDF Docum...
R44CN02_191459_CMF-P-2101.pdf 5/24/2021 1:09 PM PDF Docum...
R44CN02_191458_CMF-P-2000.pdf 6/1/2021 1:56 PM PDF Docum...
R44CN02_191457_CMF-P-1301.pdf 5/24/2021 1:07 PM PDF Docum...
R44CN02_191456_CMF-P-1202.pdf 5/24/2021 1:06 PM PDF Docum...
R44CN02_191455_CMF-P-1201.pdf 5/24/2021 1:04 PM PDF Docum...
R44CN02_191454_CMF-P-1102.pdf 5/24/2021 1:03 PM PDF Docum...
R44CN02_191453_CMF-P-1101.pdf 5/24/2021 1:02 PM PDF Docum...
R44CN02_191452_CMF-P-1000.pdf 5/24/2021 1:01 PM PDF Docum...
File
Home
Share
View
Pin to Quick access
Copy
Paste
Clipboard
Organize
New folder
New
Properties
Open
Select
« DWGS › Volume 4
Search Vol...
Name
Date modified
Type
Size
R44CN02_191480_CMF-P-9002.dwg 6/15/2021 9:52 AM DWG File
R44CN02_191479_CMF-P-9001.dwg 6/15/2021 9:51 AM DWG File
R44CN02_191478_CMF-P-7002.dwg 6/15/2021 9:51 AM DWG File
R44CN02_191477_CMF-P-7001.dwg 6/15/2021 9:49 AM DWG File
R44CN02_191476_CMF-P-6002.dwg 6/15/2021 9:48 AM DWG File
R44CN02_191475_CMF-P-6001.dwg 6/15/2021 9:48 AM DWG File
R44CN02_191474_CMF-P-4001.dwg 6/15/2021 9:47 AM DWG File
R44CN02_191473_CMF-P-2502.dwg 6/15/2021 9:44 AM DWG File
R44CN02_191472_CMF-P-2501.dwg 6/15/2021 9:43 AM DWG File
R44CN02_191471_CMF-P-2405.dwg 6/15/2021 9:42 AM DWG File
R44CN02_191470_CMF-P-2404.dwg 6/15/2021 9:41 AM DWG File
R44CN02_191469_CMF-P-2403.dwg 6/15/2021 9:40 AM DWG File
R44CN02_191468_CMF-P-2402.dwg 6/15/2021 9:38 AM DWG File
R44CN02_191467_CMF-P-2401.dwg 6/15/2021 9:37 AM DWG File
R44CN02_191466_CMF-P-2301.dwg 6/15/2021 9:35 AM DWG File
R44CN02_191465_CMF-P-2202.dwg 6/15/2021 9:33 AM DWG File
R44CN02_191464_CMF-P-2201.dwg 6/15/2021 9:32 AM DWG File
R44CN02_191463_CMF-P-2105.dwg 6/15/2021 9:30 AM DWG File
R44CN02_191462_CMF-P-2104.dwg 6/15/2021 9:28 AM DWG File
R44CN02_191461_CMF-P-2103.dwg 6/15/2021 9:25 AM DWG File
R44CN02_191460_CMF-P-2102.dwg 6/15/2021 9:24 AM DWG File
R44CN02_191459_CMF-P-2101.dwg 6/15/2021 9:23 AM DWG File
R44CN02_191458_CMF-P-2000.dwg 6/15/2021 9:22 AM DWG File
R44CN02_191457_CMF-P-1301.dwg 6/15/2021 9:20 AM DWG File
R44CN02_191456_CMF-P-1202.dwg 6/15/2021 9:19 AM DWG File
R44CN02_191455_CMF-P-1201.dwg 6/15/2021 9:18 AM DWG File
R44CN02_191454_CMF-P-1102.dwg 6/15/2021 9:16 AM DWG File
R44CN02_191453_CMF-P-1101.dwg 6/15/2021 8:43 AM DWG File
R44CN02_191452_CMF-P-1000.dwg 6/15/2021 8:41 AM DWG File

www.ingramcontent.com/pod-product-compliance
Ingram Content Group UK Ltd.
Pitfield, Milton Keynes, MK11 3LW, UK
UKHW052226270726
14059UKWH00003B/146